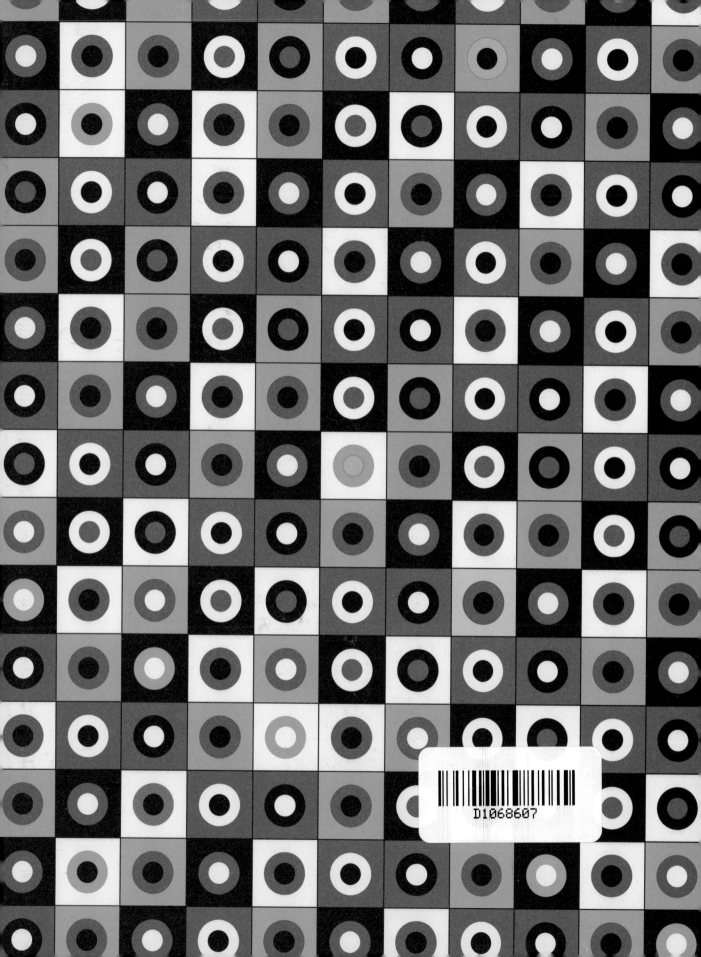

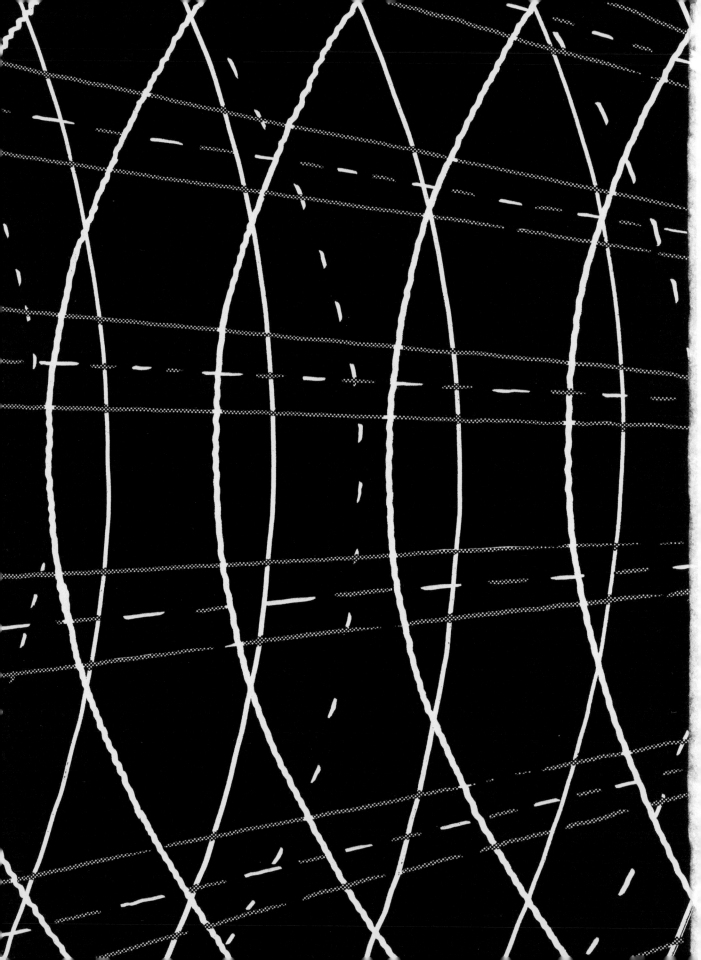

The
River at
Night

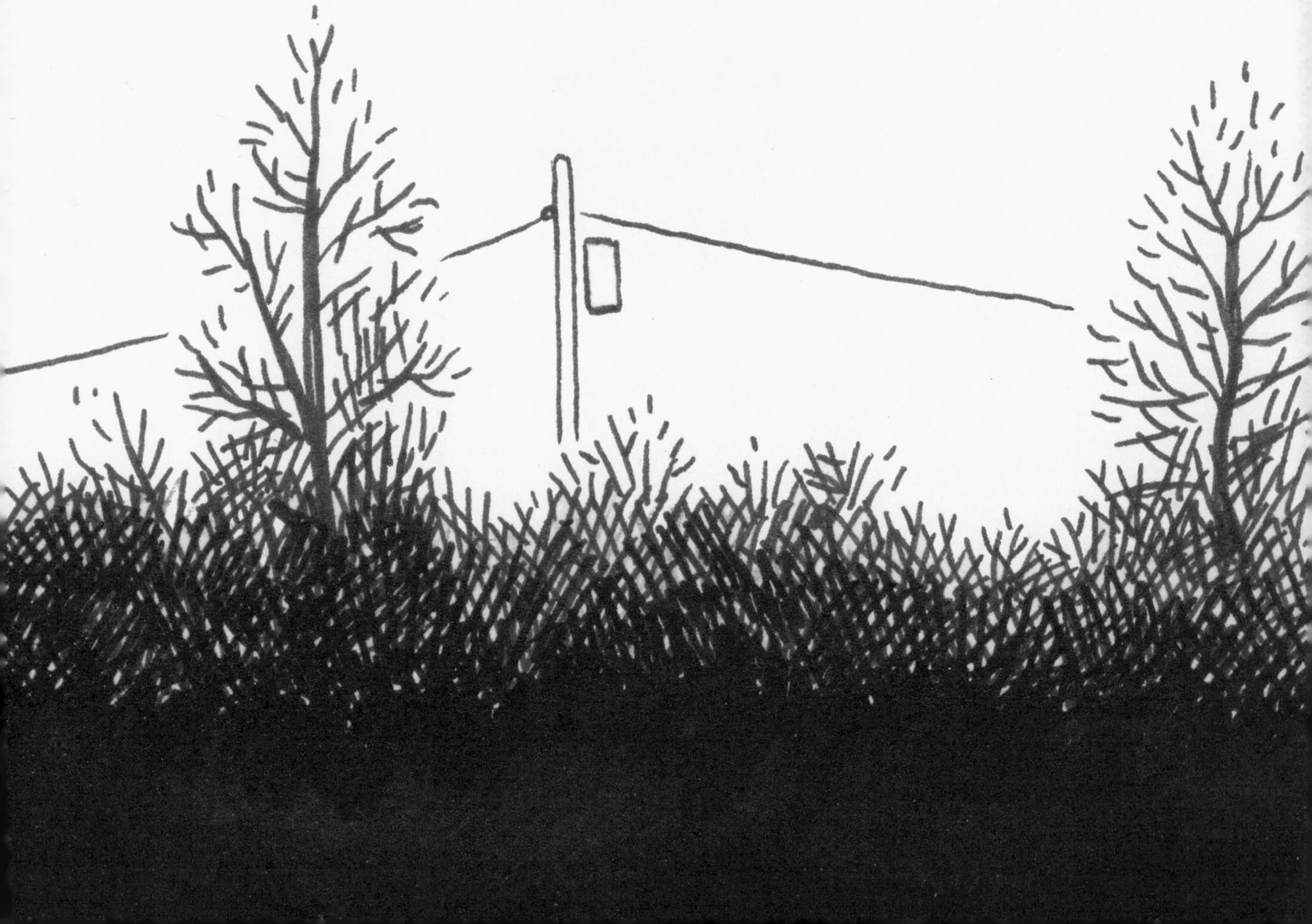

Kevin Huizenga

Glenn
GANGES

in:

"The River at Night"

2019

DRAWN & QUARTERLY

Montreal

For my family

The author would like to thank Igor Tuveri, Sammy Harkham, Kim Thompson, Ken Parille, Eric Reynolds, Chris Oliveros, Peggy Burns, Tom Devlin, Tracy Hurren, Julia Pohl-Miranda, Alison Naturale, Katherine Labarbera, John McPhee (Glenn is reading *Basin and Range*), Paul Baresh, Jordan Crane, Anne Koyama, Dan Zettwoch, Ted May and Sacha Mardou, Dan Madrigal, Dan Nadel, Emily Bucher, the MCAD Service Bureau, Iona Woolmington, John Porcellino, Jacob Berendes, Chris Ware, Frank Santoro, Anders Nilsen, and his family for their kind assistance in making this book possible.

First edition:
September 2019

Printed in China on acid-free paper

Library and Archives Canada Cataloguing in Publication
Title: *The River at Night* / Kevin Huizenga.
Names: Huizenga, Kevin, 1977– author, illustrator.
Identifiers: Canadiana 20190070587 | ISBN 9781770463745 (hardcover)
Subjects: LCGFT: Graphic novels.
Classification: LCC PN6727.H83 R58 2019 | DDC 741.5/973—DC23

Published in the USA by Drawn & Quarterly, a client publisher of Farrar, Straus and Giroux
Published in Canada by Drawn & Quarterly, a client publisher of Raincoast Books
Published in the United Kingdom by Drawn & Quarterly, a client publisher of Publishers Group UK

THANK YOU / DON'T FORGET

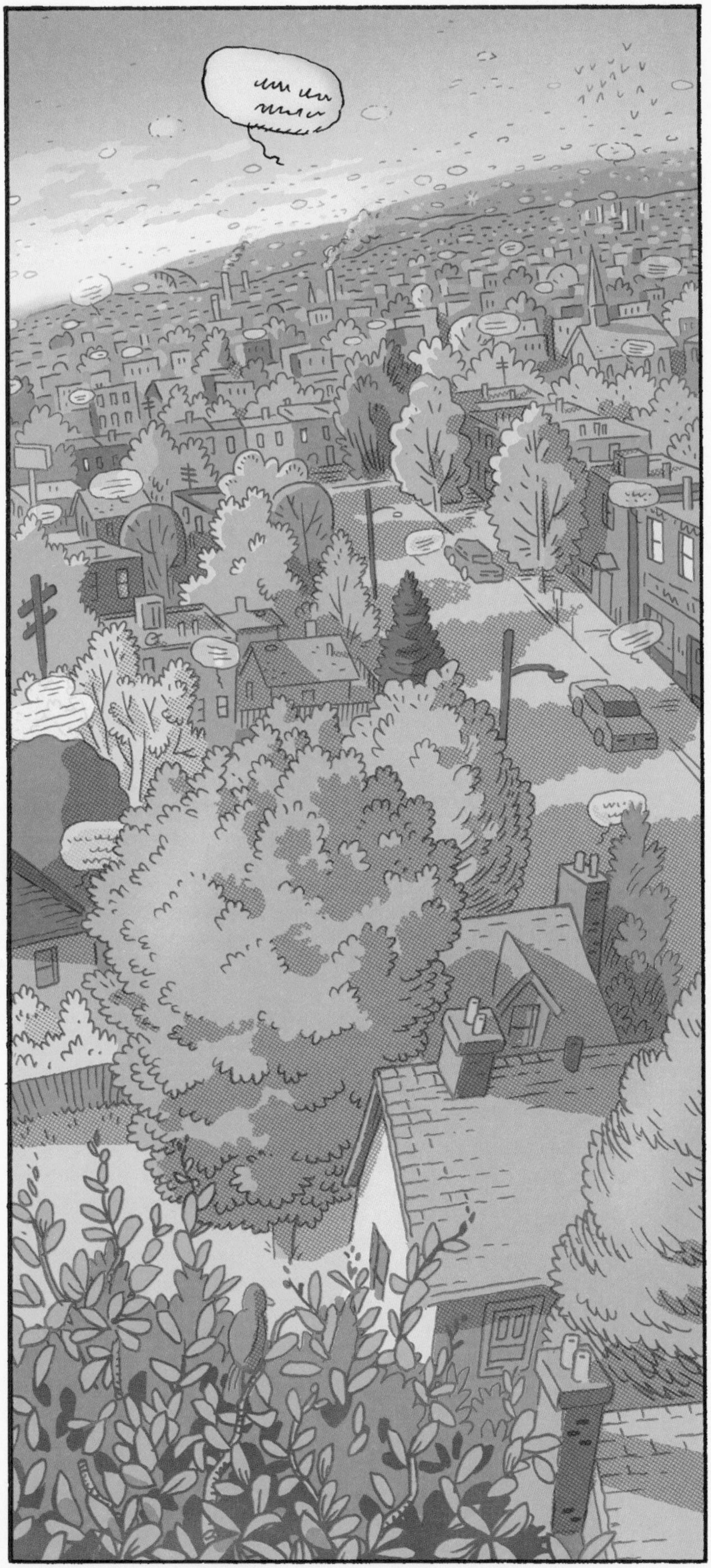

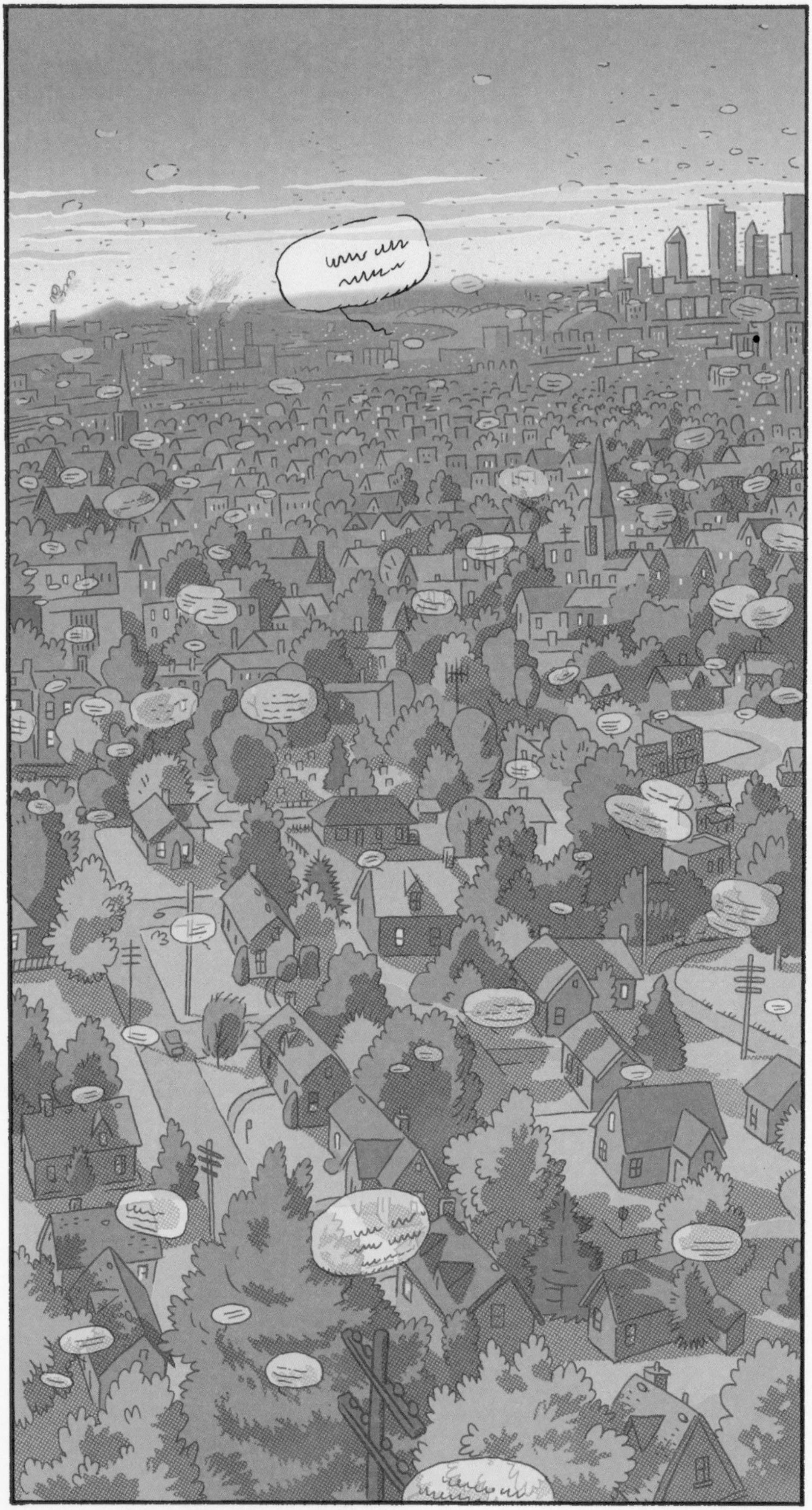

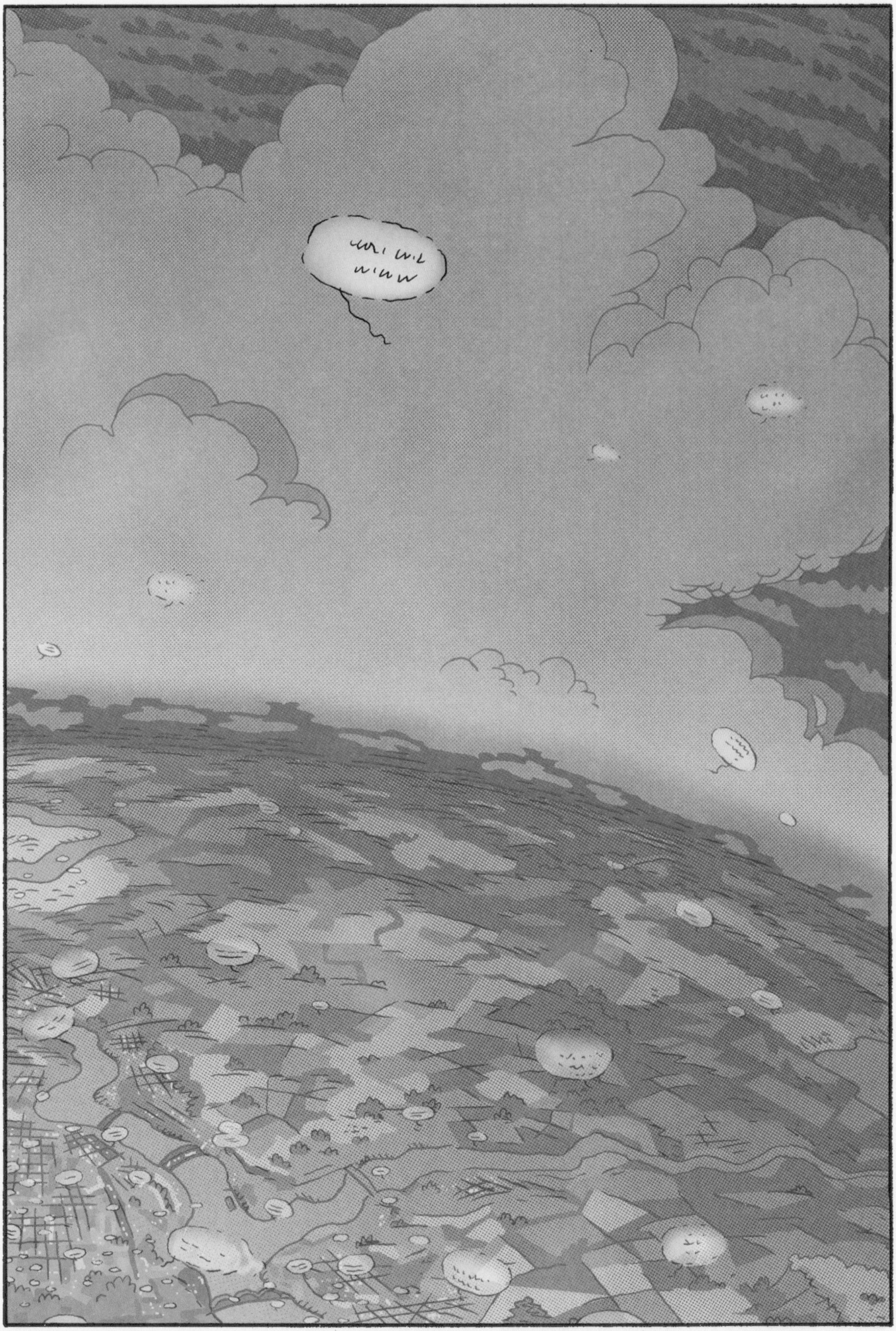

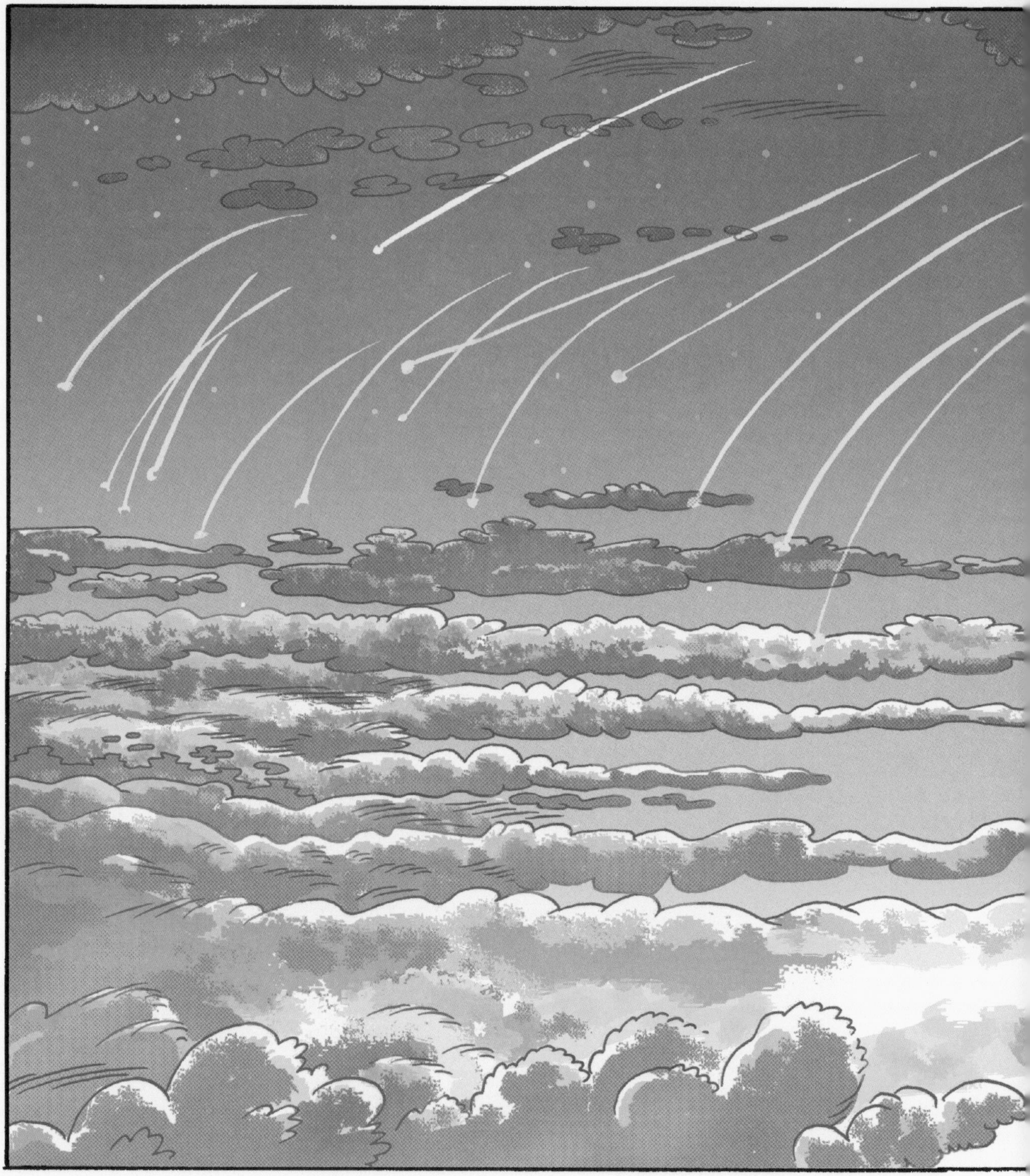

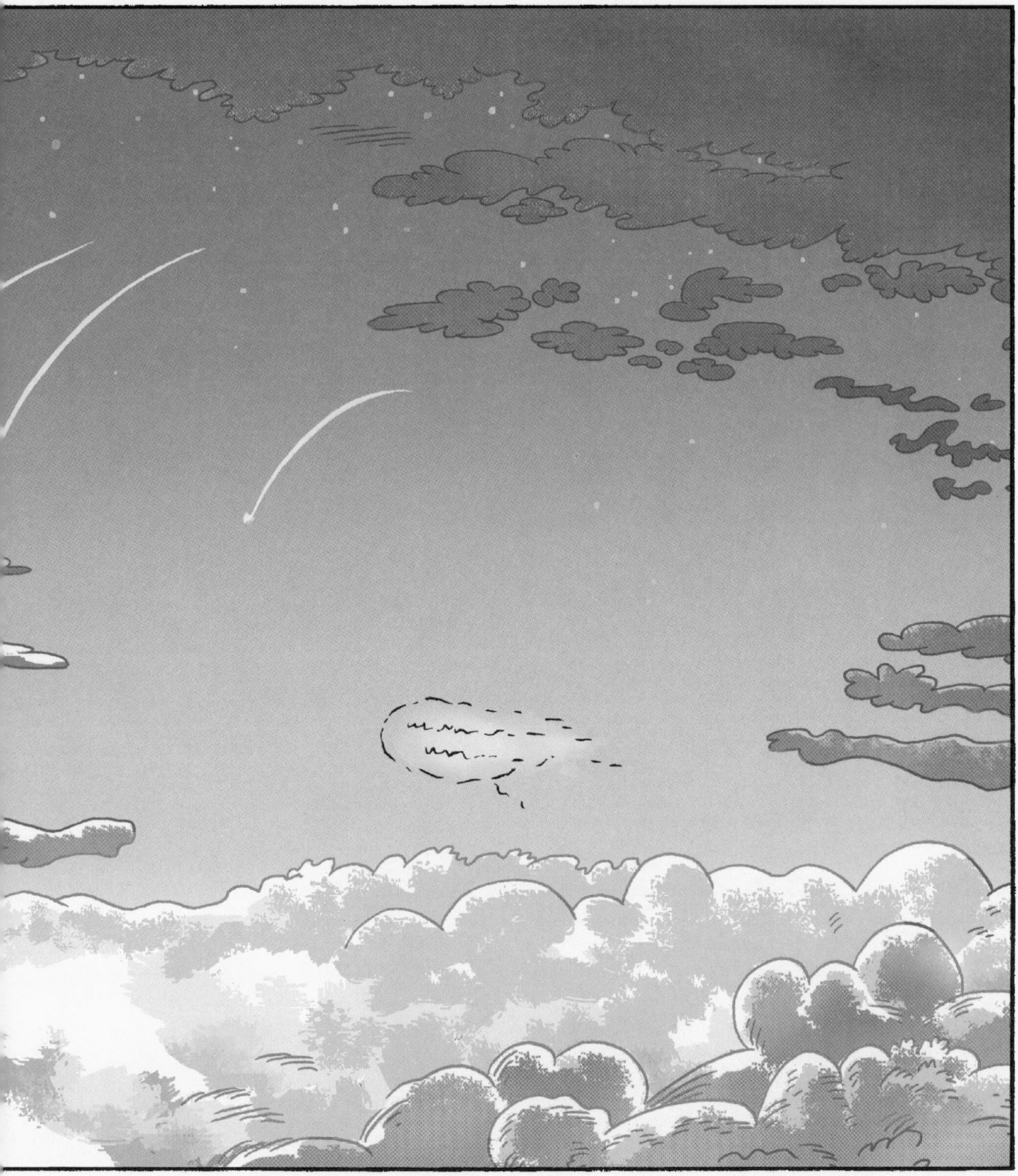

THE END

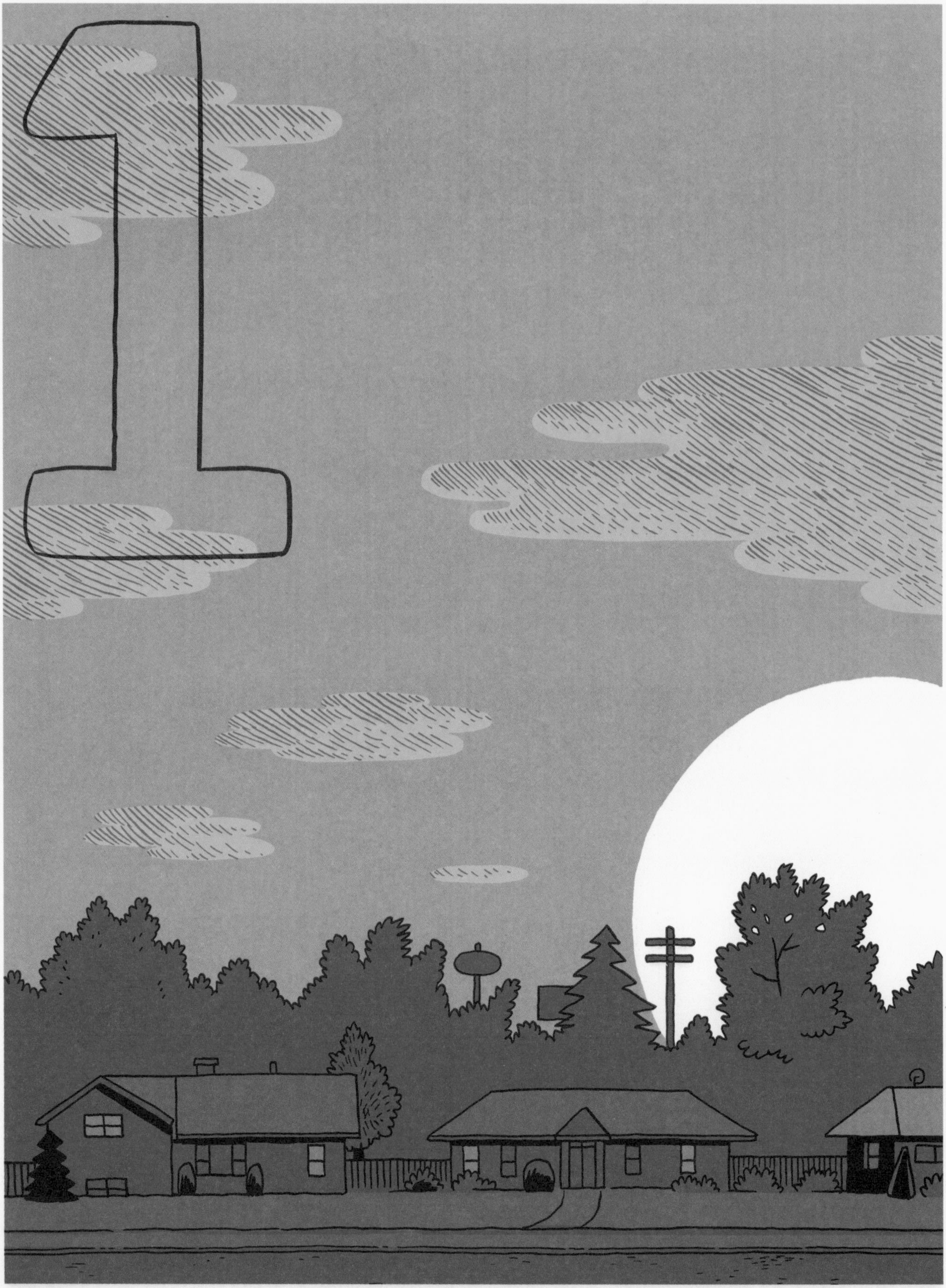
1

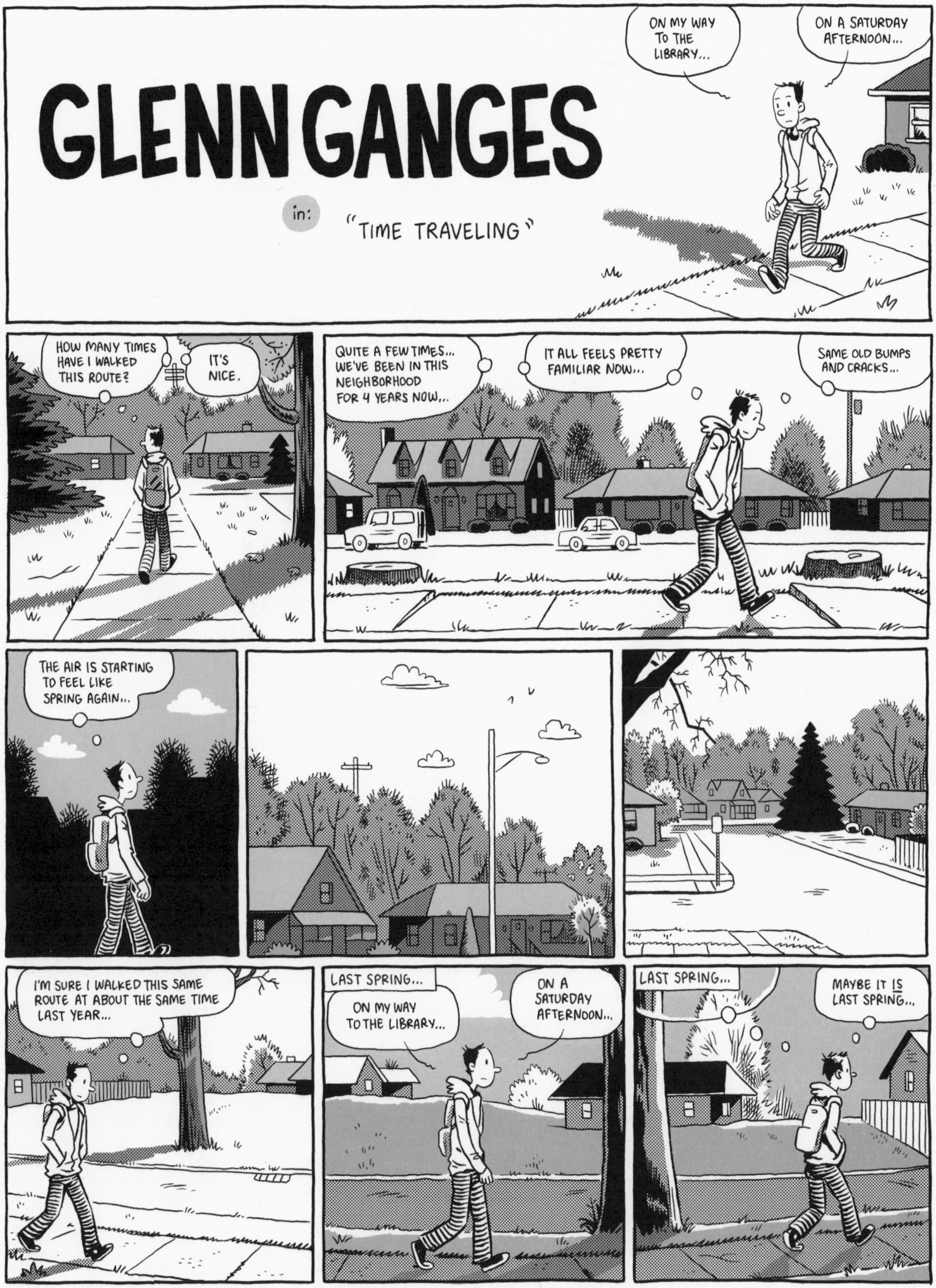
GLENN GANGES
in: "TIME TRAVELING"
ON MY WAY TO THE LIBRARY...
ON A SATURDAY AFTERNOON...
HOW MANY TIMES HAVE I WALKED THIS ROUTE?
IT'S NICE.
QUITE A FEW TIMES... WE'VE BEEN IN THIS NEIGHBORHOOD FOR 4 YEARS NOW...
IT ALL FEELS PRETTY FAMILIAR NOW...
SAME OLD BUMPS AND CRACKS...
THE AIR IS STARTING TO FEEL LIKE SPRING AGAIN...
I'M SURE I WALKED THIS SAME ROUTE AT ABOUT THE SAME TIME LAST YEAR...
LAST SPRING...
ON MY WAY TO THE LIBRARY...
ON A SATURDAY AFTERNOON...
LAST SPRING...
MAYBE IT IS LAST SPRING...

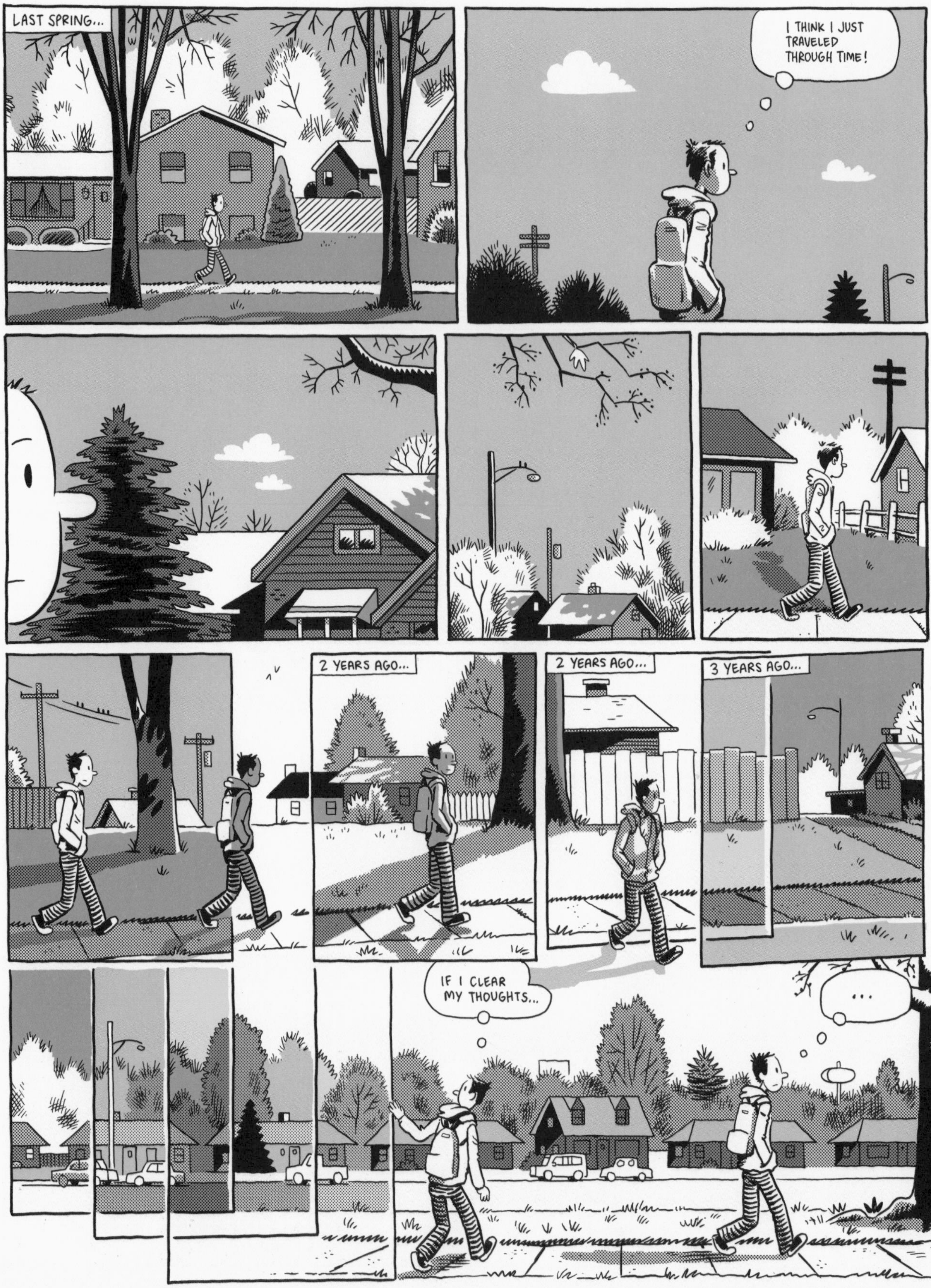
LAST SPRING...
I THINK I JUST TRAVELED THROUGH TIME!
2 YEARS AGO...
2 YEARS AGO...
3 YEARS AGO...
IF I CLEAR MY THOUGHTS...
...

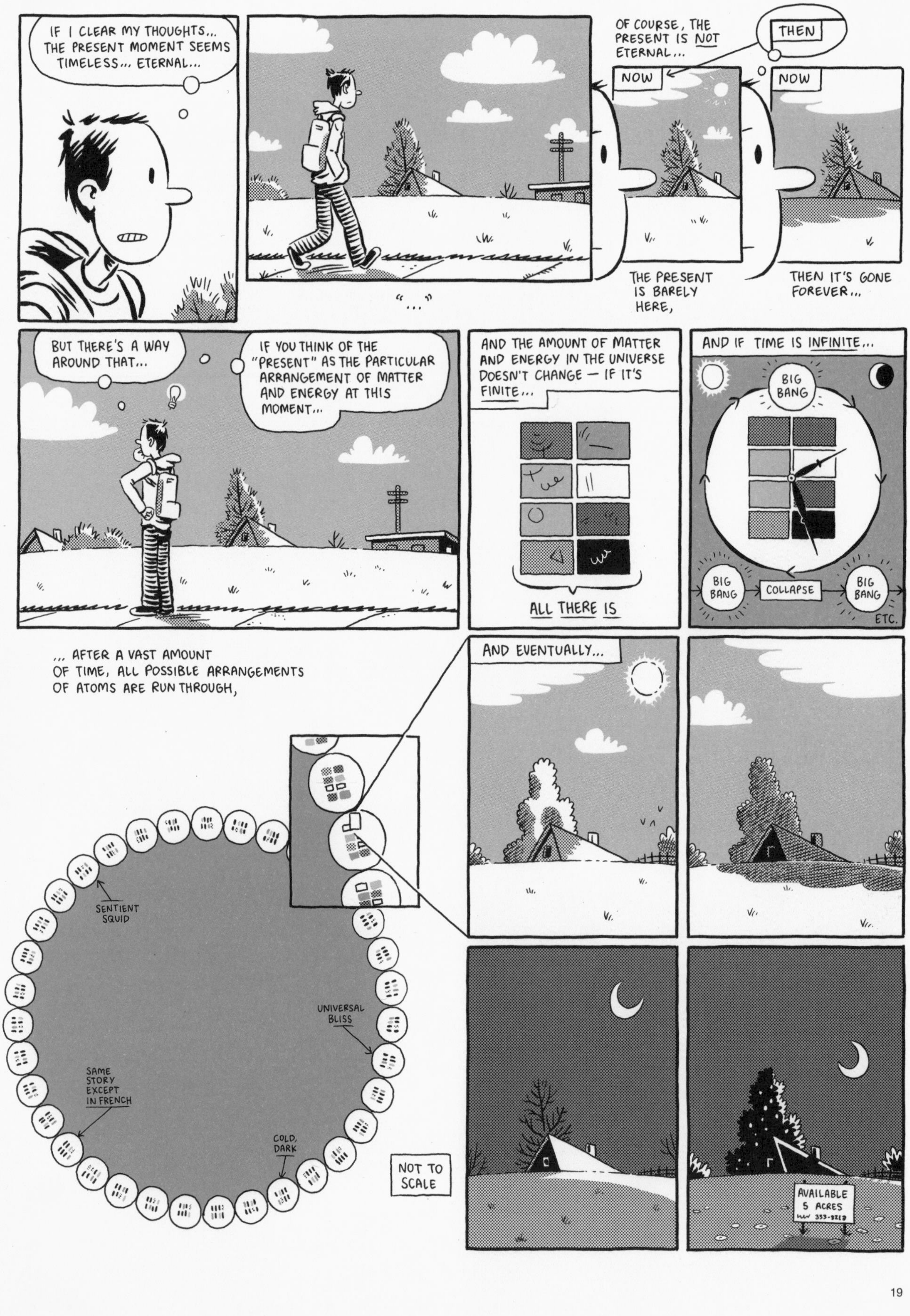

IF I CLEAR MY THOUGHTS... THE PRESENT MOMENT SEEMS TIMELESS... ETERNAL...
"..."
OF COURSE, THE PRESENT IS NOT ETERNAL...
NOW
THE PRESENT IS BARELY HERE,
THEN
NOW
THEN IT'S GONE FOREVER...
BUT THERE'S A WAY AROUND THAT...
IF YOU THINK OF THE "PRESENT" AS THE PARTICULAR ARRANGEMENT OF MATTER AND ENERGY AT THIS MOMENT...
AND THE AMOUNT OF MATTER AND ENERGY IN THE UNIVERSE DOESN'T CHANGE — IF IT'S FINITE...
ALL THERE IS
AND IF TIME IS INFINITE...
BIG BANG
BIG BANG
COLLAPSE
BIG BANG
ETC.
... AFTER A VAST AMOUNT OF TIME, ALL POSSIBLE ARRANGEMENTS OF ATOMS ARE RUN THROUGH,
SENTIENT SQUID
UNIVERSAL BLISS
SAME STORY EXCEPT IN FRENCH
COLD, DARK
NOT TO SCALE
AND EVENTUALLY...
AVAILABLE
5 ACRES

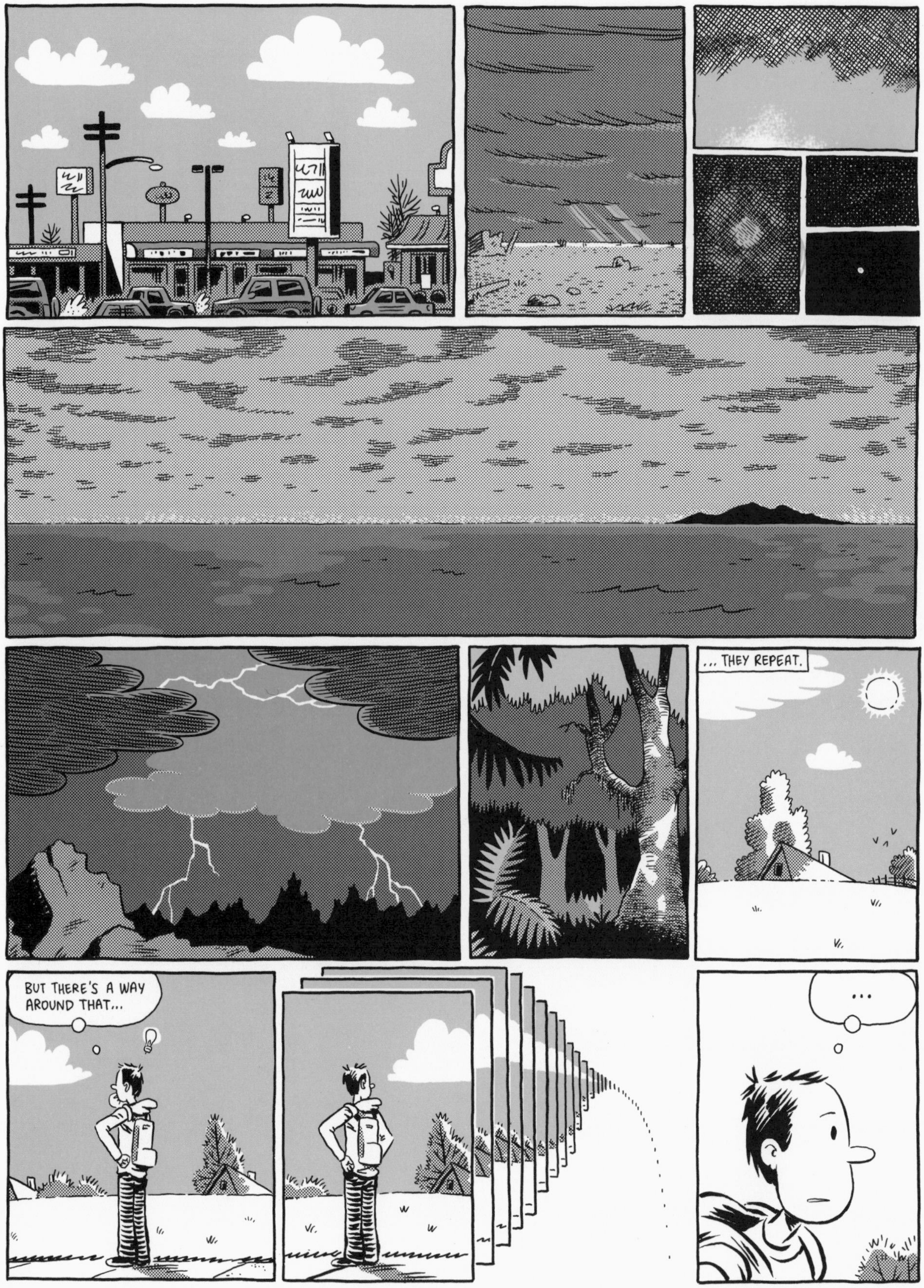
... THEY REPEAT.
BUT THERE'S A WAY AROUND THAT...
...

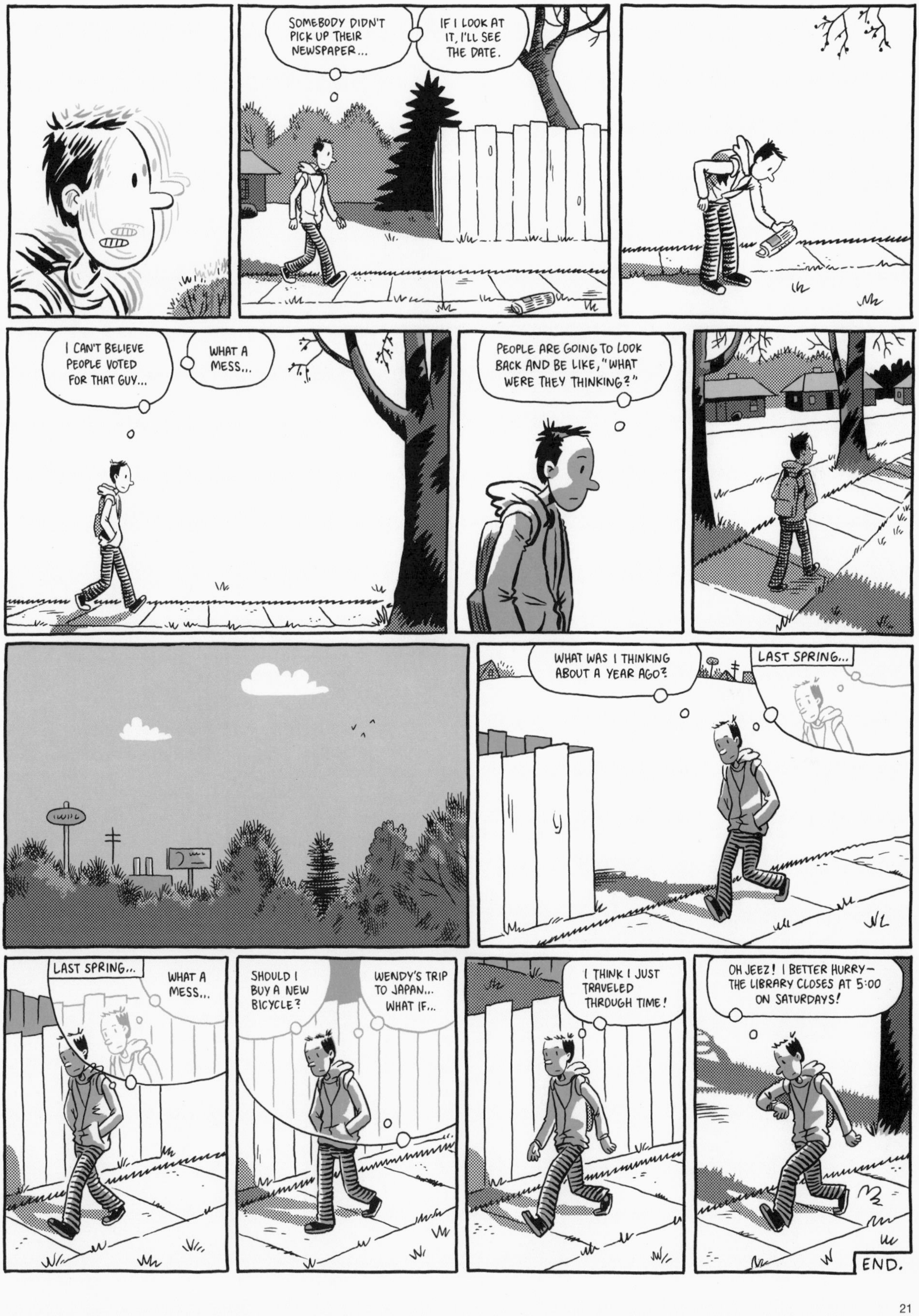
SOMEBODY DIDN'T PICK UP THEIR NEWSPAPER...
IF I LOOK AT IT, I'LL SEE THE DATE.
I CAN'T BELIEVE PEOPLE VOTED FOR THAT GUY...
WHAT A MESS...
PEOPLE ARE GOING TO LOOK BACK AND BE LIKE, "WHAT WERE THEY THINKING?"
WHAT WAS I THINKING ABOUT A YEAR AGO?
LAST SPRING...
LAST SPRING...
WHAT A MESS...
SHOULD I BUY A NEW BICYCLE?
WENDY'S TRIP TO JAPAN... WHAT IF...
I THINK I JUST TRAVELED THROUGH TIME!
OH JEEZ! I BETTER HURRY— THE LIBRARY CLOSES AT 5:00 ON SATURDAYS!
END.

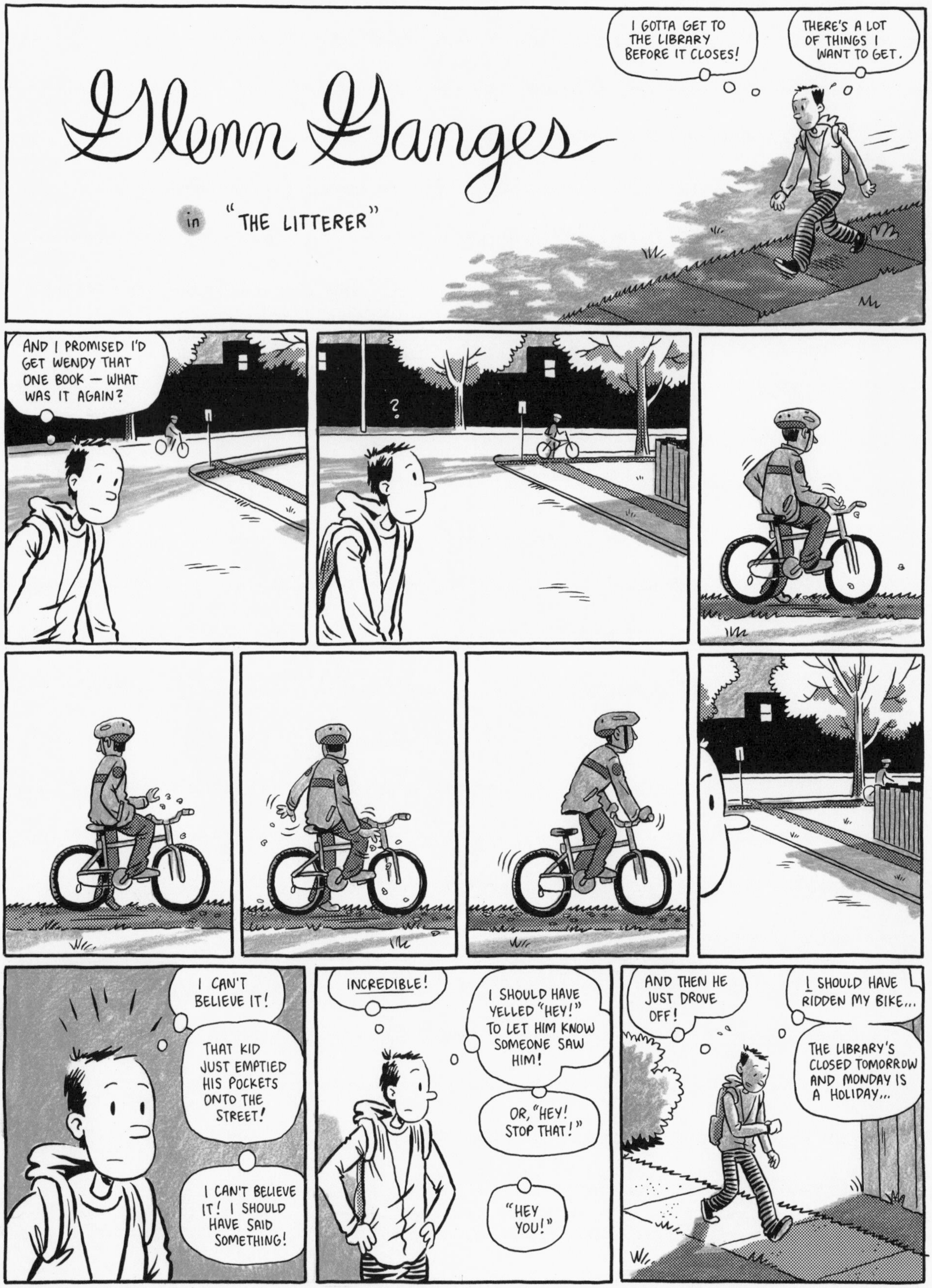
Glenn Ganges
in "THE LITTERER"
I GOTTA GET TO THE LIBRARY BEFORE IT CLOSES!
THERE'S A LOT OF THINGS I WANT TO GET.
AND I PROMISED I'D GET WENDY THAT ONE BOOK — WHAT WAS IT AGAIN?
?
I CAN'T BELIEVE IT!
THAT KID JUST EMPTIED HIS POCKETS ONTO THE STREET!
I CAN'T BELIEVE IT! I SHOULD HAVE SAID SOMETHING!
INCREDIBLE!
I SHOULD HAVE YELLED "HEY!" TO LET HIM KNOW SOMEONE SAW HIM!
OR, "HEY! STOP THAT!"
"HEY YOU!"
AND THEN HE JUST DROVE OFF!
I SHOULD HAVE RIDDEN MY BIKE...
THE LIBRARY'S CLOSED TOMORROW AND MONDAY IS A HOLIDAY...

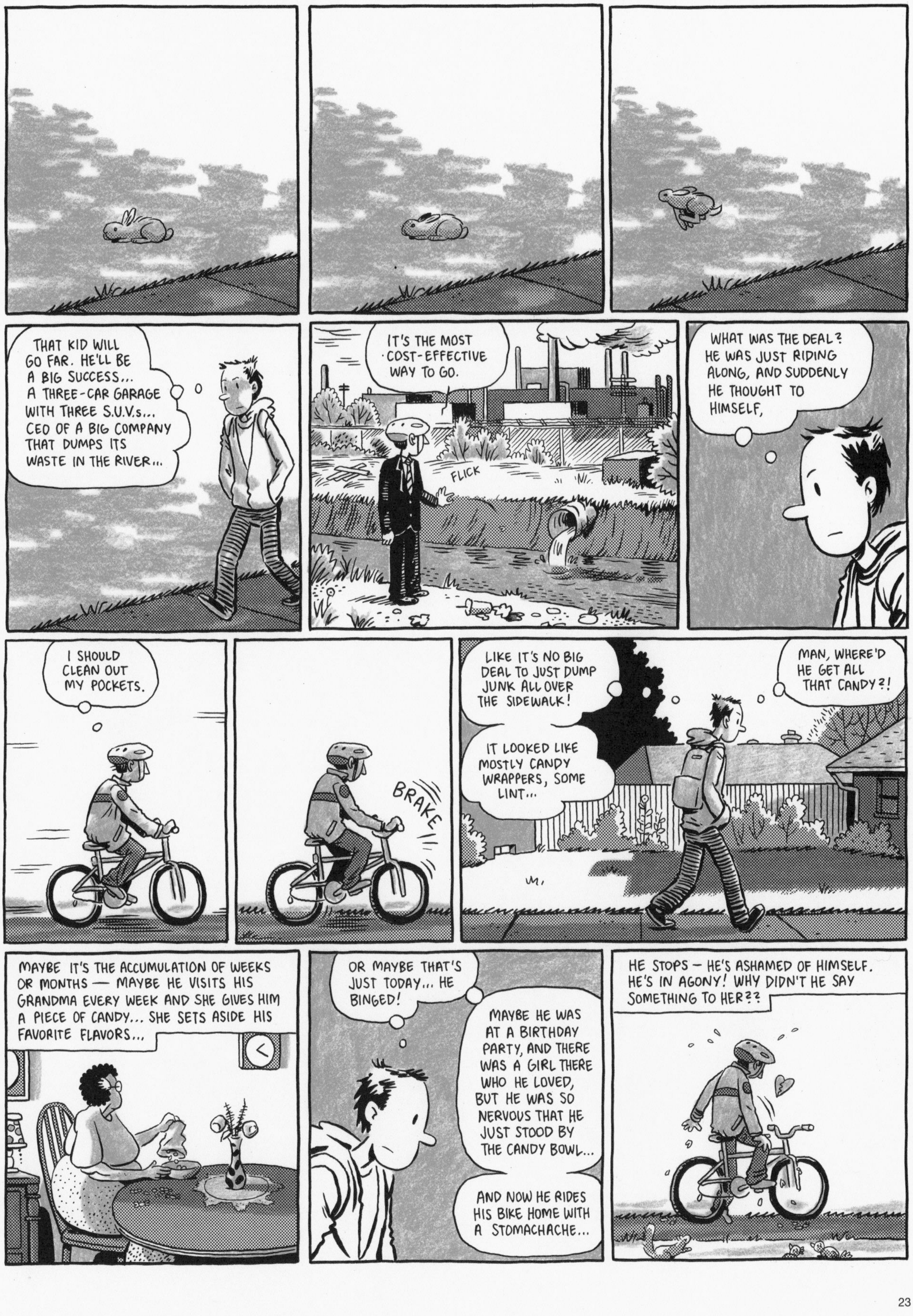
THAT KID WILL GO FAR. HE'LL BE A BIG SUCCESS... A THREE-CAR GARAGE WITH THREE S.U.V.s... CEO OF A BIG COMPANY THAT DUMPS ITS WASTE IN THE RIVER...
IT'S THE MOST COST-EFFECTIVE WAY TO GO.
FLICK
WHAT WAS THE DEAL? HE WAS JUST RIDING ALONG, AND SUDDENLY HE THOUGHT TO HIMSELF,
I SHOULD CLEAN OUT MY POCKETS.
BRAKE
LIKE IT'S NO BIG DEAL TO JUST DUMP JUNK ALL OVER THE SIDEWALK!
IT LOOKED LIKE MOSTLY CANDY WRAPPERS, SOME LINT...
MAN, WHERE'D HE GET ALL THAT CANDY?!
MAYBE IT'S THE ACCUMULATION OF WEEKS OR MONTHS — MAYBE HE VISITS HIS GRANDMA EVERY WEEK AND SHE GIVES HIM A PIECE OF CANDY... SHE SETS ASIDE HIS FAVORITE FLAVORS...
OR MAYBE THAT'S JUST TODAY... HE BINGED!
MAYBE HE WAS AT A BIRTHDAY PARTY, AND THERE WAS A GIRL THERE WHO HE LOVED, BUT HE WAS SO NERVOUS THAT HE JUST STOOD BY THE CANDY BOWL...
AND NOW HE RIDES HIS BIKE HOME WITH A STOMACHACHE...
HE STOPS — HE'S ASHAMED OF HIMSELF. HE'S IN AGONY! WHY DIDN'T HE SAY SOMETHING TO HER??

ALMOST THERE.

I DON'T KNOW...

IT WAS KIND OF TERRIFYING... MAYBE HE JUST DOES IT BECAUSE HE _CAN_. WHY NOT? WHO IS GOING TO STOP HIM?

THERE IS NO ONE AROUND...AS FAR AS HE KNOWS.

DOES HE FEEL A LITTLE THRILL, KNOWING HE'S GOING TO GET AWAY WITH IT?

MAYBE HE'S DONE THIS KIND OF THING BEFORE — LITTLE CRIMES, MISCHIEF... HE'S A BAD KID, THAT'S WHO HE IS...

HE'S NONCHALANT ABOUT IT — THE OTHER KIDS ARE WEAKER AND FEAR HIM...

HE DOES WHATEVER HE WANTS, HE DOESN'T CARE... HE KNOWS THERE'S NO GOD TO PUNISH HIM...

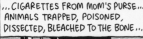

HE RIDES AWAY WITHOUT A CARE, GUILTLESS...

A GIANT...

...CIGARETTES FROM MOM'S PURSE... ANIMALS TRAPPED, POISONED, DISSECTED, BLEACHED TO THE BONE...

... THE CORRUPTION AND PSYCH- OLOGICAL DISSOLUTION OF A YOUNGER NEIGHBOR BOY...

BIGGER SCHEMES, MORE BODIES... THE YEARS PASS...

... THE RIGHT CONNECTIONS ARE MADE, ALL THE PIECES ARE IN PLACE...

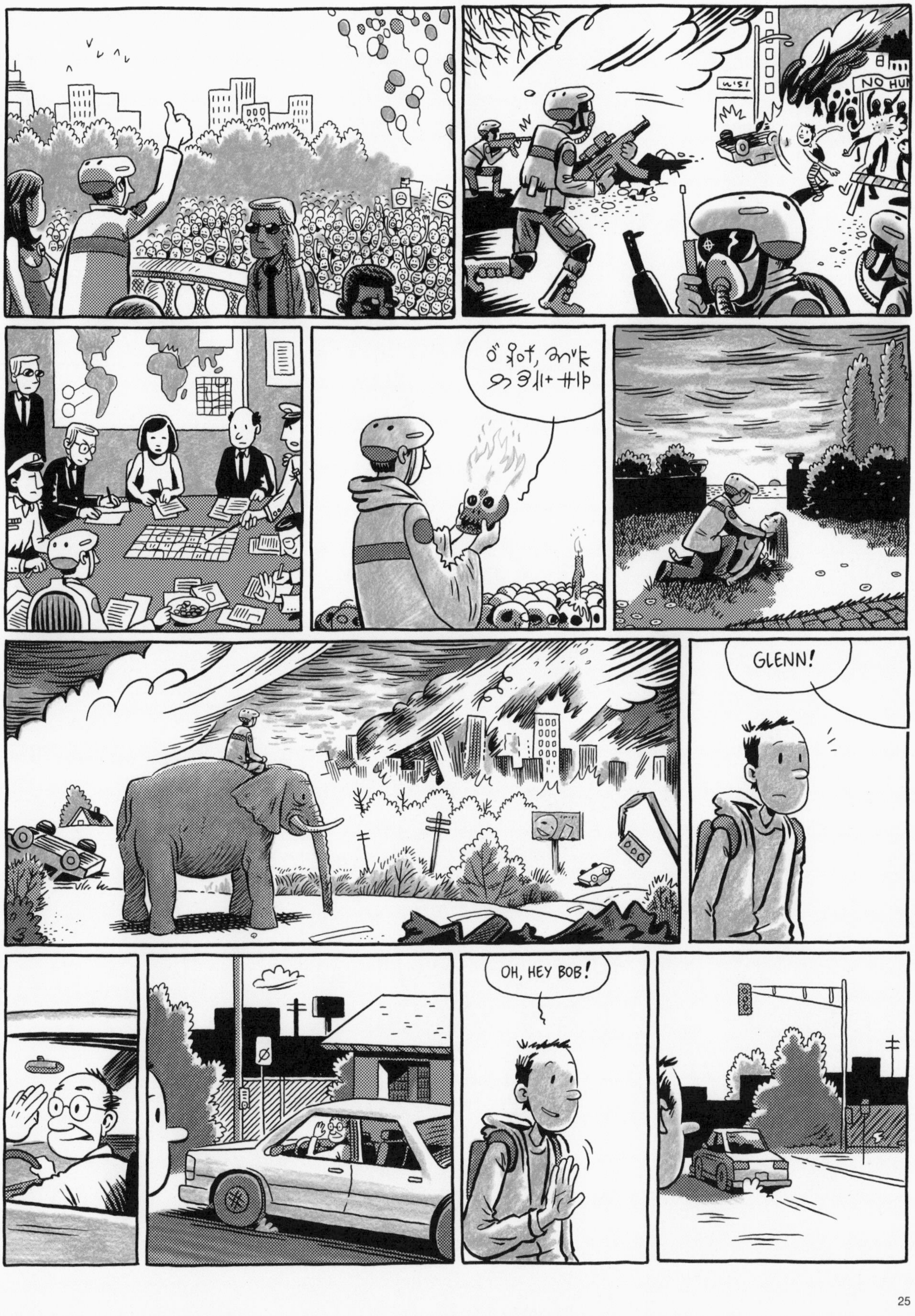
NO HU
GLENN!
OH, HEY BOB!

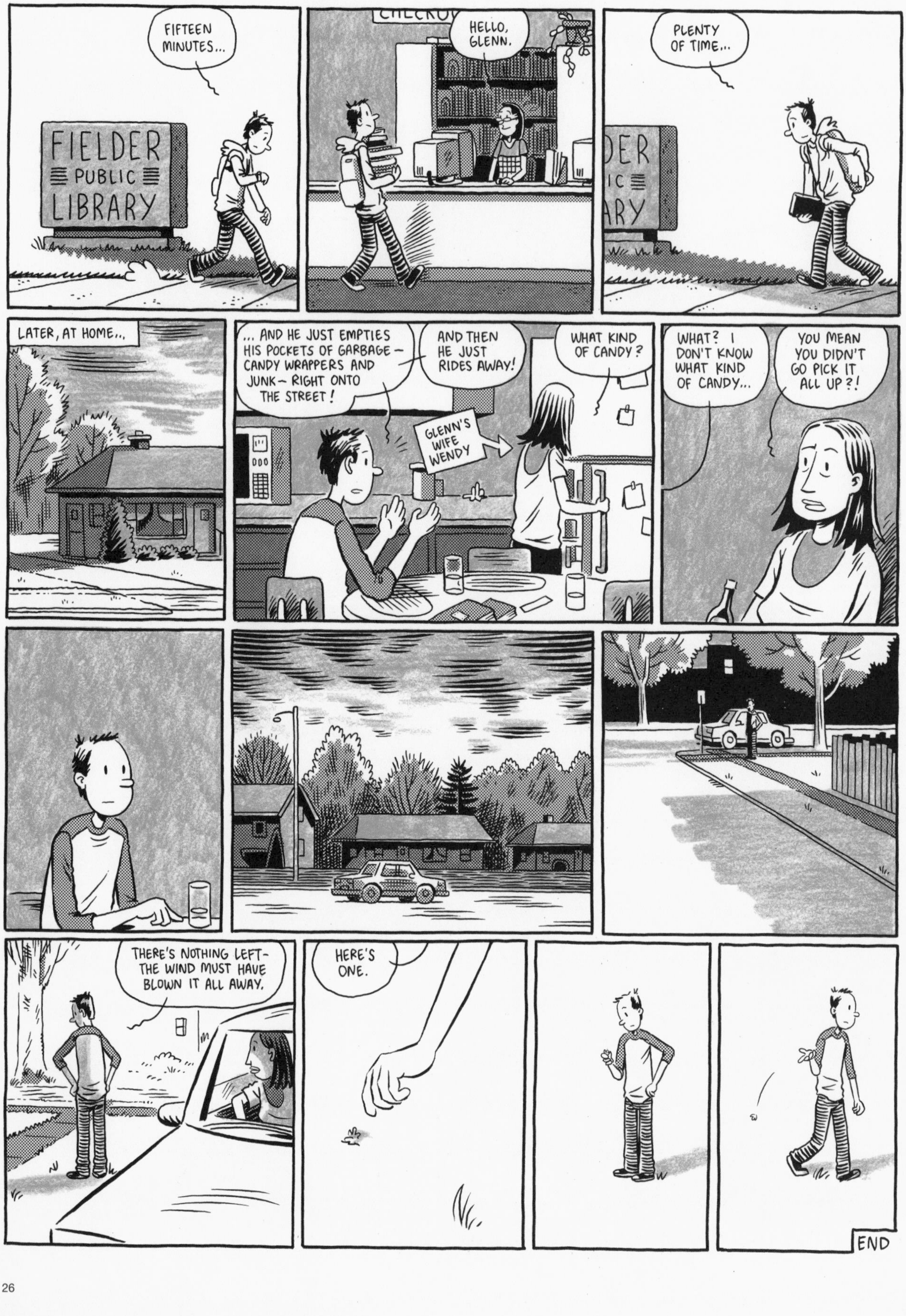
FIFTEEN MINUTES...
FIELDER PUBLIC LIBRARY
HELLO, GLENN.
PLENTY OF TIME...
LATER, AT HOME...
... AND HE JUST EMPTIES HIS POCKETS OF GARBAGE — CANDY WRAPPERS AND JUNK — RIGHT ONTO THE STREET!
AND THEN HE JUST RIDES AWAY!
WHAT KIND OF CANDY?
GLENN'S WIFE WENDY
WHAT? I DON'T KNOW WHAT KIND OF CANDY...
YOU MEAN YOU DIDN'T GO PICK IT ALL UP?!
THERE'S NOTHING LEFT— THE WIND MUST HAVE BLOWN IT ALL AWAY.
HERE'S ONE.
END

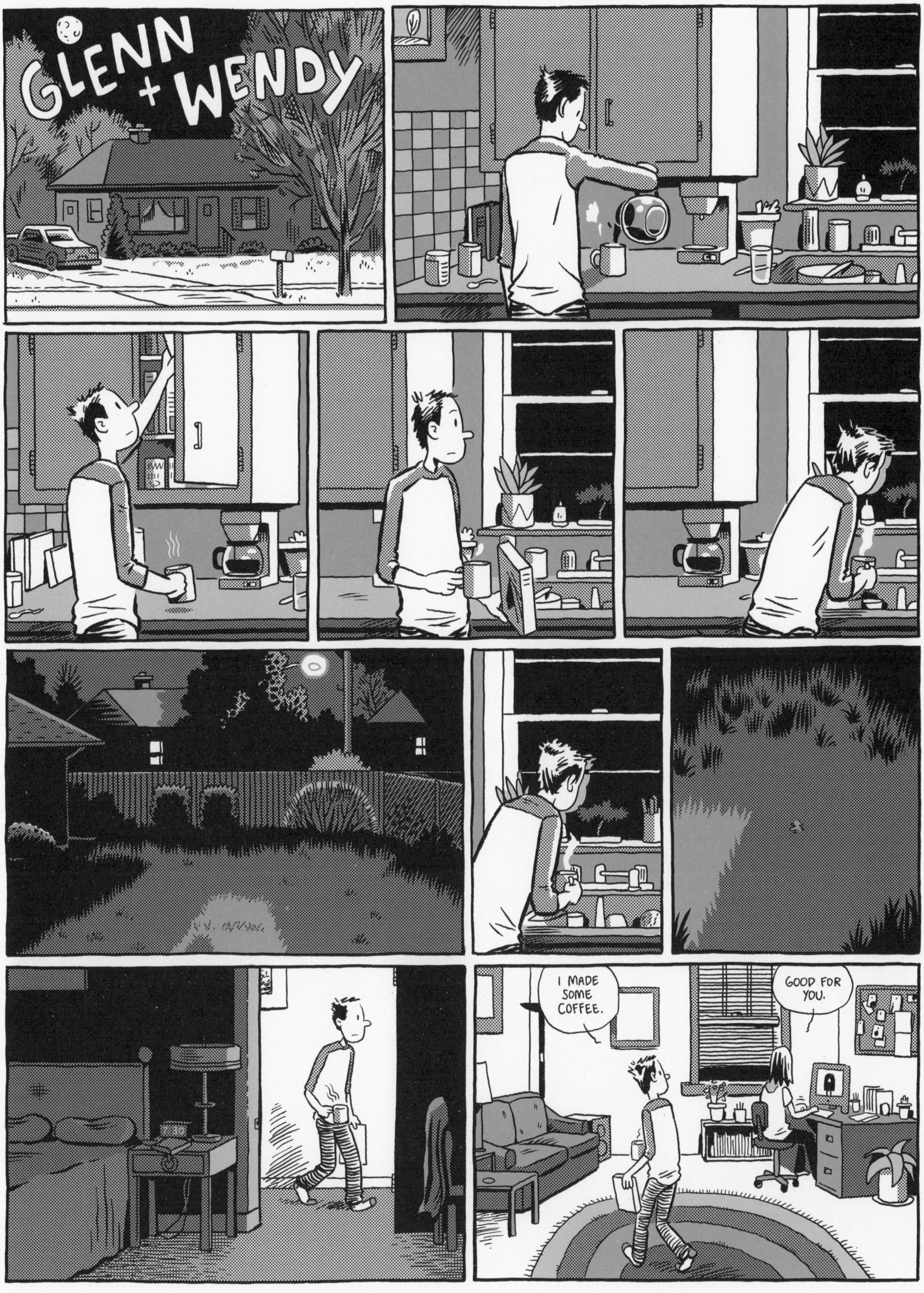
GLENN + WENDY
I MADE SOME COFFEE.
GOOD FOR YOU.

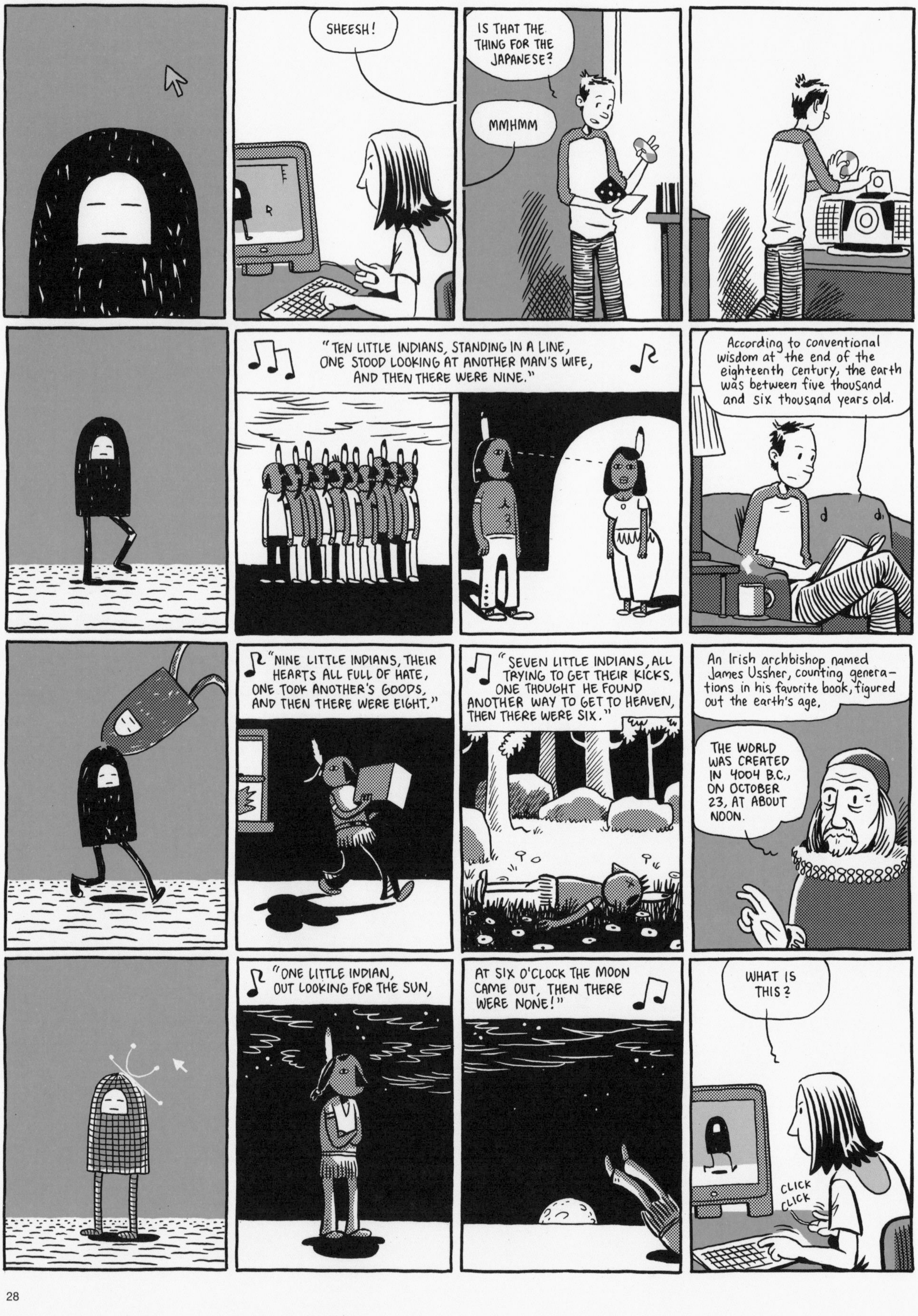
SHEESH!
IS THAT THE THING FOR THE JAPANESE?
MMHMM
"TEN LITTLE INDIANS, STANDING IN A LINE, ONE STOOD LOOKING AT ANOTHER MAN'S WIFE, AND THEN THERE WERE NINE."
According to conventional wisdom at the end of the eighteenth century, the earth was between five thousand and six thousand years old.
"NINE LITTLE INDIANS, THEIR HEARTS ALL FULL OF HATE, ONE TOOK ANOTHER'S GOODS, AND THEN THERE WERE EIGHT."
"SEVEN LITTLE INDIANS, ALL TRYING TO GET THEIR KICKS, ONE THOUGHT HE FOUND ANOTHER WAY TO GET TO HEAVEN, THEN THERE WERE SIX."
An Irish archbishop named James Ussher, counting generations in his favorite book, figured out the earth's age.
THE WORLD WAS CREATED IN 4004 B.C., ON OCTOBER 23, AT ABOUT NOON.
"ONE LITTLE INDIAN, OUT LOOKING FOR THE SUN,
AT SIX O'CLOCK THE MOON CAME OUT, THEN THERE WERE NONE!"
WHAT IS THIS?
CLICK CLICK

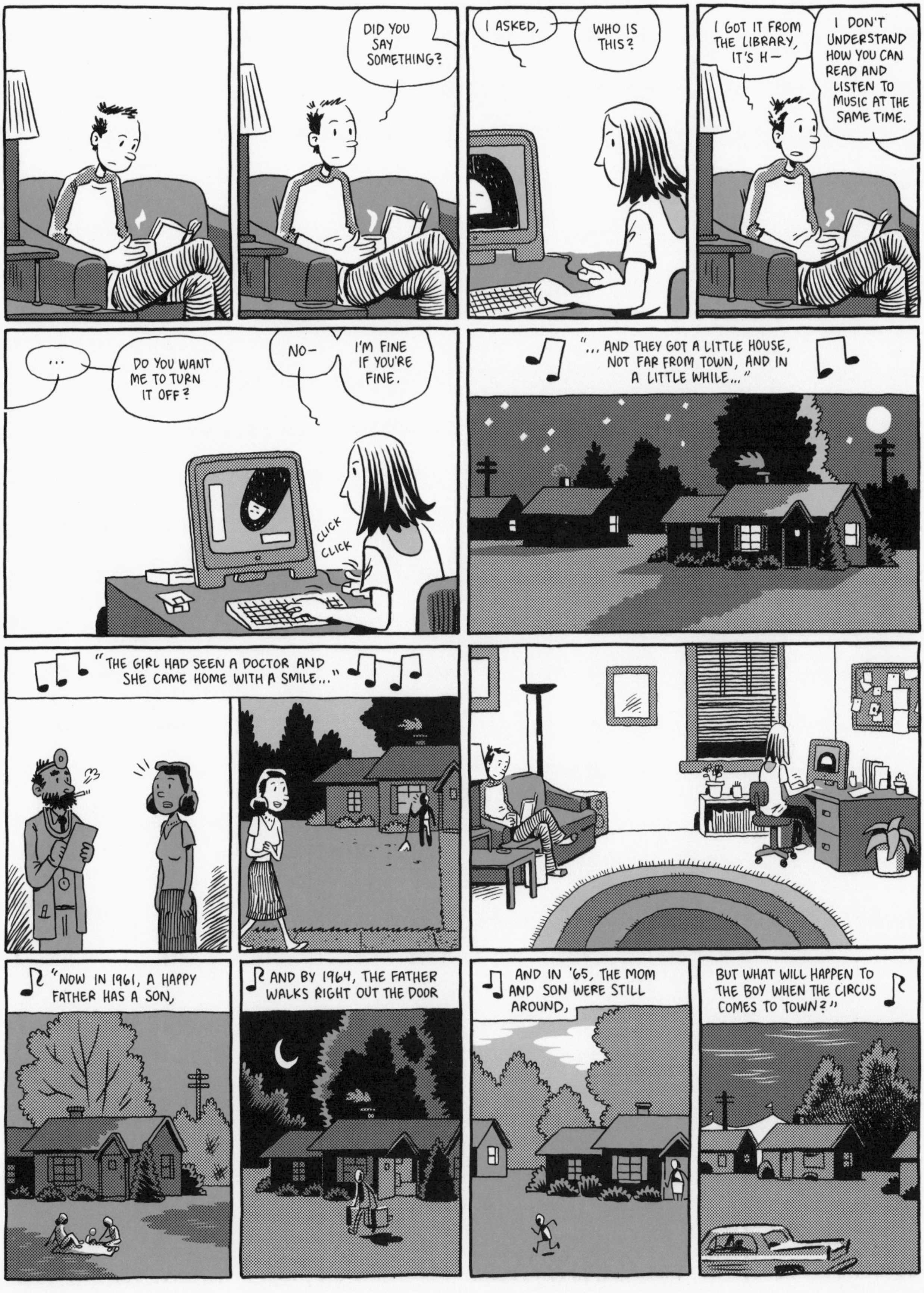
DID YOU SAY SOMETHING?
I ASKED,
WHO IS THIS?
I GOT IT FROM THE LIBRARY, IT'S H—
I DON'T UNDERSTAND HOW YOU CAN READ AND LISTEN TO MUSIC AT THE SAME TIME.
...
DO YOU WANT ME TO TURN IT OFF?
NO—
I'M FINE IF YOU'RE FINE.
CLICK
CLICK
"... AND THEY GOT A LITTLE HOUSE, NOT FAR FROM TOWN, AND IN A LITTLE WHILE..."
"THE GIRL HAD SEEN A DOCTOR AND SHE CAME HOME WITH A SMILE..."
"NOW IN 1961, A HAPPY FATHER HAS A SON,
AND BY 1964, THE FATHER WALKS RIGHT OUT THE DOOR
AND IN '65, THE MOM AND SON WERE STILL AROUND,
BUT WHAT WILL HAPPEN TO THE BOY WHEN THE CIRCUS COMES TO TOWN?"

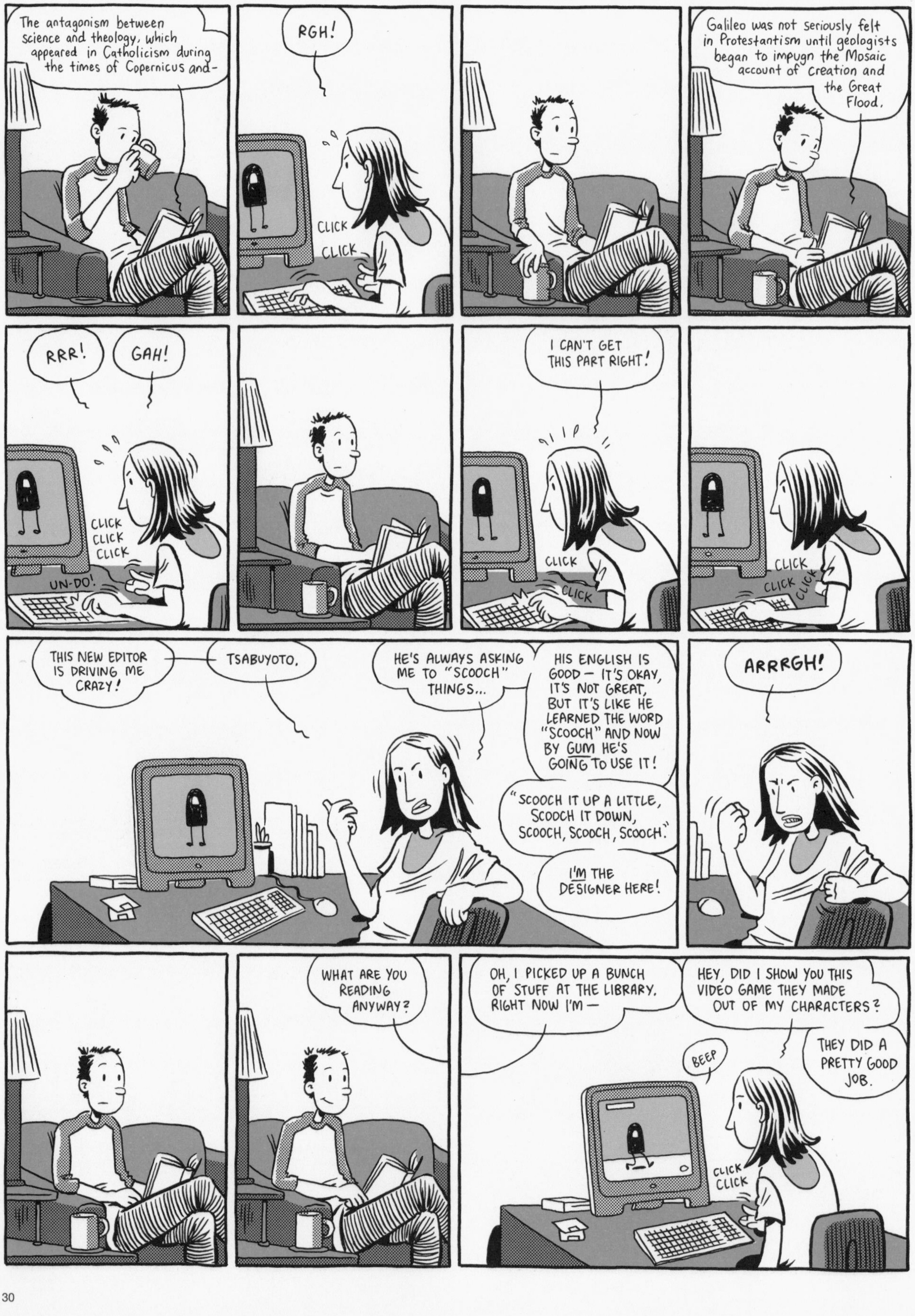
The antagonism between science and theology, which appeared in Catholicism during the times of Copernicus and-
RGH!
CLICK
CLICK
Galileo was not seriously felt in Protestantism until geologists began to impugn the Mosaic account of creation and the Great Flood.
RRR!
GAH!
CLICK CLICK CLICK
UN-DO!
I CAN'T GET THIS PART RIGHT!
CLICK
CLICK
CLICK
CLICK
CLICK
THIS NEW EDITOR IS DRIVING ME CRAZY!
TSABUYOTO.
HE'S ALWAYS ASKING ME TO "SCOOCH" THINGS...
HIS ENGLISH IS GOOD — IT'S OKAY, IT'S NOT GREAT, BUT IT'S LIKE HE LEARNED THE WORD "SCOOCH" AND NOW BY GUM HE'S GOING TO USE IT!
"SCOOCH IT UP A LITTLE, SCOOCH IT DOWN, SCOOCH, SCOOCH, SCOOCH."
I'M THE DESIGNER HERE!
ARRRGH!
WHAT ARE YOU READING ANYWAY?
OH, I PICKED UP A BUNCH OF STUFF AT THE LIBRARY. RIGHT NOW I'M —
HEY, DID I SHOW YOU THIS VIDEO GAME THEY MADE OUT OF MY CHARACTERS?
BEEP
THEY DID A PRETTY GOOD JOB.
CLICK CLICK

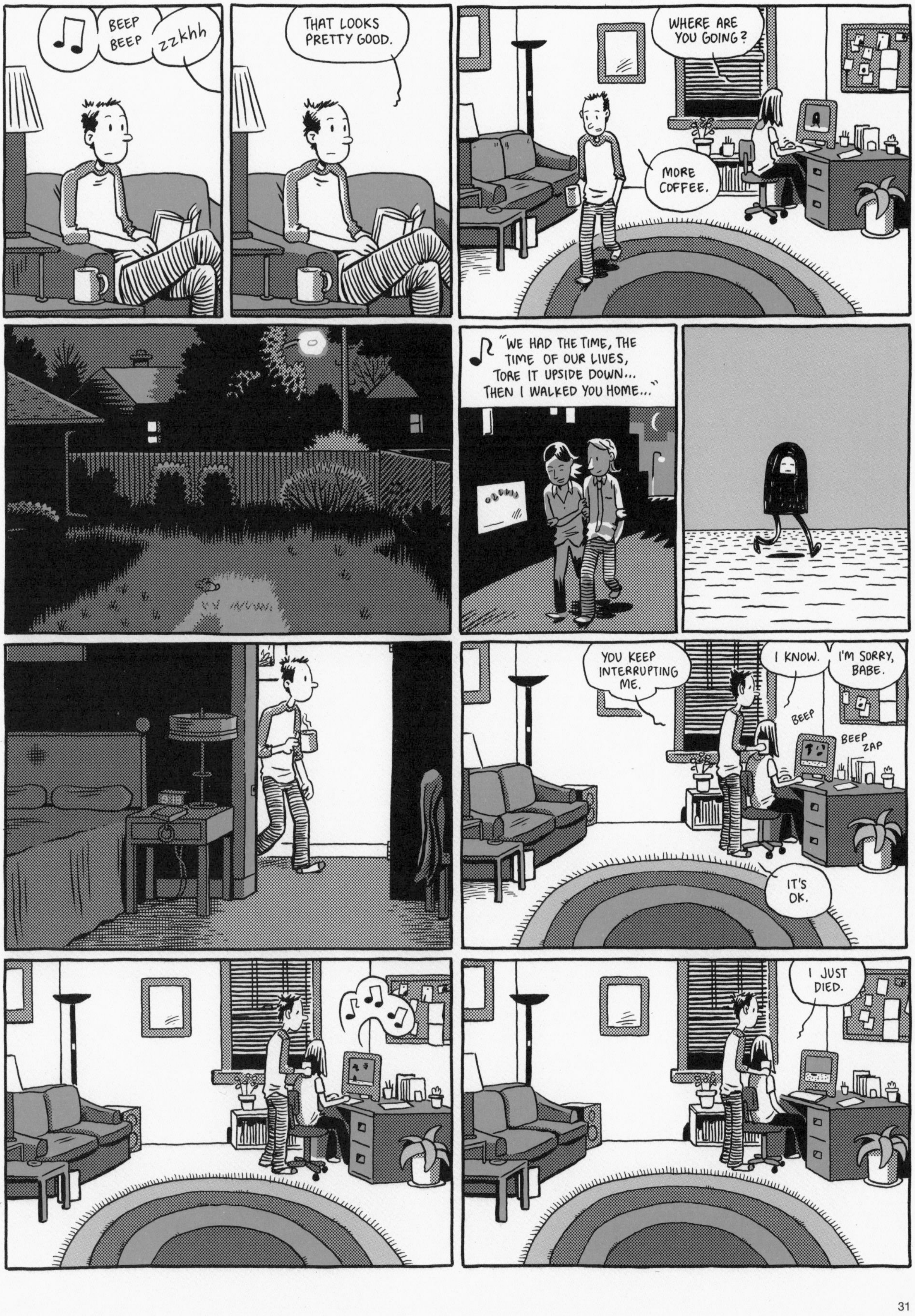

BEEP BEEP
zzkhh
THAT LOOKS PRETTY GOOD.
WHERE ARE YOU GOING?
MORE COFFEE.
"WE HAD THE TIME, THE TIME OF OUR LIVES, TORE IT UPSIDE DOWN... THEN I WALKED YOU HOME..."
YOU KEEP INTERRUPTING ME.
I KNOW.
I'M SORRY, BABE.
BEEP
BEEP
ZAP
IT'S OK.
I JUST DIED.

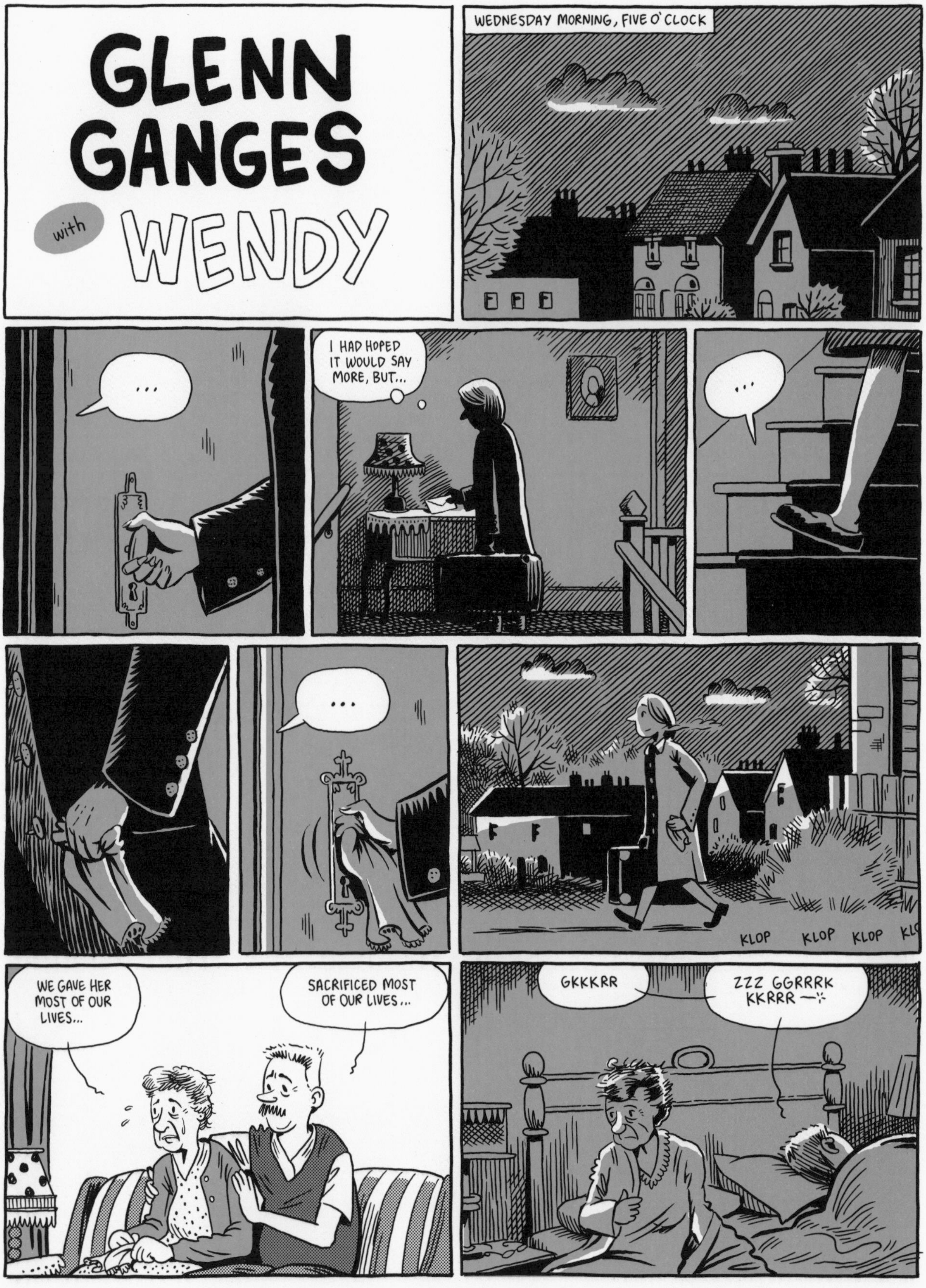
GLENN GANGES
with WENDY
WEDNESDAY MORNING, FIVE O' CLOCK
...
I HAD HOPED IT WOULD SAY MORE, BUT...
...
...
KLOP KLOP KLOP
WE GAVE HER MOST OF OUR LIVES...
SACRIFICED MOST OF OUR LIVES...
GKKKR
ZZZ GGRRRK KKRRR

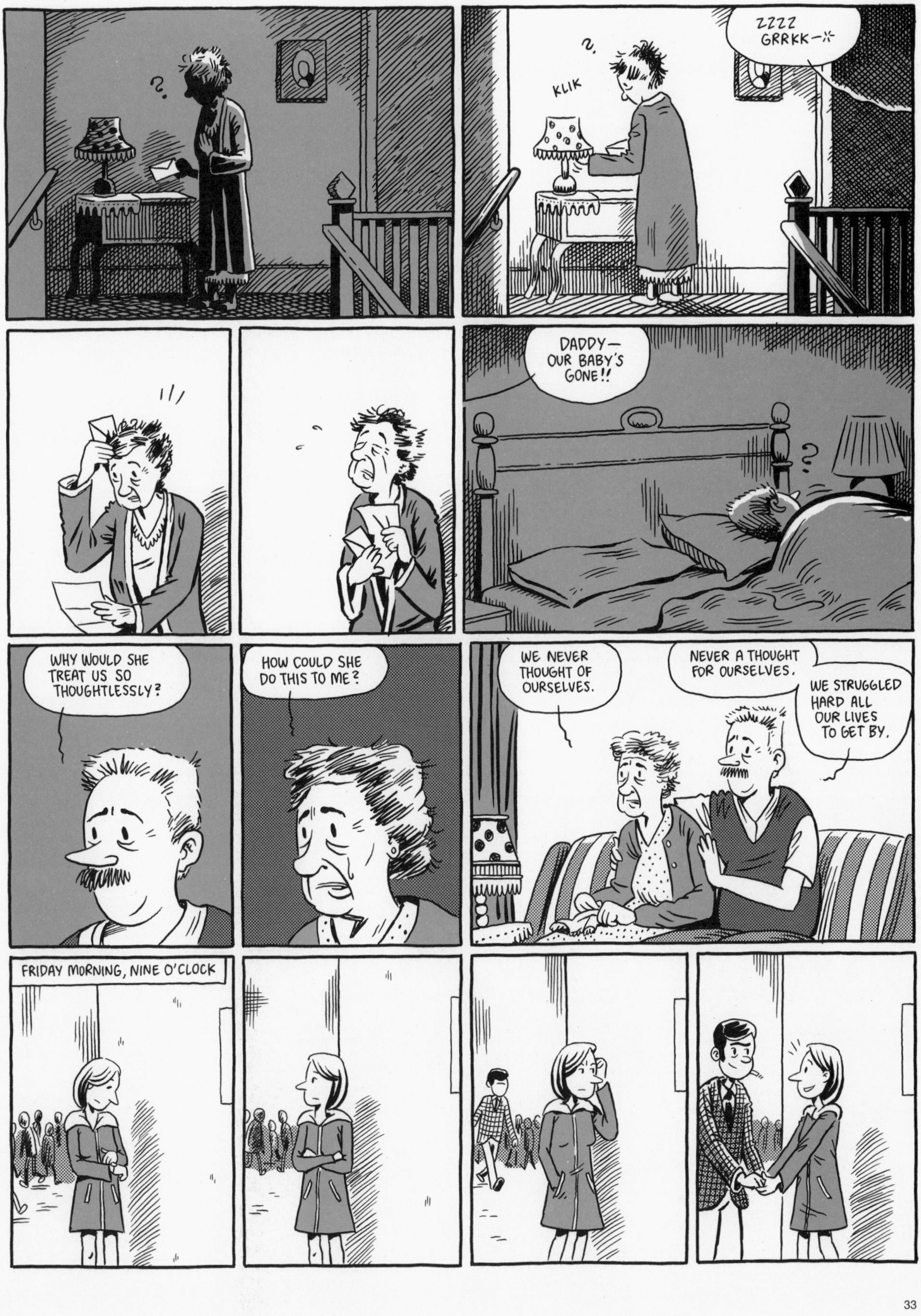
ZZZZ GRRKK—
KLIK
DADDY— OUR BABY'S GONE!!
WHY WOULD SHE TREAT US SO THOUGHTLESSLY?
HOW COULD SHE DO THIS TO ME?
WE NEVER THOUGHT OF OURSELVES.
NEVER A THOUGHT FOR OURSELVES.
WE STRUGGLED HARD ALL OUR LIVES TO GET BY.
FRIDAY MORNING, NINE O'CLOCK

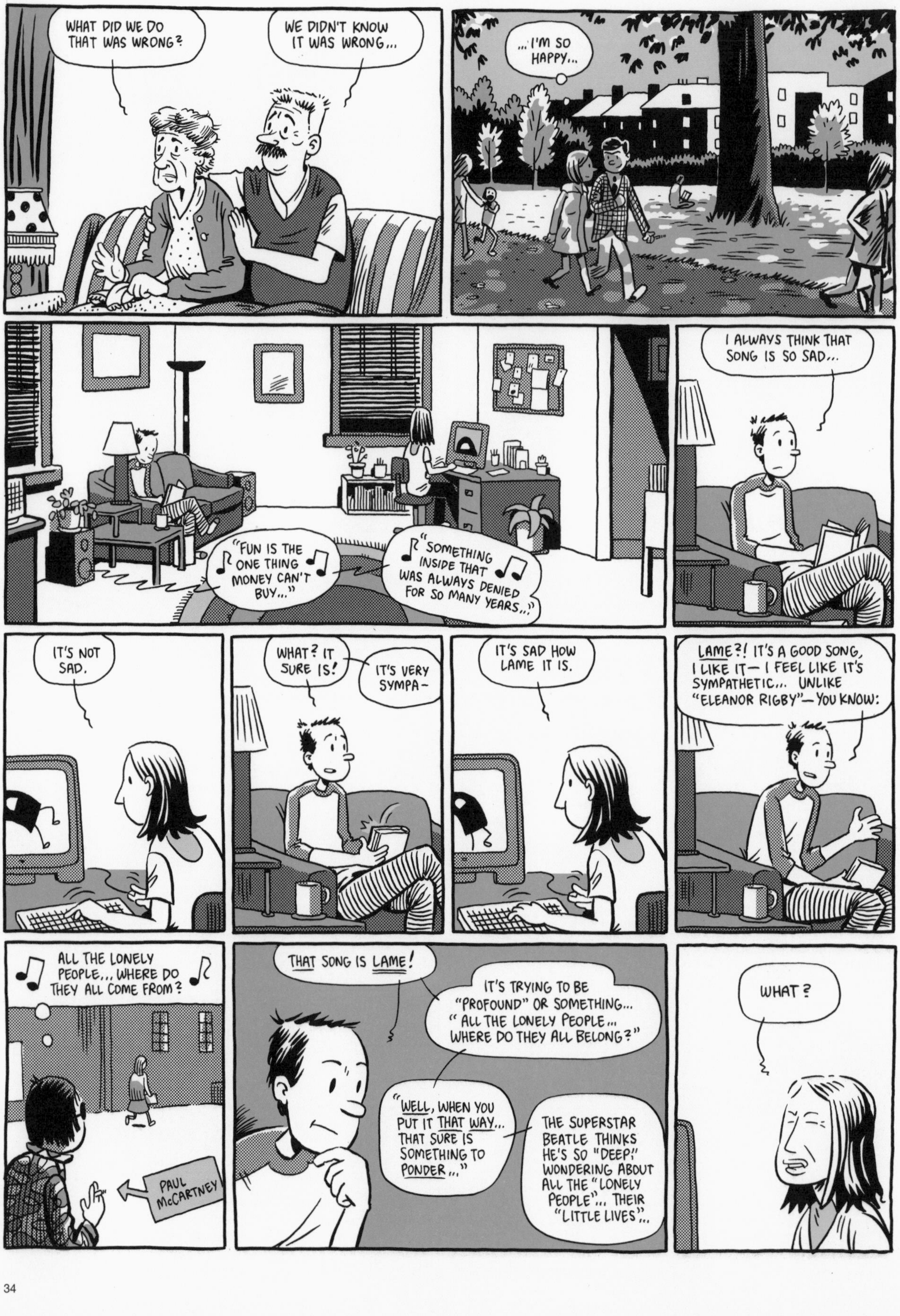
WHAT DID WE DO THAT WAS WRONG?
WE DIDN'T KNOW IT WAS WRONG...
...I'M SO HAPPY...
"FUN IS THE ONE THING MONEY CAN'T BUY..."
"SOMETHING INSIDE THAT WAS ALWAYS DENIED FOR SO MANY YEARS..."
I ALWAYS THINK THAT SONG IS SO SAD...
IT'S NOT SAD.
WHAT? IT SURE IS!
IT'S VERY SYMPA-
IT'S SAD HOW LAME IT IS.
LAME?! IT'S A GOOD SONG, I LIKE IT— I FEEL LIKE IT'S SYMPATHETIC... UNLIKE "ELEANOR RIGBY"—YOU KNOW:
ALL THE LONELY PEOPLE... WHERE DO THEY ALL COME FROM?
PAUL McCARTNEY
THAT SONG IS LAME!
IT'S TRYING TO BE "PROFOUND" OR SOMETHING... "ALL THE LONELY PEOPLE... WHERE DO THEY ALL BELONG?"
"WELL, WHEN YOU PUT IT THAT WAY... THAT SURE IS SOMETHING TO PONDER..."
THE SUPERSTAR BEATLE THINKS HE'S SO "DEEP," WONDERING ABOUT ALL THE "LONELY PEOPLE"... THEIR "LITTLE LIVES"...
WHAT?

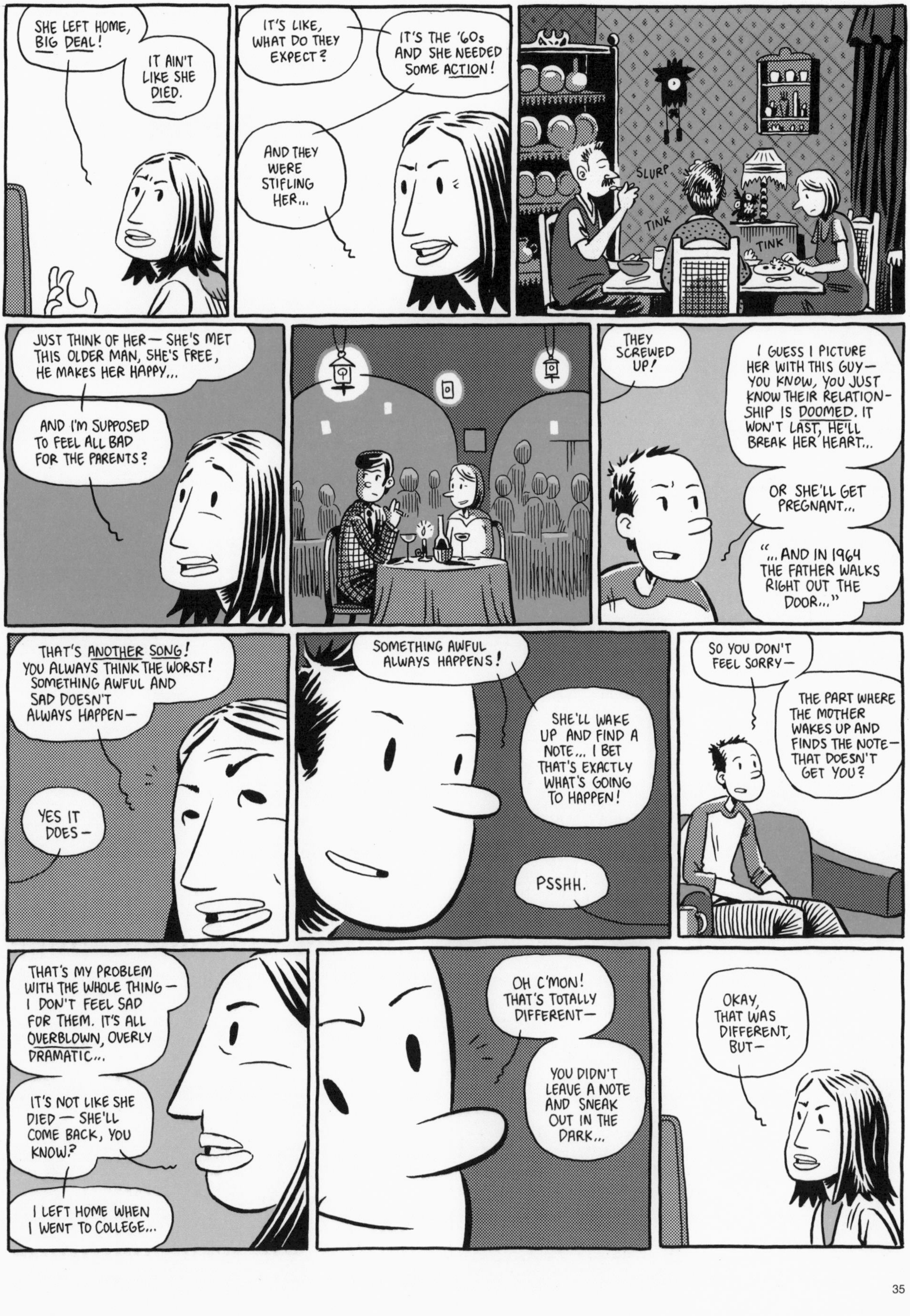
SHE LEFT HOME, BIG DEAL!
IT AIN'T LIKE SHE DIED.
IT'S LIKE, WHAT DO THEY EXPECT?
IT'S THE '60s AND SHE NEEDED SOME ACTION!
AND THEY WERE STIFLING HER...
SLURP
TINK
TINK
JUST THINK OF HER— SHE'S MET THIS OLDER MAN, SHE'S FREE, HE MAKES HER HAPPY...
AND I'M SUPPOSED TO FEEL ALL BAD FOR THE PARENTS?
THEY SCREWED UP!
I GUESS I PICTURE HER WITH THIS GUY— YOU KNOW, YOU JUST KNOW THEIR RELATIONSHIP IS DOOMED. IT WON'T LAST, HE'LL BREAK HER HEART...
OR SHE'LL GET PREGNANT...
"...AND IN 1964 THE FATHER WALKS RIGHT OUT THE DOOR..."
THAT'S ANOTHER SONG! YOU ALWAYS THINK THE WORST! SOMETHING AWFUL AND SAD DOESN'T ALWAYS HAPPEN—
YES IT DOES—
SOMETHING AWFUL ALWAYS HAPPENS!
SHE'LL WAKE UP AND FIND A NOTE... I BET THAT'S EXACTLY WHAT'S GOING TO HAPPEN!
PSSHH.
SO YOU DON'T FEEL SORRY—
THE PART WHERE THE MOTHER WAKES UP AND FINDS THE NOTE— THAT DOESN'T GET YOU?
THAT'S MY PROBLEM WITH THE WHOLE THING— I DON'T FEEL SAD FOR THEM. IT'S ALL OVERBLOWN, OVERLY DRAMATIC...
IT'S NOT LIKE SHE DIED— SHE'LL COME BACK, YOU KNOW?
I LEFT HOME WHEN I WENT TO COLLEGE...
OH C'MON! THAT'S TOTALLY DIFFERENT—
YOU DIDN'T LEAVE A NOTE AND SNEAK OUT IN THE DARK...
OKAY, THAT WAS DIFFERENT, BUT—

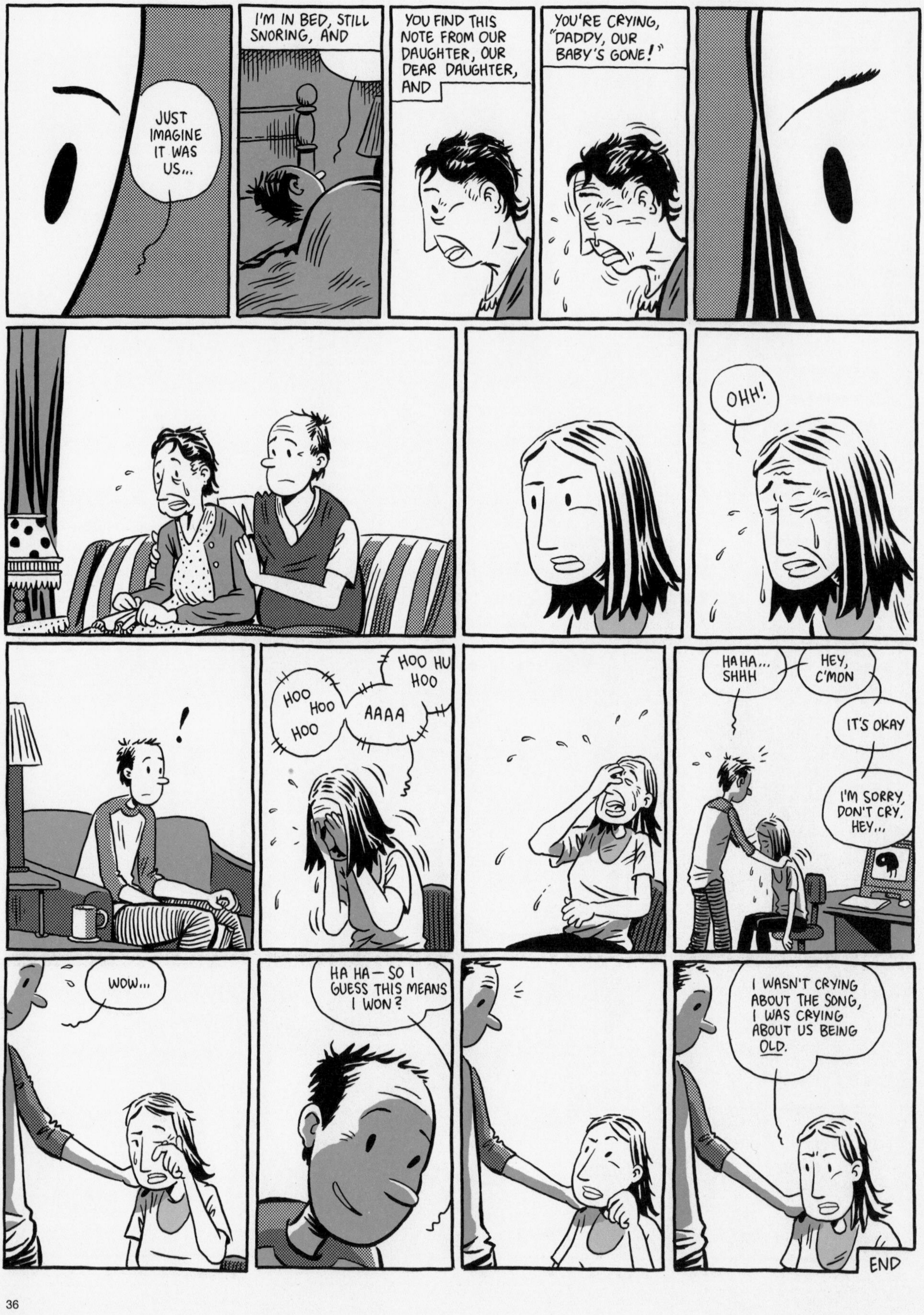
JUST IMAGINE IT WAS US...
I'M IN BED, STILL SNORING, AND
YOU FIND THIS NOTE FROM OUR DAUGHTER, OUR DEAR DAUGHTER, AND
YOU'RE CRYING, "DADDY, OUR BABY'S GONE!"
OHH!
!
HOO HOO HOO
AAAA
HOO HU HOO
HA HA... SHHH
HEY, C'MON
IT'S OKAY
I'M SORRY, DON'T CRY. HEY...
WOW...
HA HA— SO I GUESS THIS MEANS I WON?
I WASN'T CRYING ABOUT THE SONG, I WAS CRYING ABOUT US BEING OLD.
END

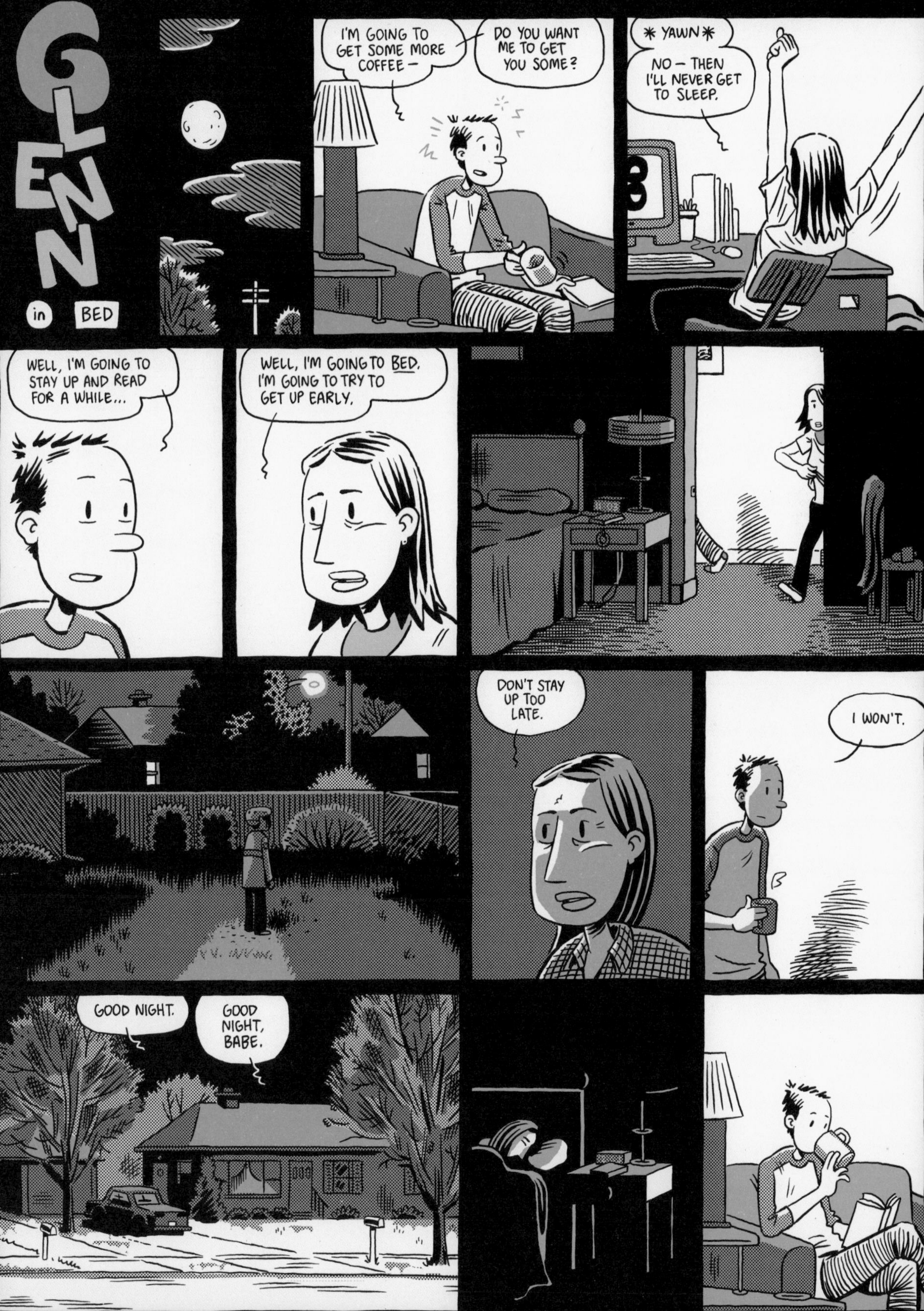
GLENN
in BED
I'M GOING TO GET SOME MORE COFFEE –
DO YOU WANT ME TO GET YOU SOME?
* YAWN *
NO – THEN I'LL NEVER GET TO SLEEP.
WELL, I'M GOING TO STAY UP AND READ FOR A WHILE...
WELL, I'M GOING TO BED. I'M GOING TO TRY TO GET UP EARLY.
DON'T STAY UP TOO LATE.
I WON'T.
GOOD NIGHT.
GOOD NIGHT, BABE.

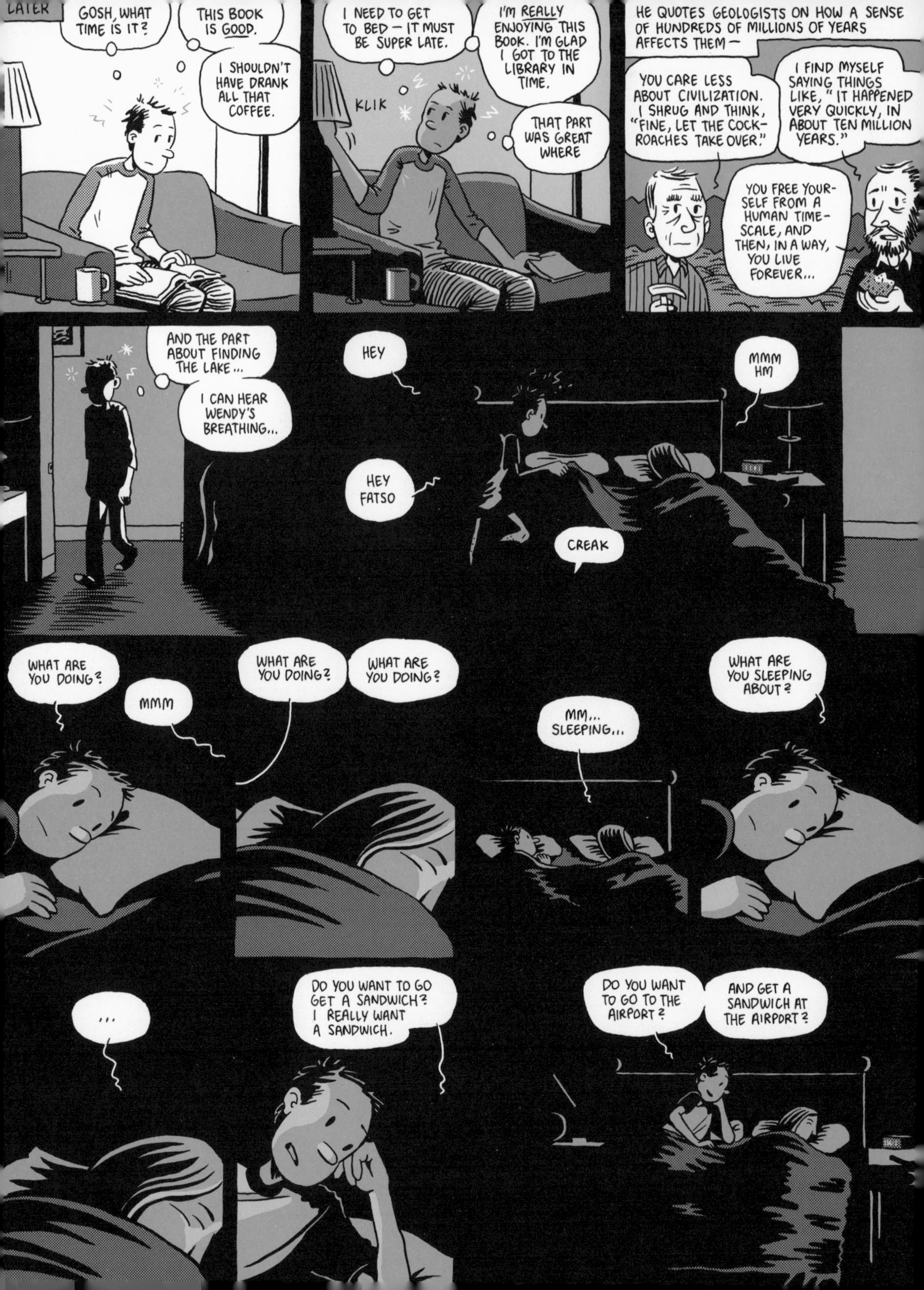
LATER
GOSH, WHAT TIME IS IT?
THIS BOOK IS GOOD.
I SHOULDN'T HAVE DRANK ALL THAT COFFEE.
I NEED TO GET TO BED — IT MUST BE SUPER LATE.
I'M REALLY ENJOYING THIS BOOK. I'M GLAD I GOT TO THE LIBRARY IN TIME.
KLIK
THAT PART WAS GREAT WHERE
HE QUOTES GEOLOGISTS ON HOW A SENSE OF HUNDREDS OF MILLIONS OF YEARS AFFECTS THEM —
YOU CARE LESS ABOUT CIVILIZATION. I SHRUG AND THINK, "FINE, LET THE COCKROACHES TAKE OVER."
I FIND MYSELF SAYING THINGS LIKE, "IT HAPPENED VERY QUICKLY, IN ABOUT TEN MILLION YEARS."
YOU FREE YOURSELF FROM A HUMAN TIME-SCALE, AND THEN, IN A WAY, YOU LIVE FOREVER...
AND THE PART ABOUT FINDING THE LAKE...
I CAN HEAR WENDY'S BREATHING...
HEY
HEY FATSO
MMM HM
CREAK
WHAT ARE YOU DOING?
MMM
WHAT ARE YOU DOING?
WHAT ARE YOU DOING?
MM... SLEEPING...
WHAT ARE YOU SLEEPING ABOUT?
...
DO YOU WANT TO GO GET A SANDWICH? I REALLY WANT A SANDWICH.
DO YOU WANT TO GO TO THE AIRPORT?
AND GET A SANDWICH AT THE AIRPORT?

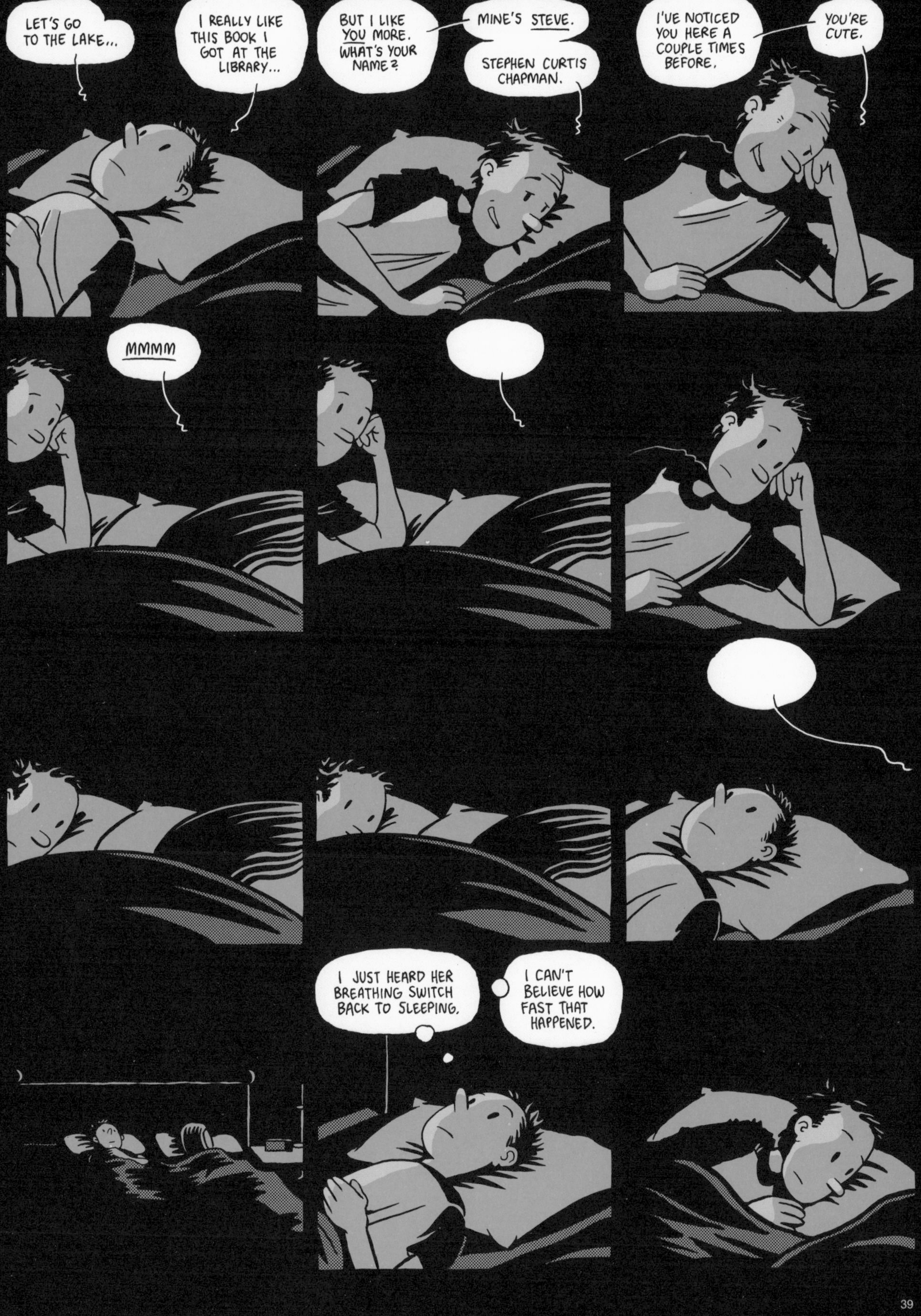
LET'S GO TO THE LAKE...
I REALLY LIKE THIS BOOK I GOT AT THE LIBRARY...
BUT I LIKE YOU MORE. WHAT'S YOUR NAME?
MINE'S STEVE.
STEPHEN CURTIS CHAPMAN.
I'VE NOTICED YOU HERE A COUPLE TIMES BEFORE.
YOU'RE CUTE.
MMMM
I JUST HEARD HER BREATHING SWITCH BACK TO SLEEPING.
I CAN'T BELIEVE HOW FAST THAT HAPPENED.

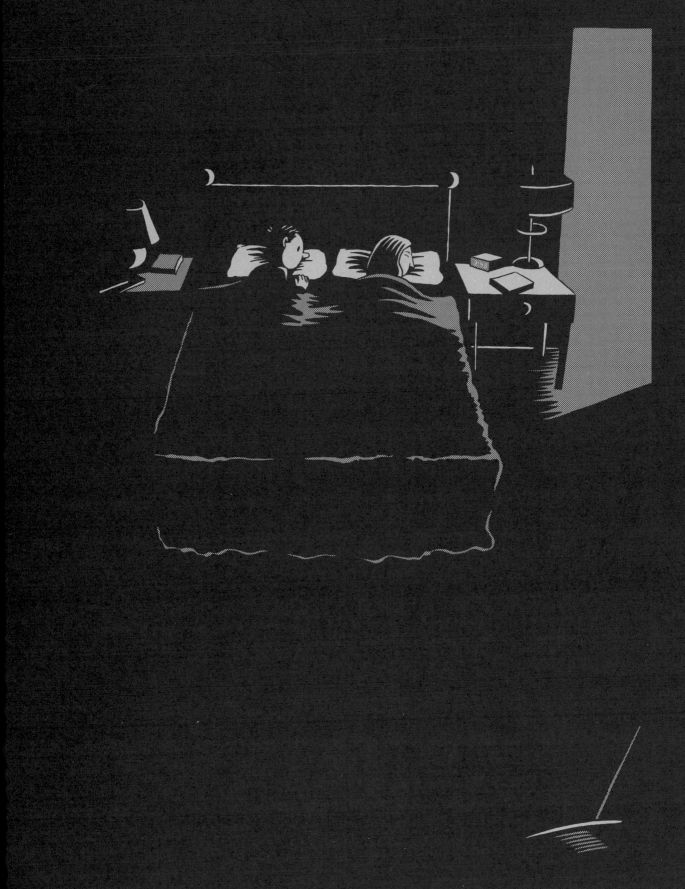

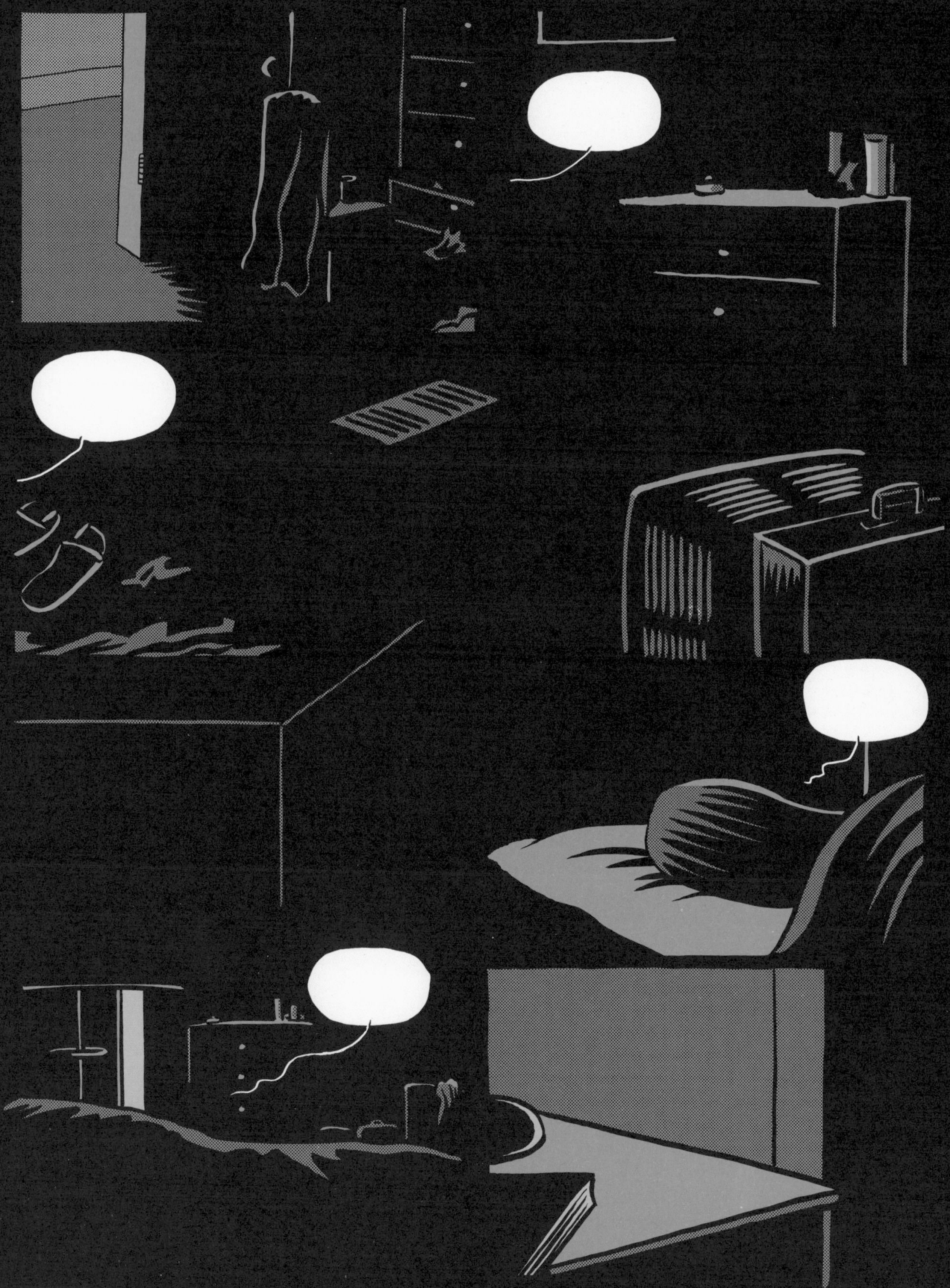

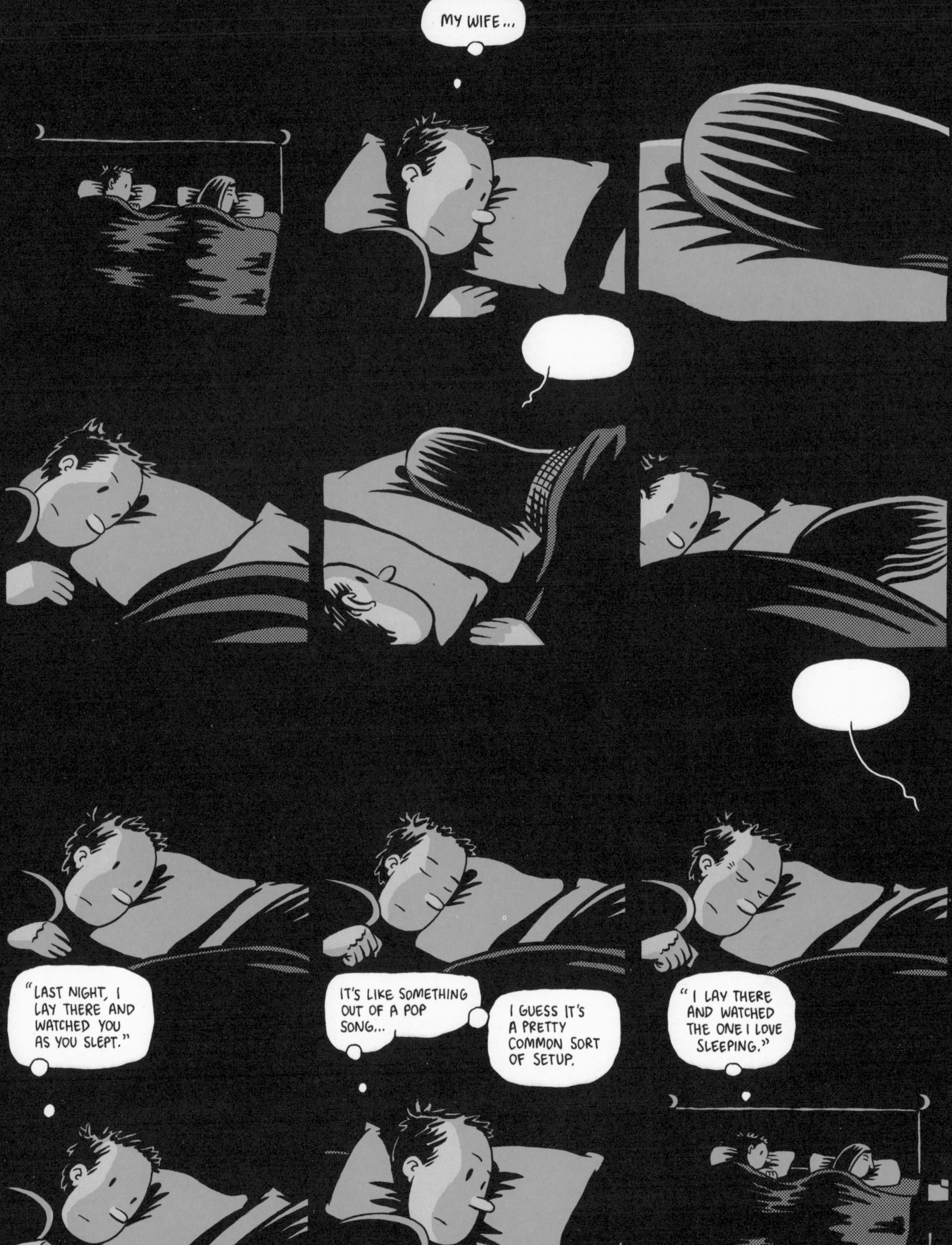
MY WIFE...
"LAST NIGHT, I LAY THERE AND WATCHED YOU AS YOU SLEPT."
IT'S LIKE SOMETHING OUT OF A POP SONG...
I GUESS IT'S A PRETTY COMMON SORT OF SETUP.
"I LAY THERE AND WATCHED THE ONE I LOVE SLEEPING."

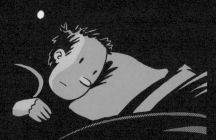

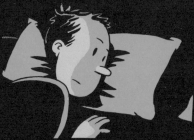

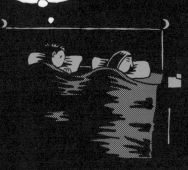

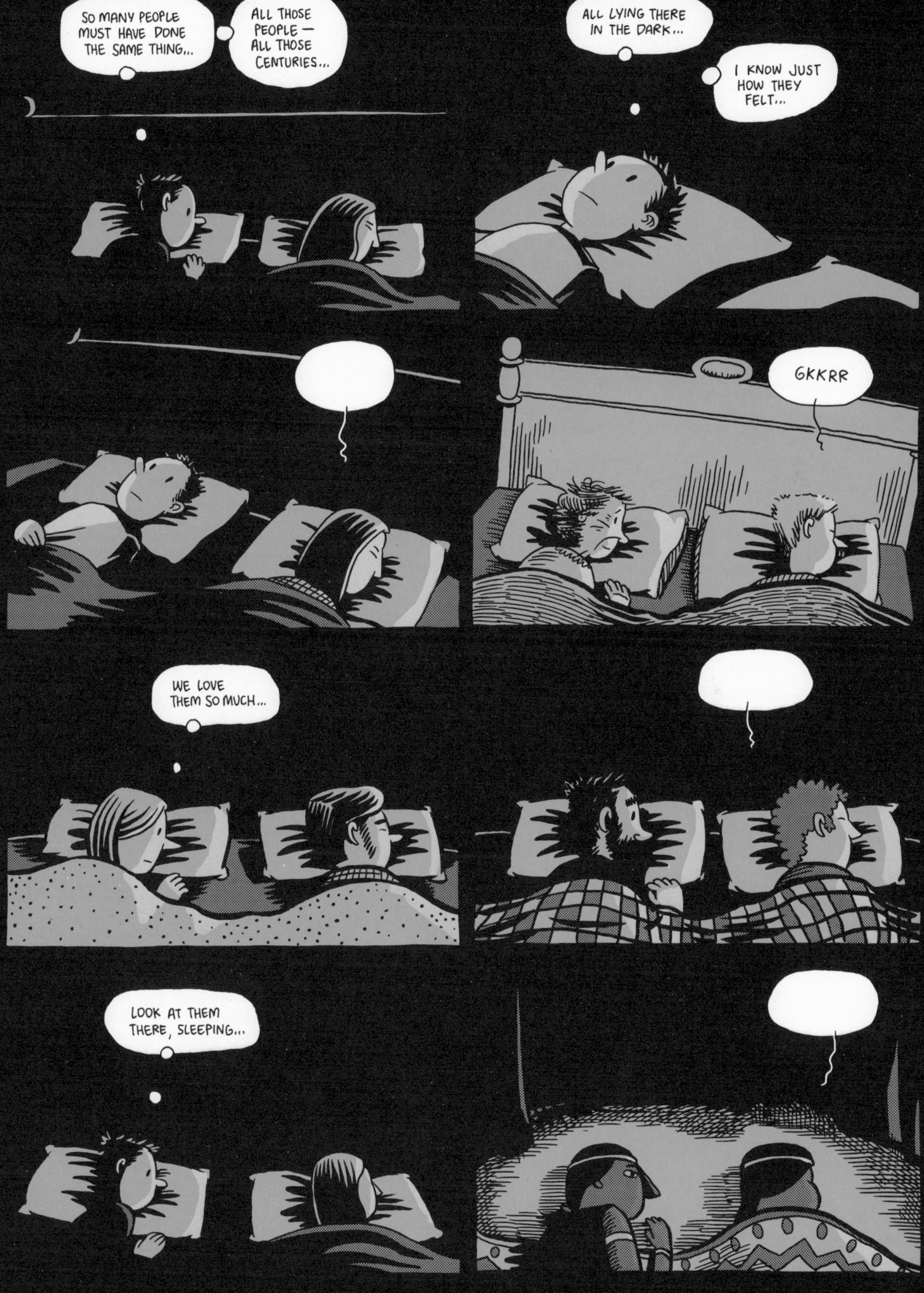
SO MANY PEOPLE MUST HAVE DONE THE SAME THING...
ALL THOSE PEOPLE — ALL THOSE CENTURIES...
ALL LYING THERE IN THE DARK...
I KNOW JUST HOW THEY FELT...
GKKRR
WE LOVE THEM SO MUCH...
LOOK AT THEM THERE, SLEEPING...

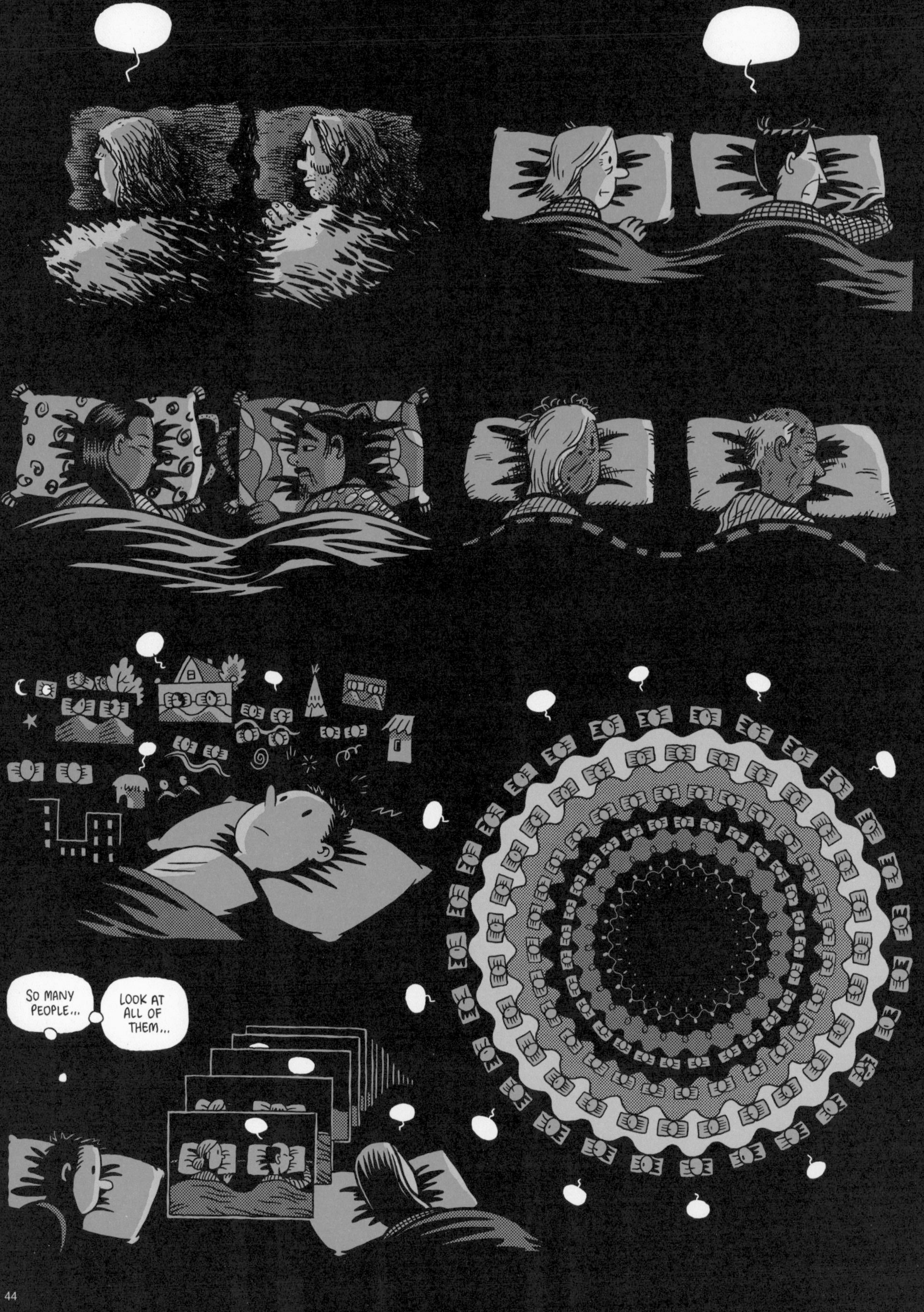
SO MANY PEOPLE...
LOOK AT ALL OF THEM...

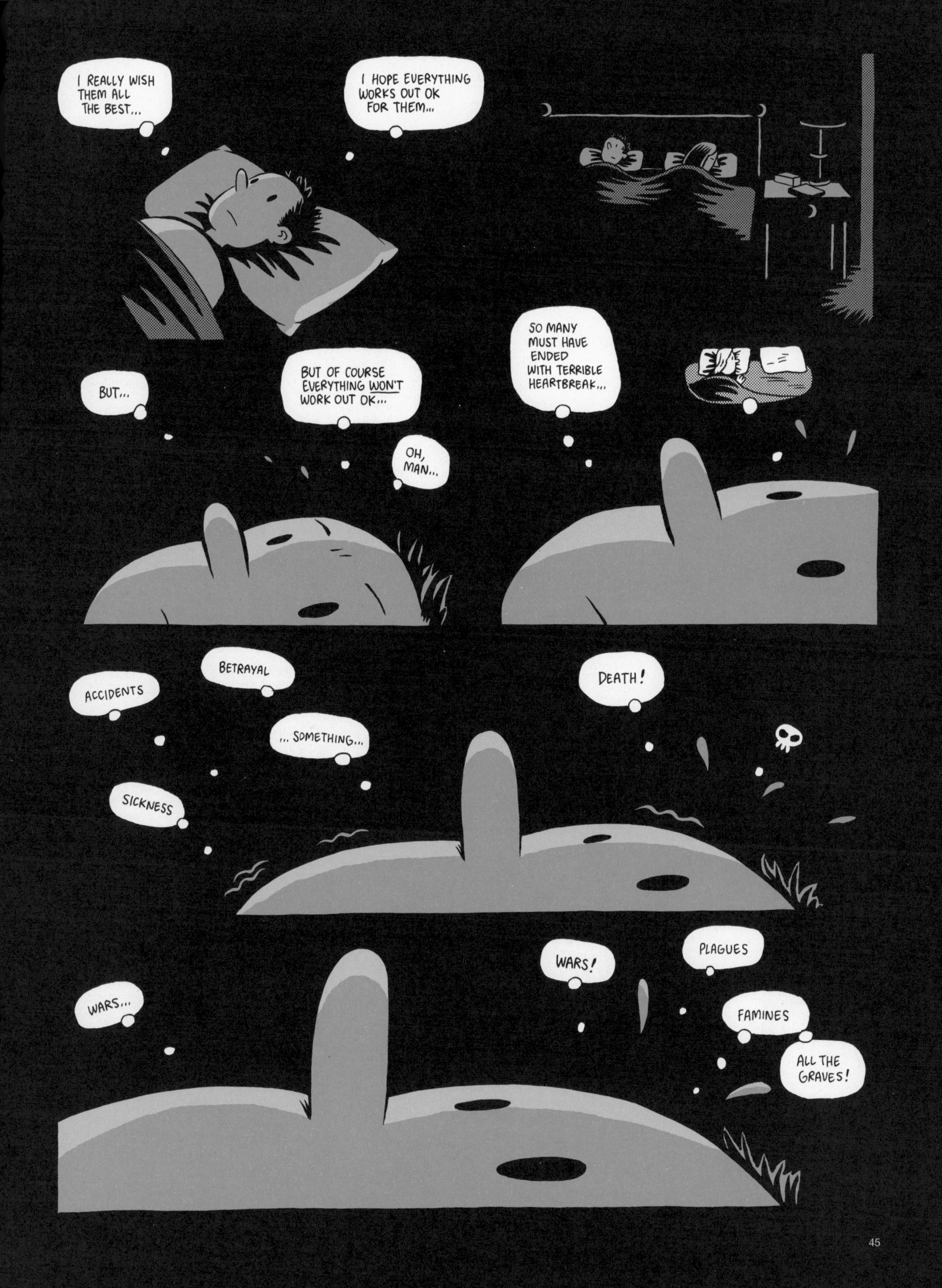

I REALLY WISH THEM ALL THE BEST...
I HOPE EVERYTHING WORKS OUT OK FOR THEM...
BUT...
BUT OF COURSE EVERYTHING WON'T WORK OUT OK...
OH, MAN...
SO MANY MUST HAVE ENDED WITH TERRIBLE HEARTBREAK...
ACCIDENTS
BETRAYAL
... SOMETHING...
SICKNESS
DEATH!
WARS...
WARS!
PLAGUES
FAMINES
ALL THE GRAVES!

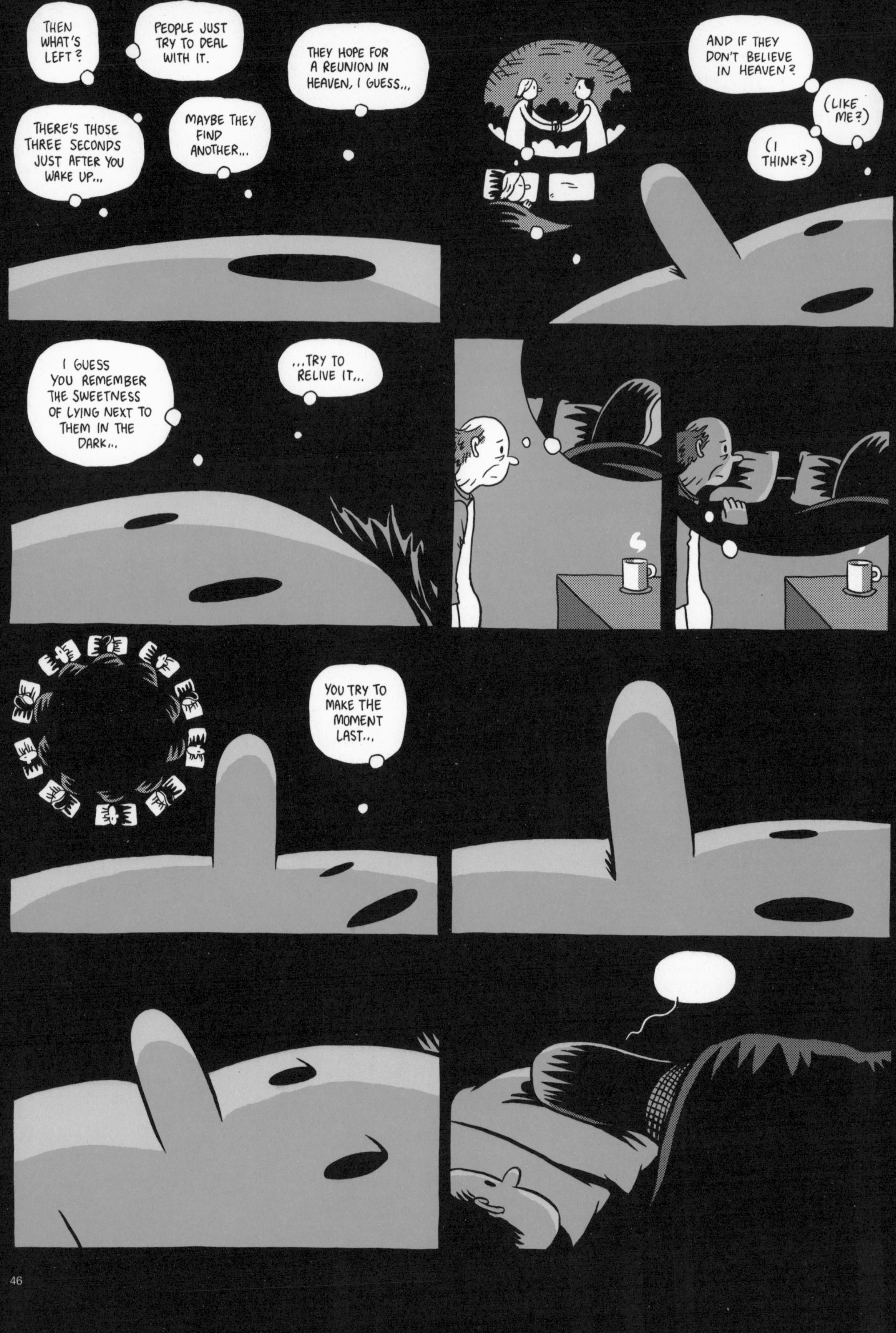
THEN WHAT'S LEFT?
PEOPLE JUST TRY TO DEAL WITH IT.
THERE'S THOSE THREE SECONDS JUST AFTER YOU WAKE UP...
MAYBE THEY FIND ANOTHER...
THEY HOPE FOR A REUNION IN HEAVEN, I GUESS...
AND IF THEY DON'T BELIEVE IN HEAVEN?
(LIKE ME?)
(I THINK?)
I GUESS YOU REMEMBER THE SWEETNESS OF LYING NEXT TO THEM IN THE DARK...
...TRY TO RELIVE IT...
YOU TRY TO MAKE THE MOMENT LAST...

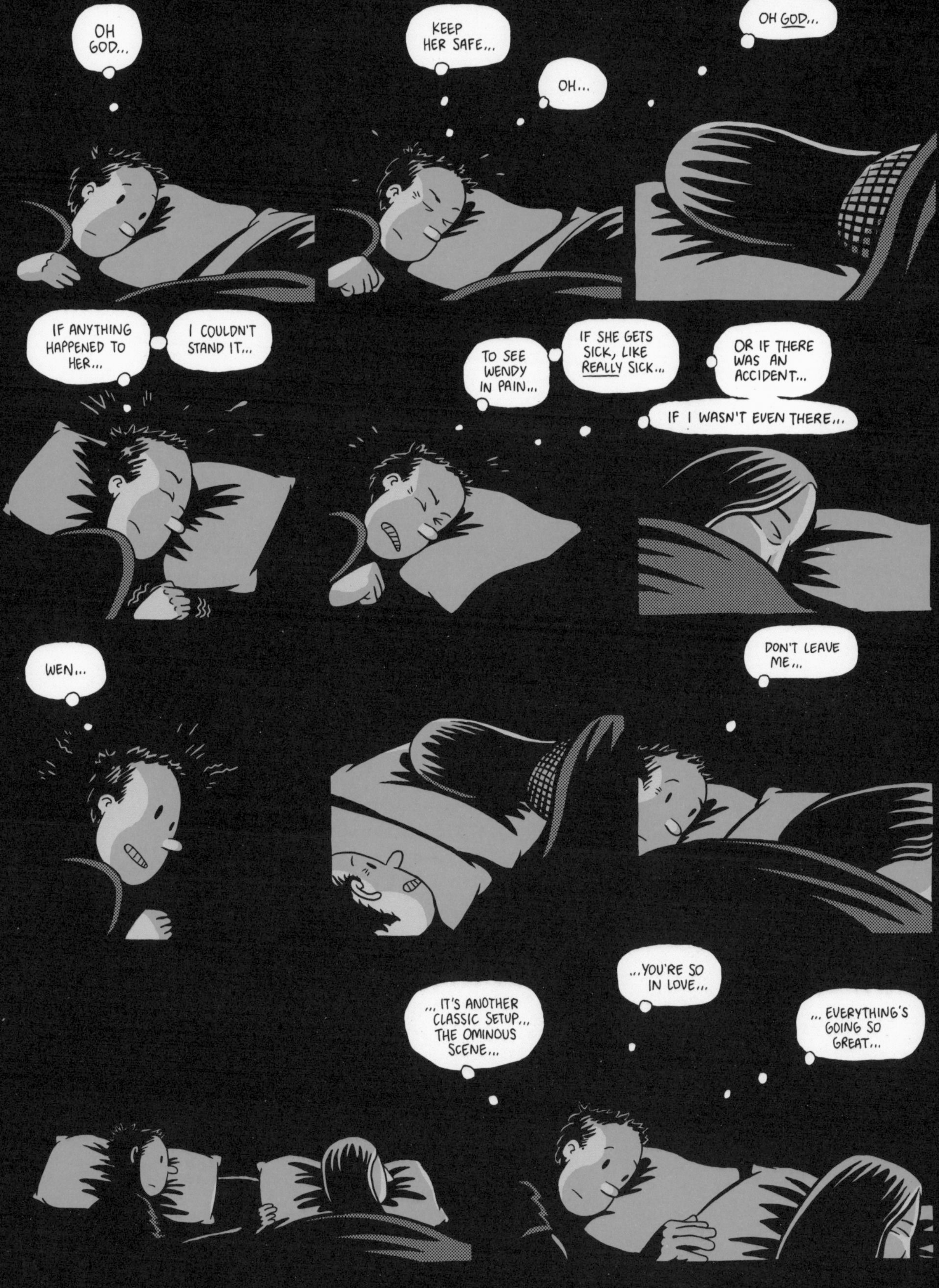
OH GOD...
KEEP HER SAFE...
OH...
OH GOD...
IF ANYTHING HAPPENED TO HER...
I COULDN'T STAND IT...
IF SHE GETS SICK, LIKE REALLY SICK...
TO SEE WENDY IN PAIN...
OR IF THERE WAS AN ACCIDENT...
IF I WASN'T EVEN THERE...
WEN...
DON'T LEAVE ME...
...IT'S ANOTHER CLASSIC SETUP... THE OMINOUS SCENE...
...YOU'RE SO IN LOVE...
...EVERYTHING'S GOING SO GREAT...

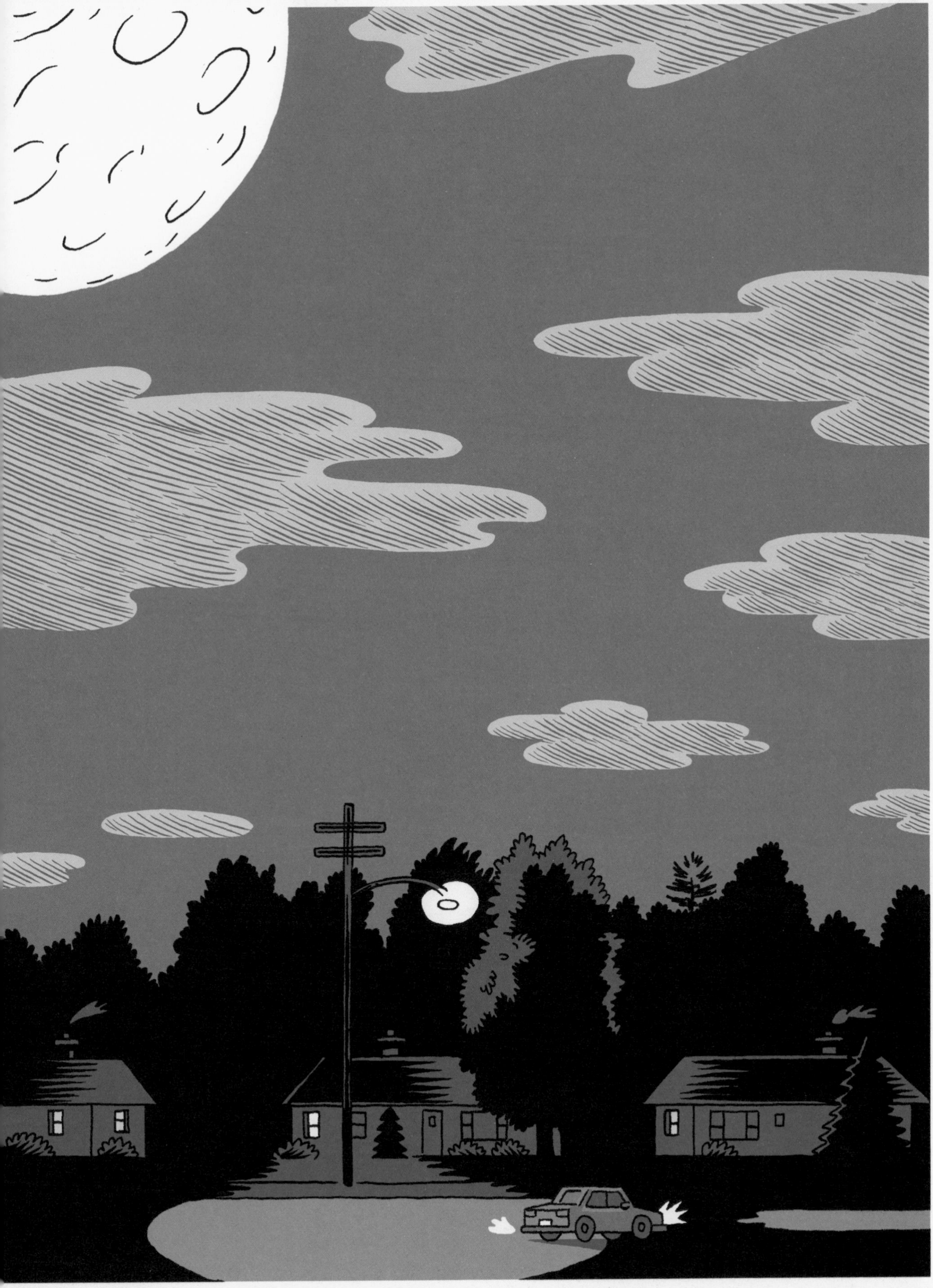

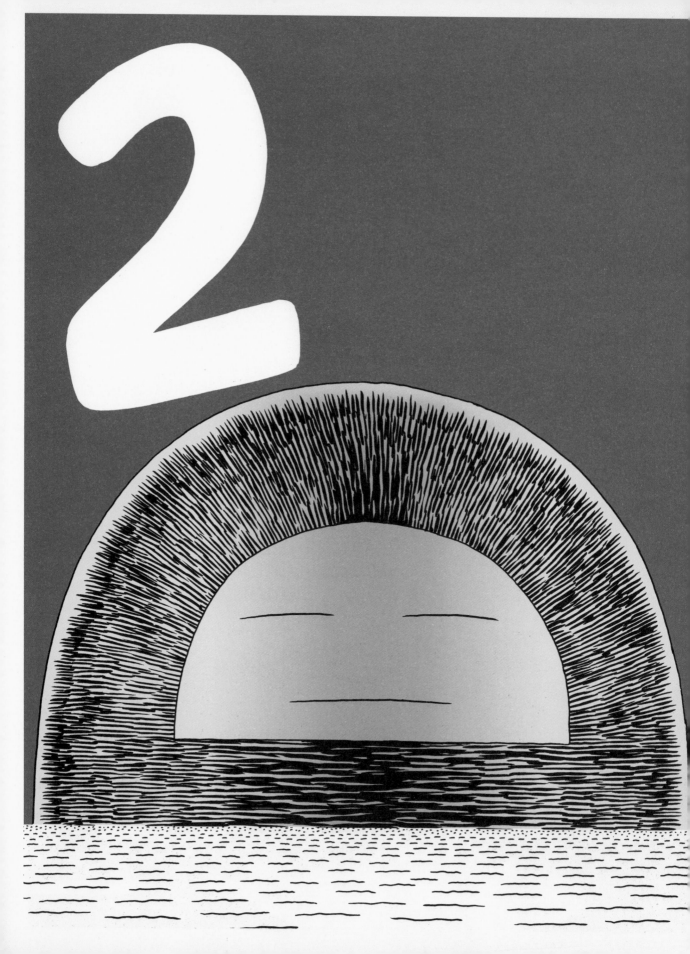

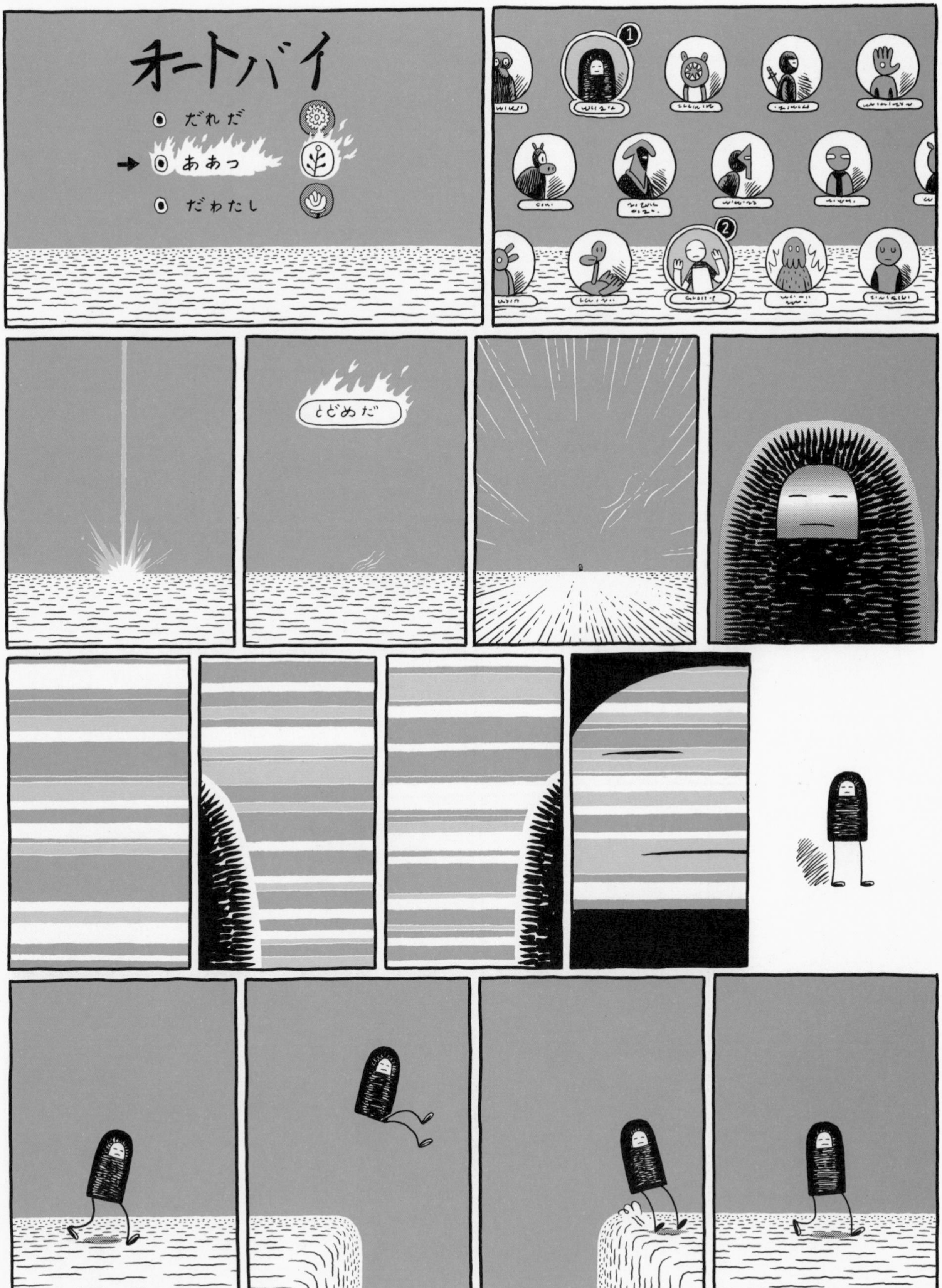
オートバイ
だれだ
ああっ
だわたし
1
2
とどめだ

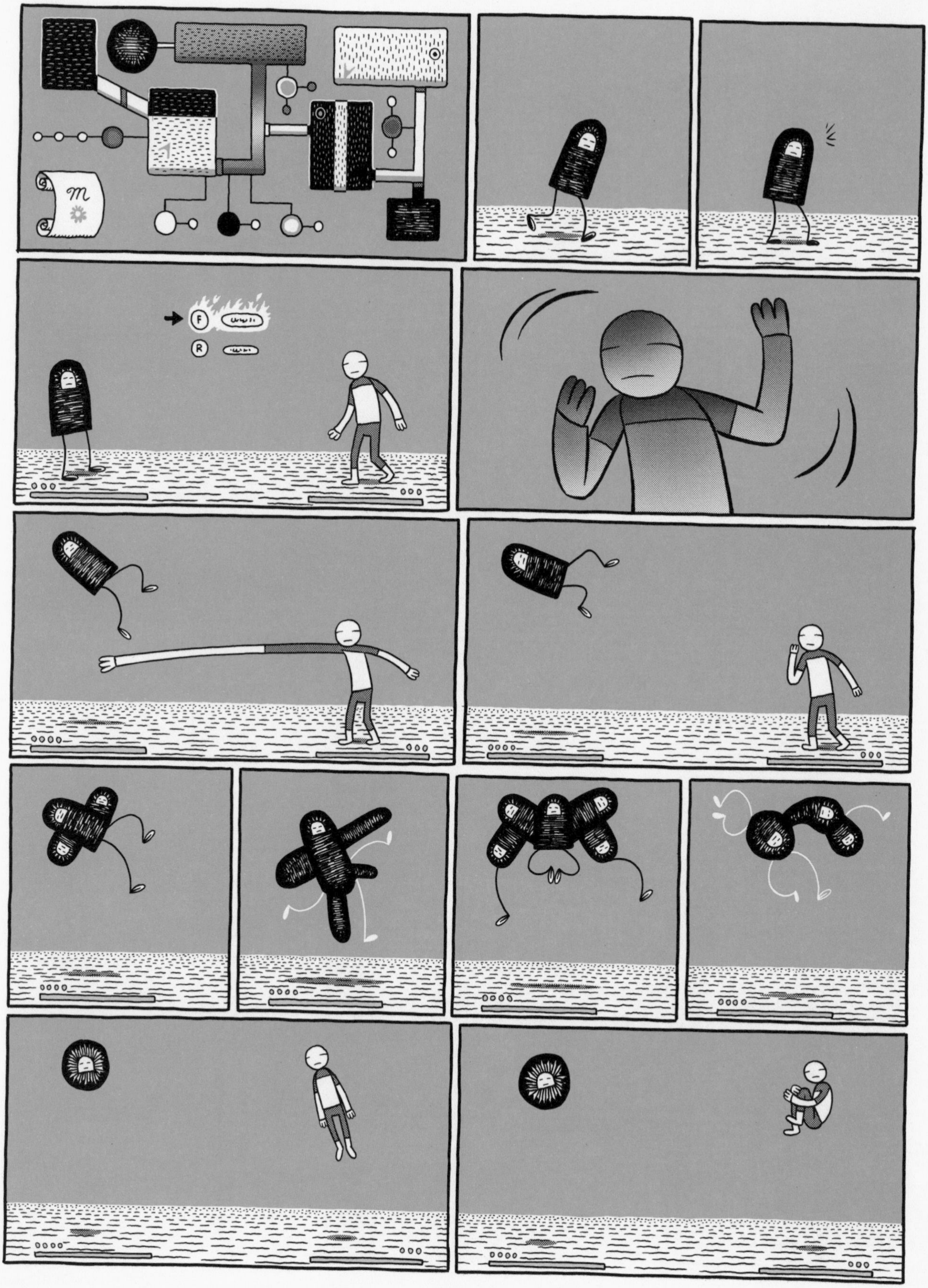
F
R

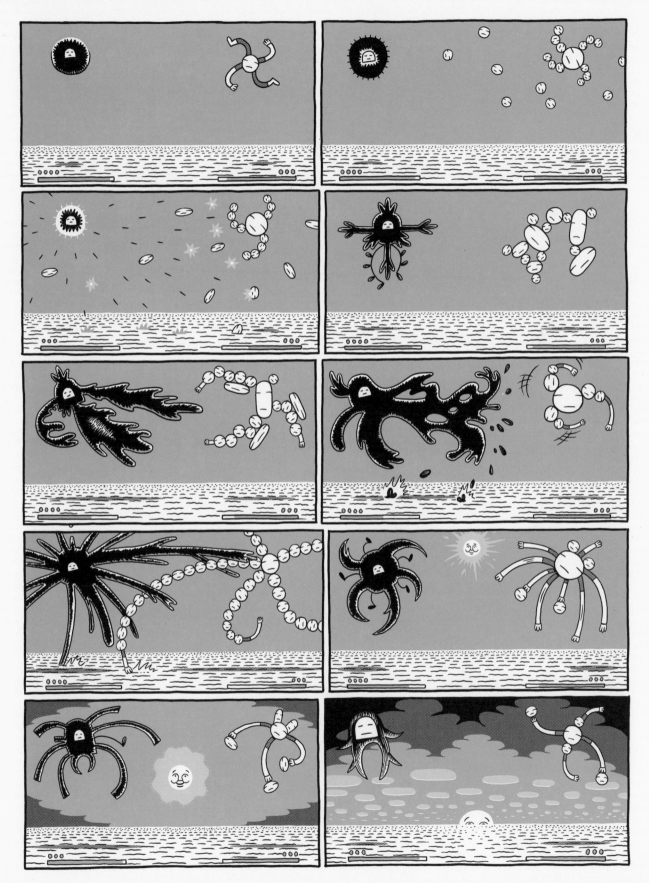

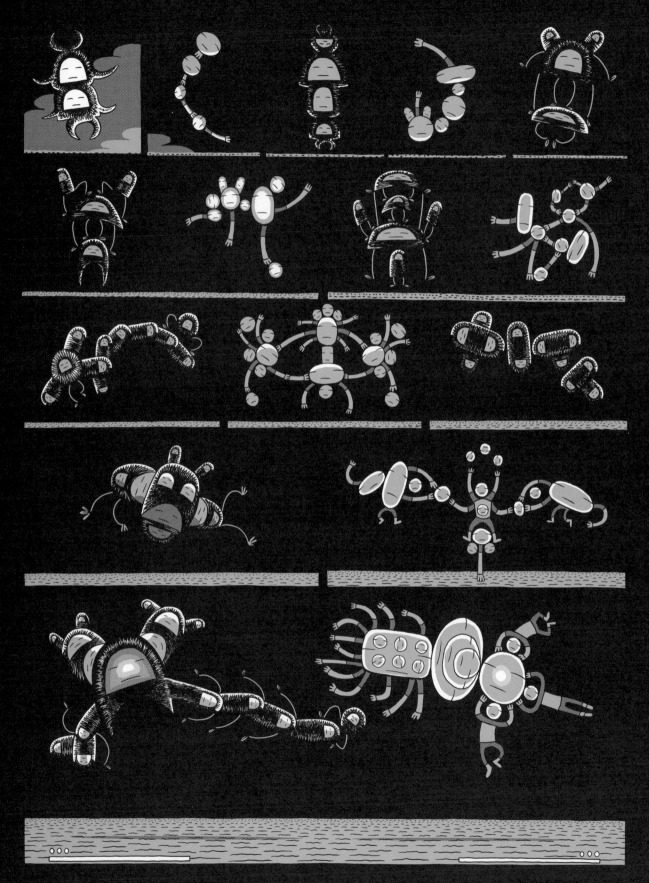

+20
↑↑↑ A
↑↓ AB
AS →→
↑↗→ B
+3
+5
+7
+7
+3
P
E
K
Z
Q
36012
M
N
Y

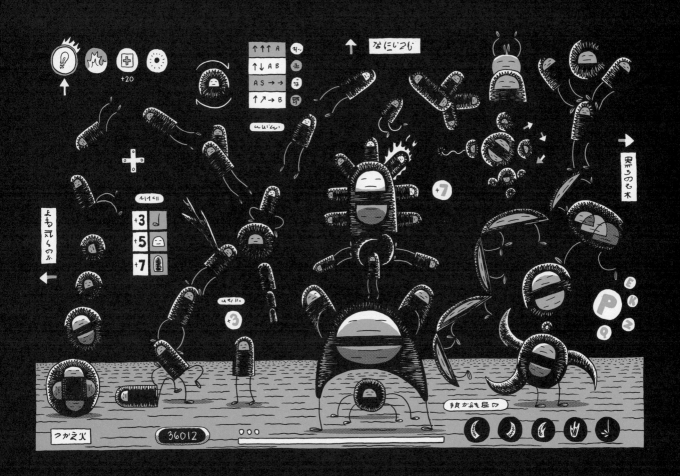

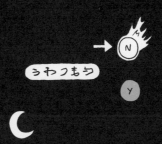

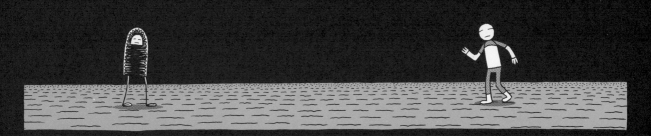

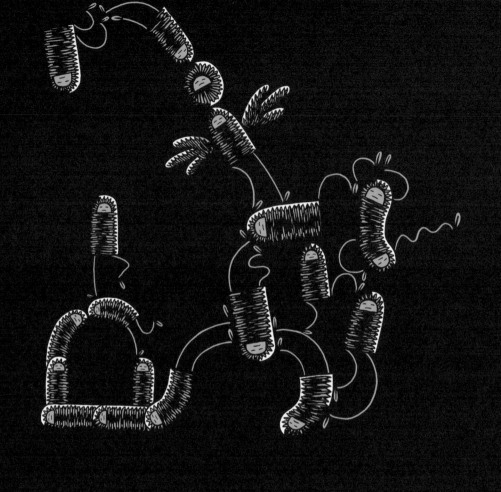

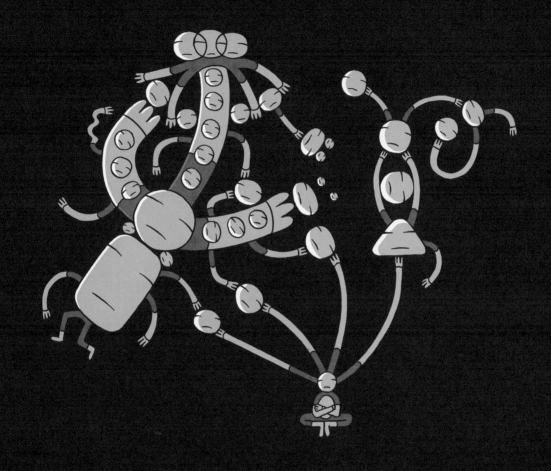

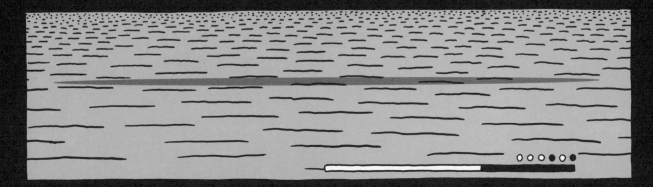

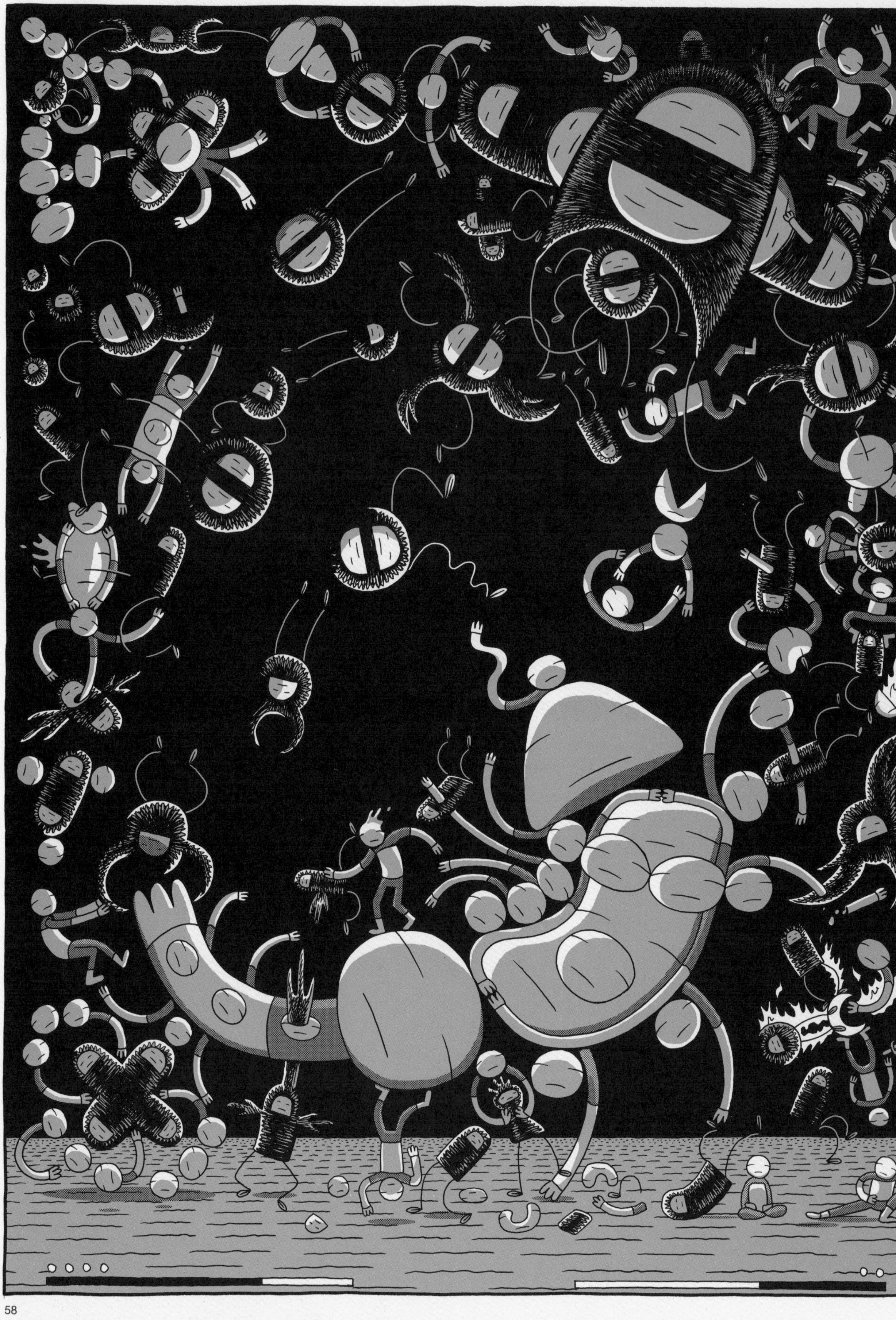

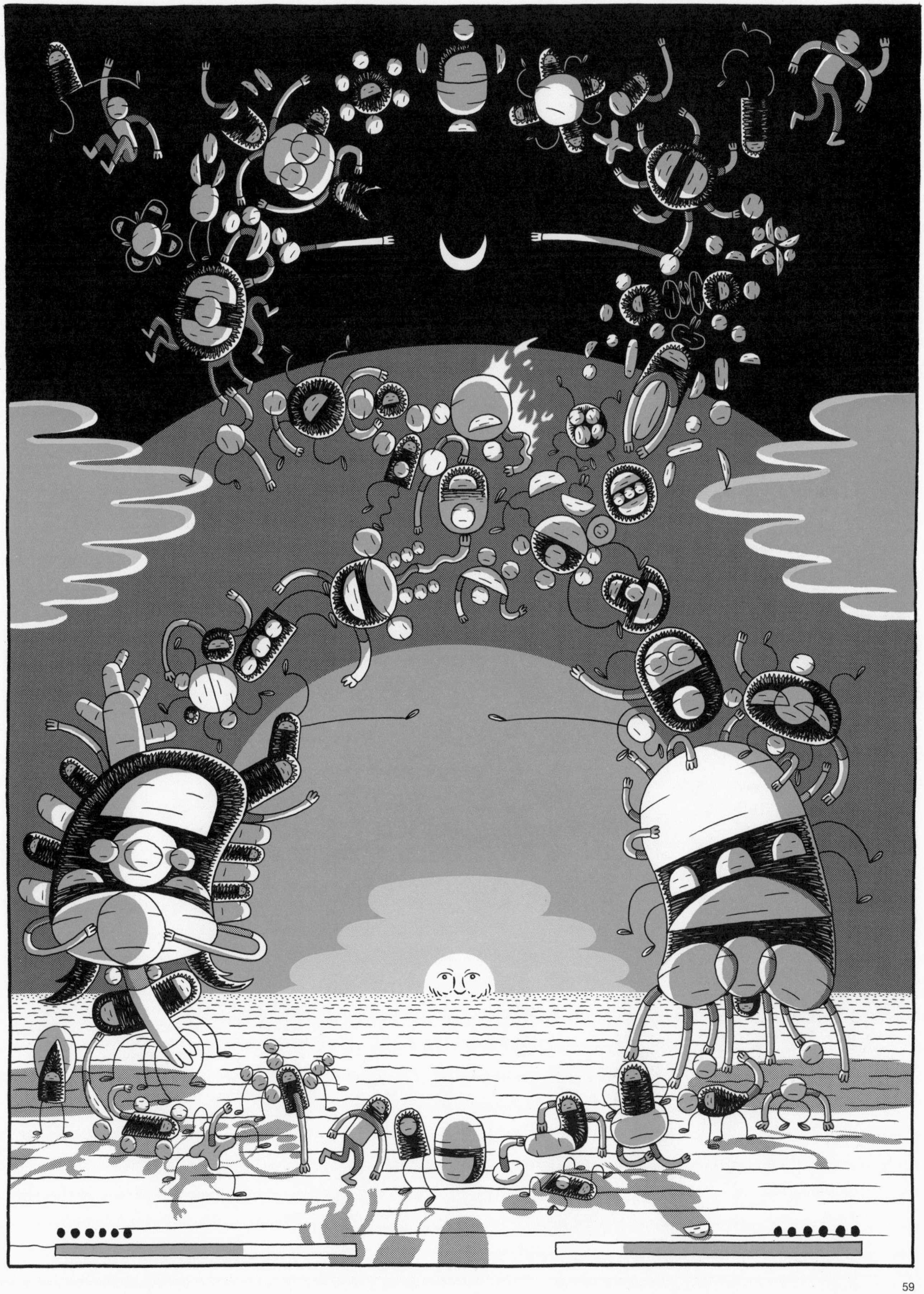

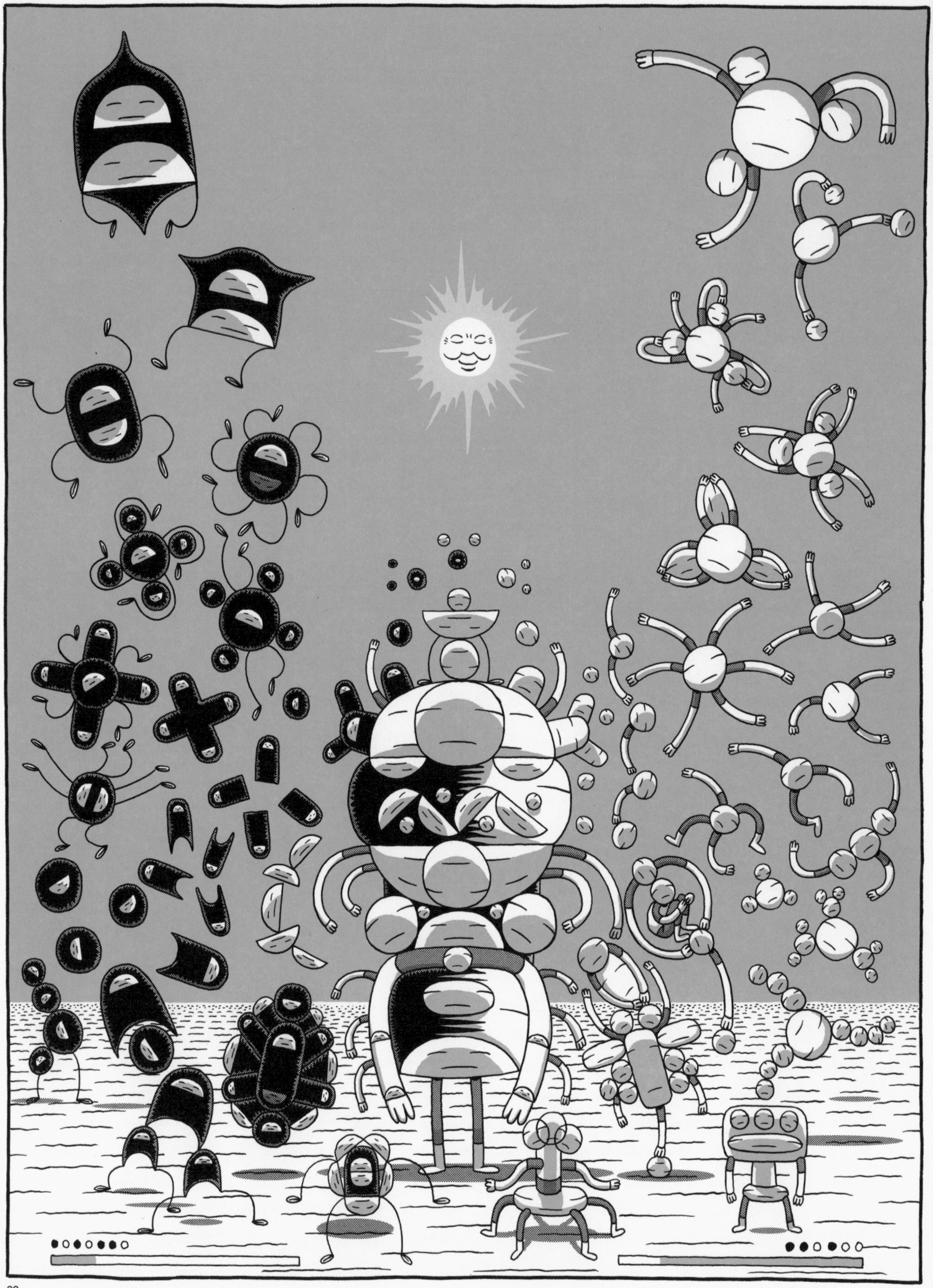

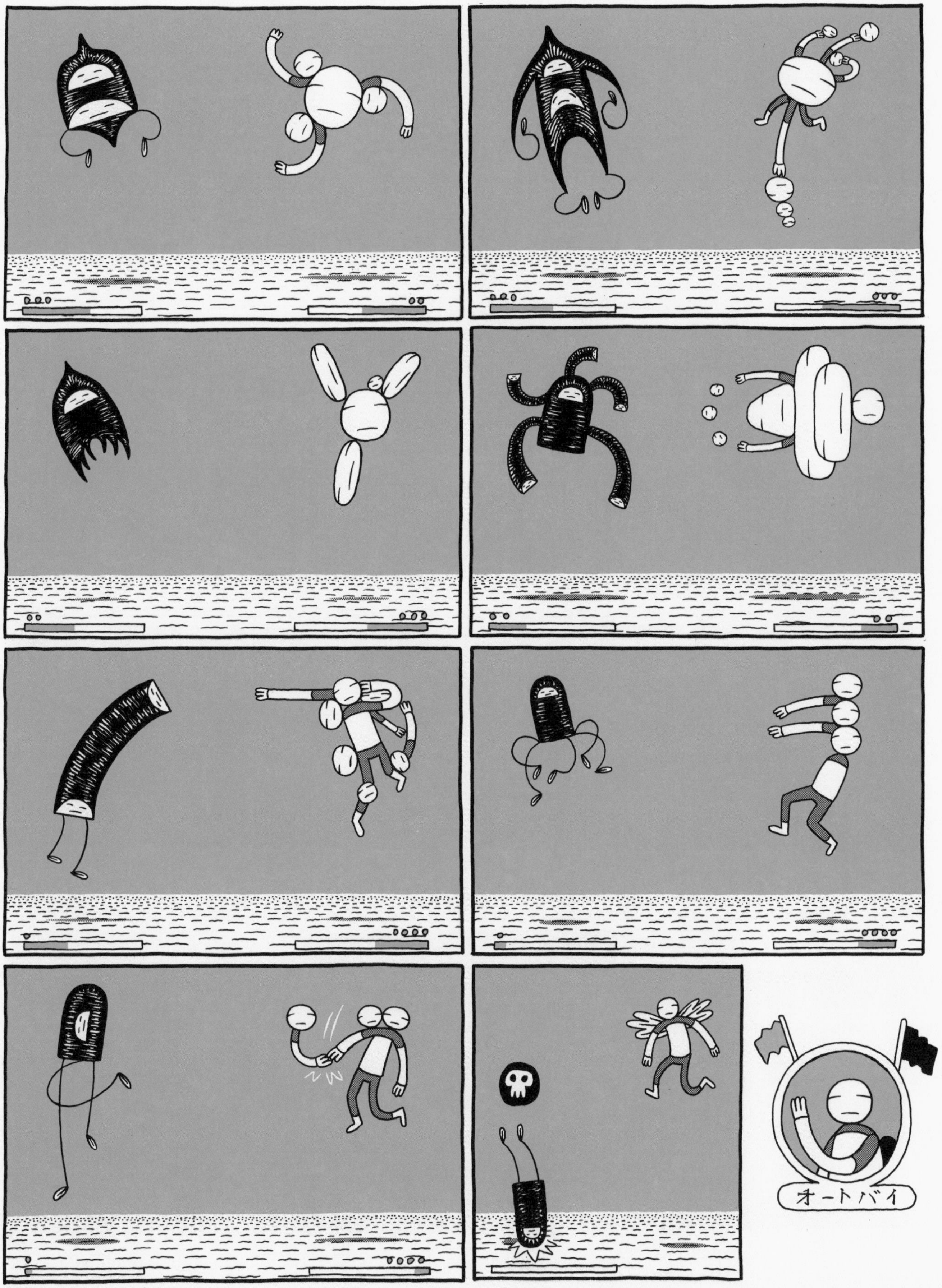
オートバイ

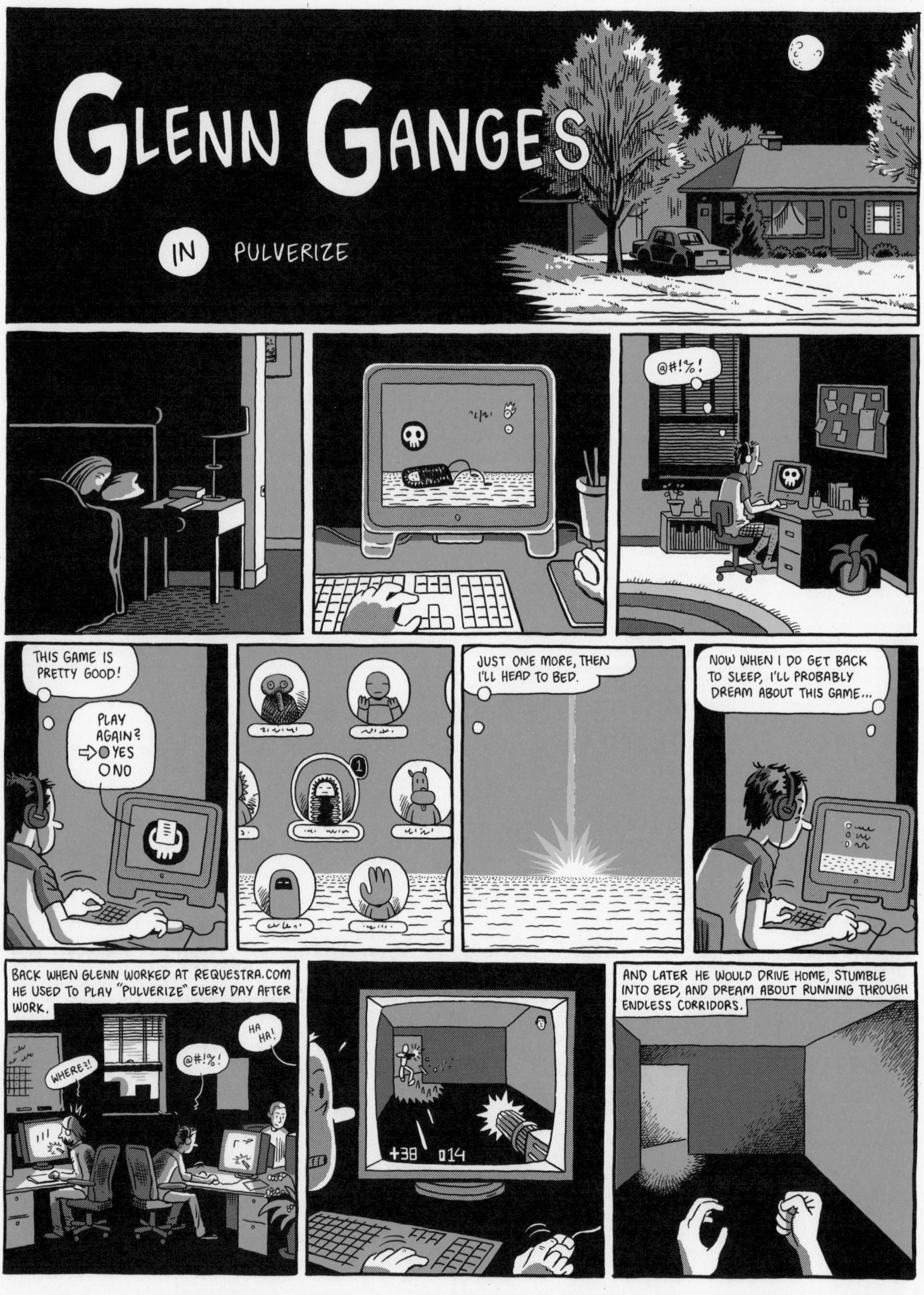
GLENN GANGES
IN PULVERIZE
@#!%!
THIS GAME IS PRETTY GOOD!
PLAY AGAIN? YES NO
JUST ONE MORE, THEN I'LL HEAD TO BED.
NOW WHEN I DO GET BACK TO SLEEP, I'LL PROBABLY DREAM ABOUT THIS GAME...
BACK WHEN GLENN WORKED AT REQUESTRA.COM HE USED TO PLAY "PULVERIZE" EVERY DAY AFTER WORK.
WHERE?!
@#!%!
HA HA!
+38 014
AND LATER HE WOULD DRIVE HOME, STUMBLE INTO BED, AND DREAM ABOUT RUNNING THROUGH ENDLESS CORRIDORS.

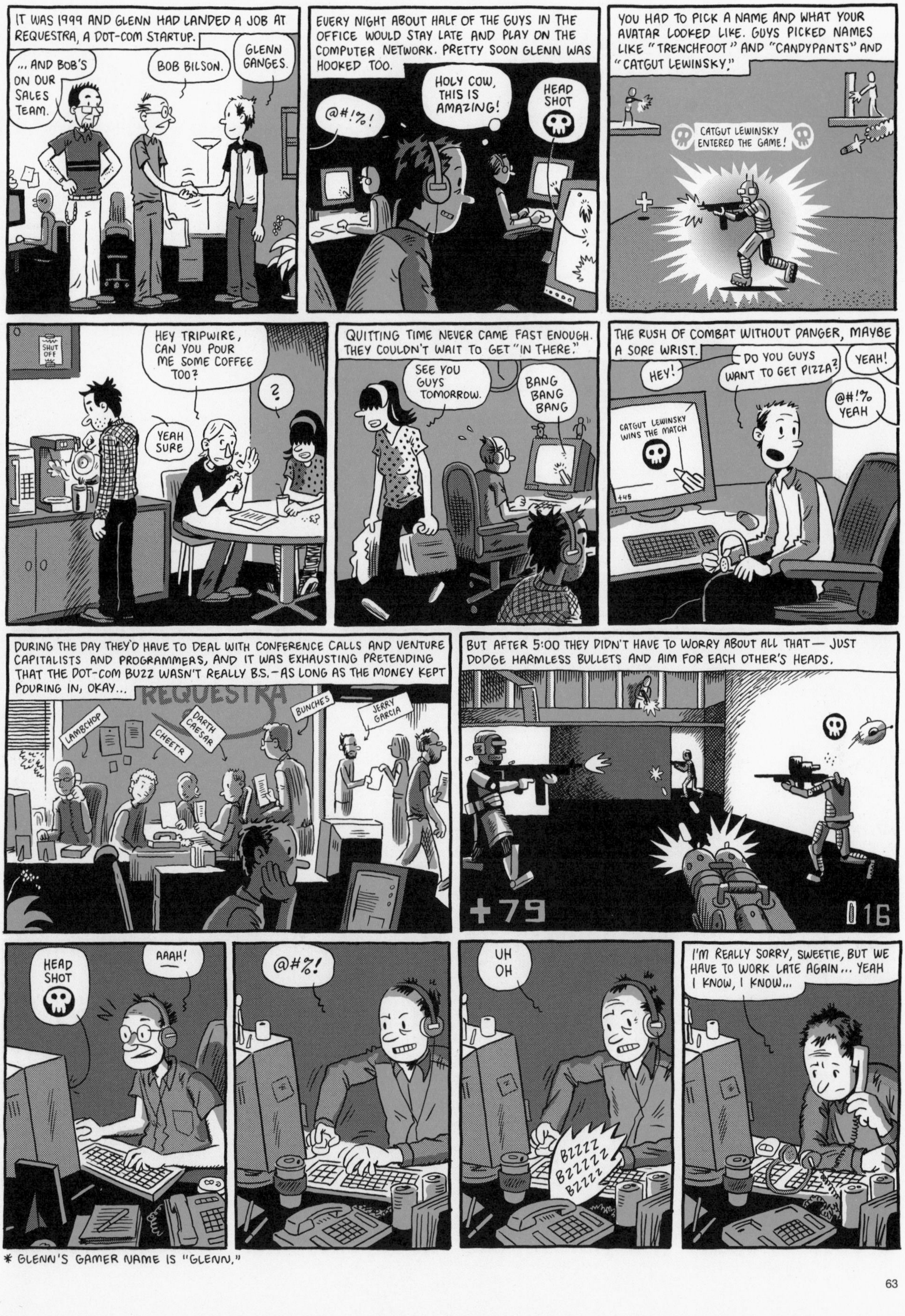
IT WAS 1999 AND GLENN HAD LANDED A JOB AT REQUESTRA, A DOT-COM STARTUP.
...AND BOB'S ON OUR SALES TEAM.
BOB BILSON.
GLENN GANGES.
EVERY NIGHT ABOUT HALF OF THE GUYS IN THE OFFICE WOULD STAY LATE AND PLAY ON THE COMPUTER NETWORK. PRETTY SOON GLENN WAS HOOKED TOO.
@#!%!
HOLY COW, THIS IS AMAZING!
HEAD SHOT
YOU HAD TO PICK A NAME AND WHAT YOUR AVATAR LOOKED LIKE. GUYS PICKED NAMES LIKE "TRENCHFOOT" AND "CANDYPANTS" AND "CATGUT LEWINSKY."
CATGUT LEWINSKY ENTERED THE GAME!
SHUT OFF
HEY TRIPWIRE, CAN YOU POUR ME SOME COFFEE TOO?
YEAH SURE
?
QUITTING TIME NEVER CAME FAST ENOUGH. THEY COULDN'T WAIT TO GET "IN THERE."
SEE YOU GUYS TOMORROW.
BANG BANG BANG
THE RUSH OF COMBAT WITHOUT DANGER, MAYBE A SORE WRIST.
HEY!
DO YOU GUYS WANT TO GET PIZZA?
YEAH!
@#!% YEAH
CATGUT LEWINSKY WINS THE MATCH
445
DURING THE DAY THEY'D HAVE TO DEAL WITH CONFERENCE CALLS AND VENTURE CAPITALISTS AND PROGRAMMERS, AND IT WAS EXHAUSTING PRETENDING THAT THE DOT-COM BUZZ WASN'T REALLY B.S.—AS LONG AS THE MONEY KEPT POURING IN, OKAY...
REQUESTRA
LAMBCHOP
CHEETR
DARTH CAESAR
BUNCHES
JERRY GARCIA
BUT AFTER 5:00 THEY DIDN'T HAVE TO WORRY ABOUT ALL THAT— JUST DODGE HARMLESS BULLETS AND AIM FOR EACH OTHER'S HEADS.
+79
016
HEAD SHOT
AAAH!
@#%!
UH OH
BZZZZ BZZZZZ BZZZZ
I'M REALLY SORRY, SWEETIE, BUT WE HAVE TO WORK LATE AGAIN... YEAH I KNOW, I KNOW...

* GLENN'S GAMER NAME IS "GLENN."

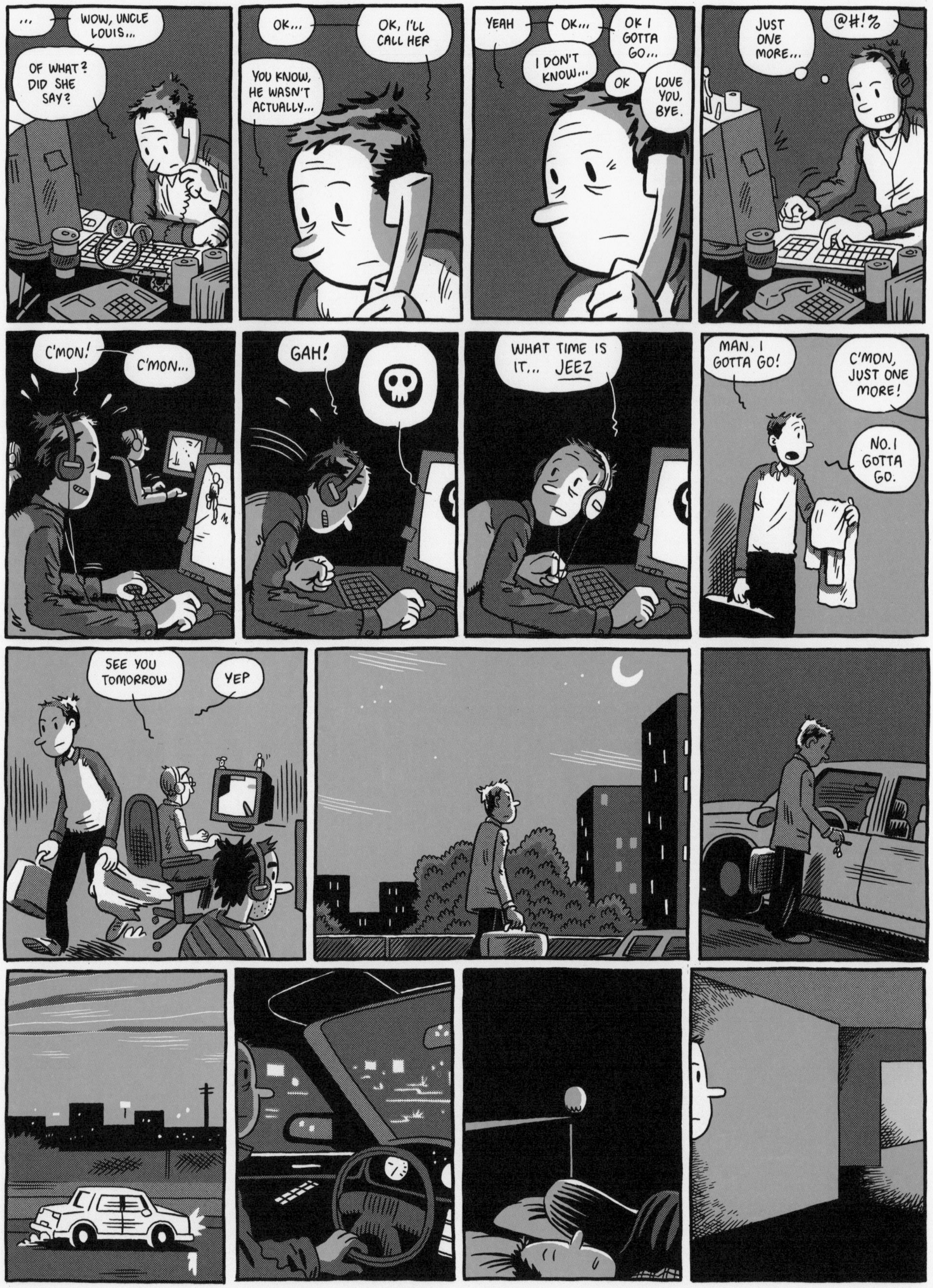
...
WOW, UNCLE LOUIS...
OF WHAT? DID SHE SAY?
OK...
OK, I'LL CALL HER
YOU KNOW, HE WASN'T ACTUALLY...
YEAH
OK...
OK I GOTTA GO...
I DON'T KNOW...
OK
LOVE YOU, BYE.
JUST ONE MORE...
@#!%
C'MON!
C'MON...
GAH!
WHAT TIME IS IT... JEEZ
MAN, I GOTTA GO!
C'MON, JUST ONE MORE!
NO. I GOTTA GO.
SEE YOU TOMORROW
YEP

WHAT'S WEIRD IS THAT GLENN DIDN'T DREAM ABOUT PLAYING A VIDEO GAME, HE DREAMT AS IF HE HAD REALLY BEEN RUNNING THROUGH ENDLESS HALLWAYS. HIS BRAIN WAS FOOLED BY THE GAME'S FIRST-PERSON POINT OF VIEW.

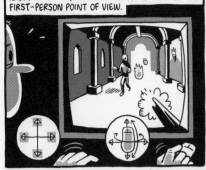

ALL HE SEES IS HIS GUN AND WHAT HE CAN SHOOT. ALL LOOKING IS ALSO AIMING. IT'S AN AGGRESSIVE AND PARANOID POINT OF VIEW—A PRETTY COMMON SORT OF SETUP.

THEY PLAYED DEATHMATCHES FOR HOURS, FIRST TO TWENTY, KILLS MINUS DEATHS. NOBODY AT THE OFFICE DOMINATED THE FIELD SO IT STAYED FUN.

GLENN CHASES CANDYPANTS UP TO THE ROOF, TRYING TO HIT HIM WITH THE SHOTGUN, BUT HE KEEPS DUCKING BEHIND CORNERS JUST IN TIME.

THIS MONASTERY IS THE "MAP" THEY PLAY MOST OFTEN. THE CHAPELS, ROOFTOPS, AND COURTYARDS MAKE FOR GREAT GUN BATTLES — THERE ARE A LOT OF HIDDEN PASSAGEWAYS, TRAPDOORS, ETC.

GLENN HESITATES. HE'S ALWAYS AMAZED BY THE VIEW UP HERE. ARE THOSE SUPPOSED TO BE THE HIMALAYAS?

@#!ª%! LEWINSKY IS UP HERE TOO!

JEEZ!

HA HA!

YOU ALMOST GAVE ME A HEART ATTACK!

HE STOPPED FIRING — I BET HE'S HEADING FOR THE BELLTOWER!

NOT IF I GET THERE FIRST!

ATOP THE BELLTOWER IS THE MOST POWERFUL GUN IN THE GAME — THE "ALLSLAYER," WHICH KILLS WITH ONE SHOT (THOUGH YOU HAVE TO WAIT 5 SECONDS BEFORE YOU CAN FIRE AGAIN).

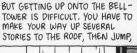

IT'S ALSO A GOOD SPOT FOR USING THE SNIPER RIFLE, IF YOU PICKED IT UP IN THE CHAPEL.

BUT GETTING UP ONTO THE BELL-TOWER IS DIFFICULT. YOU HAVE TO MAKE YOUR WAY UP SEVERAL STORIES TO THE ROOF, THEN JUMP,

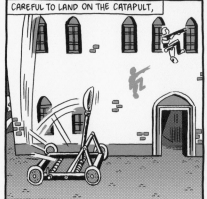

CAREFUL TO LAND ON THE CATAPULT,

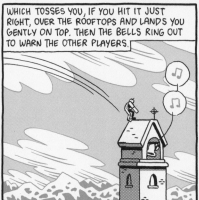

WHICH TOSSES YOU, IF YOU HIT IT JUST RIGHT, OVER THE ROOFTOPS AND LANDS YOU GENTLY ON TOP. THEN THE BELLS RING OUT TO WARN THE OTHER PLAYERS.

IF YOU MISS THE BELLTOWER, YOU'LL PLUNGE INTO THE VALLEY BELOW,

AS YOU FALL, YOU SEE THAT THE VALLEY IS REALLY AN ILLUSION — IT'S A FLAT IMAGE OF A VALLEY THAT RUSHES UP TO YOU, GROWING MORE PIXELATED, AND YOU EVEN START TO SEE THE SEAMS OF THE BACKDROP RIGHT BEFORE IMPACT.

WHEN GLENN JUMPS OFF THE ROOF, LEWINSKY IS RIGHT BEHIND HIM.

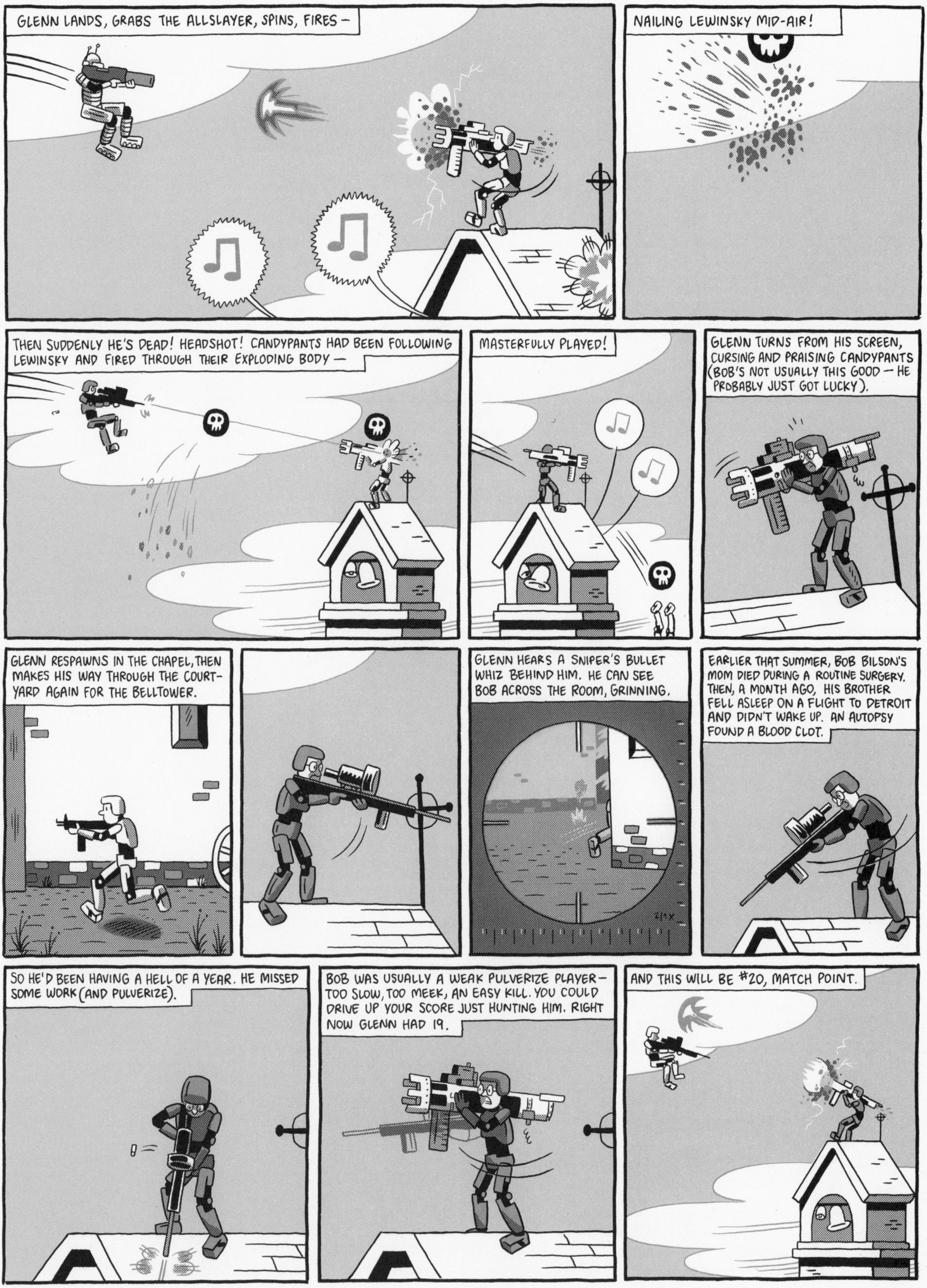
GLENN LANDS, GRABS THE ALLSLAYER, SPINS, FIRES —
NAILING LEWINSKY MID-AIR!
THEN SUDDENLY HE'S DEAD! HEADSHOT! CANDYPANTS HAD BEEN FOLLOWING LEWINSKY AND FIRED THROUGH THEIR EXPLODING BODY —
MASTERFULLY PLAYED!
GLENN TURNS FROM HIS SCREEN, CURSING AND PRAISING CANDYPANTS (BOB'S NOT USUALLY THIS GOOD — HE PROBABLY JUST GOT LUCKY).
GLENN RESPAWNS IN THE CHAPEL, THEN MAKES HIS WAY THROUGH THE COURTYARD AGAIN FOR THE BELLTOWER.
GLENN HEARS A SNIPER'S BULLET WHIZ BEHIND HIM. HE CAN SEE BOB ACROSS THE ROOM, GRINNING.
EARLIER THAT SUMMER, BOB BILSON'S MOM DIED DURING A ROUTINE SURGERY. THEN, A MONTH AGO, HIS BROTHER FELL ASLEEP ON A FLIGHT TO DETROIT AND DIDN'T WAKE UP. AN AUTOPSY FOUND A BLOOD CLOT.
SO HE'D BEEN HAVING A HELL OF A YEAR. HE MISSED SOME WORK (AND PULVERIZE).
BOB WAS USUALLY A WEAK PULVERIZE PLAYER — TOO SLOW, TOO MEEK, AN EASY KILL. YOU COULD DRIVE UP YOUR SCORE JUST HUNTING HIM. RIGHT NOW GLENN HAD 19.
AND THIS WILL BE #20, MATCH POINT.

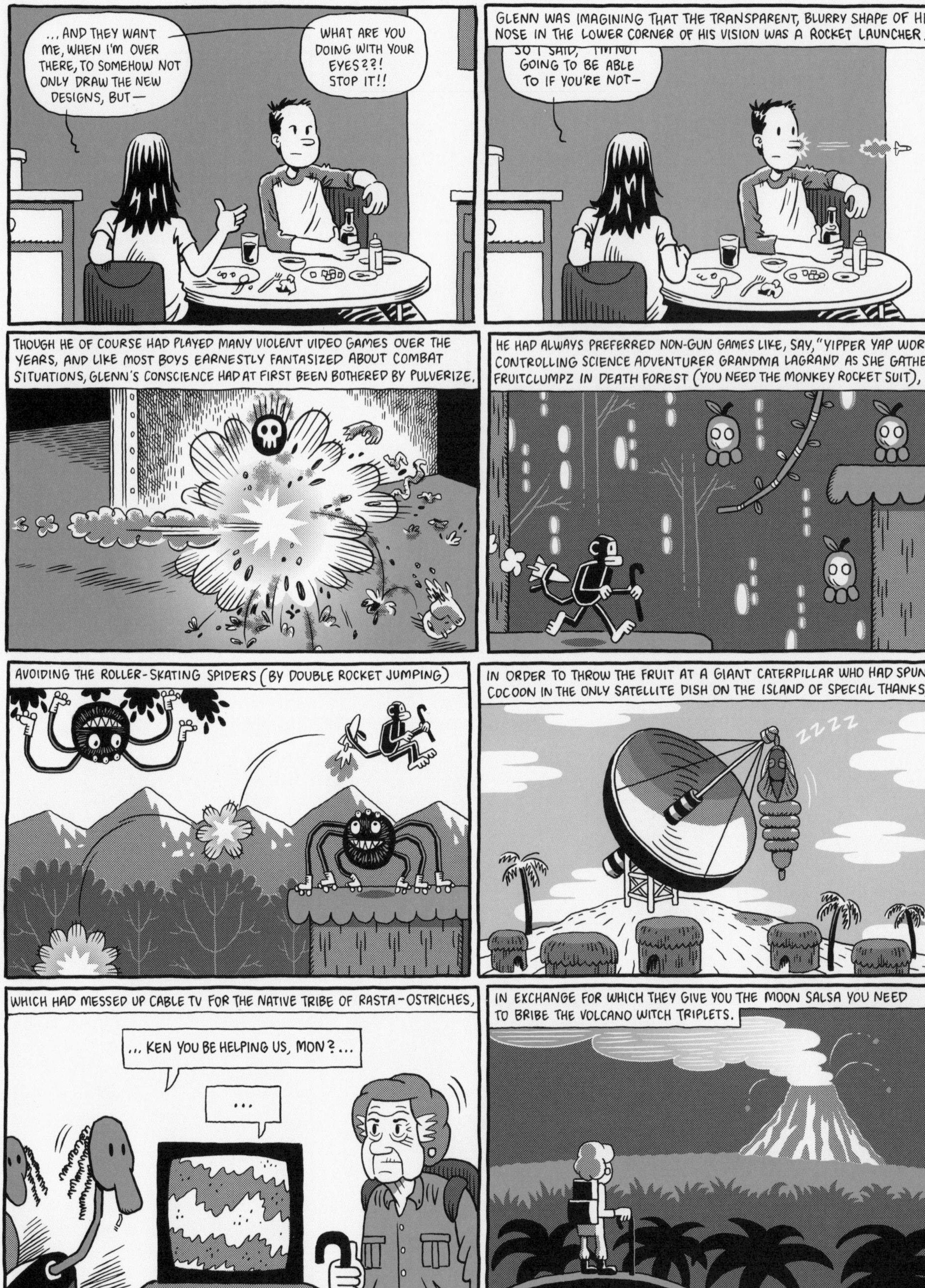
...AND THEY WANT ME, WHEN I'M OVER THERE, TO SOMEHOW NOT ONLY DRAW THE NEW DESIGNS, BUT—
WHAT ARE YOU DOING WITH YOUR EYES??! STOP IT!!
GLENN WAS IMAGINING THAT THE TRANSPARENT, BLURRY SHAPE OF HIS NOSE IN THE LOWER CORNER OF HIS VISION WAS A ROCKET LAUNCHER.
SO I SAID, "I'M NOT GOING TO BE ABLE TO IF YOU'RE NOT—
THOUGH HE OF COURSE HAD PLAYED MANY VIOLENT VIDEO GAMES OVER THE YEARS, AND LIKE MOST BOYS EARNESTLY FANTASIZED ABOUT COMBAT SITUATIONS, GLENN'S CONSCIENCE HAD AT FIRST BEEN BOTHERED BY PULVERIZE.
HE HAD ALWAYS PREFERRED NON-GUN GAMES LIKE, SAY, "YIPPER YAP WORLD," CONTROLLING SCIENCE ADVENTURER GRANDMA LAGRAND AS SHE GATHERS FRUITCLUMPZ IN DEATH FOREST (YOU NEED THE MONKEY ROCKET SUIT),
AVOIDING THE ROLLER-SKATING SPIDERS (BY DOUBLE ROCKET JUMPING)
IN ORDER TO THROW THE FRUIT AT A GIANT CATERPILLAR WHO HAD SPUN A COCOON IN THE ONLY SATELLITE DISH ON THE ISLAND OF SPECIAL THANKS,
ZZZZ
WHICH HAD MESSED UP CABLE TV FOR THE NATIVE TRIBE OF RASTA-OSTRICHES,
...KEN YOU BE HELPING US, MON?...
...
IN EXCHANGE FOR WHICH THEY GIVE YOU THE MOON SALSA YOU NEED TO BRIBE THE VOLCANO WITCH TRIPLETS.

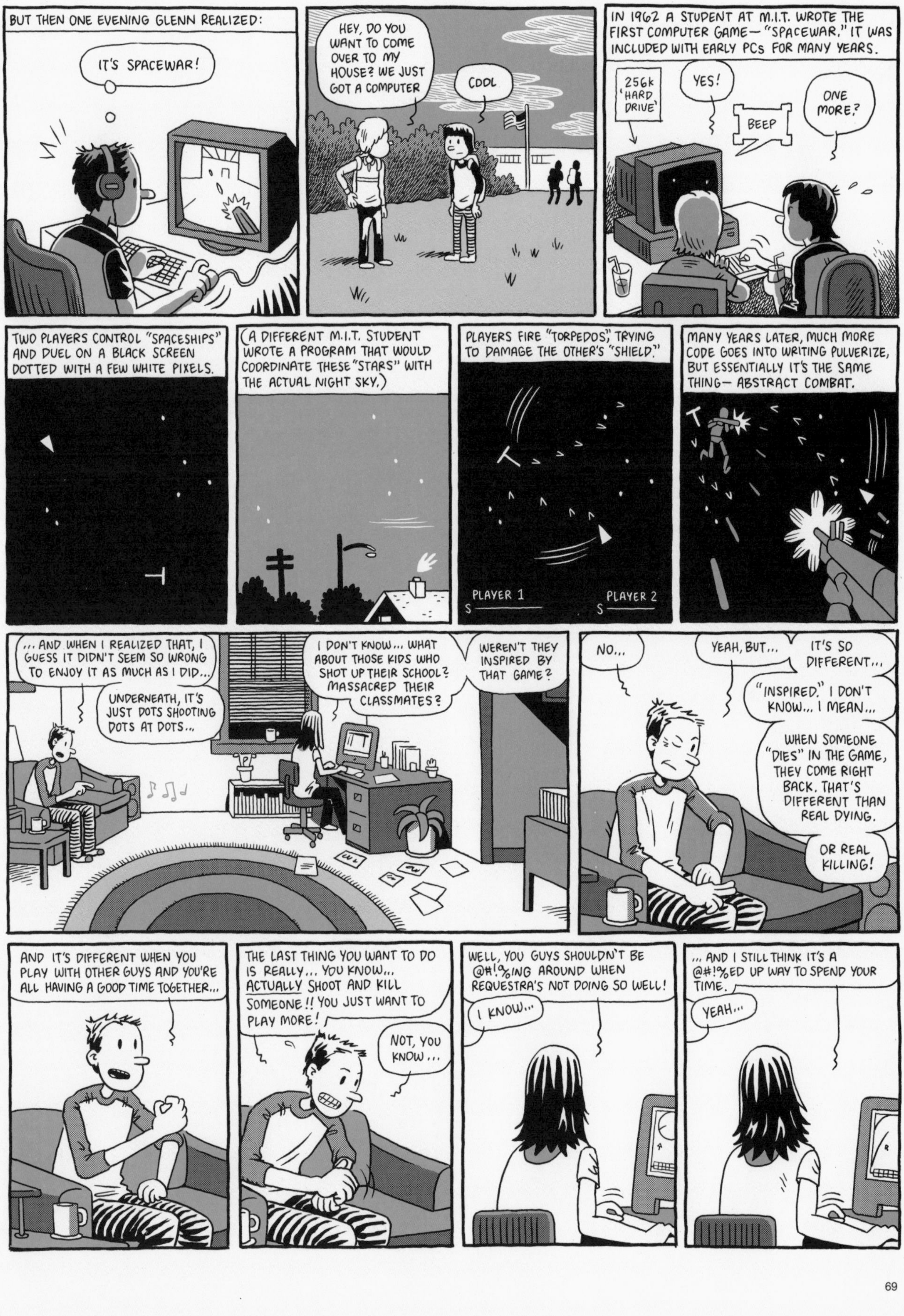
BUT THEN ONE EVENING GLENN REALIZED:
IT'S SPACEWAR!
HEY, DO YOU WANT TO COME OVER TO MY HOUSE? WE JUST GOT A COMPUTER
COOL
IN 1962 A STUDENT AT M.I.T. WROTE THE FIRST COMPUTER GAME— "SPACEWAR." IT WAS INCLUDED WITH EARLY PCs FOR MANY YEARS.
256k 'HARD DRIVE'
YES!
BEEP
ONE MORE?
TWO PLAYERS CONTROL "SPACESHIPS" AND DUEL ON A BLACK SCREEN DOTTED WITH A FEW WHITE PIXELS.
(A DIFFERENT M.I.T. STUDENT WROTE A PROGRAM THAT WOULD COORDINATE THESE "STARS" WITH THE ACTUAL NIGHT SKY.)
PLAYERS FIRE "TORPEDOS," TRYING TO DAMAGE THE OTHER'S "SHIELD."
PLAYER 1
PLAYER 2
MANY YEARS LATER, MUCH MORE CODE GOES INTO WRITING PULVERIZE, BUT ESSENTIALLY IT'S THE SAME THING— ABSTRACT COMBAT.
...AND WHEN I REALIZED THAT, I GUESS IT DIDN'T SEEM SO WRONG TO ENJOY IT AS MUCH AS I DID...
UNDERNEATH, IT'S JUST DOTS SHOOTING DOTS AT DOTS...
I DON'T KNOW... WHAT ABOUT THOSE KIDS WHO SHOT UP THEIR SCHOOL? MASSACRED THEIR CLASSMATES?
WEREN'T THEY INSPIRED BY THAT GAME?
NO...
YEAH, BUT...
IT'S SO DIFFERENT...
"INSPIRED." I DON'T KNOW... I MEAN...
WHEN SOMEONE "DIES" IN THE GAME, THEY COME RIGHT BACK. THAT'S DIFFERENT THAN REAL DYING.
OR REAL KILLING!
AND IT'S DIFFERENT WHEN YOU PLAY WITH OTHER GUYS AND YOU'RE ALL HAVING A GOOD TIME TOGETHER...
THE LAST THING YOU WANT TO DO IS REALLY... YOU KNOW... ACTUALLY SHOOT AND KILL SOMEONE!! YOU JUST WANT TO PLAY MORE!
NOT, YOU KNOW...
WELL, YOU GUYS SHOULDN'T BE @#!%ING AROUND WHEN REQUESTRA'S NOT DOING SO WELL!
I KNOW...
...AND I STILL THINK IT'S A @#!%ED UP WAY TO SPEND YOUR TIME.
YEAH...

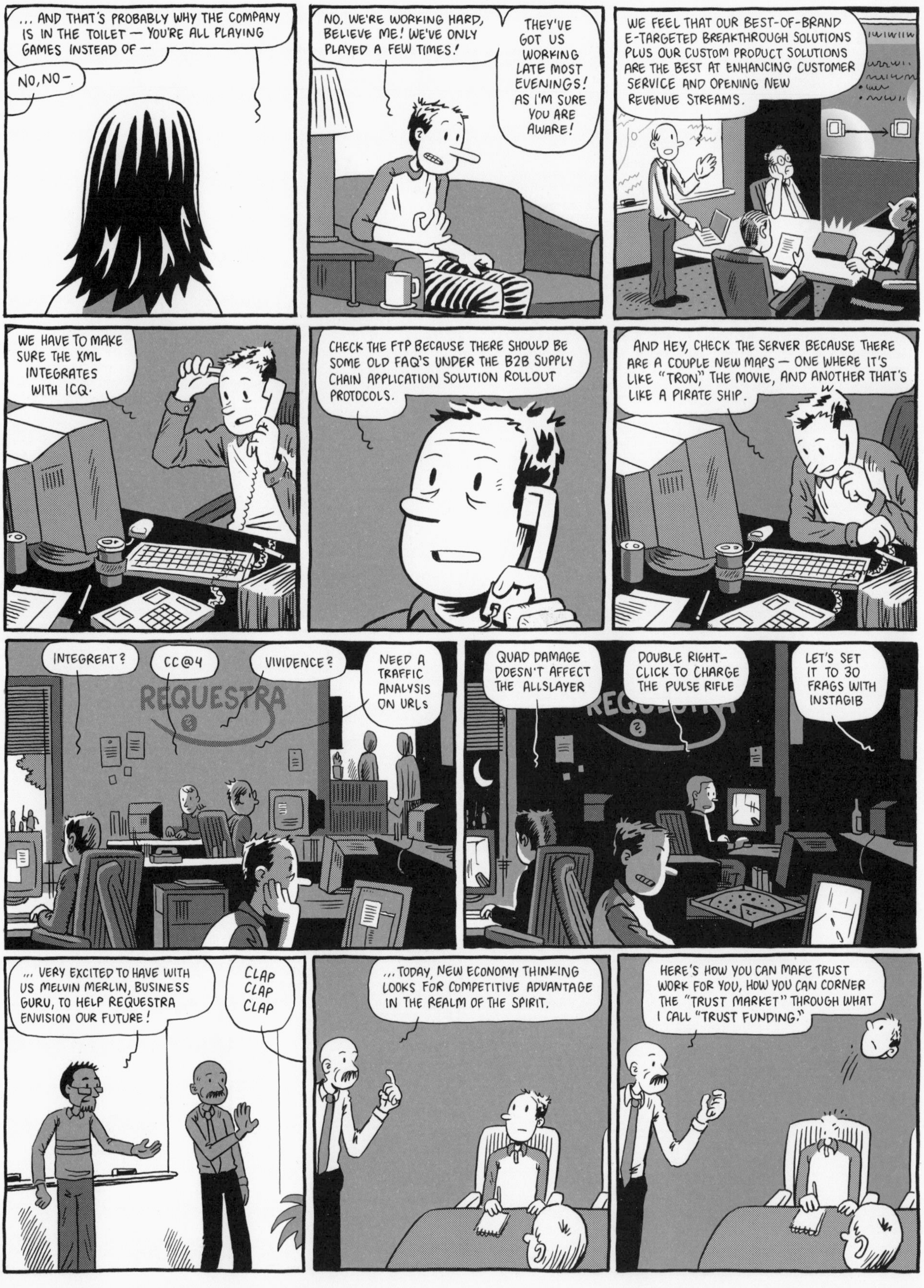
... AND THAT'S PROBABLY WHY THE COMPANY IS IN THE TOILET — YOU'RE ALL PLAYING GAMES INSTEAD OF —
NO, NO—.
NO, WE'RE WORKING HARD, BELIEVE ME! WE'VE ONLY PLAYED A FEW TIMES!
THEY'VE GOT US WORKING LATE MOST EVENINGS! AS I'M SURE YOU ARE AWARE!
WE FEEL THAT OUR BEST-OF-BRAND E-TARGETED BREAKTHROUGH SOLUTIONS PLUS OUR CUSTOM PRODUCT SOLUTIONS ARE THE BEST AT ENHANCING CUSTOMER SERVICE AND OPENING NEW REVENUE STREAMS.
WE HAVE TO MAKE SURE THE XML INTEGRATES WITH ICQ.
CHECK THE FTP BECAUSE THERE SHOULD BE SOME OLD FAQ'S UNDER THE B2B SUPPLY CHAIN APPLICATION SOLUTION ROLLOUT PROTOCOLS.
AND HEY, CHECK THE SERVER BECAUSE THERE ARE A COUPLE NEW MAPS — ONE WHERE IT'S LIKE "TRON," THE MOVIE, AND ANOTHER THAT'S LIKE A PIRATE SHIP.
INTEGREAT?
CC@4
VIVIDENCE?
NEED A TRAFFIC ANALYSIS ON URLs
REQUESTRA
QUAD DAMAGE DOESN'T AFFECT THE ALLSLAYER
DOUBLE RIGHT-CLICK TO CHARGE THE PULSE RIFLE
LET'S SET IT TO 30 FRAGS WITH INSTAGIB
... VERY EXCITED TO HAVE WITH US MELVIN MERLIN, BUSINESS GURU, TO HELP REQUESTRA ENVISION OUR FUTURE!
CLAP CLAP CLAP
... TODAY, NEW ECONOMY THINKING LOOKS FOR COMPETITIVE ADVANTAGE IN THE REALM OF THE SPIRIT.
HERE'S HOW YOU CAN MAKE TRUST WORK FOR YOU, HOW YOU CAN CORNER THE "TRUST MARKET" THROUGH WHAT I CALL "TRUST FUNDING."

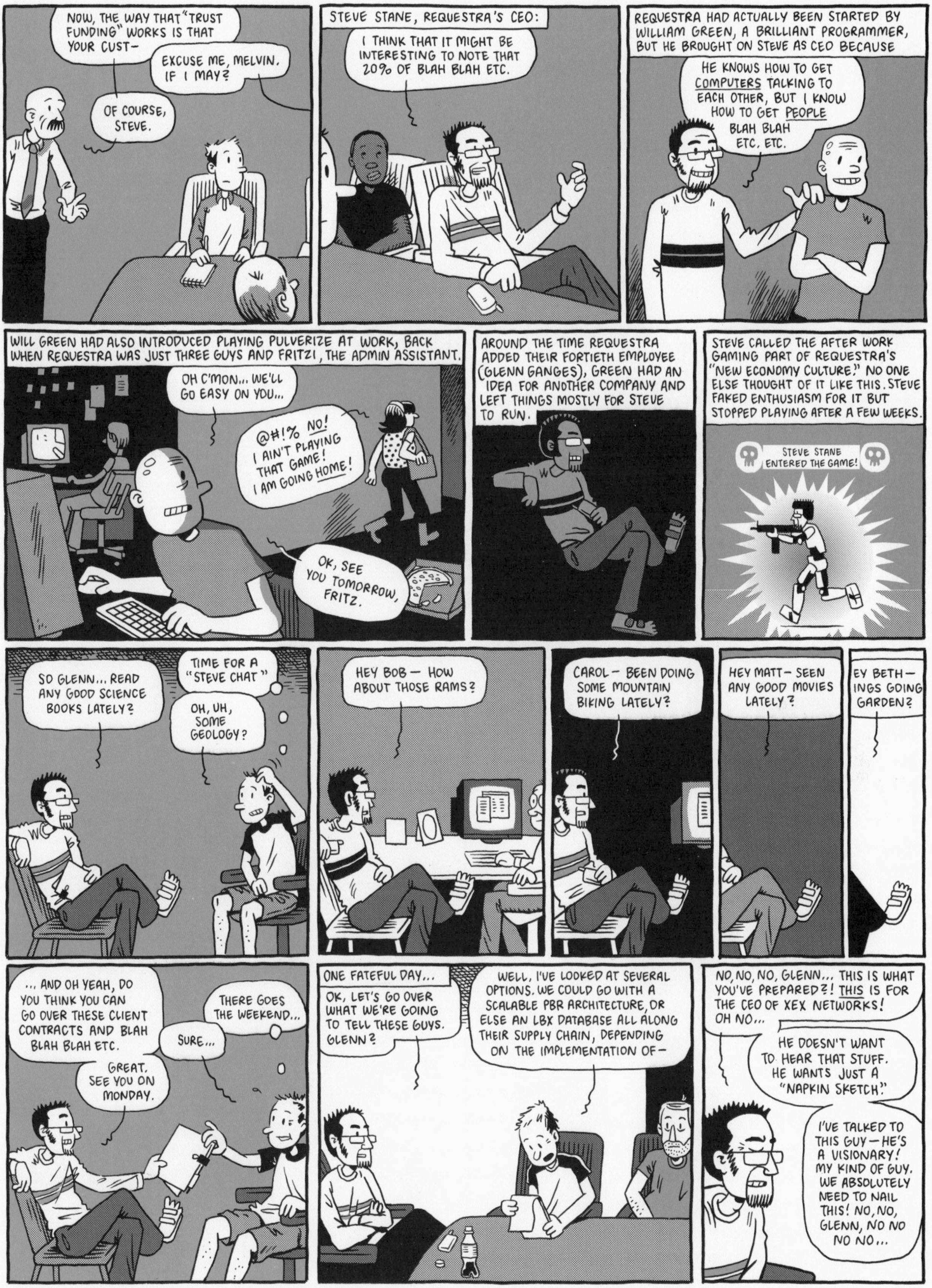

NOW, THE WAY THAT "TRUST FUNDING" WORKS IS THAT YOUR CUST-
EXCUSE ME, MELVIN. IF I MAY?
OF COURSE, STEVE.
STEVE STANE, REQUESTRA'S CEO:
I THINK THAT IT MIGHT BE INTERESTING TO NOTE THAT 20% OF BLAH BLAH ETC.
REQUESTRA HAD ACTUALLY BEEN STARTED BY WILLIAM GREEN, A BRILLIANT PROGRAMMER, BUT HE BROUGHT ON STEVE AS CEO BECAUSE
HE KNOWS HOW TO GET COMPUTERS TALKING TO EACH OTHER, BUT I KNOW HOW TO GET PEOPLE BLAH BLAH ETC. ETC.
WILL GREEN HAD ALSO INTRODUCED PLAYING PULVERIZE AT WORK, BACK WHEN REQUESTRA WAS JUST THREE GUYS AND FRITZI, THE ADMIN ASSISTANT.
OH C'MON... WE'LL GO EASY ON YOU...
@#!% NO! I AIN'T PLAYING THAT GAME! I AM GOING HOME!
OK, SEE YOU TOMORROW, FRITZ.
AROUND THE TIME REQUESTRA ADDED THEIR FORTIETH EMPLOYEE (GLENN GANGES), GREEN HAD AN IDEA FOR ANOTHER COMPANY AND LEFT THINGS MOSTLY FOR STEVE TO RUN.
STEVE CALLED THE AFTER WORK GAMING PART OF REQUESTRA'S "NEW ECONOMY CULTURE." NO ONE ELSE THOUGHT OF IT LIKE THIS. STEVE FAKED ENTHUSIASM FOR IT BUT STOPPED PLAYING AFTER A FEW WEEKS.
STEVE STANE ENTERED THE GAME!
SO GLENN... READ ANY GOOD SCIENCE BOOKS LATELY?
TIME FOR A "STEVE CHAT"
OH, UH, SOME GEOLOGY?
HEY BOB— HOW ABOUT THOSE RAMS?
CAROL— BEEN DOING SOME MOUNTAIN BIKING LATELY?
HEY MATT— SEEN ANY GOOD MOVIES LATELY?
EY BETH— INGS GOING GARDEN?
... AND OH YEAH, DO YOU THINK YOU CAN GO OVER THESE CLIENT CONTRACTS AND BLAH BLAH BLAH ETC.
THERE GOES THE WEEKEND...
SURE...
GREAT. SEE YOU ON MONDAY.
ONE FATEFUL DAY...
OK, LET'S GO OVER WHAT WE'RE GOING TO TELL THESE GUYS. GLENN?
WELL, I'VE LOOKED AT SEVERAL OPTIONS. WE COULD GO WITH A SCALABLE PBR ARCHITECTURE, OR ELSE AN LBX DATABASE ALL ALONG THEIR SUPPLY CHAIN, DEPENDING ON THE IMPLEMENTATION OF—
NO, NO, NO, GLENN... THIS IS WHAT YOU'VE PREPARED?! THIS IS FOR THE CEO OF XEX NETWORKS! OH NO...
HE DOESN'T WANT TO HEAR THAT STUFF. HE WANTS JUST A "NAPKIN SKETCH."
I'VE TALKED TO THIS GUY—HE'S A VISIONARY! MY KIND OF GUY. WE ABSOLUTELY NEED TO NAIL THIS! NO, NO, GLENN, NO NO NO NO...

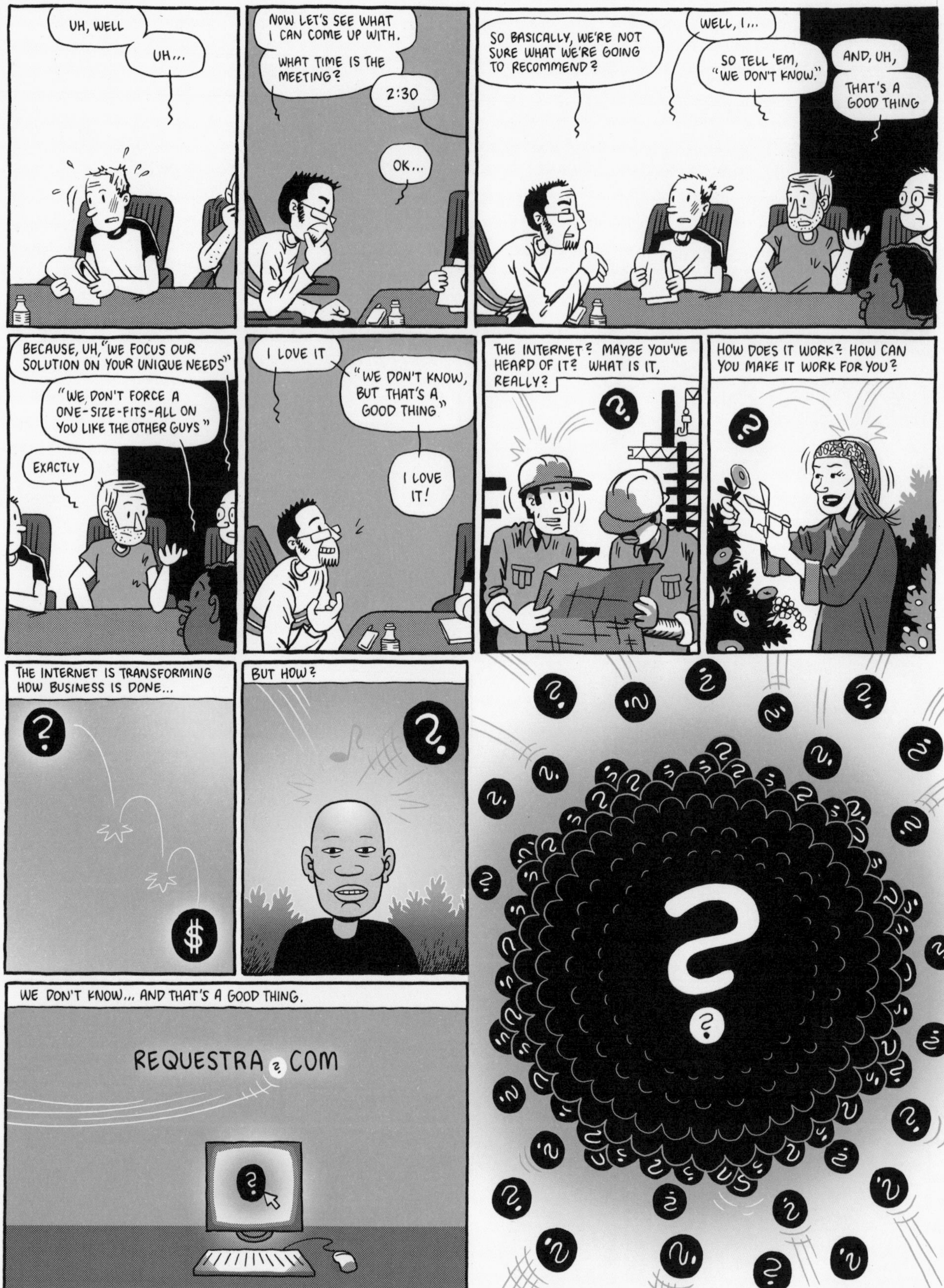
UH, WELL
UH...
NOW LET'S SEE WHAT I CAN COME UP WITH.
WHAT TIME IS THE MEETING?
2:30
OK...
SO BASICALLY, WE'RE NOT SURE WHAT WE'RE GOING TO RECOMMEND?
WELL, I...
SO TELL 'EM, "WE DON'T KNOW."
AND, UH,
THAT'S A GOOD THING
BECAUSE, UH, "WE FOCUS OUR SOLUTION ON YOUR UNIQUE NEEDS"
"WE DON'T FORCE A ONE-SIZE-FITS-ALL ON YOU LIKE THE OTHER GUYS"
EXACTLY
I LOVE IT
"WE DON'T KNOW, BUT THAT'S A GOOD THING"
I LOVE IT!
THE INTERNET? MAYBE YOU'VE HEARD OF IT? WHAT IS IT, REALLY?
HOW DOES IT WORK? HOW CAN YOU MAKE IT WORK FOR YOU?
THE INTERNET IS TRANSFORMING HOW BUSINESS IS DONE...
BUT HOW?
WE DON'T KNOW... AND THAT'S A GOOD THING.
REQUESTRA ? COM

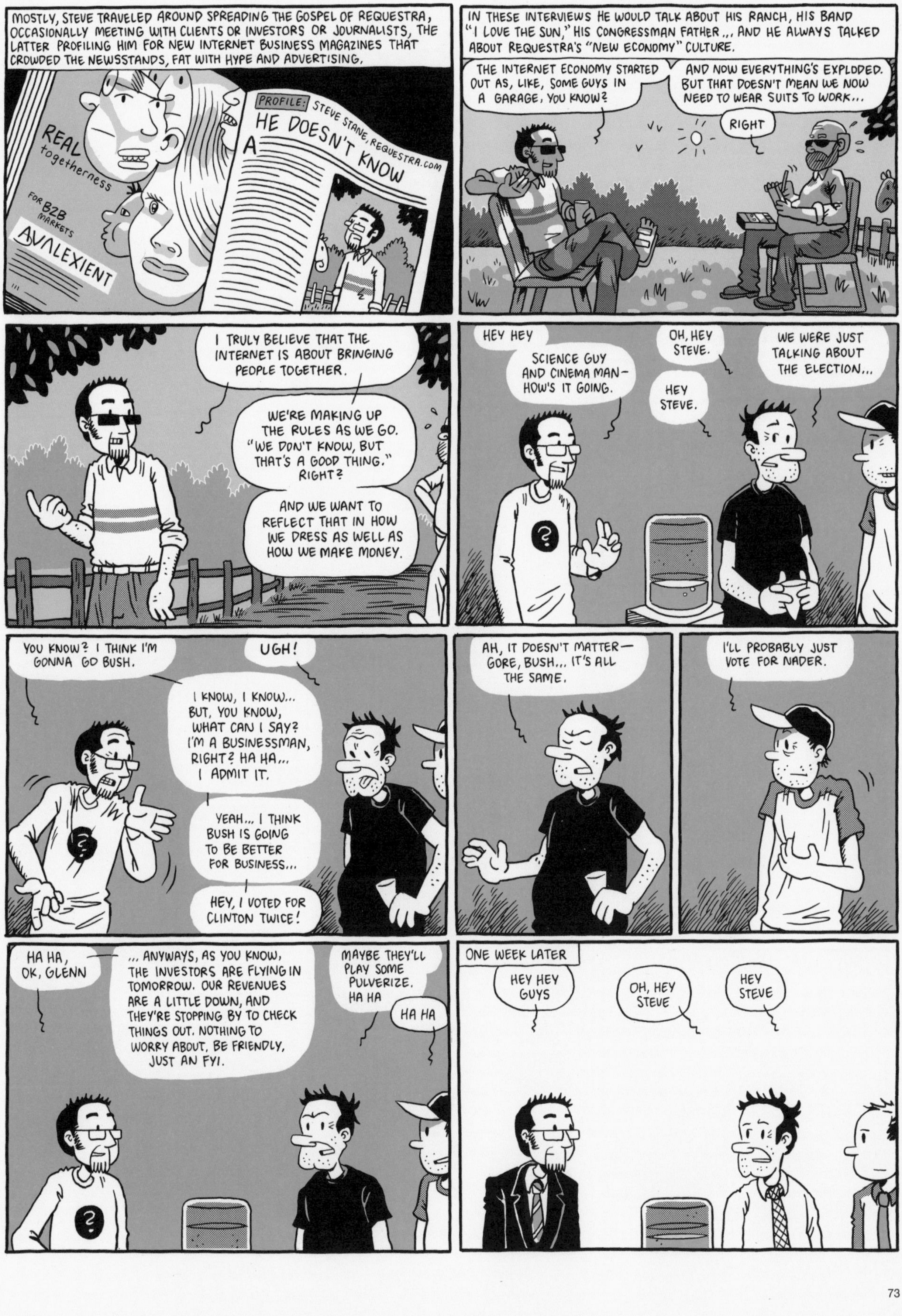

MOSTLY, STEVE TRAVELED AROUND SPREADING THE GOSPEL OF REQUESTRA, OCCASIONALLY MEETING WITH CLIENTS OR INVESTORS OR JOURNALISTS, THE LATTER PROFILING HIM FOR NEW INTERNET BUSINESS MAGAZINES THAT CROWDED THE NEWSSTANDS, FAT WITH HYPE AND ADVERTISING.
REAL togetherness
FOR B2B MARKETS
AVALEXIENT
PROFILE: STEVE STANE, REQUESTRA.COM
HE DOESN'T KNOW
IN THESE INTERVIEWS HE WOULD TALK ABOUT HIS RANCH, HIS BAND "I LOVE THE SUN," HIS CONGRESSMAN FATHER... AND HE ALWAYS TALKED ABOUT REQUESTRA'S "NEW ECONOMY" CULTURE.
THE INTERNET ECONOMY STARTED OUT AS, LIKE, SOME GUYS IN A GARAGE, YOU KNOW?
AND NOW EVERYTHING'S EXPLODED. BUT THAT DOESN'T MEAN WE NOW NEED TO WEAR SUITS TO WORK...
RIGHT
I TRULY BELIEVE THAT THE INTERNET IS ABOUT BRINGING PEOPLE TOGETHER.
WE'RE MAKING UP THE RULES AS WE GO. "WE DON'T KNOW, BUT THAT'S A GOOD THING." RIGHT?
AND WE WANT TO REFLECT THAT IN HOW WE DRESS AS WELL AS HOW WE MAKE MONEY.
HEY HEY
SCIENCE GUY AND CINEMA MAN— HOW'S IT GOING.
OH, HEY STEVE.
HEY STEVE.
WE WERE JUST TALKING ABOUT THE ELECTION...
YOU KNOW? I THINK I'M GONNA GO BUSH.
UGH!
I KNOW, I KNOW... BUT, YOU KNOW, WHAT CAN I SAY? I'M A BUSINESSMAN, RIGHT? HA HA... I ADMIT IT.
YEAH... I THINK BUSH IS GOING TO BE BETTER FOR BUSINESS...
HEY, I VOTED FOR CLINTON TWICE!
AH, IT DOESN'T MATTER— GORE, BUSH... IT'S ALL THE SAME.
I'LL PROBABLY JUST VOTE FOR NADER.
HA HA, OK, GLENN
... ANYWAYS, AS YOU KNOW, THE INVESTORS ARE FLYING IN TOMORROW. OUR REVENUES ARE A LITTLE DOWN, AND THEY'RE STOPPING BY TO CHECK THINGS OUT. NOTHING TO WORRY ABOUT. BE FRIENDLY. JUST AN FYI.
MAYBE THEY'LL PLAY SOME PULVERIZE. HA HA
HA HA
ONE WEEK LATER
HEY HEY GUYS
OH, HEY STEVE
HEY STEVE

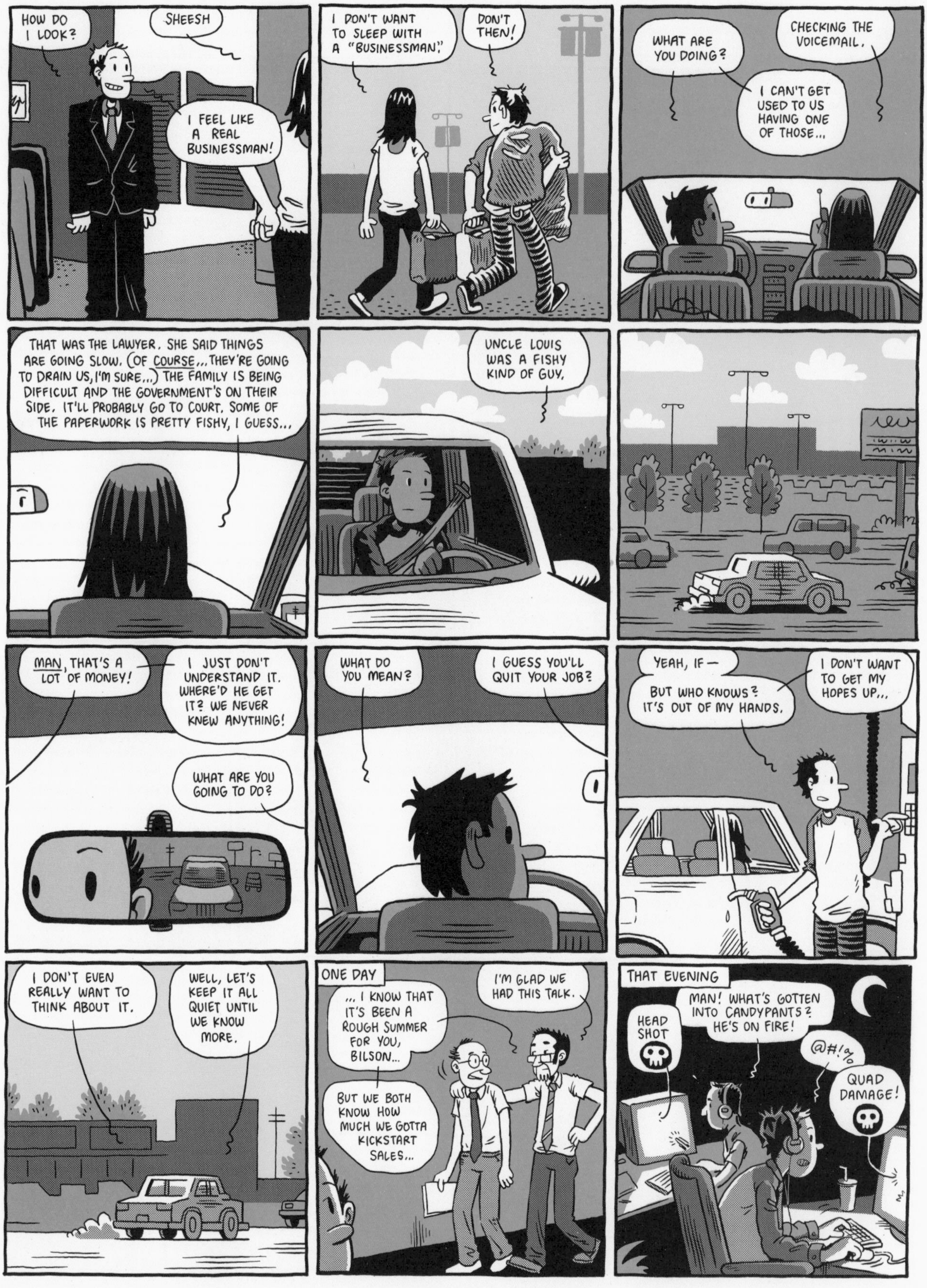
HOW DO I LOOK?
SHEESH
I FEEL LIKE A REAL BUSINESSMAN!
I DON'T WANT TO SLEEP WITH A "BUSINESSMAN."
DON'T THEN!
WHAT ARE YOU DOING?
CHECKING THE VOICEMAIL.
I CAN'T GET USED TO US HAVING ONE OF THOSE...
THAT WAS THE LAWYER. SHE SAID THINGS ARE GOING SLOW. (OF COURSE... THEY'RE GOING TO DRAIN US, I'M SURE...) THE FAMILY IS BEING DIFFICULT AND THE GOVERNMENT'S ON THEIR SIDE. IT'LL PROBABLY GO TO COURT. SOME OF THE PAPERWORK IS PRETTY FISHY, I GUESS...
UNCLE LOUIS WAS A FISHY KIND OF GUY.
MAN, THAT'S A LOT OF MONEY!
I JUST DON'T UNDERSTAND IT. WHERE'D HE GET IT? WE NEVER KNEW ANYTHING!
WHAT ARE YOU GOING TO DO?
WHAT DO YOU MEAN?
I GUESS YOU'LL QUIT YOUR JOB?
YEAH, IF—
BUT WHO KNOWS? IT'S OUT OF MY HANDS.
I DON'T WANT TO GET MY HOPES UP...
I DON'T EVEN REALLY WANT TO THINK ABOUT IT.
WELL, LET'S KEEP IT ALL QUIET UNTIL WE KNOW MORE.
ONE DAY
...I KNOW THAT IT'S BEEN A ROUGH SUMMER FOR YOU, BILSON...
BUT WE BOTH KNOW HOW MUCH WE GOTTA KICKSTART SALES...
I'M GLAD WE HAD THIS TALK.
THAT EVENING
HEAD SHOT
MAN! WHAT'S GOTTEN INTO CANDYPANTS? HE'S ON FIRE!
@#!%
QUAD DAMAGE!

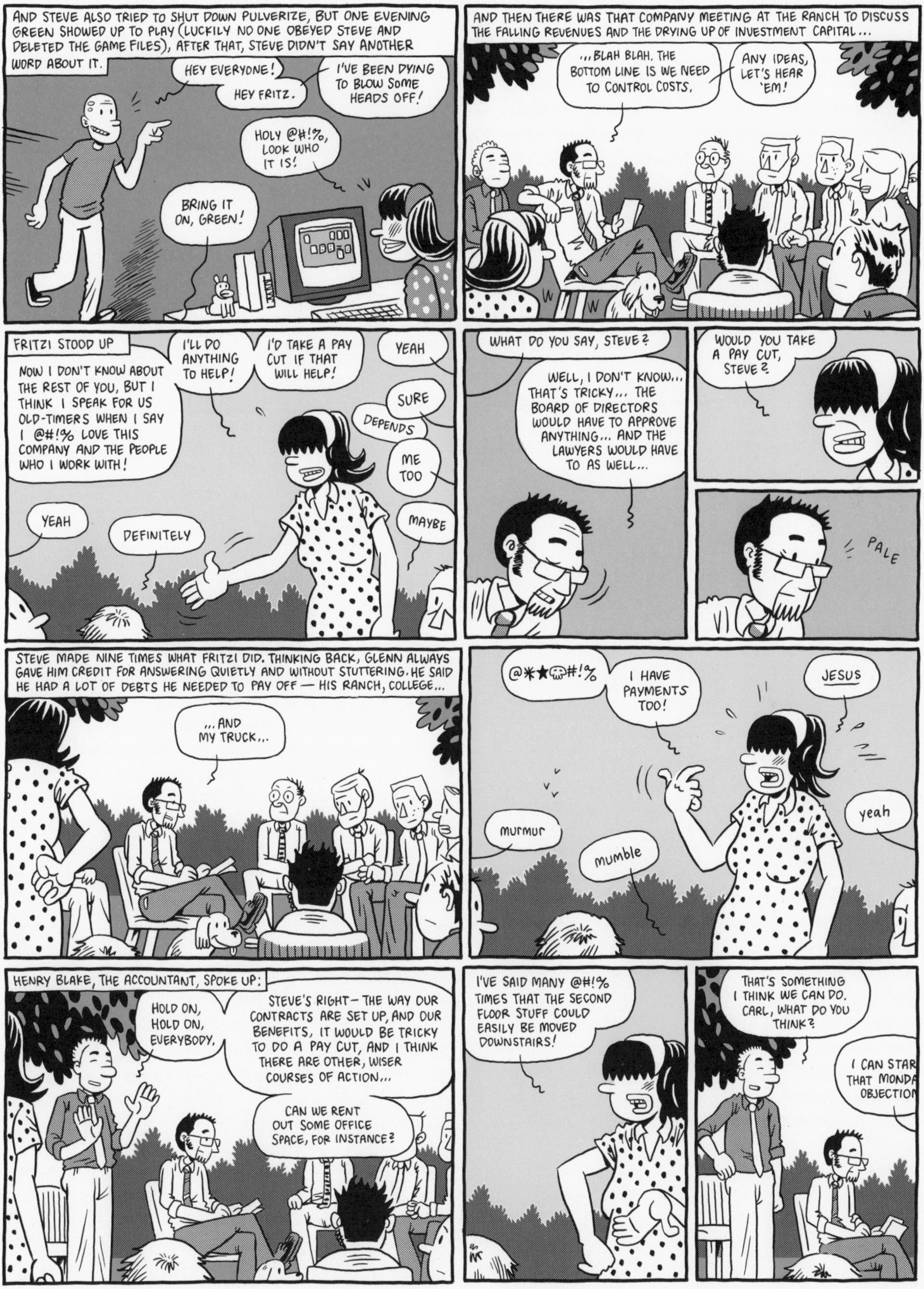

AND STEVE ALSO TRIED TO SHUT DOWN PULVERIZE, BUT ONE EVENING GREEN SHOWED UP TO PLAY (LUCKILY NO ONE OBEYED STEVE AND DELETED THE GAME FILES), AFTER THAT, STEVE DIDN'T SAY ANOTHER WORD ABOUT IT.
HEY EVERYONE!
HEY FRITZ.
I'VE BEEN DYING TO BLOW SOME HEADS OFF!
HOLY @#!%, LOOK WHO IT IS!
BRING IT ON, GREEN!
AND THEN THERE WAS THAT COMPANY MEETING AT THE RANCH TO DISCUSS THE FALLING REVENUES AND THE DRYING UP OF INVESTMENT CAPITAL...
...BLAH BLAH. THE BOTTOM LINE IS WE NEED TO CONTROL COSTS.
ANY IDEAS, LET'S HEAR 'EM!
FRITZI STOOD UP
NOW I DON'T KNOW ABOUT THE REST OF YOU, BUT I THINK I SPEAK FOR US OLD-TIMERS WHEN I SAY I @#!% LOVE THIS COMPANY AND THE PEOPLE WHO I WORK WITH!
I'LL DO ANYTHING TO HELP!
I'D TAKE A PAY CUT IF THAT WILL HELP!
YEAH
SURE
DEPENDS
ME TOO
YEAH
DEFINITELY
MAYBE
WHAT DO YOU SAY, STEVE?
WELL, I DON'T KNOW... THAT'S TRICKY... THE BOARD OF DIRECTORS WOULD HAVE TO APPROVE ANYTHING... AND THE LAWYERS WOULD HAVE TO AS WELL...
WOULD YOU TAKE A PAY CUT, STEVE?
PALE
STEVE MADE NINE TIMES WHAT FRITZI DID. THINKING BACK, GLENN ALWAYS GAVE HIM CREDIT FOR ANSWERING QUIETLY AND WITHOUT STUTTERING. HE SAID HE HAD A LOT OF DEBTS HE NEEDED TO PAY OFF — HIS RANCH, COLLEGE...
...AND MY TRUCK...
@✱★#!%
I HAVE PAYMENTS TOO!
JESUS
yeah
murmur
mumble
HENRY BLAKE, THE ACCOUNTANT, SPOKE UP:
HOLD ON, HOLD ON, EVERYBODY.
STEVE'S RIGHT— THE WAY OUR CONTRACTS ARE SET UP, AND OUR BENEFITS, IT WOULD BE TRICKY TO DO A PAY CUT, AND I THINK THERE ARE OTHER, WISER COURSES OF ACTION...
CAN WE RENT OUT SOME OFFICE SPACE, FOR INSTANCE?
I'VE SAID MANY @#!% TIMES THAT THE SECOND FLOOR STUFF COULD EASILY BE MOVED DOWNSTAIRS!
THAT'S SOMETHING I THINK WE CAN DO. CARL, WHAT DO YOU THINK?
I CAN STAR THAT MONDA OBJECTION

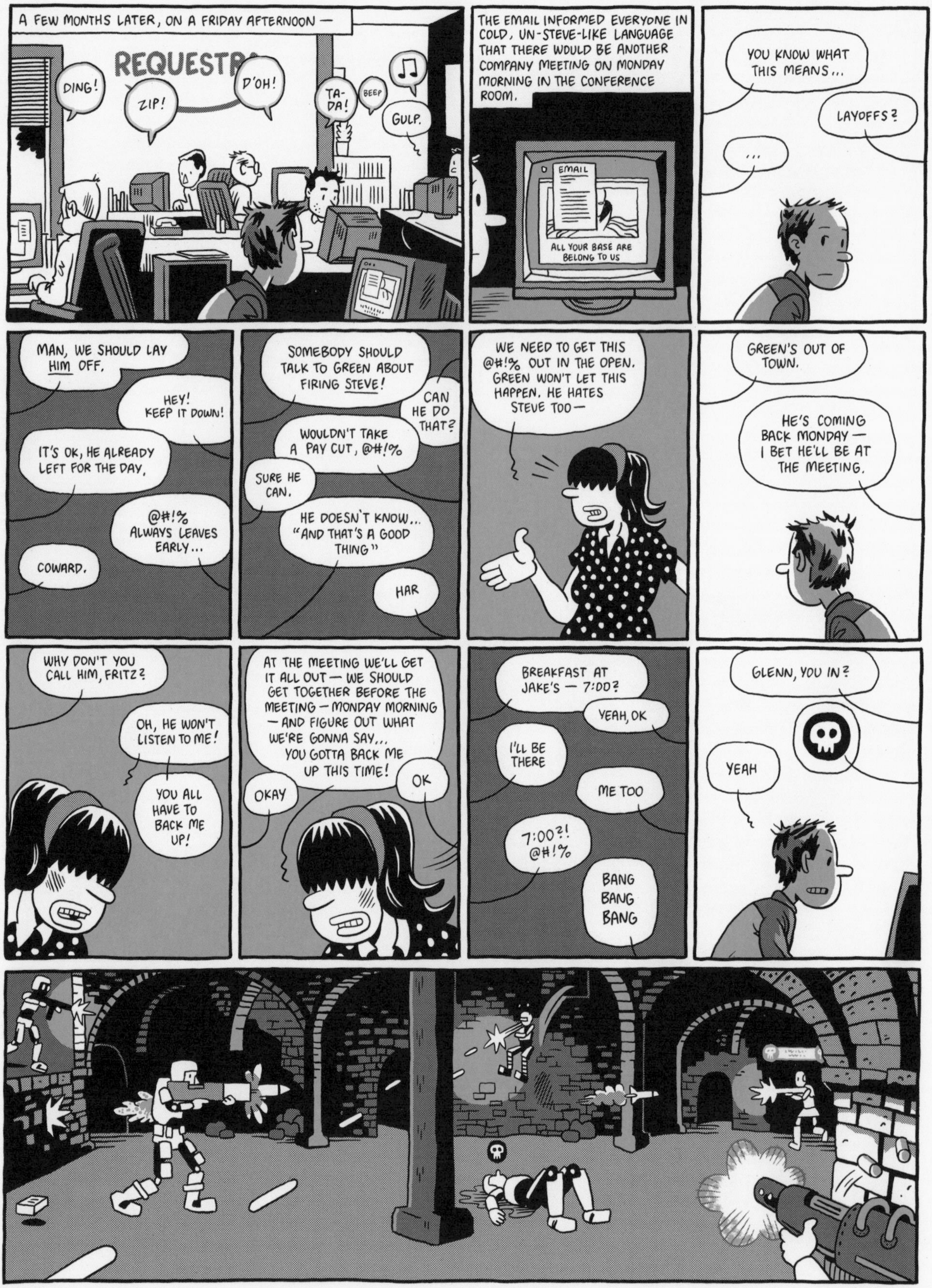
A FEW MONTHS LATER, ON A FRIDAY AFTERNOON —
REQUESTR
DING!
ZIP!
D'OH!
TA-DA!
BEEP
GULP.
THE EMAIL INFORMED EVERYONE IN COLD, UN-STEVE-LIKE LANGUAGE THAT THERE WOULD BE ANOTHER COMPANY MEETING ON MONDAY MORNING IN THE CONFERENCE ROOM.
EMAIL
ALL YOUR BASE ARE BELONG TO US
YOU KNOW WHAT THIS MEANS...
LAYOFFS?
...
MAN, WE SHOULD LAY HIM OFF.
HEY! KEEP IT DOWN!
IT'S OK, HE ALREADY LEFT FOR THE DAY.
@#!% ALWAYS LEAVES EARLY...
COWARD.
SOMEBODY SHOULD TALK TO GREEN ABOUT FIRING STEVE!
CAN HE DO THAT?
WOULDN'T TAKE A PAY CUT, @#!%
SURE HE CAN.
HE DOESN'T KNOW... "AND THAT'S A GOOD THING"
HAR
WE NEED TO GET THIS @#!% OUT IN THE OPEN. GREEN WON'T LET THIS HAPPEN. HE HATES STEVE TOO—
GREEN'S OUT OF TOWN.
HE'S COMING BACK MONDAY — I BET HE'LL BE AT THE MEETING.
WHY DON'T YOU CALL HIM, FRITZ?
OH, HE WON'T LISTEN TO ME!
YOU ALL HAVE TO BACK ME UP!
AT THE MEETING WE'LL GET IT ALL OUT — WE SHOULD GET TOGETHER BEFORE THE MEETING — MONDAY MORNING — AND FIGURE OUT WHAT WE'RE GONNA SAY... YOU GOTTA BACK ME UP THIS TIME!
OKAY
OK
BREAKFAST AT JAKE'S — 7:00?
YEAH, OK
I'LL BE THERE
ME TOO
7:00?! @#!%
BANG BANG BANG
GLENN, YOU IN?
YEAH

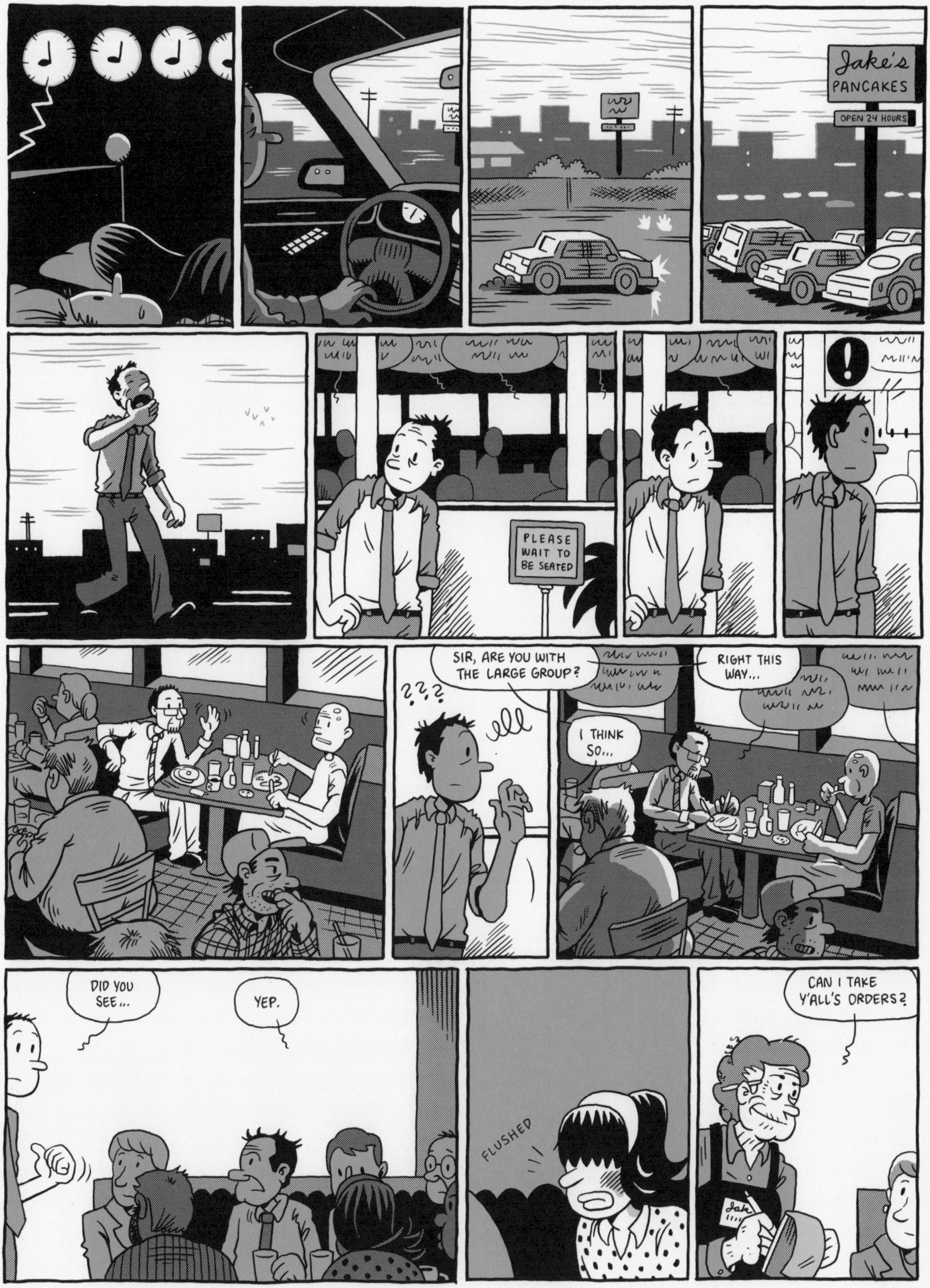
Jake's
PANCAKES
OPEN 24 HOURS
PLEASE WAIT TO BE SEATED
!
SIR, ARE YOU WITH THE LARGE GROUP?
???
I THINK SO...
RIGHT THIS WAY...
DID YOU SEE...
YEP.
FLUSHED
CAN I TAKE Y'ALL'S ORDERS?

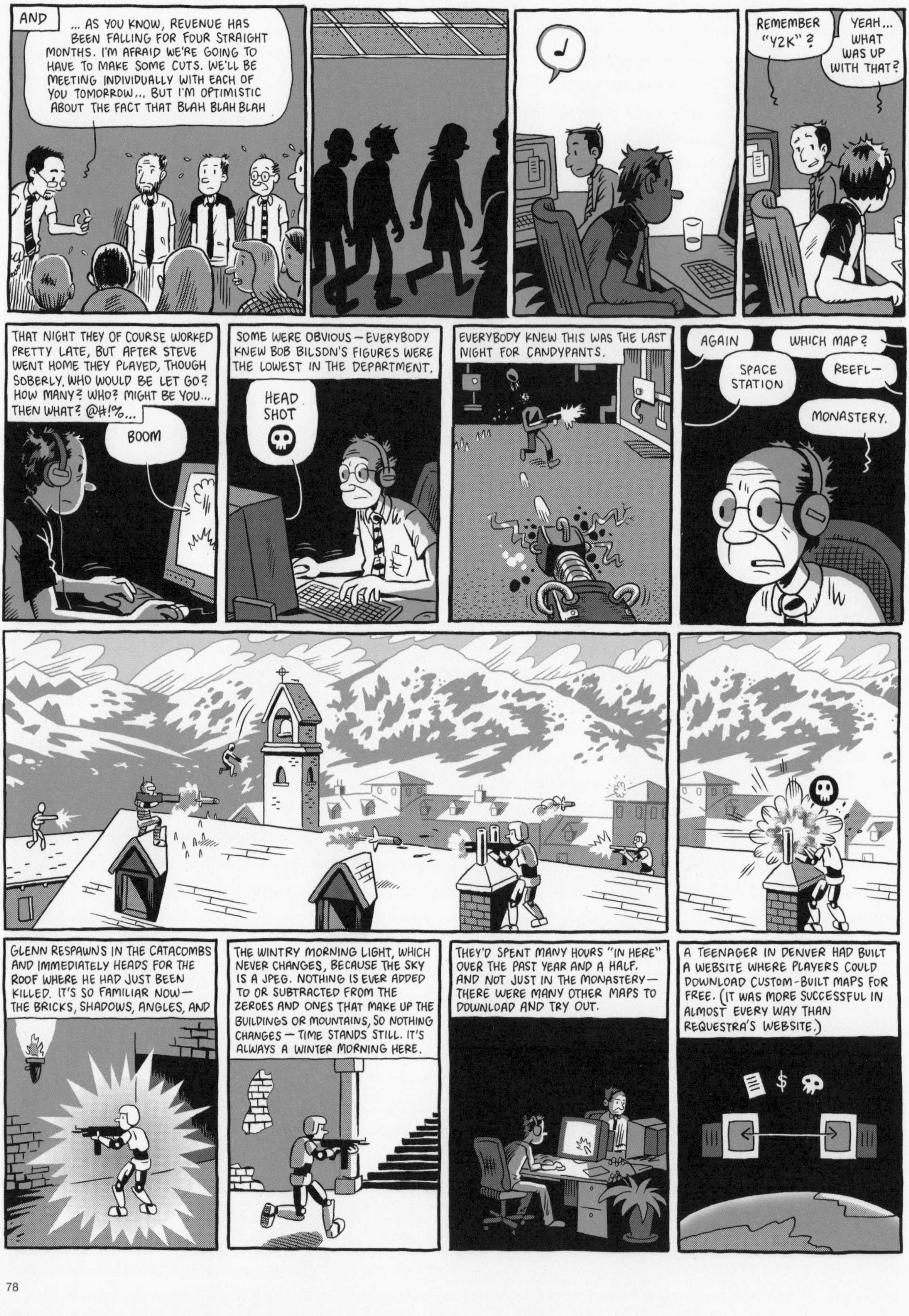
AND
... AS YOU KNOW, REVENUE HAS BEEN FALLING FOR FOUR STRAIGHT MONTHS. I'M AFRAID WE'RE GOING TO HAVE TO MAKE SOME CUTS. WE'LL BE MEETING INDIVIDUALLY WITH EACH OF YOU TOMORROW... BUT I'M OPTIMISTIC ABOUT THE FACT THAT BLAH BLAH BLAH
REMEMBER "Y2K"?
YEAH... WHAT WAS UP WITH THAT?
THAT NIGHT THEY OF COURSE WORKED PRETTY LATE, BUT AFTER STEVE WENT HOME THEY PLAYED, THOUGH SOBERLY. WHO WOULD BE LET GO? HOW MANY? WHO? MIGHT BE YOU... THEN WHAT? @#!%...
BOOM
SOME WERE OBVIOUS—EVERYBODY KNEW BOB BILSON'S FIGURES WERE THE LOWEST IN THE DEPARTMENT.
HEAD SHOT
EVERYBODY KNEW THIS WAS THE LAST NIGHT FOR CANDYPANTS.
AGAIN
WHICH MAP?
SPACE STATION
REEFL—
MONASTERY.
GLENN RESPAWNS IN THE CATACOMBS AND IMMEDIATELY HEADS FOR THE ROOF WHERE HE HAD JUST BEEN KILLED. IT'S SO FAMILIAR NOW—THE BRICKS, SHADOWS, ANGLES, AND
THE WINTRY MORNING LIGHT, WHICH NEVER CHANGES, BECAUSE THE SKY IS A JPEG. NOTHING IS EVER ADDED TO OR SUBTRACTED FROM THE ZEROES AND ONES THAT MAKE UP THE BUILDINGS OR MOUNTAINS, SO NOTHING CHANGES—TIME STANDS STILL. IT'S ALWAYS A WINTER MORNING HERE.
THEY'D SPENT MANY HOURS "IN HERE" OVER THE PAST YEAR AND A HALF. AND NOT JUST IN THE MONASTERY—THERE WERE MANY OTHER MAPS TO DOWNLOAD AND TRY OUT.
A TEENAGER IN DENVER HAD BUILT A WEBSITE WHERE PLAYERS COULD DOWNLOAD CUSTOM-BUILT MAPS FOR FREE. (IT WAS MORE SUCCESSFUL IN ALMOST EVERY WAY THAN REQUESTRA'S WEBSITE.)

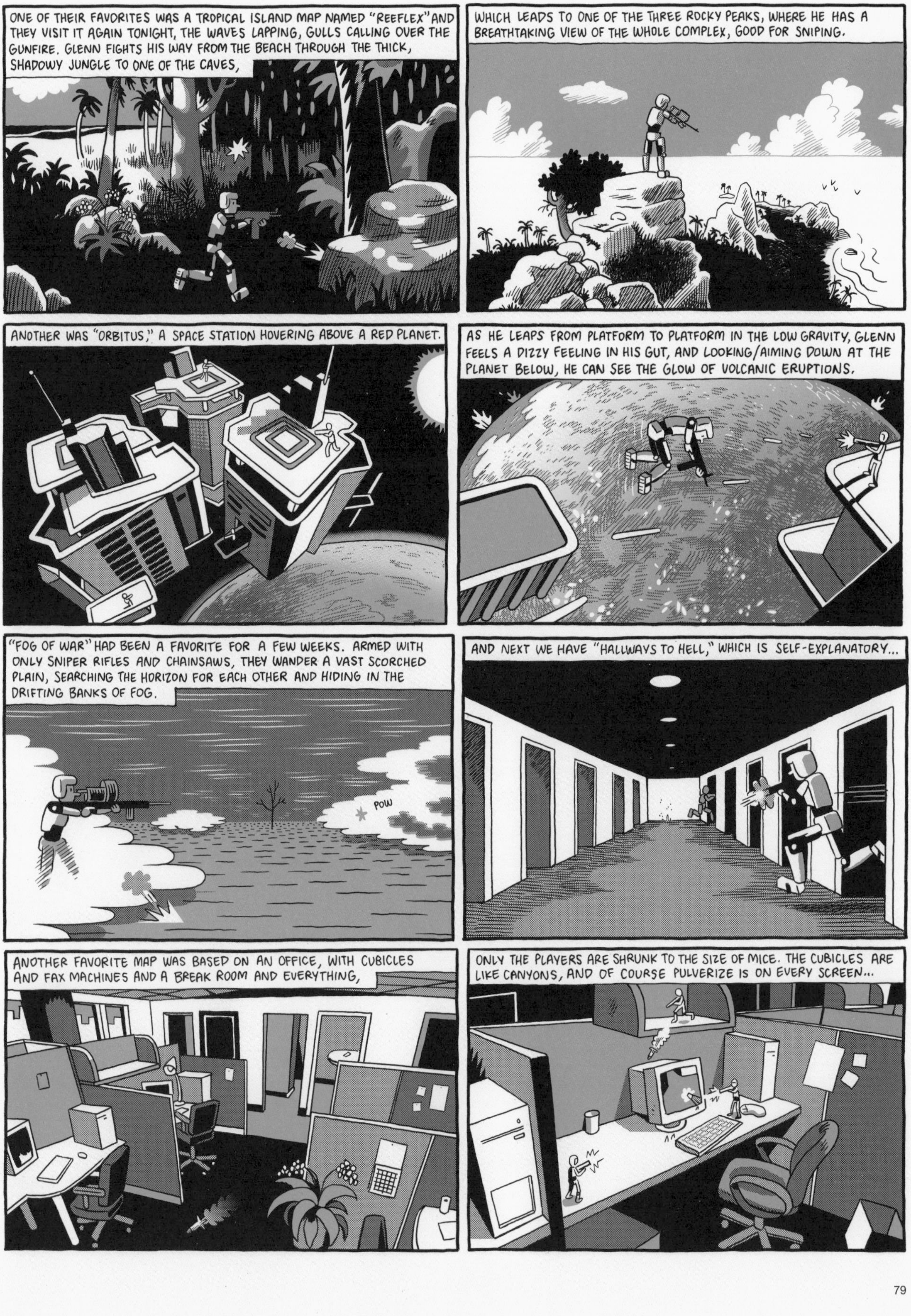
ONE OF THEIR FAVORITES WAS A TROPICAL ISLAND MAP NAMED "REEFLEX" AND THEY VISIT IT AGAIN TONIGHT, THE WAVES LAPPING, GULLS CALLING OVER THE GUNFIRE. GLENN FIGHTS HIS WAY FROM THE BEACH THROUGH THE THICK, SHADOWY JUNGLE TO ONE OF THE CAVES,
WHICH LEADS TO ONE OF THE THREE ROCKY PEAKS, WHERE HE HAS A BREATHTAKING VIEW OF THE WHOLE COMPLEX, GOOD FOR SNIPING.
ANOTHER WAS "ORBITUS," A SPACE STATION HOVERING ABOVE A RED PLANET.
AS HE LEAPS FROM PLATFORM TO PLATFORM IN THE LOW GRAVITY, GLENN FEELS A DIZZY FEELING IN HIS GUT, AND LOOKING/AIMING DOWN AT THE PLANET BELOW, HE CAN SEE THE GLOW OF VOLCANIC ERUPTIONS.
"FOG OF WAR" HAD BEEN A FAVORITE FOR A FEW WEEKS. ARMED WITH ONLY SNIPER RIFLES AND CHAINSAWS, THEY WANDER A VAST SCORCHED PLAIN, SEARCHING THE HORIZON FOR EACH OTHER AND HIDING IN THE DRIFTING BANKS OF FOG.
POW
AND NEXT WE HAVE "HALLWAYS TO HELL," WHICH IS SELF-EXPLANATORY...
ANOTHER FAVORITE MAP WAS BASED ON AN OFFICE, WITH CUBICLES AND FAX MACHINES AND A BREAK ROOM AND EVERYTHING,
ONLY THE PLAYERS ARE SHRUNK TO THE SIZE OF MICE. THE CUBICLES ARE LIKE CANYONS, AND OF COURSE PULVERIZE IS ON EVERY SCREEN...

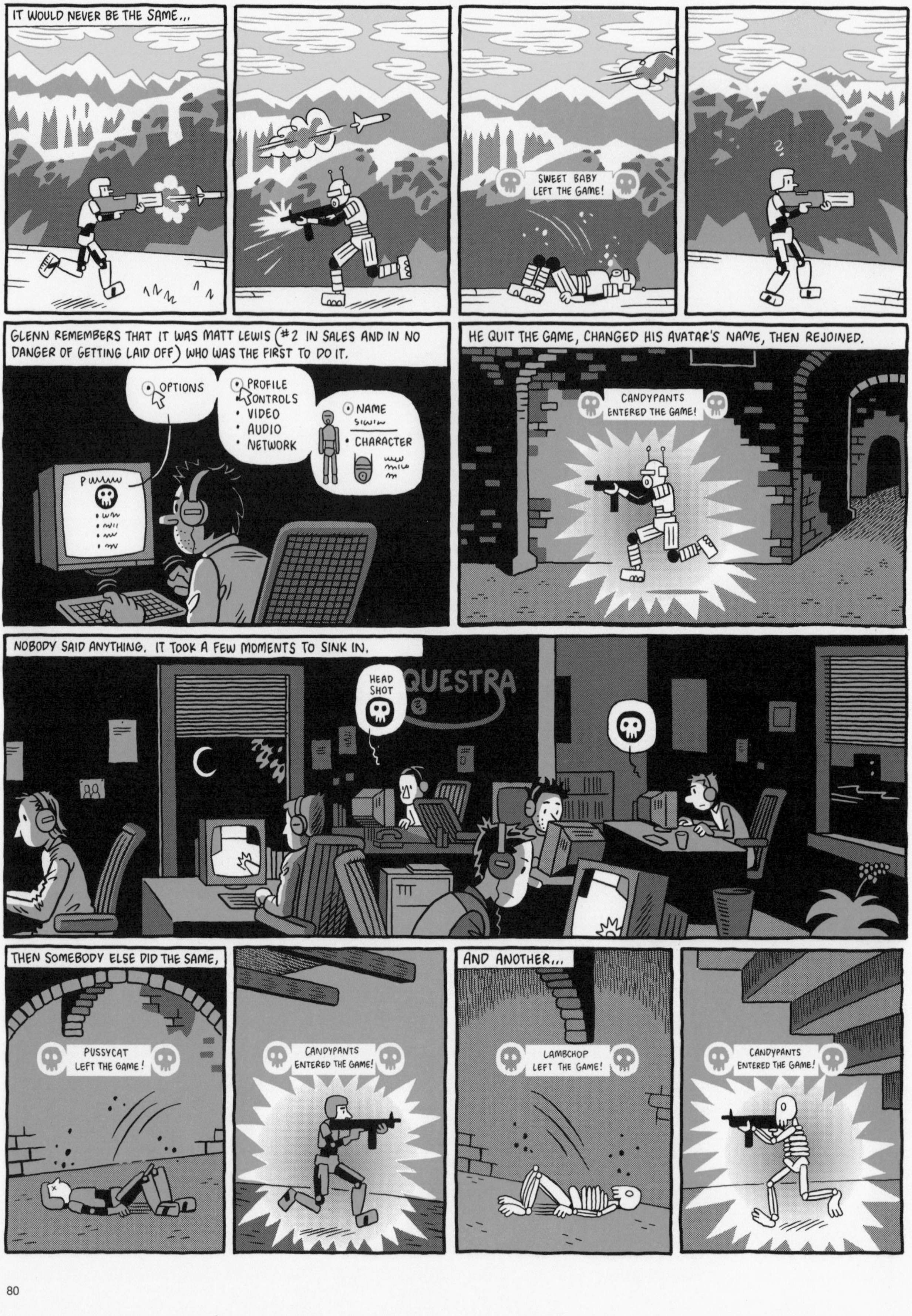
IT WOULD NEVER BE THE SAME...
SWEET BABY LEFT THE GAME!
GLENN REMEMBERS THAT IT WAS MATT LEWIS (#2 IN SALES AND IN NO DANGER OF GETTING LAID OFF) WHO WAS THE FIRST TO DO IT.
OPTIONS
PROFILE
CONTROLS
VIDEO
AUDIO
NETWORK
NAME
CHARACTER
HE QUIT THE GAME, CHANGED HIS AVATAR'S NAME, THEN REJOINED.
CANDYPANTS ENTERED THE GAME!
NOBODY SAID ANYTHING. IT TOOK A FEW MOMENTS TO SINK IN.
HEAD SHOT
QUESTRA
THEN SOMEBODY ELSE DID THE SAME,
PUSSYCAT LEFT THE GAME!
CANDYPANTS ENTERED THE GAME!
AND ANOTHER...
LAMBCHOP LEFT THE GAME!
CANDYPANTS ENTERED THE GAME!

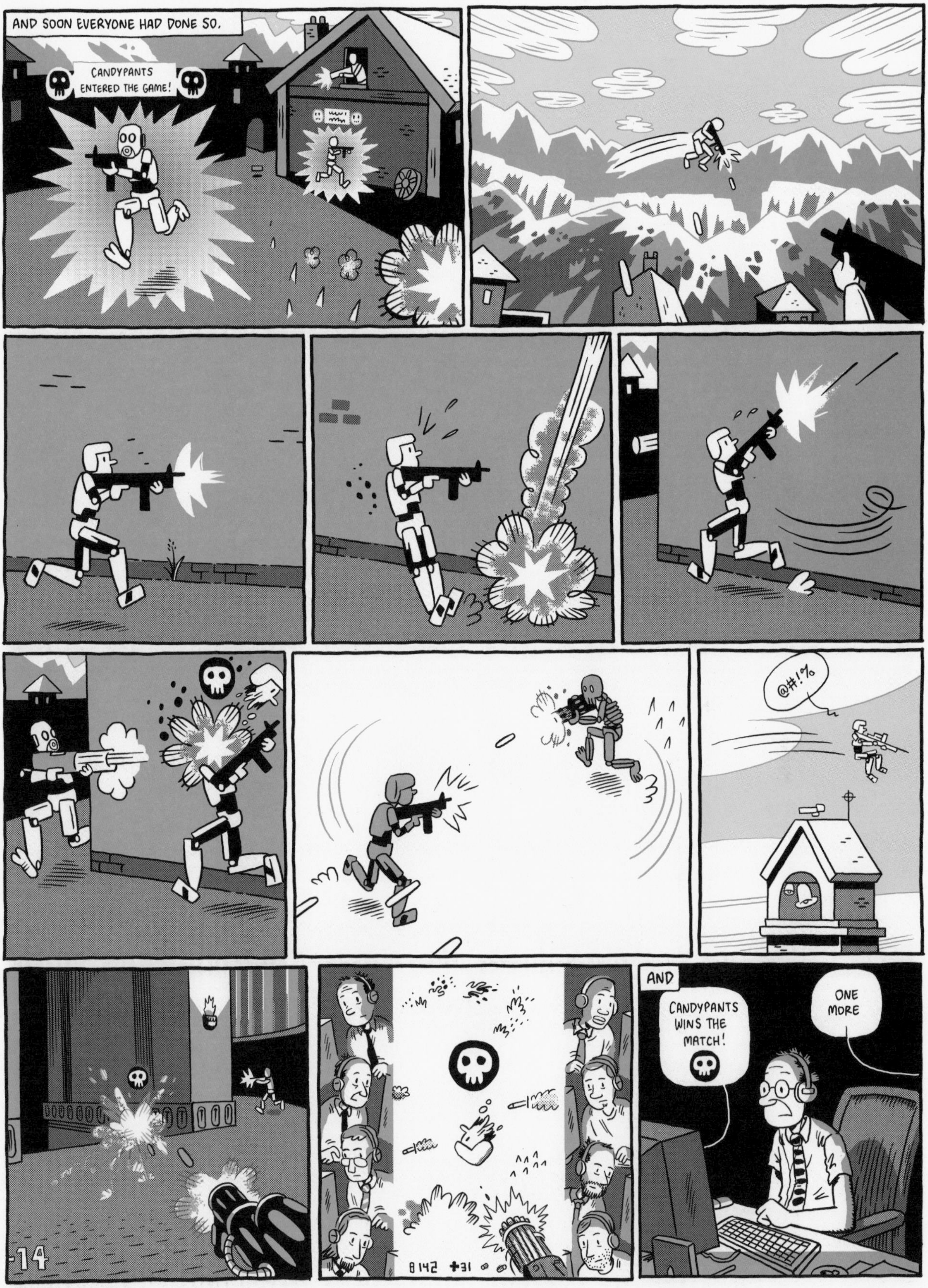
AND SOON EVERYONE HAD DONE SO.
CANDYPANTS ENTERED THE GAME!
@#!%
-14
8142 +31
AND
CANDYPANTS WINS THE MATCH!
ONE MORE

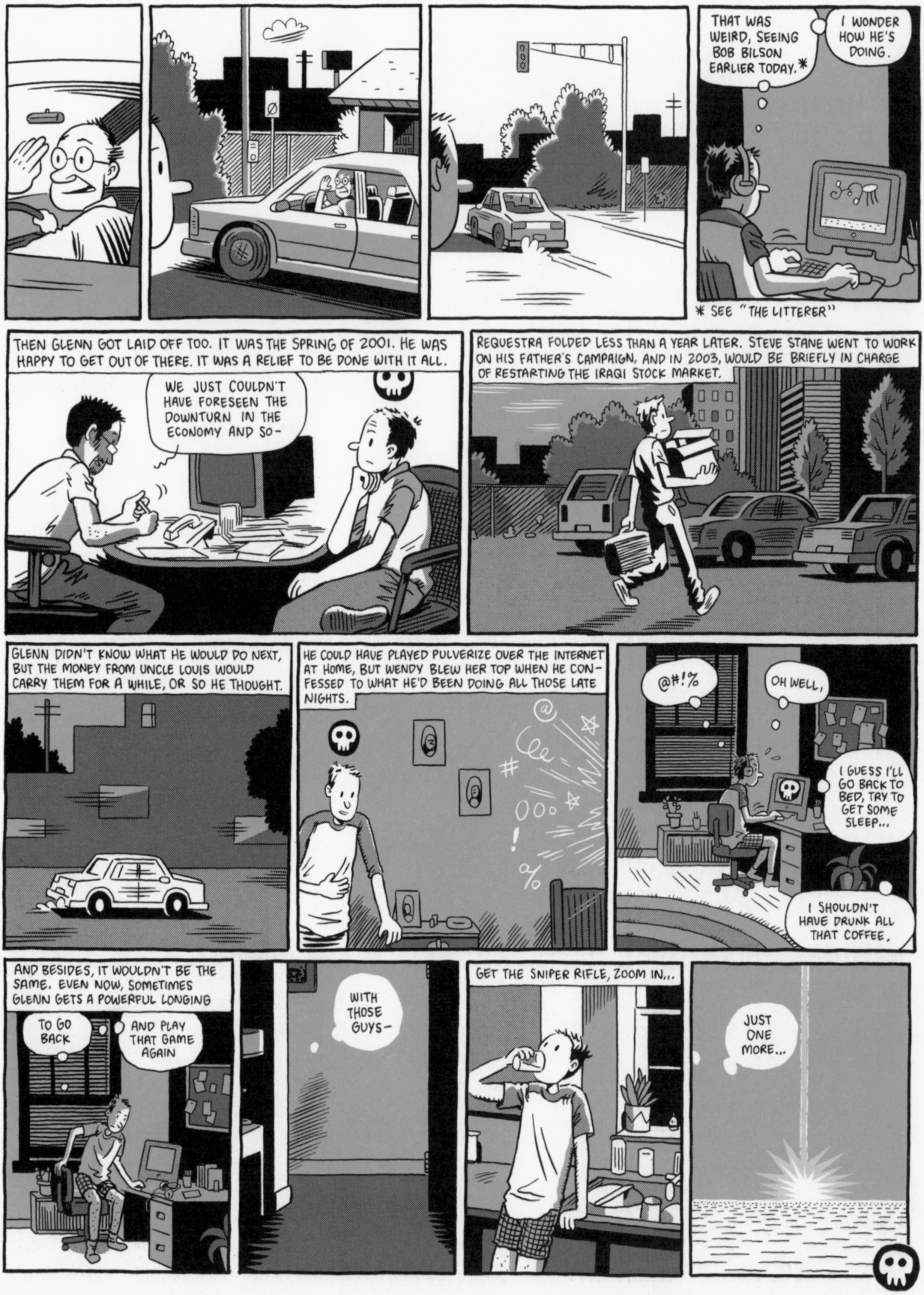
THAT WAS WEIRD, SEEING BOB BILSON EARLIER TODAY.*
I WONDER HOW HE'S DOING.
* SEE "THE LITTERER"
THEN GLENN GOT LAID OFF TOO. IT WAS THE SPRING OF 2001. HE WAS HAPPY TO GET OUT OF THERE. IT WAS A RELIEF TO BE DONE WITH IT ALL.
WE JUST COULDN'T HAVE FORESEEN THE DOWNTURN IN THE ECONOMY AND SO-
REQUESTRA FOLDED LESS THAN A YEAR LATER. STEVE STANE WENT TO WORK ON HIS FATHER'S CAMPAIGN, AND IN 2003, WOULD BE BRIEFLY IN CHARGE OF RESTARTING THE IRAQI STOCK MARKET.
GLENN DIDN'T KNOW WHAT HE WOULD DO NEXT, BUT THE MONEY FROM UNCLE LOUIS WOULD CARRY THEM FOR A WHILE, OR SO HE THOUGHT.
HE COULD HAVE PLAYED PULVERIZE OVER THE INTERNET AT HOME, BUT WENDY BLEW HER TOP WHEN HE CONFESSED TO WHAT HE'D BEEN DOING ALL THOSE LATE NIGHTS.
@#!%
OH WELL,
I GUESS I'LL GO BACK TO BED, TRY TO GET SOME SLEEP...
I SHOULDN'T HAVE DRUNK ALL THAT COFFEE.
AND BESIDES, IT WOULDN'T BE THE SAME. EVEN NOW, SOMETIMES GLENN GETS A POWERFUL LONGING
TO GO BACK
AND PLAY THAT GAME AGAIN
WITH THOSE GUYS-
GET THE SNIPER RIFLE, ZOOM IN...
JUST ONE MORE...

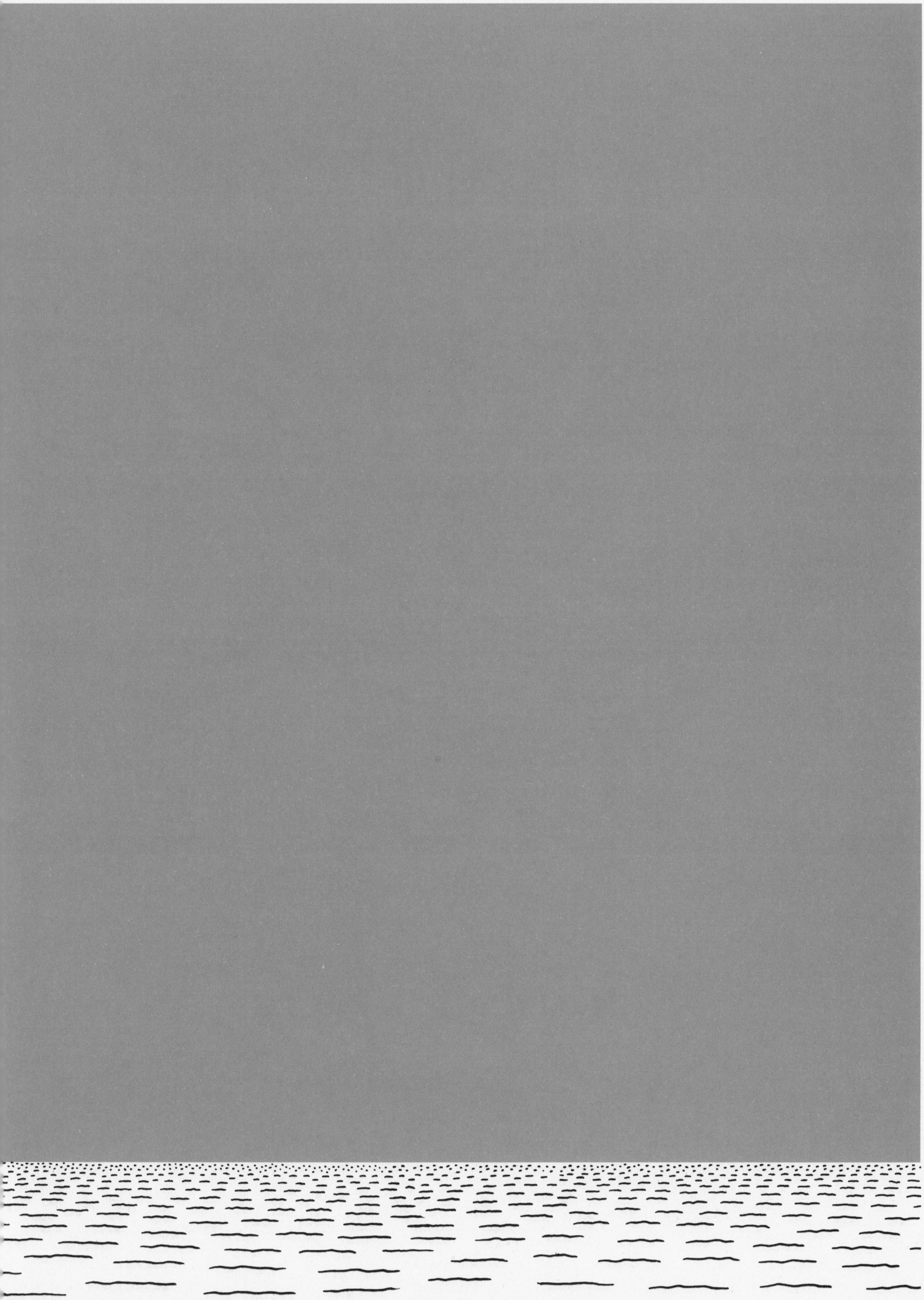

BACK TO BED...
3
...GLAD I DON'T HAVE TO WORK TOMORROW...
SIGH...
NOW I REALLY CAN'T GET TO SLEEP...
WHAT TIME IS IT? I DON'T WANT TO LOOK...
I'LL JUST TRY TO LIE HERE AND REST... RELAX MY MUSCLES, CLEAR MY HEAD... BREATHE...
(THAT STUFF I LEARNED ABOUT IN "HEALTH CLASS...")
OK, CONCENTRATE ON MY BREATH...

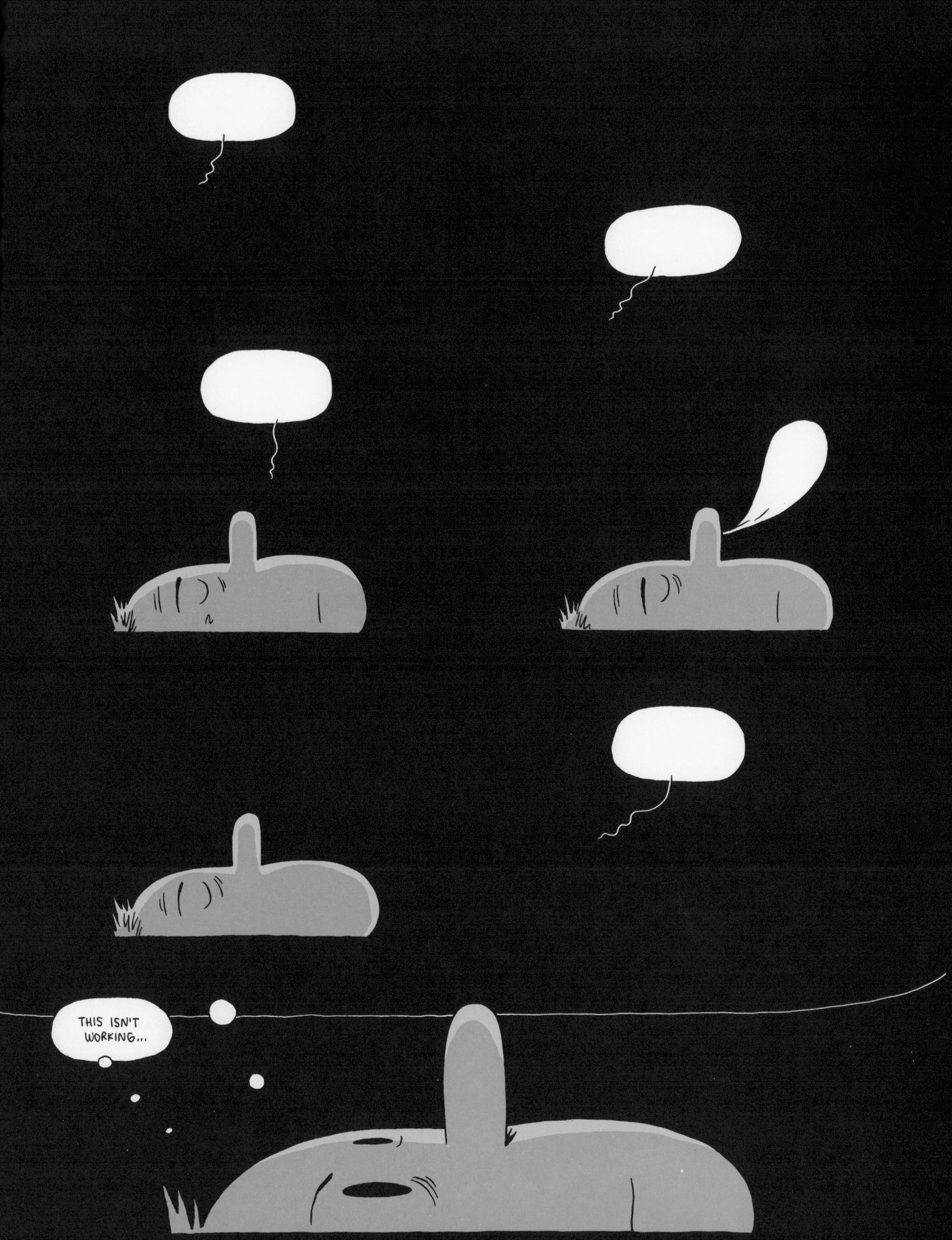
THIS ISN'T WORKING...

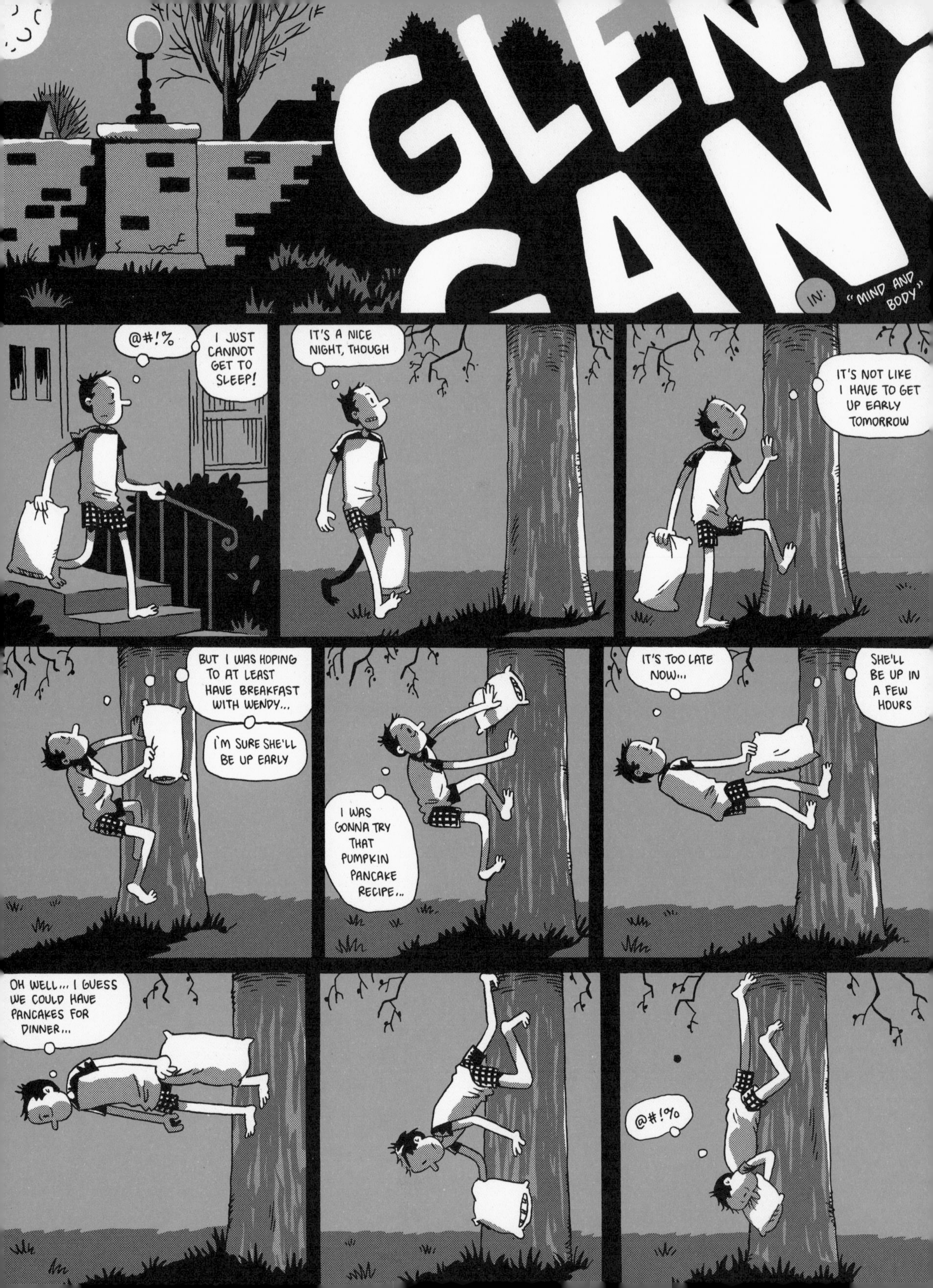
GLENN GANG
IN: "MIND AND BODY"
@#!%
I JUST CANNOT GET TO SLEEP!
IT'S A NICE NIGHT, THOUGH
IT'S NOT LIKE I HAVE TO GET UP EARLY TOMORROW
BUT I WAS HOPING TO AT LEAST HAVE BREAKFAST WITH WENDY...
I'M SURE SHE'LL BE UP EARLY
I WAS GONNA TRY THAT PUMPKIN PANCAKE RECIPE...
IT'S TOO LATE NOW...
SHE'LL BE UP IN A FEW HOURS
OH WELL... I GUESS WE COULD HAVE PANCAKES FOR DINNER...
@#!%

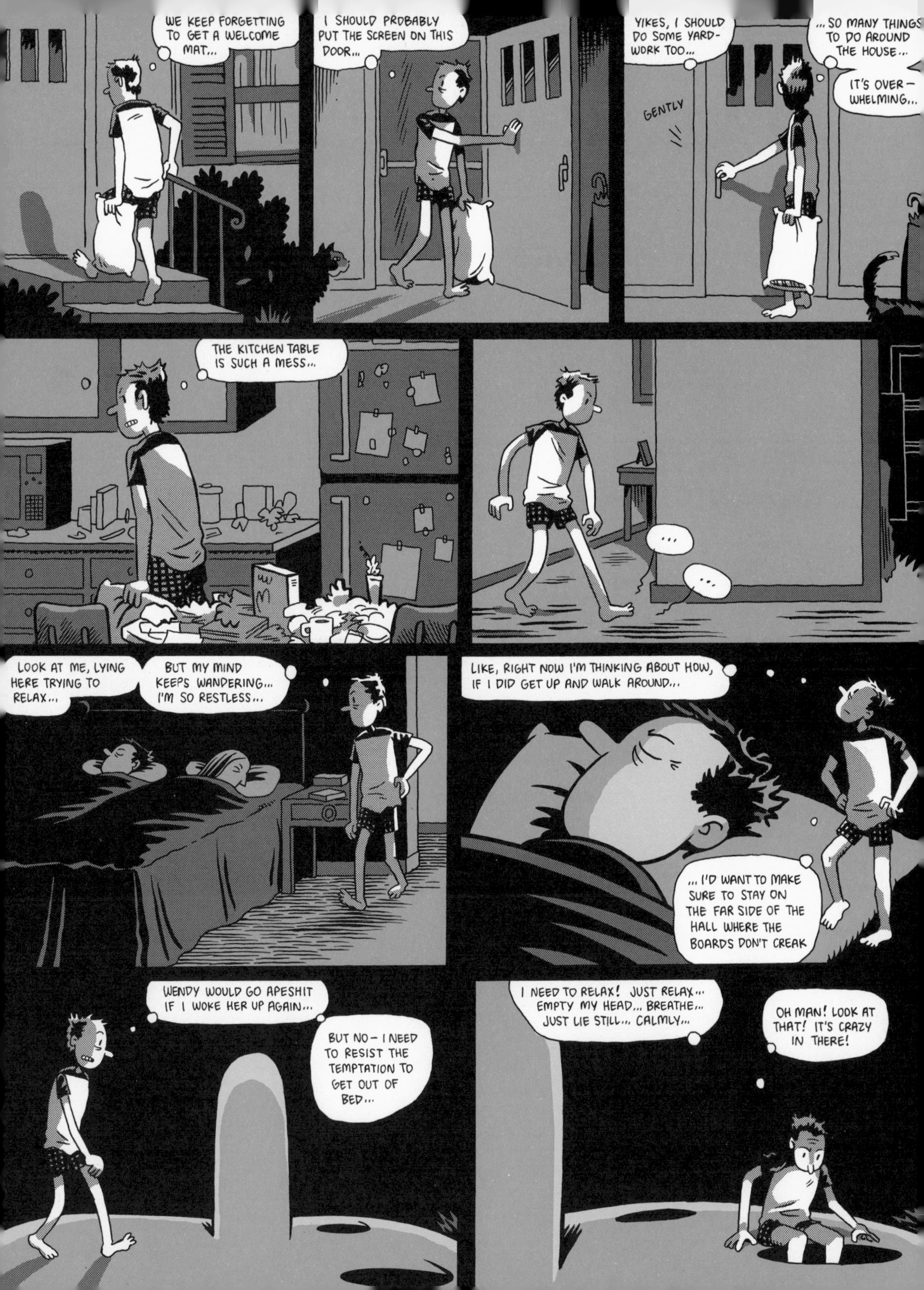
WE KEEP FORGETTING TO GET A WELCOME MAT...
I SHOULD PROBABLY PUT THE SCREEN ON THIS DOOR...
YIKES, I SHOULD DO SOME YARD-WORK TOO...
GENTLY
...SO MANY THINGS TO DO AROUND THE HOUSE...
IT'S OVER-WHELMING...
THE KITCHEN TABLE IS SUCH A MESS...
...
...
LOOK AT ME, LYING HERE TRYING TO RELAX...
BUT MY MIND KEEPS WANDERING... I'M SO RESTLESS...
LIKE, RIGHT NOW I'M THINKING ABOUT HOW, IF I DID GET UP AND WALK AROUND...
...I'D WANT TO MAKE SURE TO STAY ON THE FAR SIDE OF THE HALL WHERE THE BOARDS DON'T CREAK
WENDY WOULD GO APESHIT IF I WOKE HER UP AGAIN...
BUT NO- I NEED TO RESIST THE TEMPTATION TO GET OUT OF BED...
I NEED TO RELAX! JUST RELAX... EMPTY MY HEAD... BREATHE... JUST LIE STILL... CALMLY...
OH MAN! LOOK AT THAT! IT'S CRAZY IN THERE!

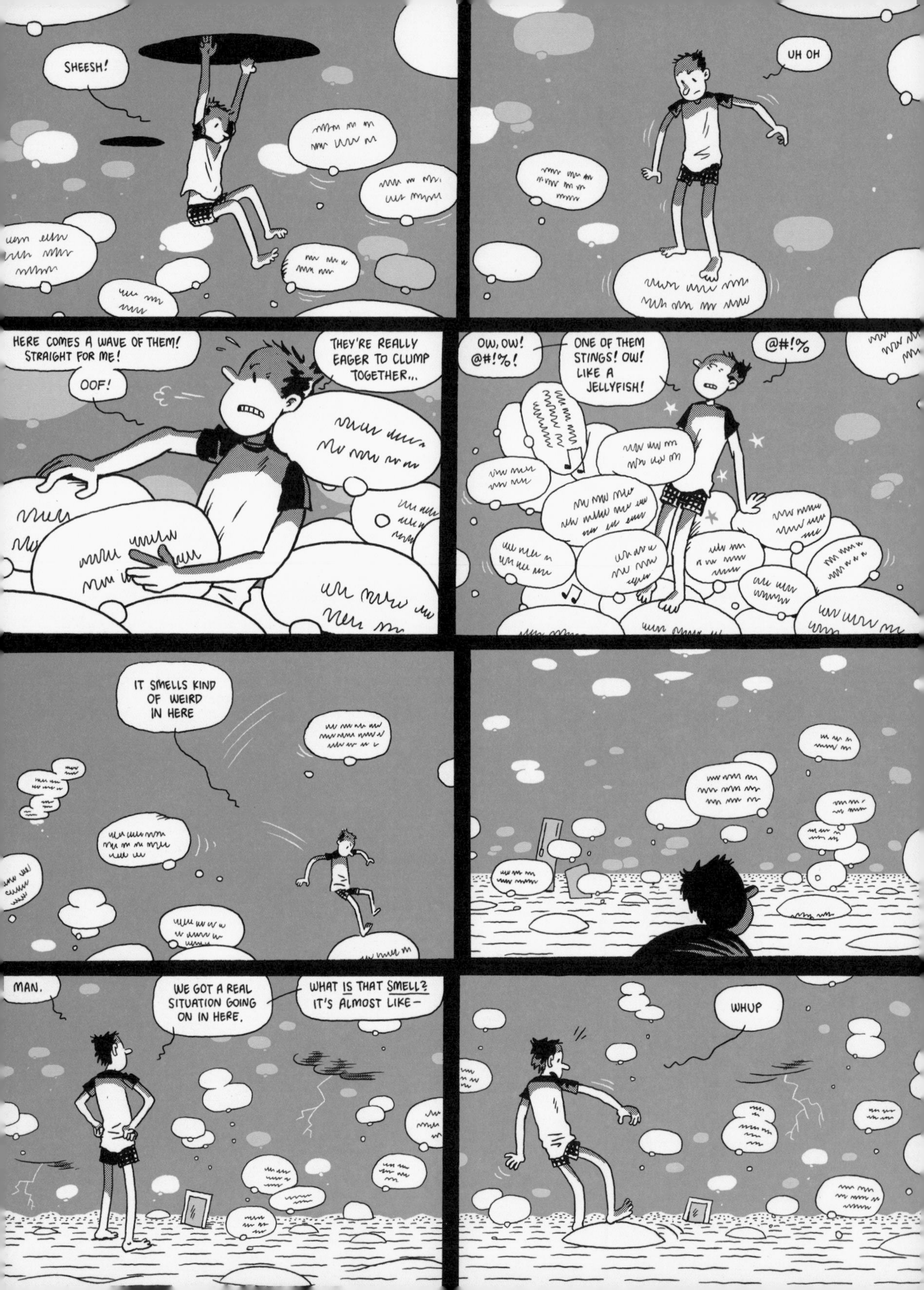
SHEESH!
UH OH
HERE COMES A WAVE OF THEM! STRAIGHT FOR ME!
OOF!
THEY'RE REALLY EAGER TO CLUMP TOGETHER...
OW, OW! @#!%!
ONE OF THEM STINGS! OW! LIKE A JELLYFISH!
@#!%
IT SMELLS KIND OF WEIRD IN HERE
MAN.
WE GOT A REAL SITUATION GOING ON IN HERE.
WHAT IS THAT SMELL? IT'S ALMOST LIKE—
WHUP

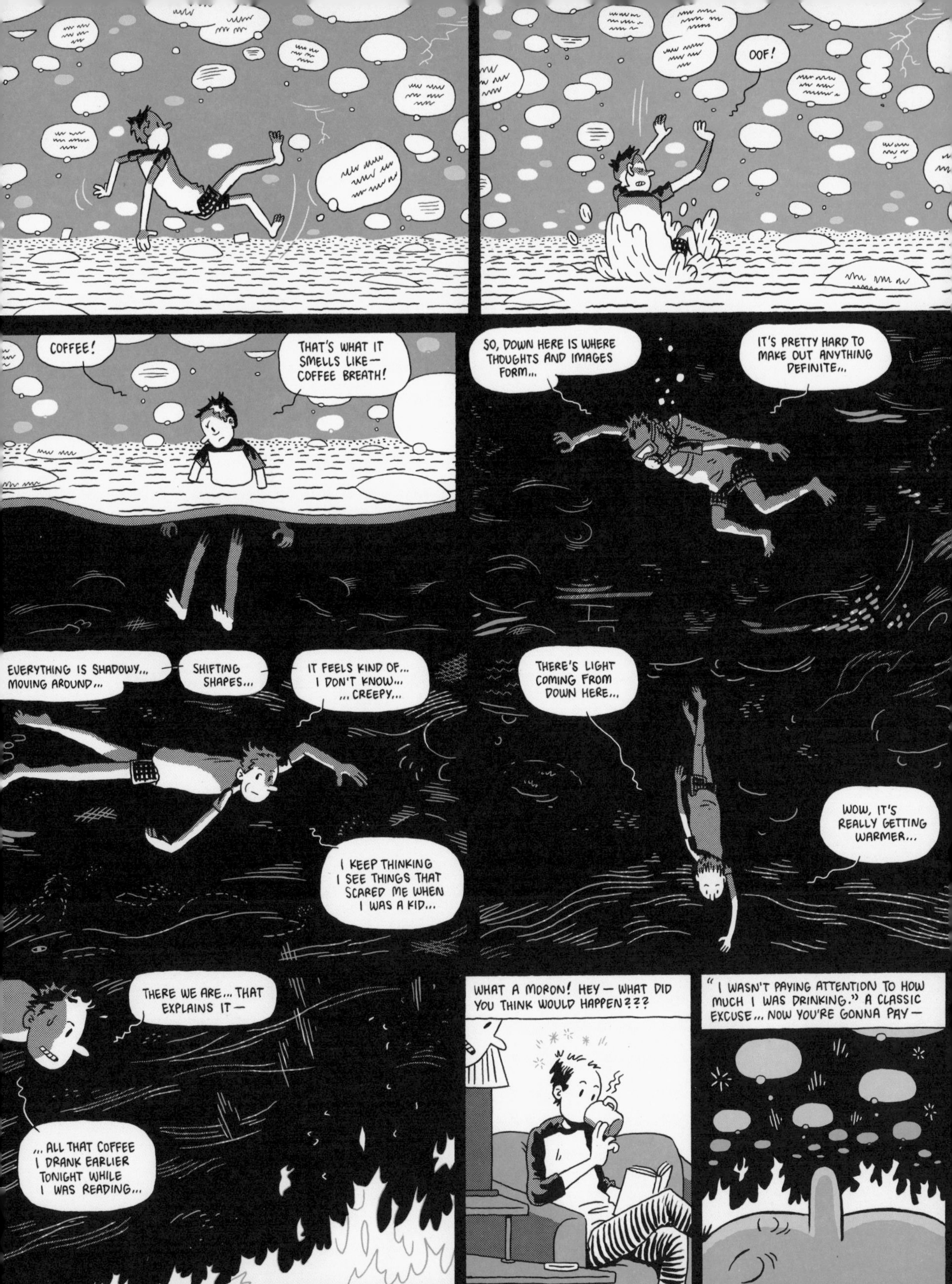
OOF!
COFFEE!
THAT'S WHAT IT SMELLS LIKE— COFFEE BREATH!
SO, DOWN HERE IS WHERE THOUGHTS AND IMAGES FORM...
IT'S PRETTY HARD TO MAKE OUT ANYTHING DEFINITE...
EVERYTHING IS SHADOWY... MOVING AROUND...
SHIFTING SHAPES...
IT FEELS KIND OF... I DON'T KNOW... ...CREEPY...
I KEEP THINKING I SEE THINGS THAT SCARED ME WHEN I WAS A KID...
THERE'S LIGHT COMING FROM DOWN HERE...
WOW, IT'S REALLY GETTING WARMER...
THERE WE ARE... THAT EXPLAINS IT—
...ALL THAT COFFEE I DRANK EARLIER TONIGHT WHILE I WAS READING...
WHAT A MORON! HEY— WHAT DID YOU THINK WOULD HAPPEN???
"I WASN'T PAYING ATTENTION TO HOW MUCH I WAS DRINKING." A CLASSIC EXCUSE... NOW YOU'RE GONNA PAY—

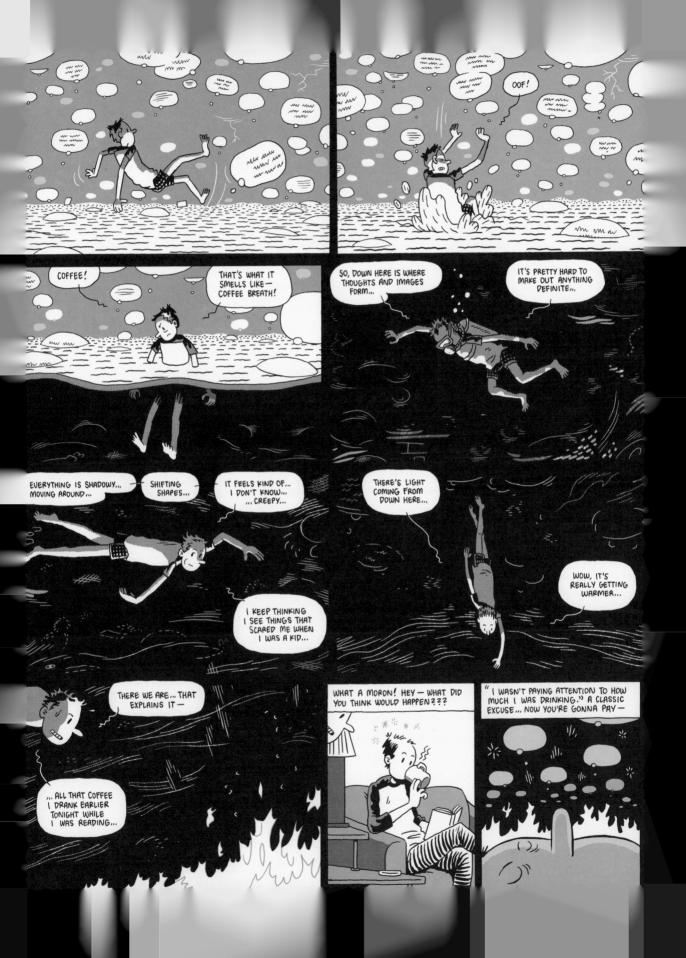

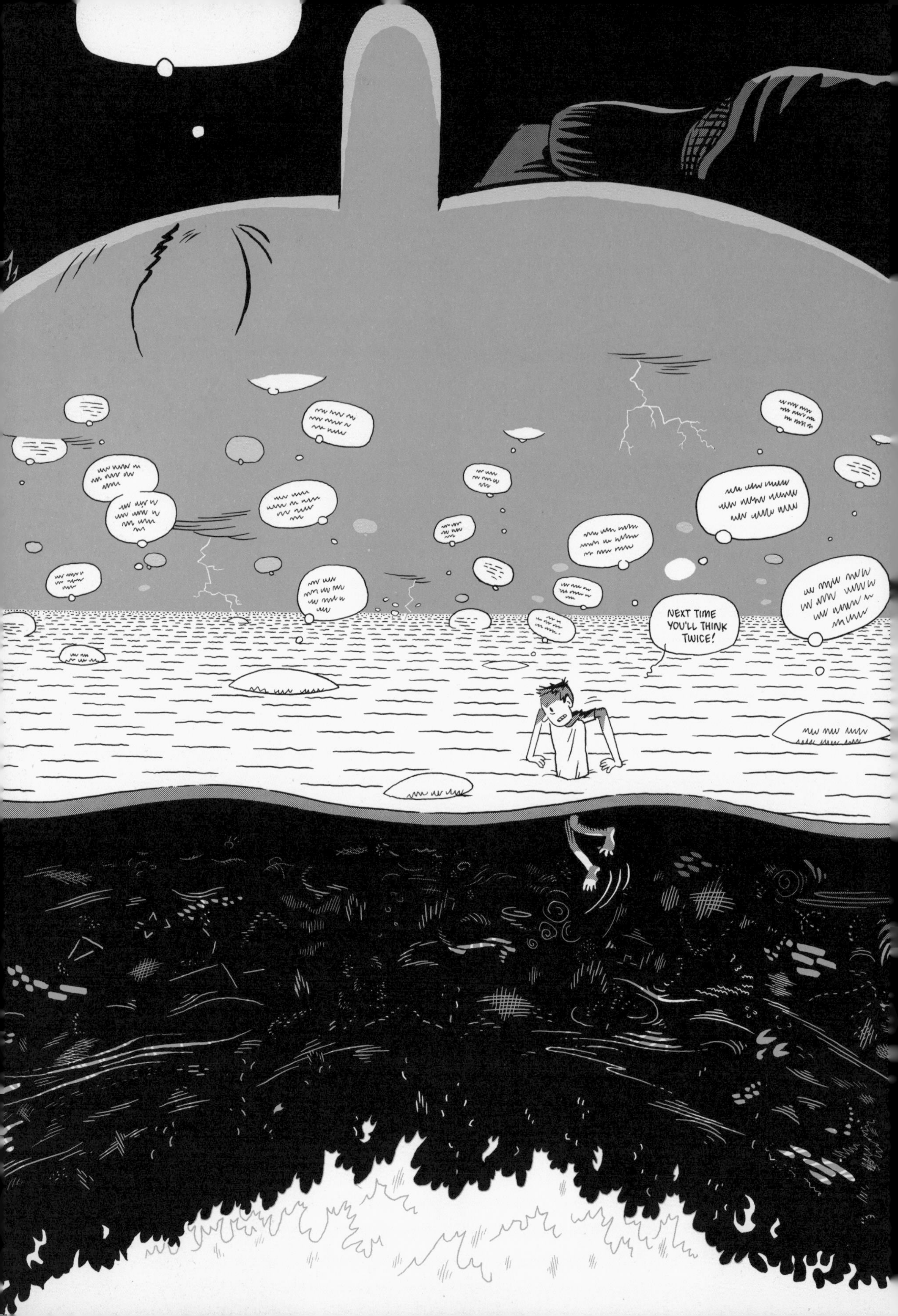
NEXT TIME YOU'LL THINK TWICE!

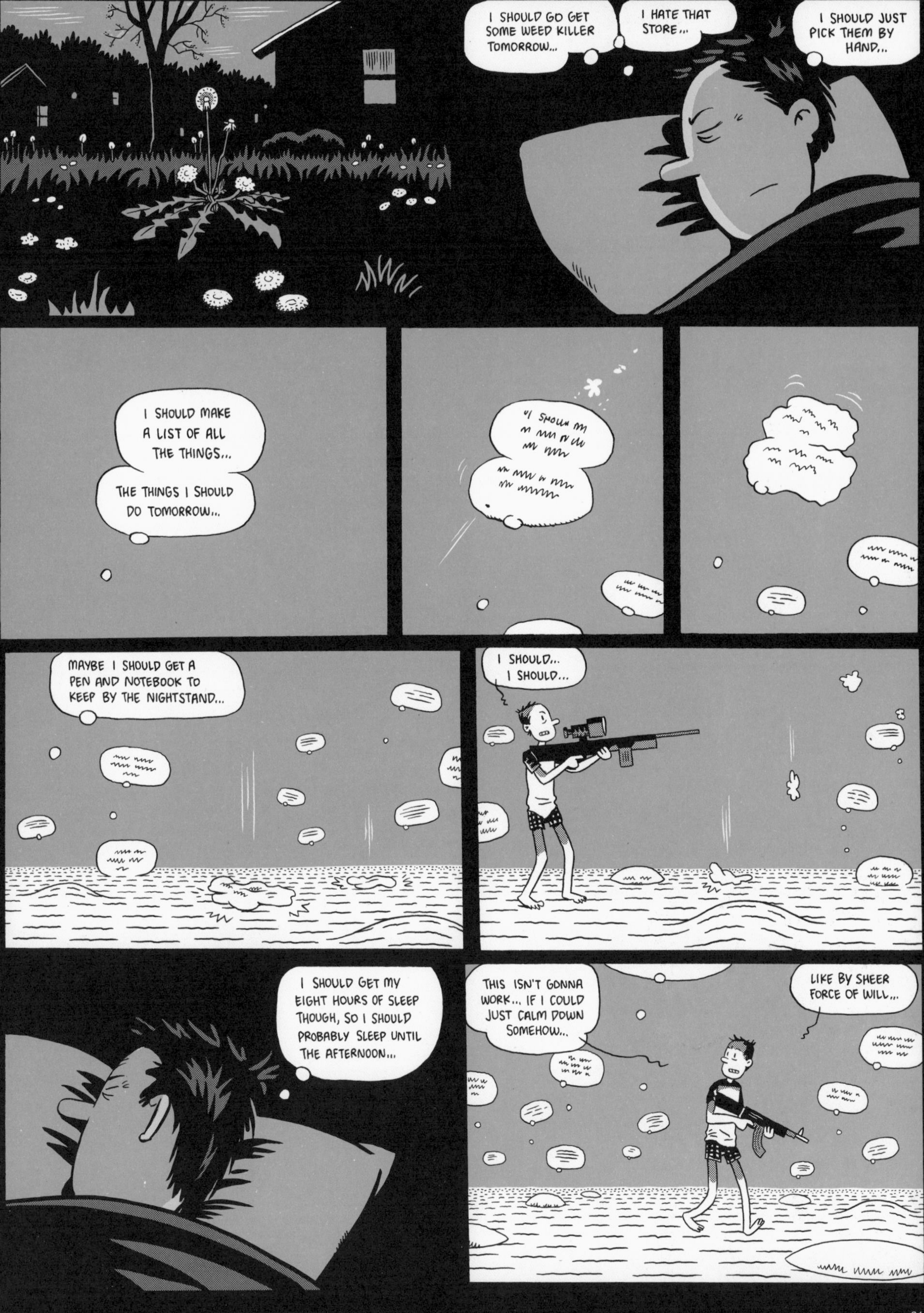

I SHOULD GO GET SOME WEED KILLER TOMORROW...
I HATE THAT STORE...
I SHOULD JUST PICK THEM BY HAND...
I SHOULD MAKE A LIST OF ALL THE THINGS...
THE THINGS I SHOULD DO TOMORROW...
MAYBE I SHOULD GET A PEN AND NOTEBOOK TO KEEP BY THE NIGHTSTAND...
I SHOULD... I SHOULD...
I SHOULD GET MY EIGHT HOURS OF SLEEP THOUGH, SO I SHOULD PROBABLY SLEEP UNTIL THE AFTERNOON...
THIS ISN'T GONNA WORK... IF I COULD JUST CALM DOWN SOMEHOW...
LIKE BY SHEER FORCE OF WILL...

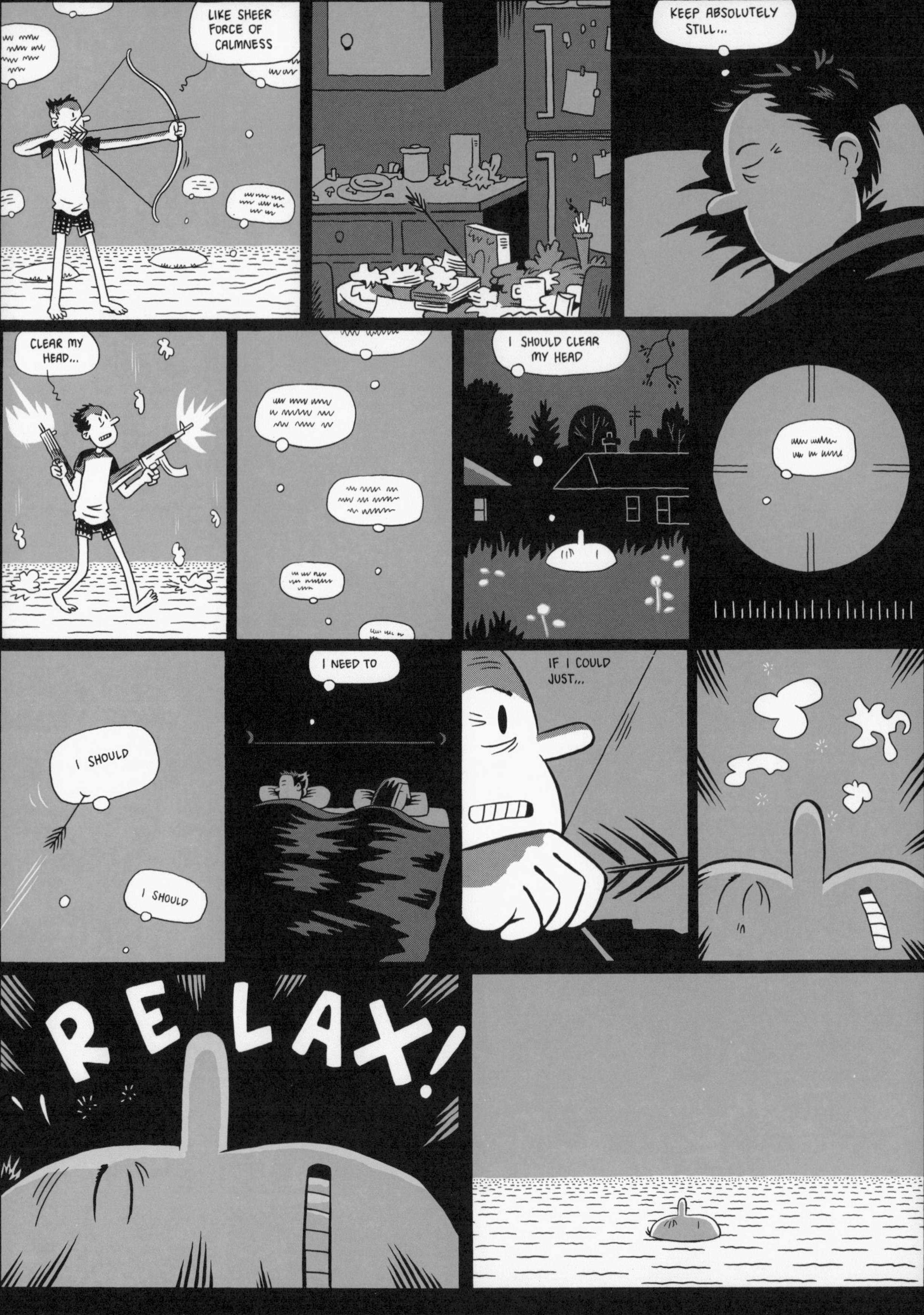
LIKE SHEER FORCE OF CALMNESS
KEEP ABSOLUTELY STILL...
CLEAR MY HEAD...
I SHOULD CLEAR MY HEAD
I SHOULD
I SHOULD
I NEED TO
IF I COULD JUST...
RELAX!

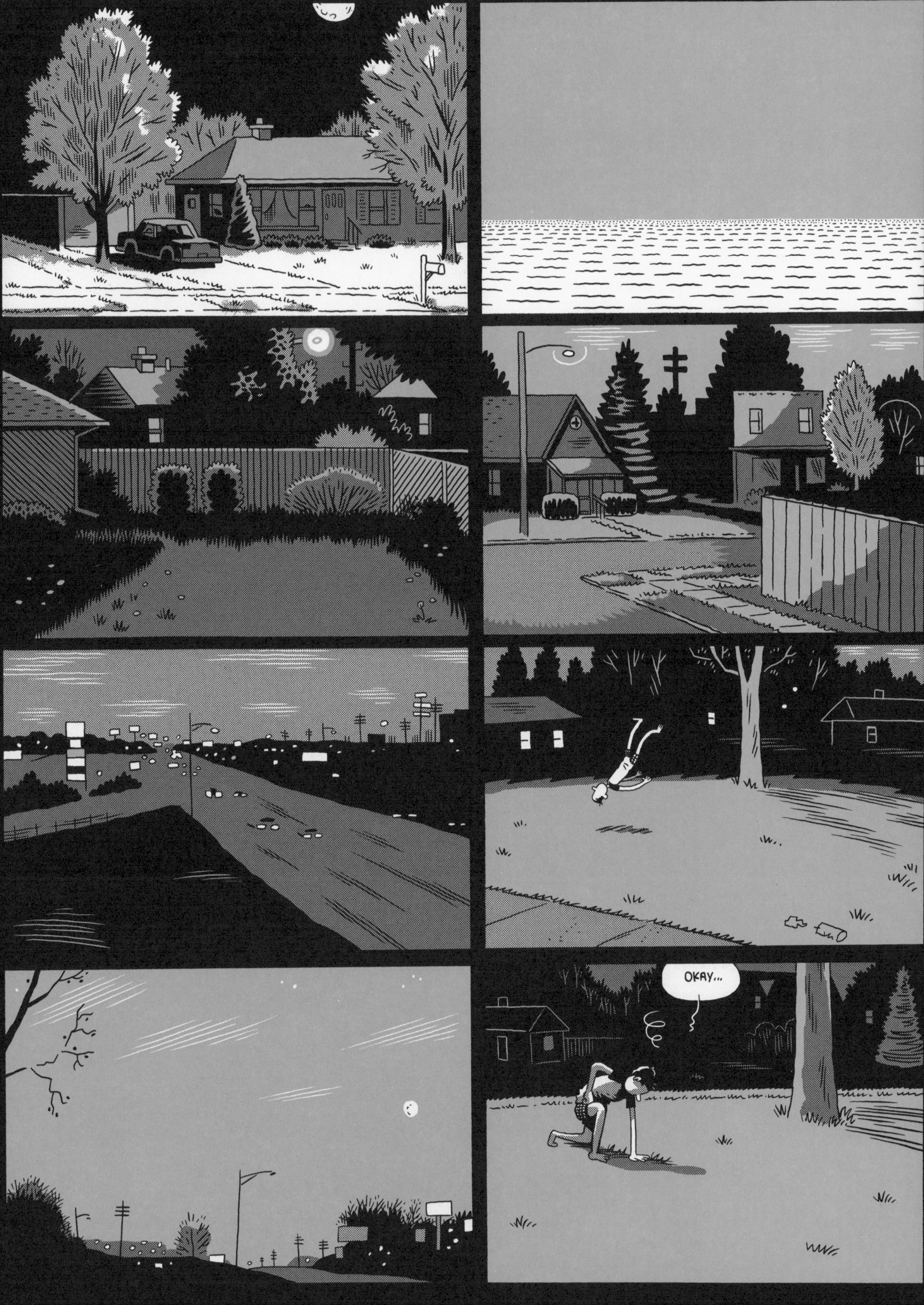
OKAY...

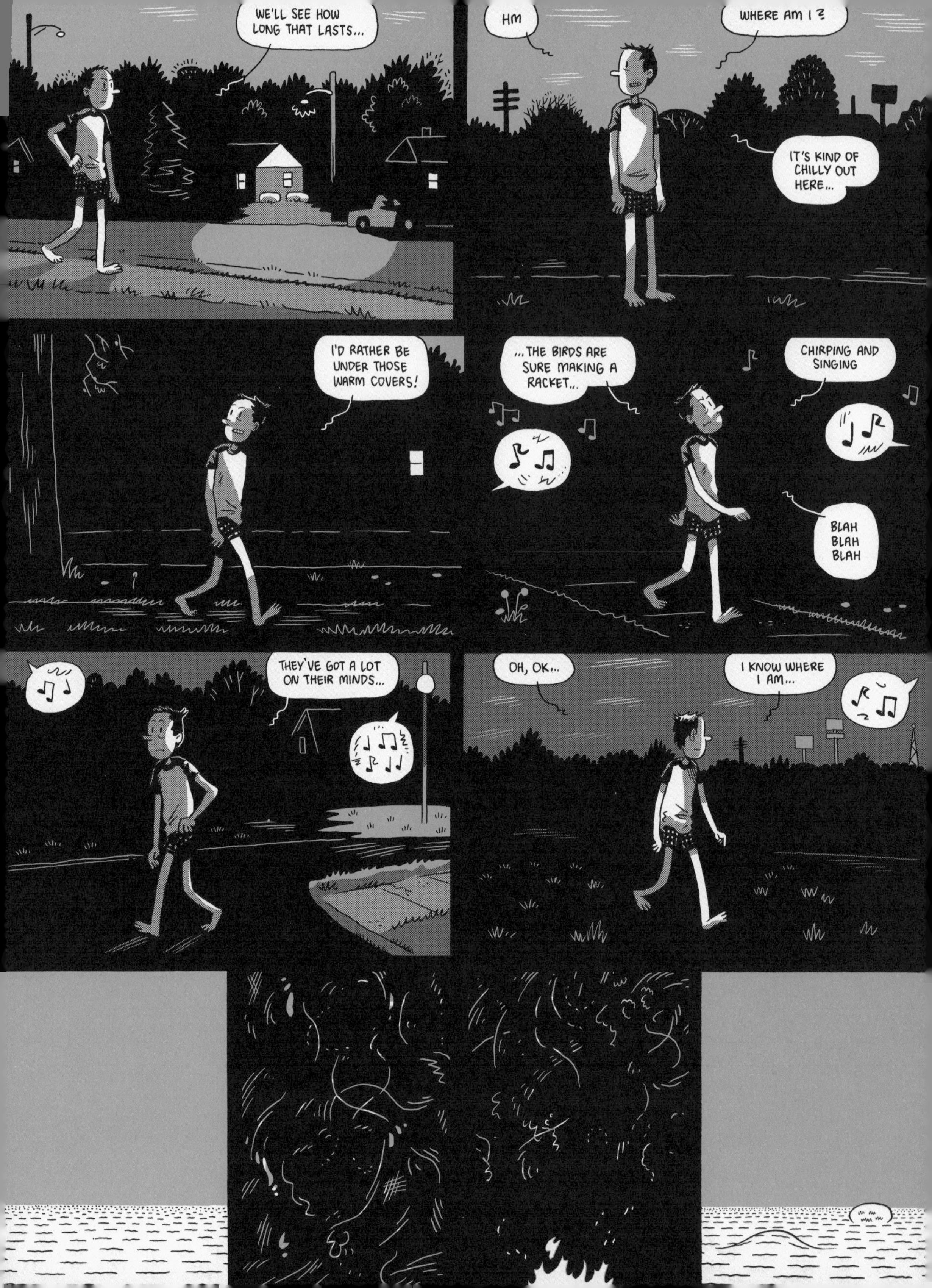

WE'LL SEE HOW LONG THAT LASTS...
HM
WHERE AM I?
IT'S KIND OF CHILLY OUT HERE...
I'D RATHER BE UNDER THOSE WARM COVERS!
...THE BIRDS ARE SURE MAKING A RACKET...
CHIRPING AND SINGING
BLAH BLAH BLAH
THEY'VE GOT A LOT ON THEIR MINDS...
OH, OK...
I KNOW WHERE I AM...

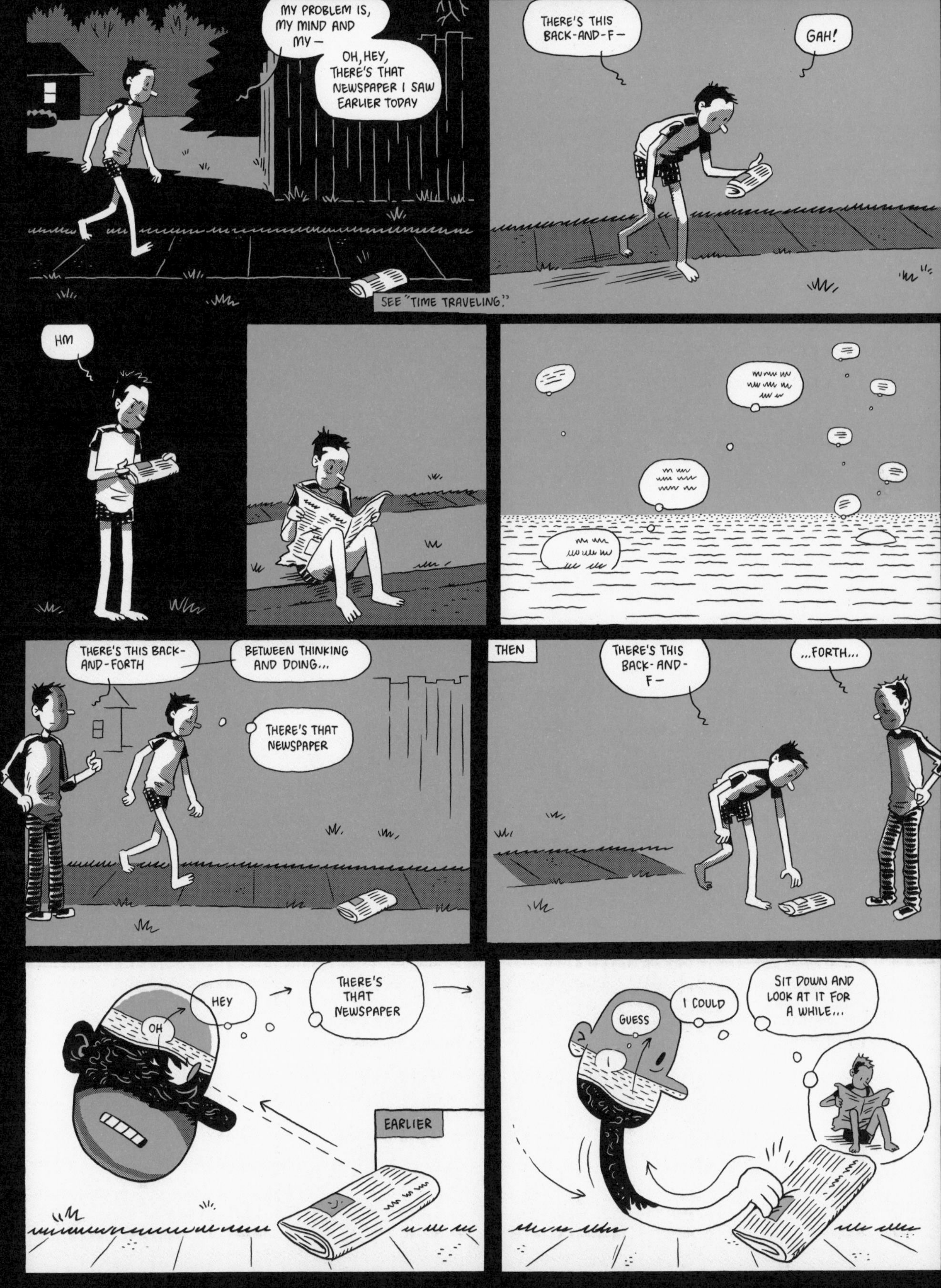
MY PROBLEM IS, MY MIND AND MY—
OH, HEY, THERE'S THAT NEWSPAPER I SAW EARLIER TODAY
SEE "TIME TRAVELING."
THERE'S THIS BACK-AND-F—
GAH!
HM
THERE'S THIS BACK-AND-FORTH
BETWEEN THINKING AND DOING...
THERE'S THAT NEWSPAPER
THEN
THERE'S THIS BACK-AND-F—
...FORTH...
OH
HEY
THERE'S THAT NEWSPAPER
EARLIER
GUESS
I COULD
SIT DOWN AND LOOK AT IT FOR A WHILE...

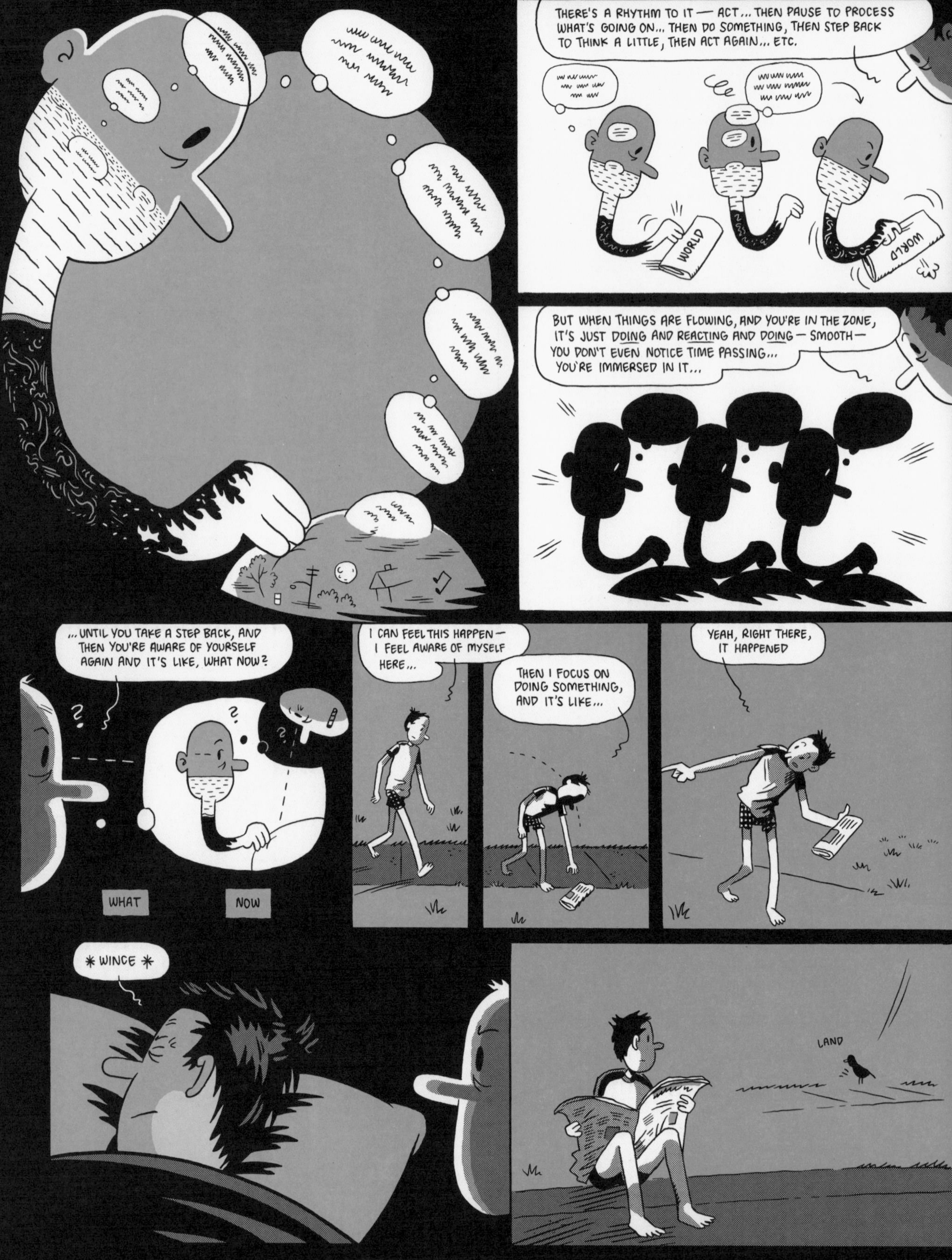
THERE'S A RHYTHM TO IT — ACT... THEN PAUSE TO PROCESS WHAT'S GOING ON... THEN DO SOMETHING, THEN STEP BACK TO THINK A LITTLE, THEN ACT AGAIN... ETC.
WORLD
WORLD
BUT WHEN THINGS ARE FLOWING, AND YOU'RE IN THE ZONE, IT'S JUST DOING AND REACTING AND DOING — SMOOTH — YOU DON'T EVEN NOTICE TIME PASSING... YOU'RE IMMERSED IN IT...
...UNTIL YOU TAKE A STEP BACK, AND THEN YOU'RE AWARE OF YOURSELF AGAIN AND IT'S LIKE, WHAT NOW?
WHAT
NOW
I CAN FEEL THIS HAPPEN — I FEEL AWARE OF MYSELF HERE...
THEN I FOCUS ON DOING SOMETHING, AND IT'S LIKE...
YEAH, RIGHT THERE, IT HAPPENED
* WINCE *
LAND

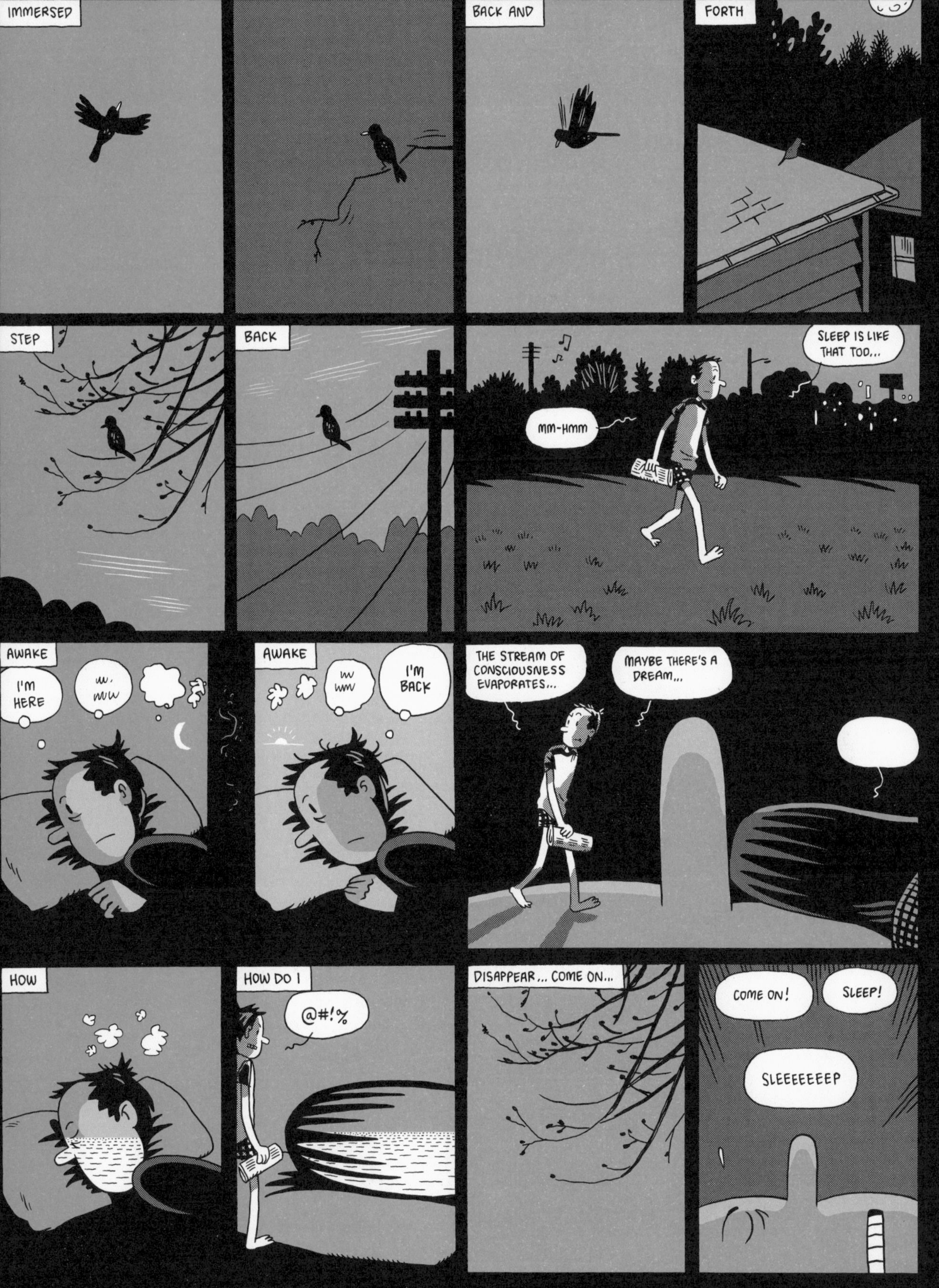
IMMERSED
BACK AND
FORTH
STEP
BACK
MM-HMM
SLEEP IS LIKE THAT TOO...
AWAKE
I'M HERE
AWAKE
I'M BACK
THE STREAM OF CONSCIOUSNESS EVAPORATES...
MAYBE THERE'S A DREAM...
HOW
HOW DO I
@#!%
DISAPPEAR... COME ON...
COME ON!
SLEEP!
SLEEEEEEEP

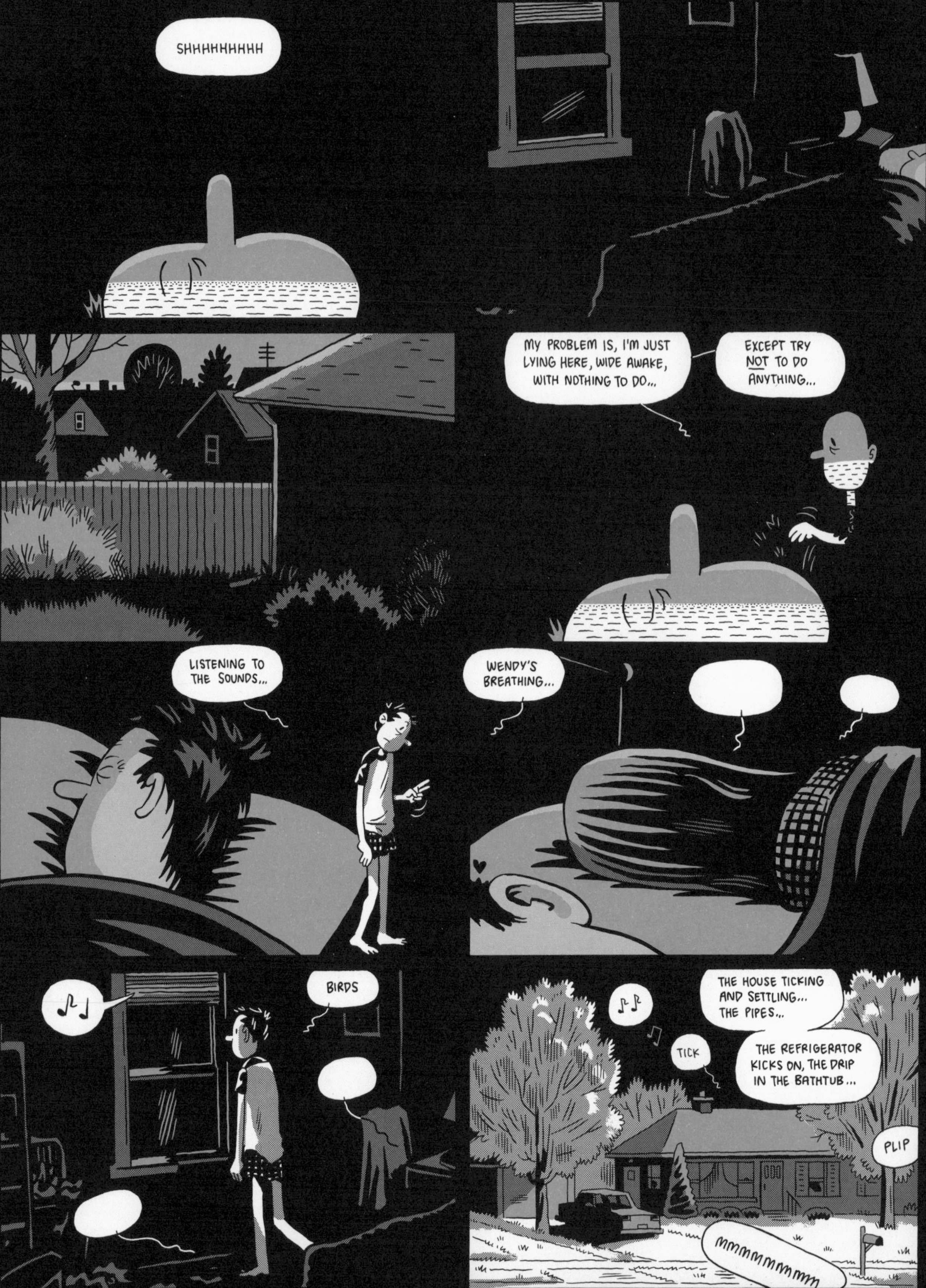
SHHHHHHHHH
MY PROBLEM IS, I'M JUST LYING HERE, WIDE AWAKE, WITH NOTHING TO DO...
EXCEPT TRY NOT TO DO ANYTHING...
LISTENING TO THE SOUNDS...
WENDY'S BREATHING...
BIRDS
THE HOUSE TICKING AND SETTLING... THE PIPES...
TICK
THE REFRIGERATOR KICKS ON, THE DRIP IN THE BATHTUB...
PLIP
MMMMMMMMM

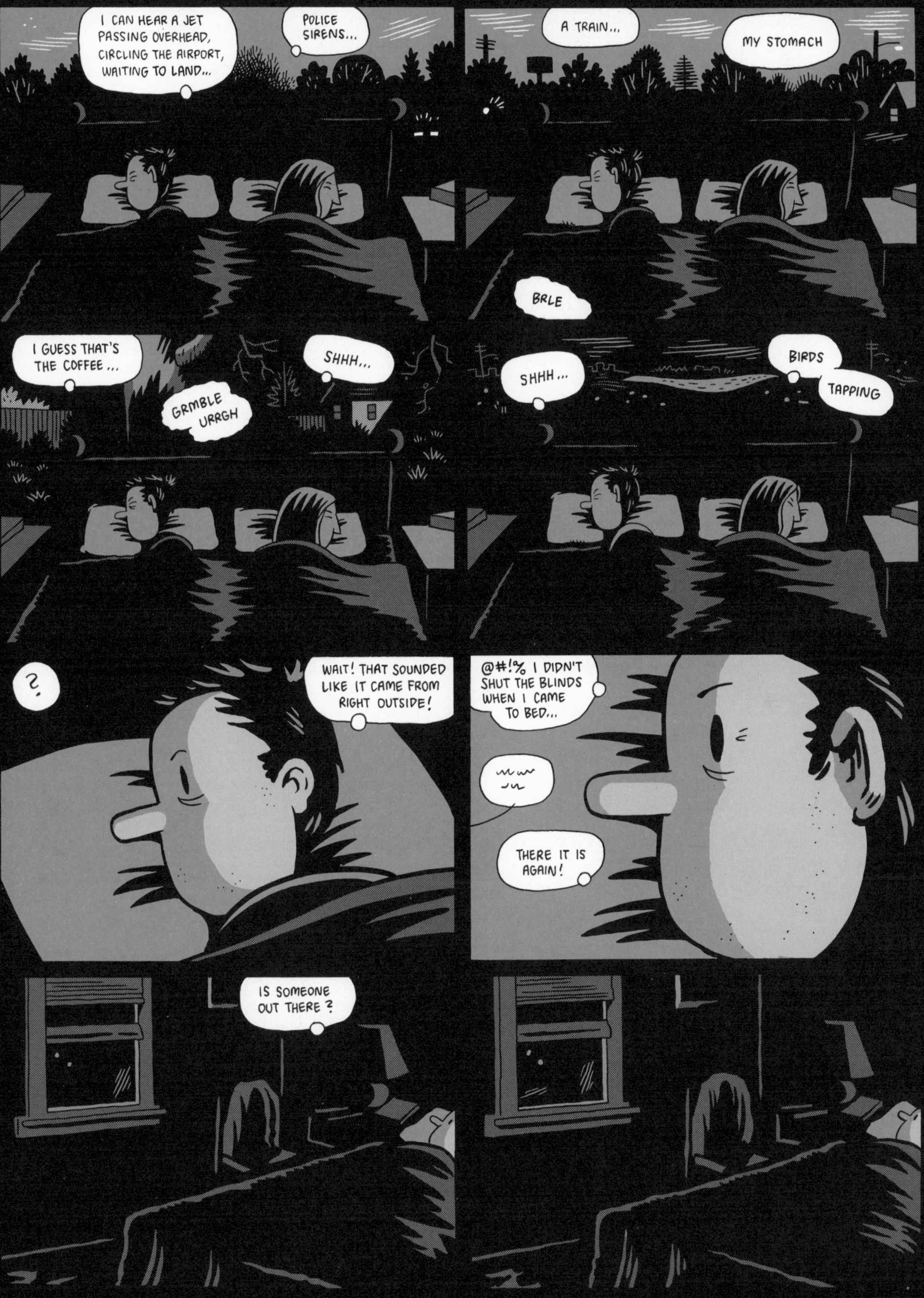
I CAN HEAR A JET PASSING OVERHEAD, CIRCLING THE AIRPORT, WAITING TO LAND...
POLICE SIRENS...
A TRAIN...
MY STOMACH
BRLE
I GUESS THAT'S THE COFFEE...
GRMBLE URRGH
SHHH...
SHHH...
BIRDS
TAPPING
?
WAIT! THAT SOUNDED LIKE IT CAME FROM RIGHT OUTSIDE!
@#!% I DIDN'T SHUT THE BLINDS WHEN I CAME TO BED...
THERE IT IS AGAIN!
IS SOMEONE OUT THERE?

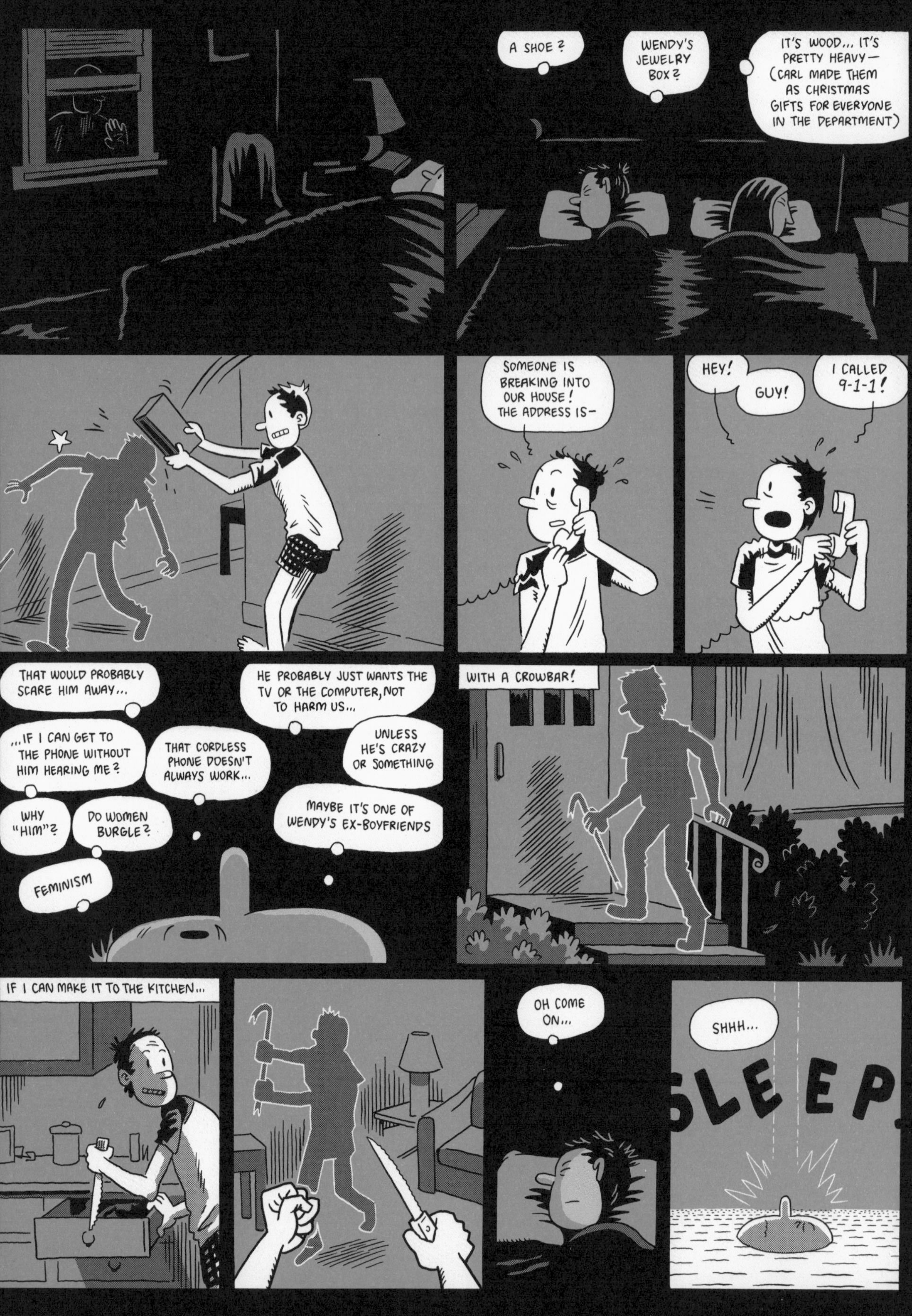
A SHOE?
WENDY'S JEWELRY BOX?
IT'S WOOD... IT'S PRETTY HEAVY— (CARL MADE THEM AS CHRISTMAS GIFTS FOR EVERYONE IN THE DEPARTMENT)
SOMEONE IS BREAKING INTO OUR HOUSE! THE ADDRESS IS—
HEY!
GUY!
I CALLED 9-1-1!
THAT WOULD PROBABLY SCARE HIM AWAY...
...IF I CAN GET TO THE PHONE WITHOUT HIM HEARING ME?
THAT CORDLESS PHONE DOESN'T ALWAYS WORK...
WHY "HIM"?
DO WOMEN BURGLE?
FEMINISM
HE PROBABLY JUST WANTS THE TV OR THE COMPUTER, NOT TO HARM US...
UNLESS HE'S CRAZY OR SOMETHING
MAYBE IT'S ONE OF WENDY'S EX-BOYFRIENDS
WITH A CROWBAR!
IF I CAN MAKE IT TO THE KITCHEN...
OH COME ON...
SHHH...
SLEEP.

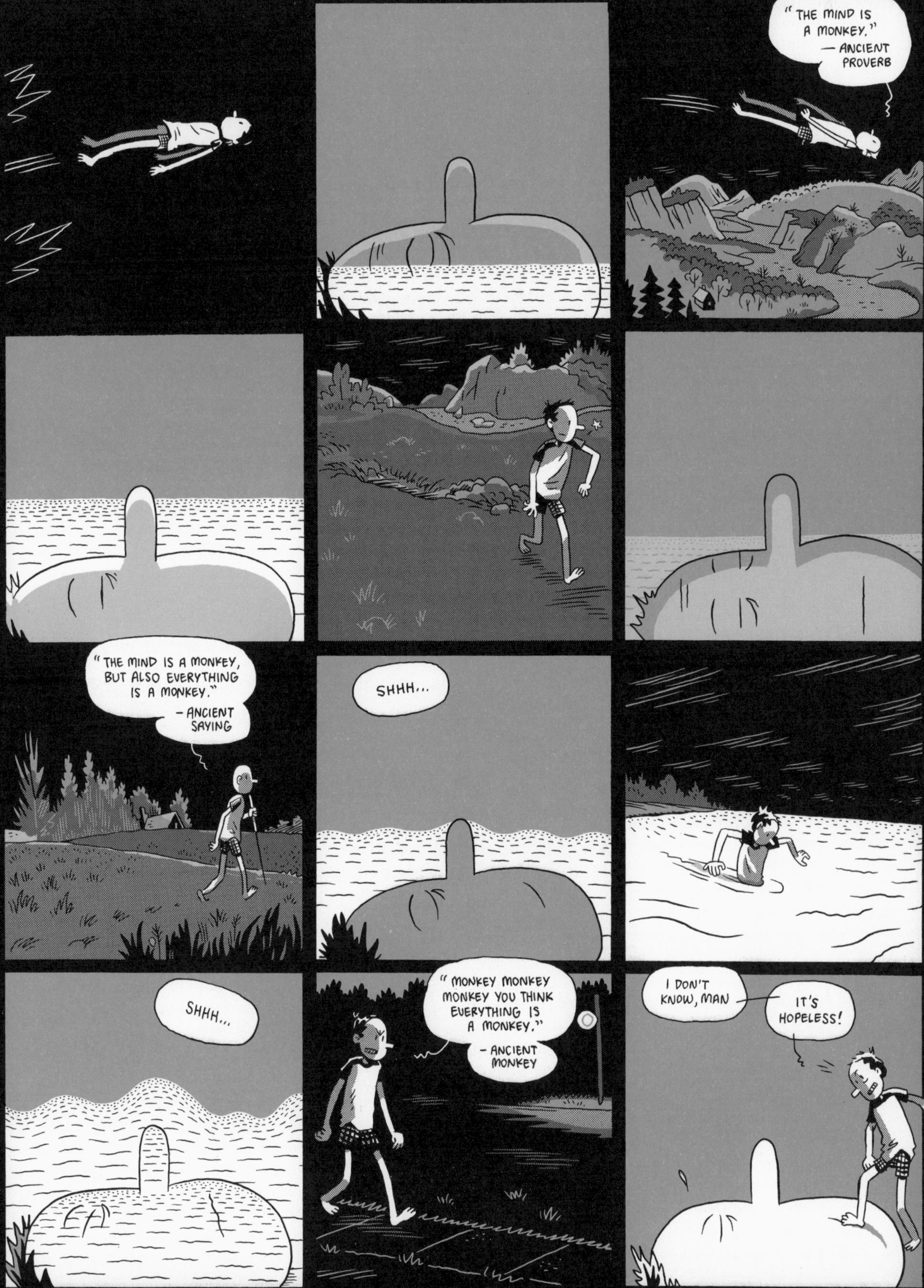
"THE MIND IS A MONKEY." — ANCIENT PROVERB
"THE MIND IS A MONKEY, BUT ALSO EVERYTHING IS A MONKEY." — ANCIENT SAYING
SHHH...
SHHH...
"MONKEY MONKEY MONKEY YOU THINK EVERYTHING IS A MONKEY." — ANCIENT MONKEY
I DON'T KNOW, MAN
IT'S HOPELESS!

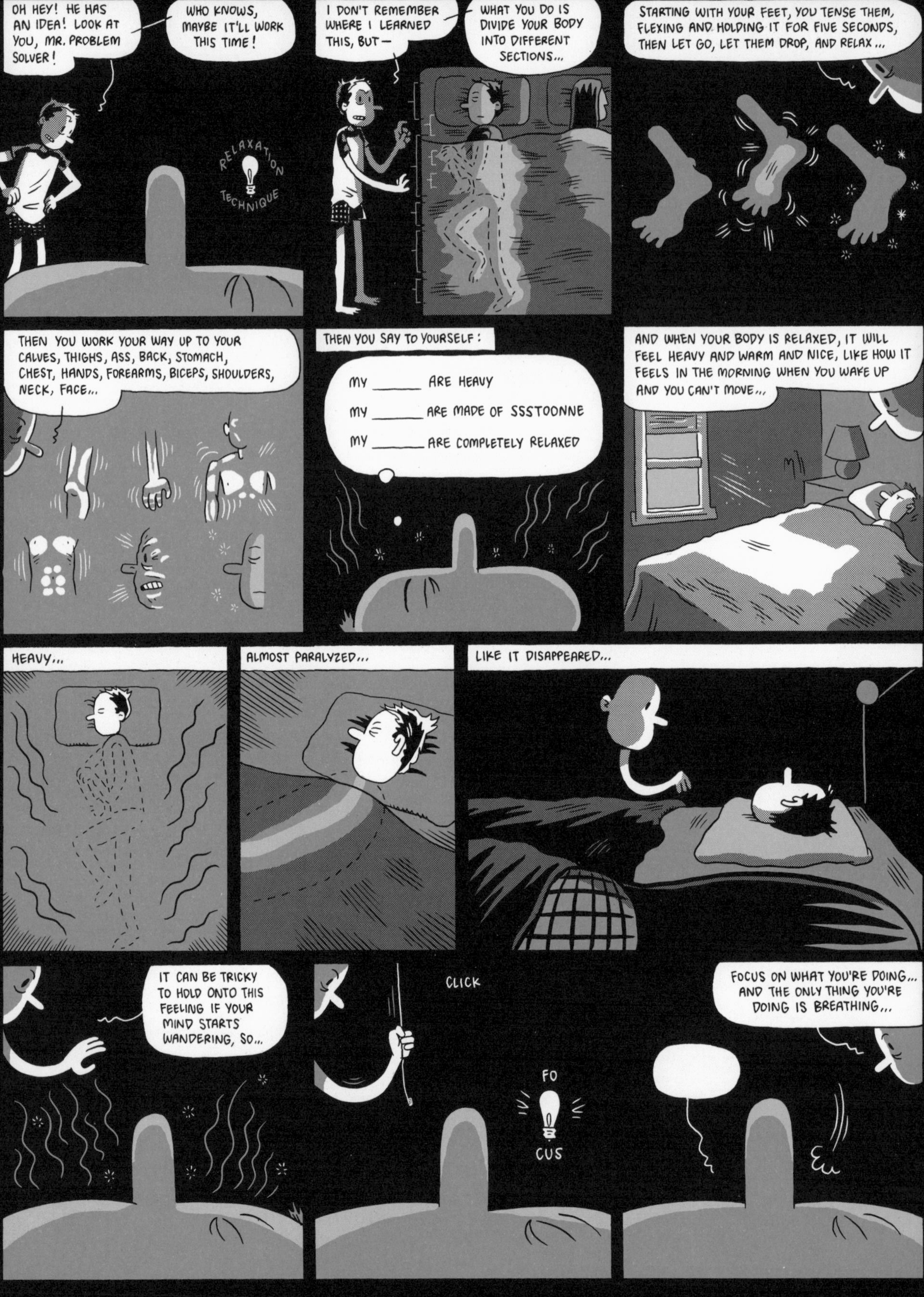
OH HEY! HE HAS AN IDEA! LOOK AT YOU, MR. PROBLEM SOLVER!
WHO KNOWS, MAYBE IT'LL WORK THIS TIME!
RELAXATION TECHNIQUE
I DON'T REMEMBER WHERE I LEARNED THIS, BUT—
WHAT YOU DO IS DIVIDE YOUR BODY INTO DIFFERENT SECTIONS...
STARTING WITH YOUR FEET, YOU TENSE THEM, FLEXING AND HOLDING IT FOR FIVE SECONDS, THEN LET GO, LET THEM DROP, AND RELAX...
THEN YOU WORK YOUR WAY UP TO YOUR CALVES, THIGHS, ASS, BACK, STOMACH, CHEST, HANDS, FOREARMS, BICEPS, SHOULDERS, NECK, FACE...
THEN YOU SAY TO YOURSELF:
MY ______ ARE HEAVY
MY ______ ARE MADE OF SSSTOONNE
MY ______ ARE COMPLETELY RELAXED
AND WHEN YOUR BODY IS RELAXED, IT WILL FEEL HEAVY AND WARM AND NICE, LIKE HOW IT FEELS IN THE MORNING WHEN YOU WAKE UP AND YOU CAN'T MOVE...
HEAVY...
ALMOST PARALYZED...
LIKE IT DISAPPEARED...
IT CAN BE TRICKY TO HOLD ONTO THIS FEELING IF YOUR MIND STARTS WANDERING, SO...
CLICK
FO
CUS
FOCUS ON WHAT YOU'RE DOING... AND THE ONLY THING YOU'RE DOING IS BREATHING...

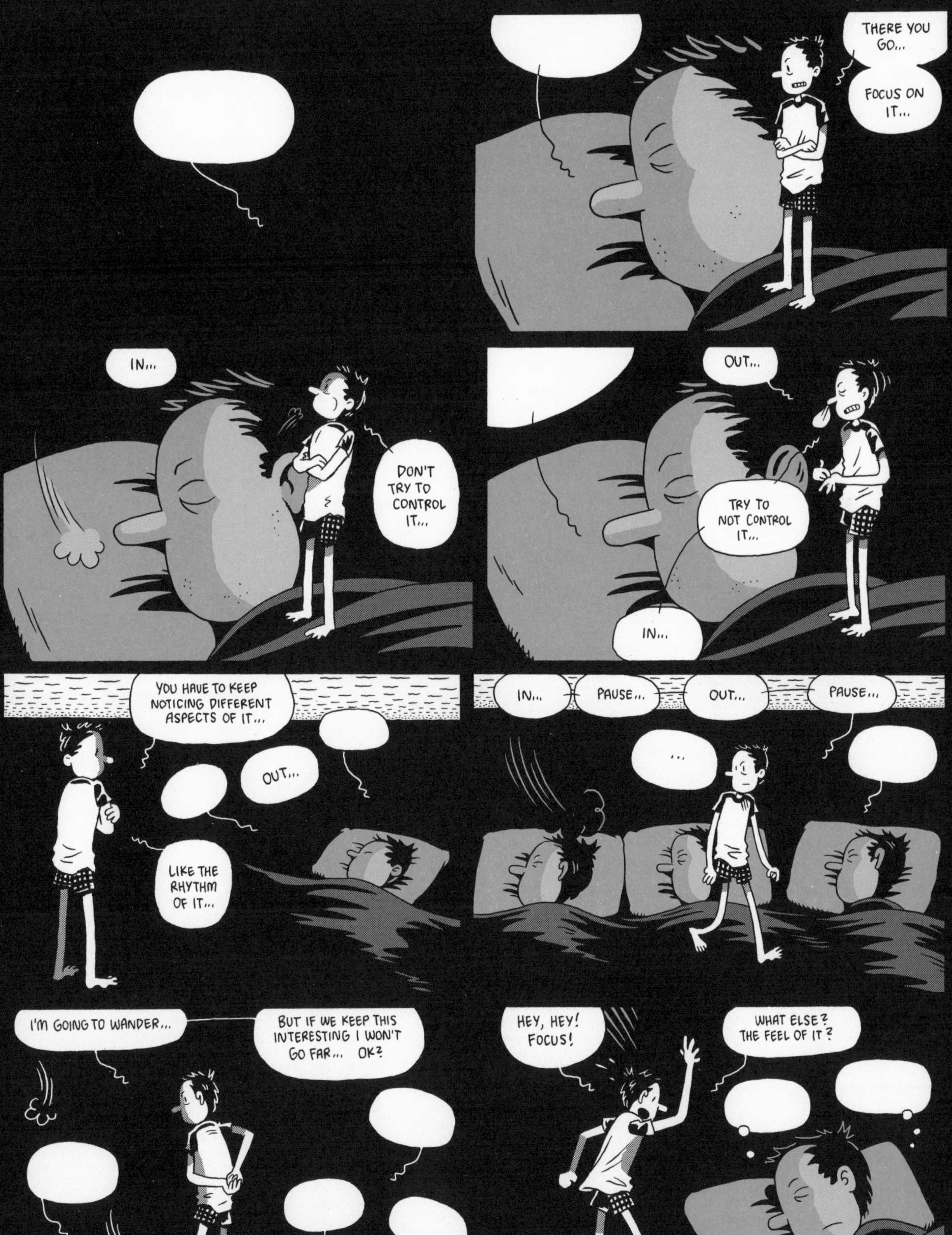
THERE YOU GO...
FOCUS ON IT...
IN...
DON'T TRY TO CONTROL IT...
OUT...
TRY TO NOT CONTROL IT...
IN...
YOU HAVE TO KEEP NOTICING DIFFERENT ASPECTS OF IT...
OUT...
LIKE THE RHYTHM OF IT...
IN...
PAUSE...
OUT...
PAUSE...
...
I'M GOING TO WANDER...
BUT IF WE KEEP THIS INTERESTING I WON'T GO FAR... OK?
HEY, HEY! FOCUS!
WHAT ELSE? THE FEEL OF IT?

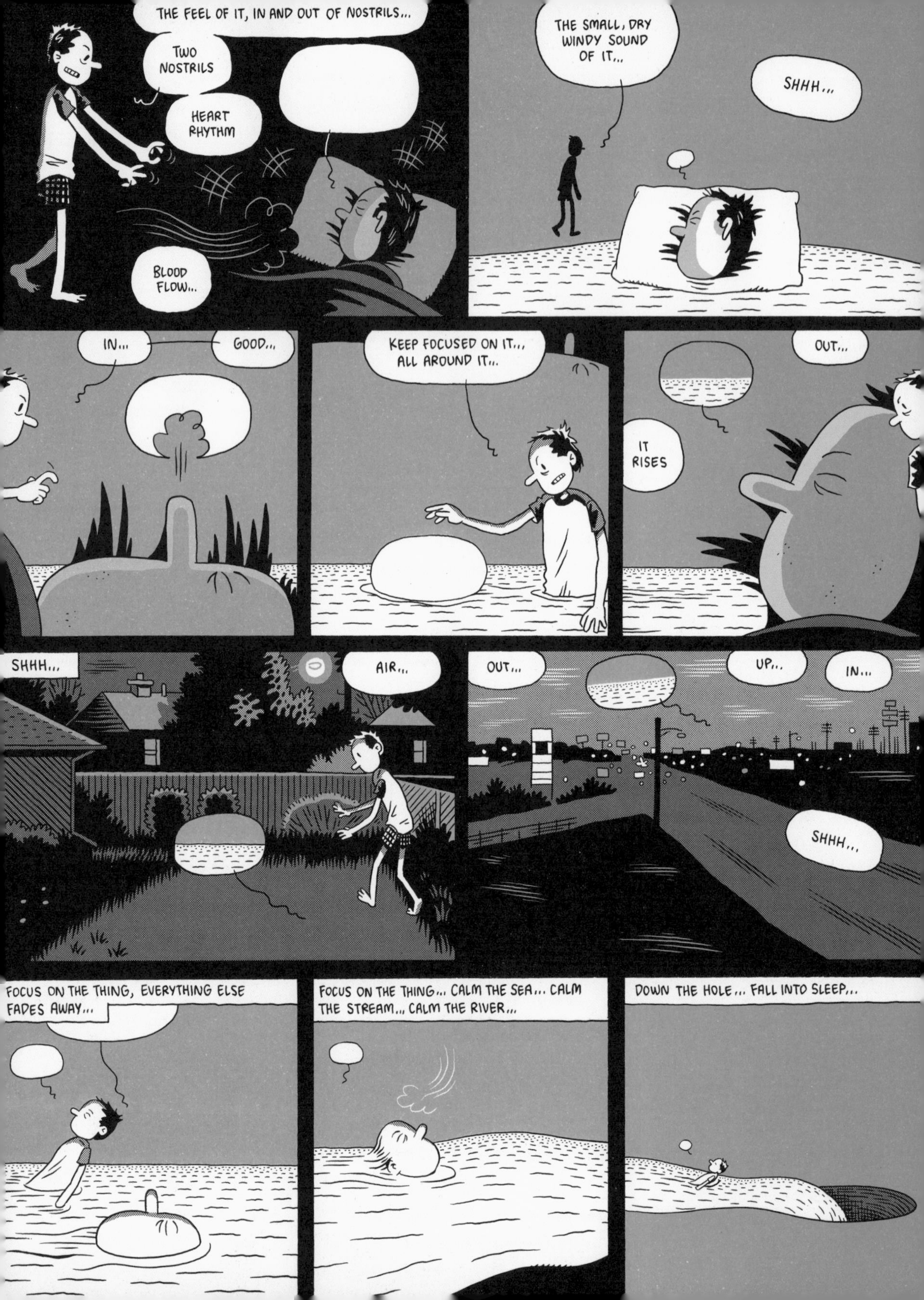
THE FEEL OF IT, IN AND OUT OF NOSTRILS...
TWO NOSTRILS
HEART RHYTHM
BLOOD FLOW...
THE SMALL, DRY WINDY SOUND OF IT...
SHHH...
IN...
GOOD...
KEEP FOCUSED ON IT... ALL AROUND IT...
OUT...
IT RISES
SHHH...
AIR...
OUT...
UP...
IN...
SHHH...
FOCUS ON THE THING, EVERYTHING ELSE FADES AWAY...
FOCUS ON THE THING... CALM THE SEA... CALM THE STREAM... CALM THE RIVER...
DOWN THE HOLE... FALL INTO SLEEP...

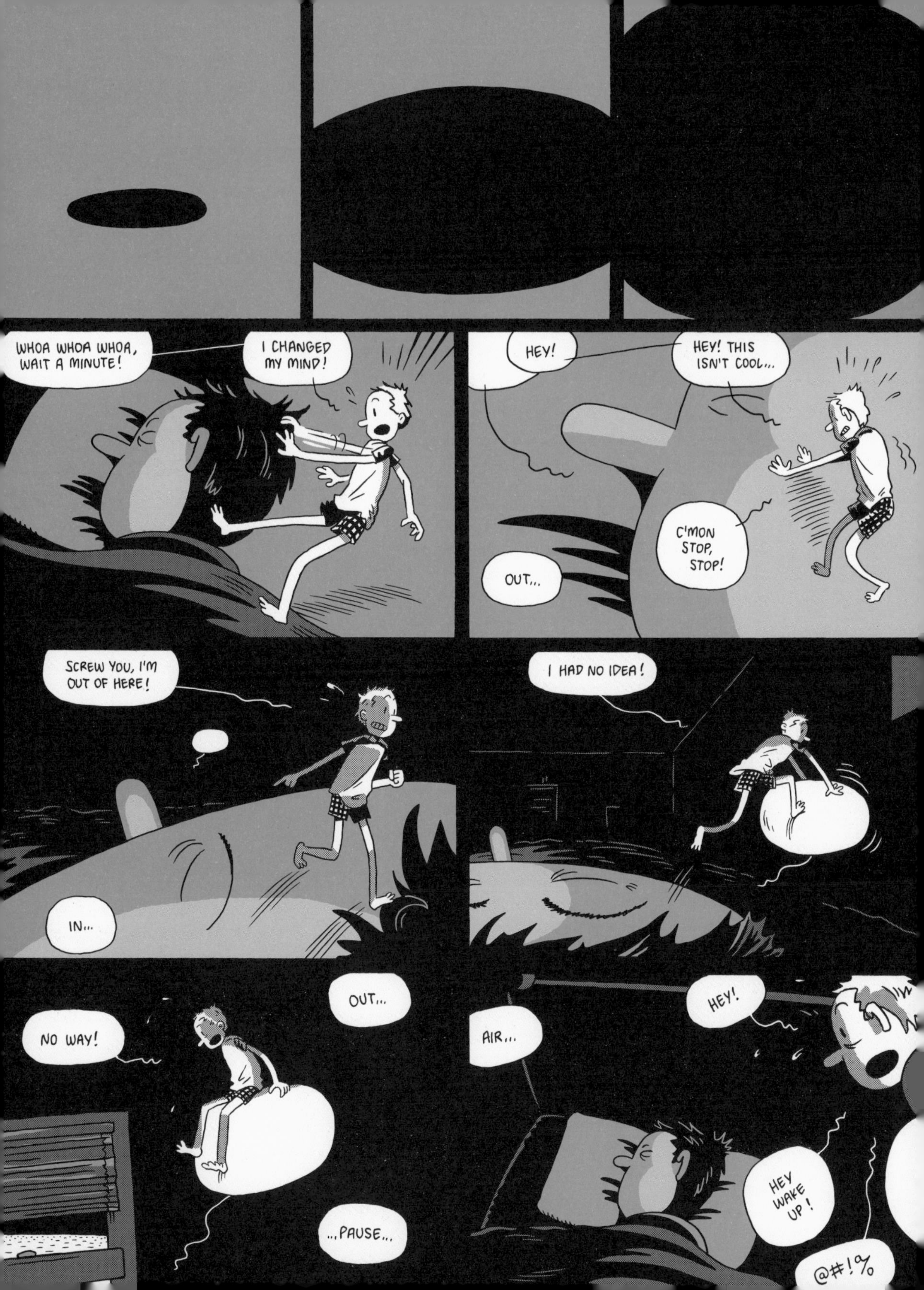
WHOA WHOA WHOA, WAIT A MINUTE!
I CHANGED MY MIND!
HEY!
HEY! THIS ISN'T COOL...
C'MON STOP, STOP!
OUT...
SCREW YOU, I'M OUT OF HERE!
IN...
I HAD NO IDEA!
NO WAY!
OUT...
...PAUSE...
AIR...
HEY!
HEY WAKE UP!
@#!%

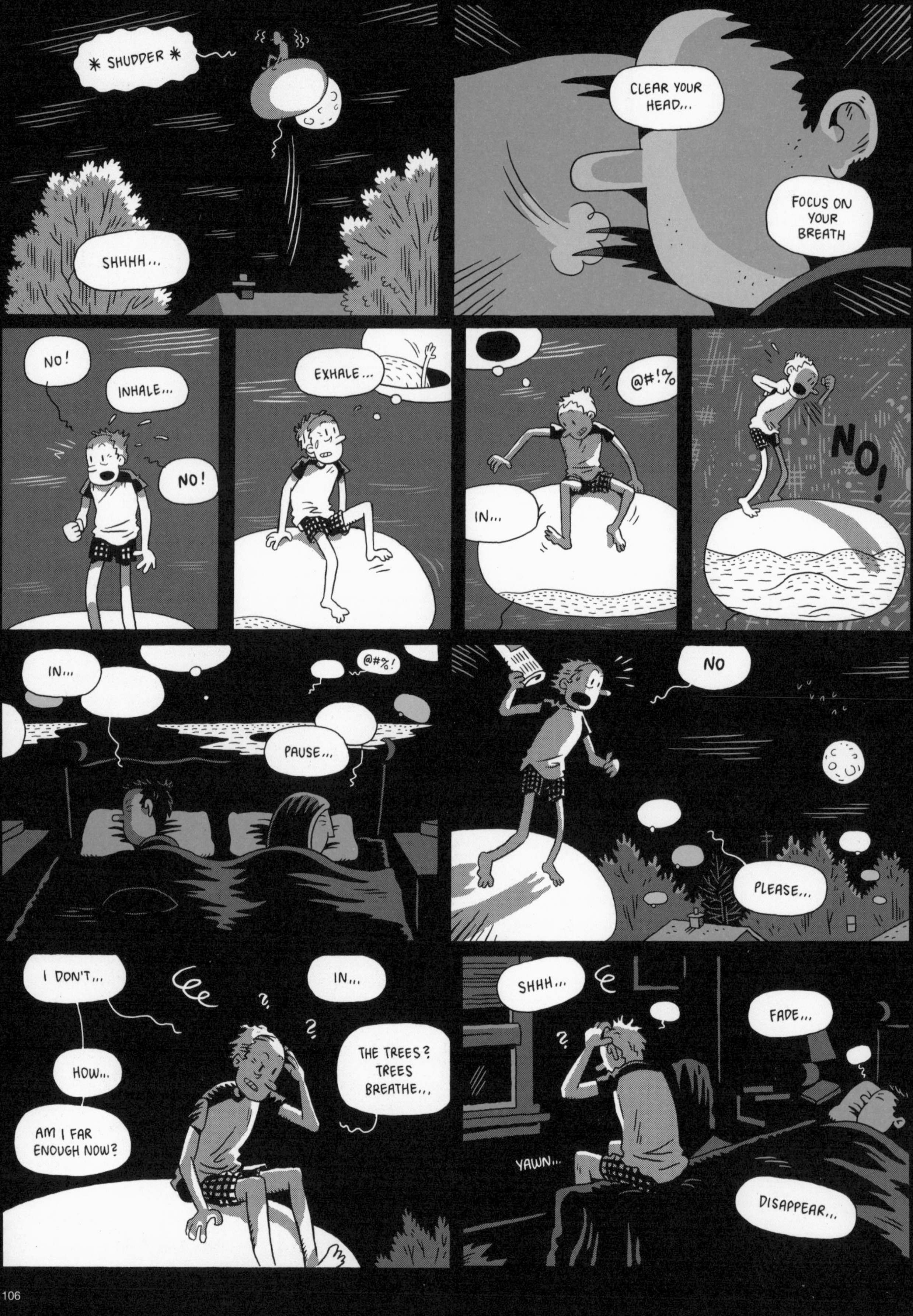

* SHUDDER *
SHHHH...
CLEAR YOUR HEAD...
FOCUS ON YOUR BREATH
NO!
INHALE...
NO!
EXHALE...
@#!%
IN...
NO!
IN...
@#%!
PAUSE...
NO
PLEASE...
I DON'T...
HOW...
AM I FAR ENOUGH NOW?
IN...
THE TREES? TREES BREATHE...
SHHH...
FADE...
YAWN...
DISAPPEAR...

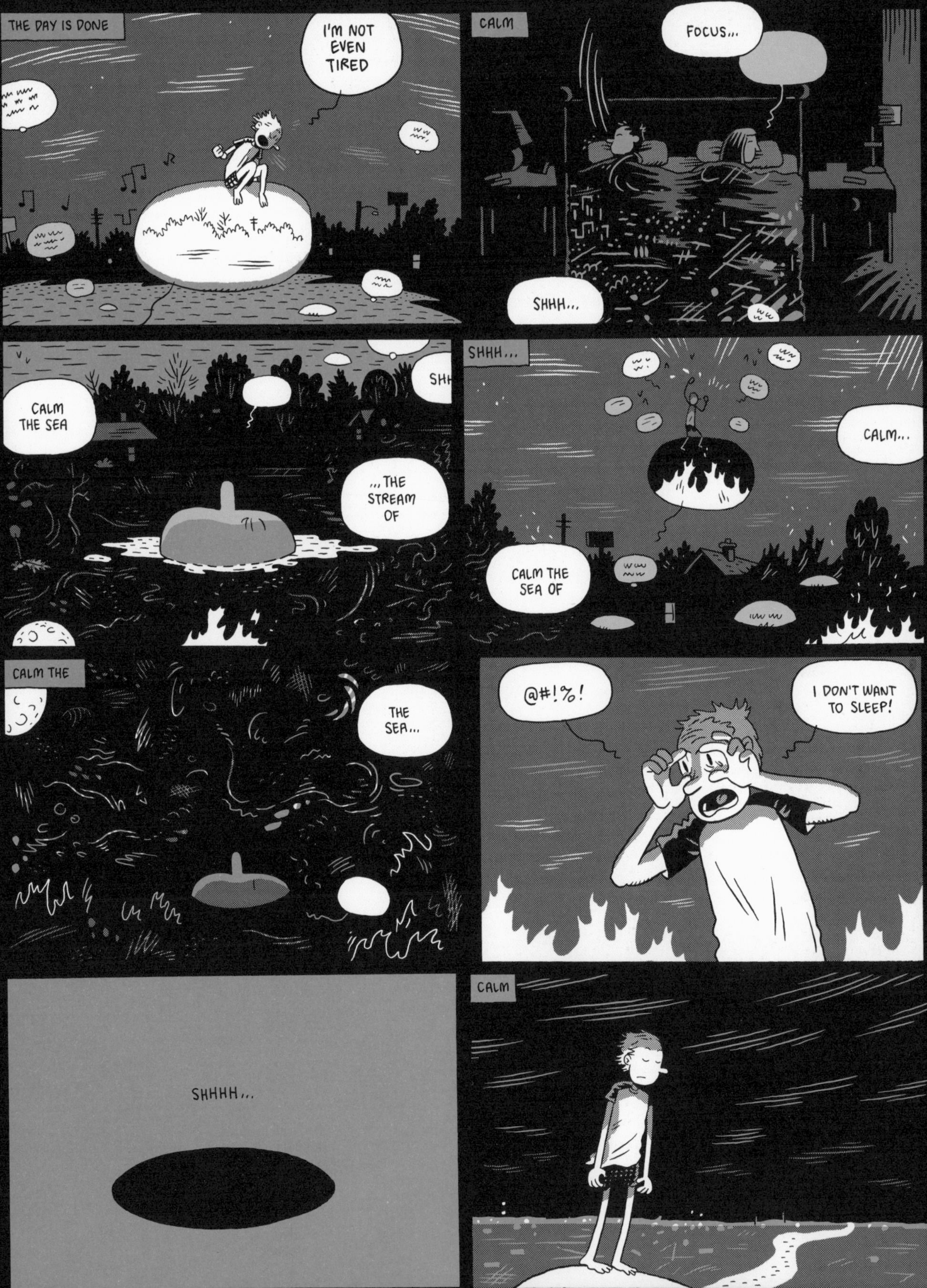

THE DAY IS DONE
I'M NOT EVEN TIRED
CALM
FOCUS...
SHHH...
CALM THE SEA
...THE STREAM OF
SHHH...
CALM...
CALM THE SEA OF
CALM THE
THE SEA...
@#!%!
I DON'T WANT TO SLEEP!
SHHHH...
CALM

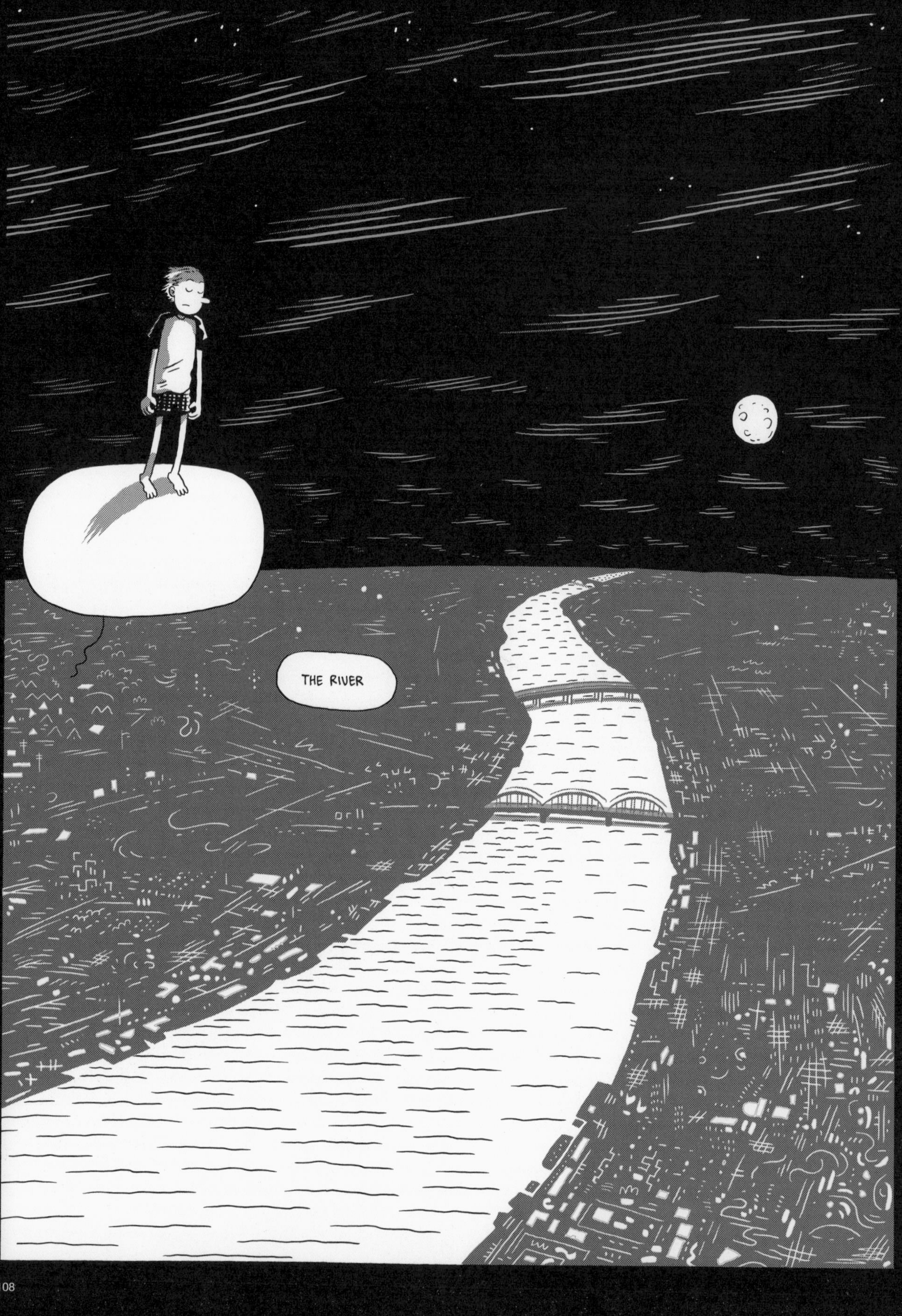
THE RIVER

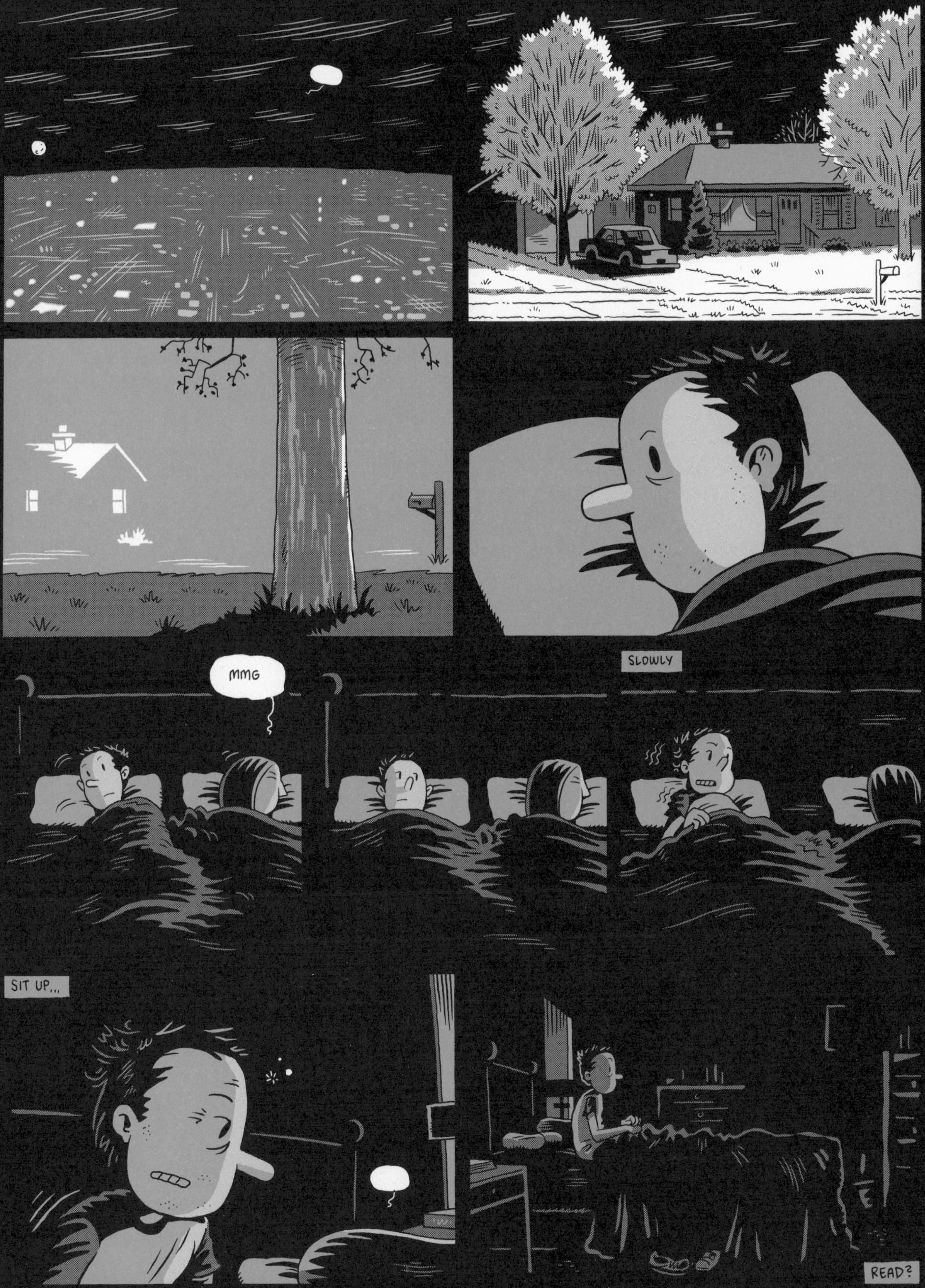
MMG
SLOWLY
SIT UP...
READ?

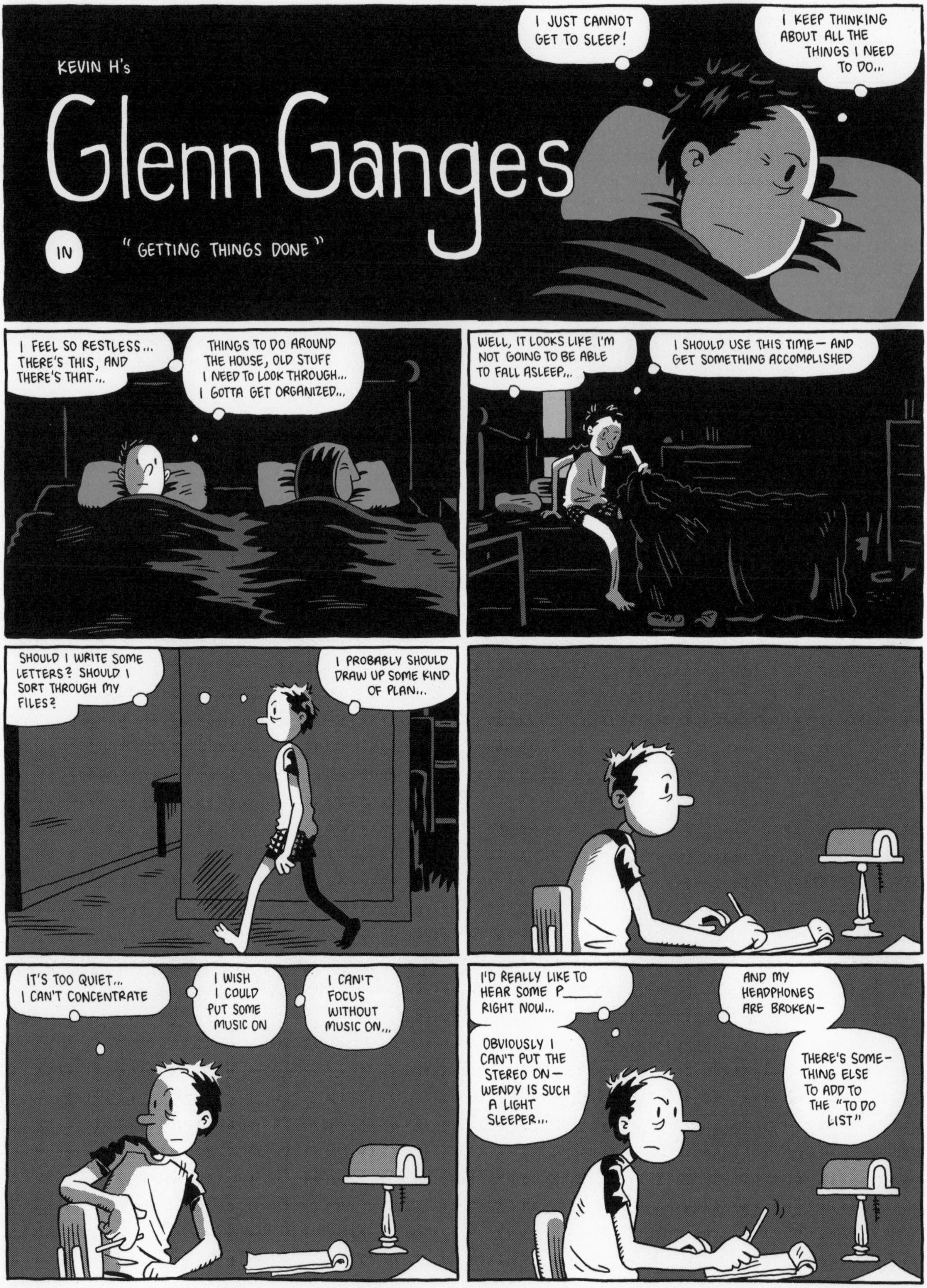
KEVIN H's
Glenn Ganges
IN "GETTING THINGS DONE"
I JUST CANNOT GET TO SLEEP!
I KEEP THINKING ABOUT ALL THE THINGS I NEED TO DO...
I FEEL SO RESTLESS... THERE'S THIS, AND THERE'S THAT...
THINGS TO DO AROUND THE HOUSE, OLD STUFF I NEED TO LOOK THROUGH... I GOTTA GET ORGANIZED...
WELL, IT LOOKS LIKE I'M NOT GOING TO BE ABLE TO FALL ASLEEP...
I SHOULD USE THIS TIME— AND GET SOMETHING ACCOMPLISHED
SHOULD I WRITE SOME LETTERS? SHOULD I SORT THROUGH MY FILES?
I PROBABLY SHOULD DRAW UP SOME KIND OF PLAN...
IT'S TOO QUIET... I CAN'T CONCENTRATE
I WISH I COULD PUT SOME MUSIC ON
I CAN'T FOCUS WITHOUT MUSIC ON...
I'D REALLY LIKE TO HEAR SOME P_____ RIGHT NOW...
AND MY HEADPHONES ARE BROKEN—
OBVIOUSLY I CAN'T PUT THE STEREO ON— WENDY IS SUCH A LIGHT SLEEPER...
THERE'S SOMETHING ELSE TO ADD TO THE "TO DO LIST"

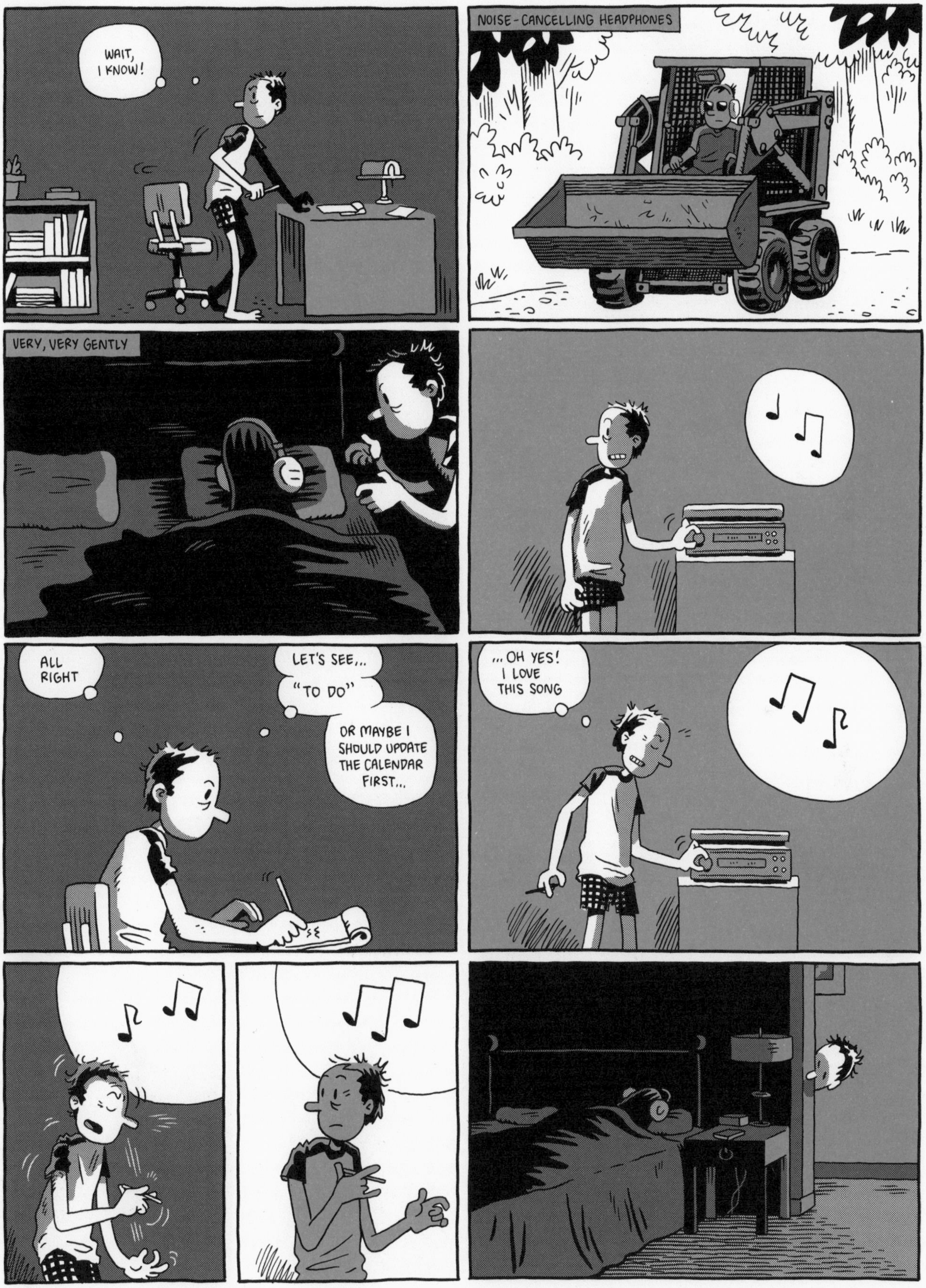
WAIT, I KNOW!
NOISE-CANCELLING HEADPHONES
VERY, VERY GENTLY
ALL RIGHT
LET'S SEE,...
"TO DO"
OR MAYBE I SHOULD UPDATE THE CALENDAR FIRST...
...OH YES! I LOVE THIS SONG

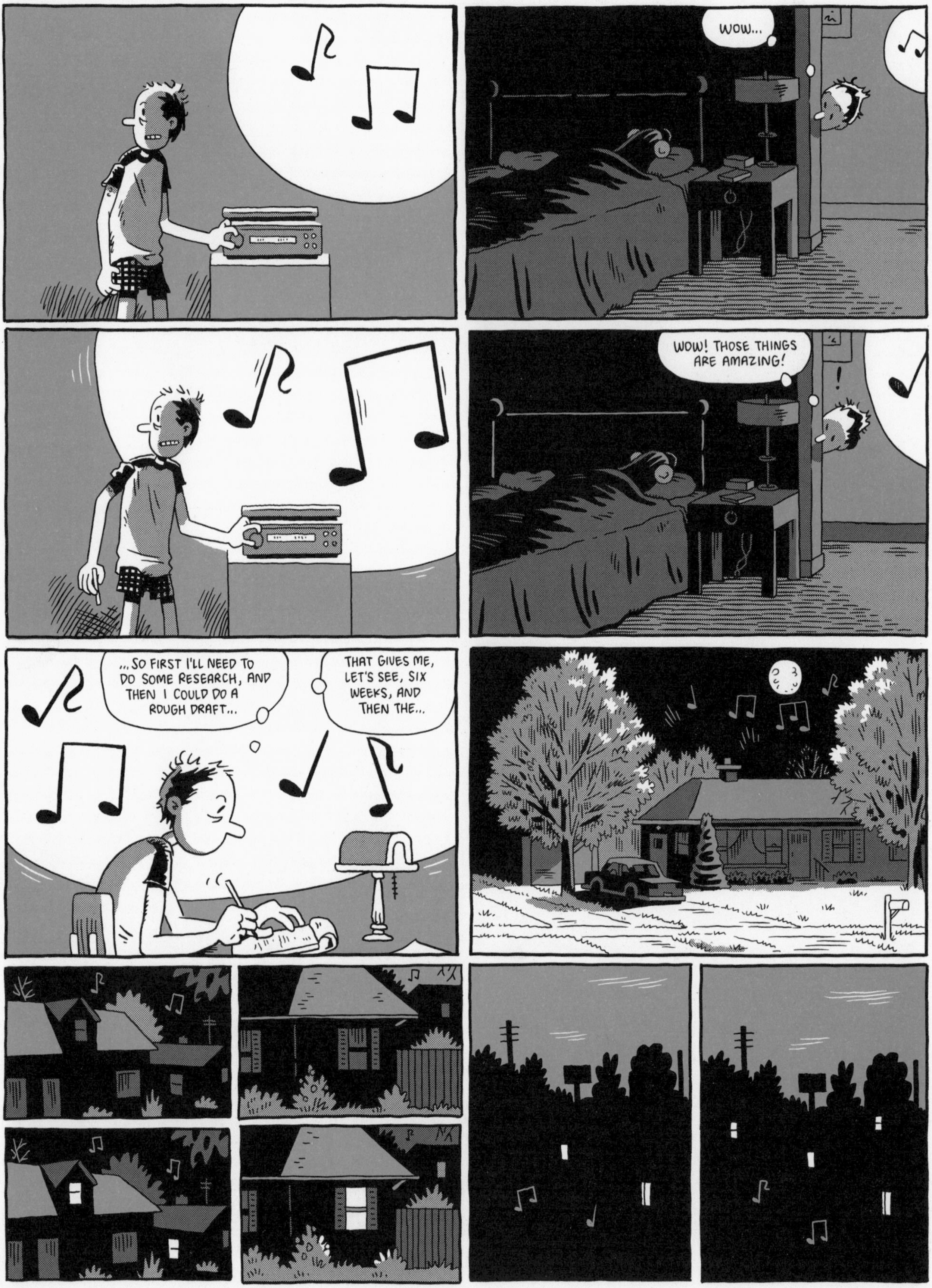
WOW...
WOW! THOSE THINGS ARE AMAZING!
!
...SO FIRST I'LL NEED TO DO SOME RESEARCH, AND THEN I COULD DO A ROUGH DRAFT...
THAT GIVES ME, LET'S SEE, SIX WEEKS, AND THEN THE...

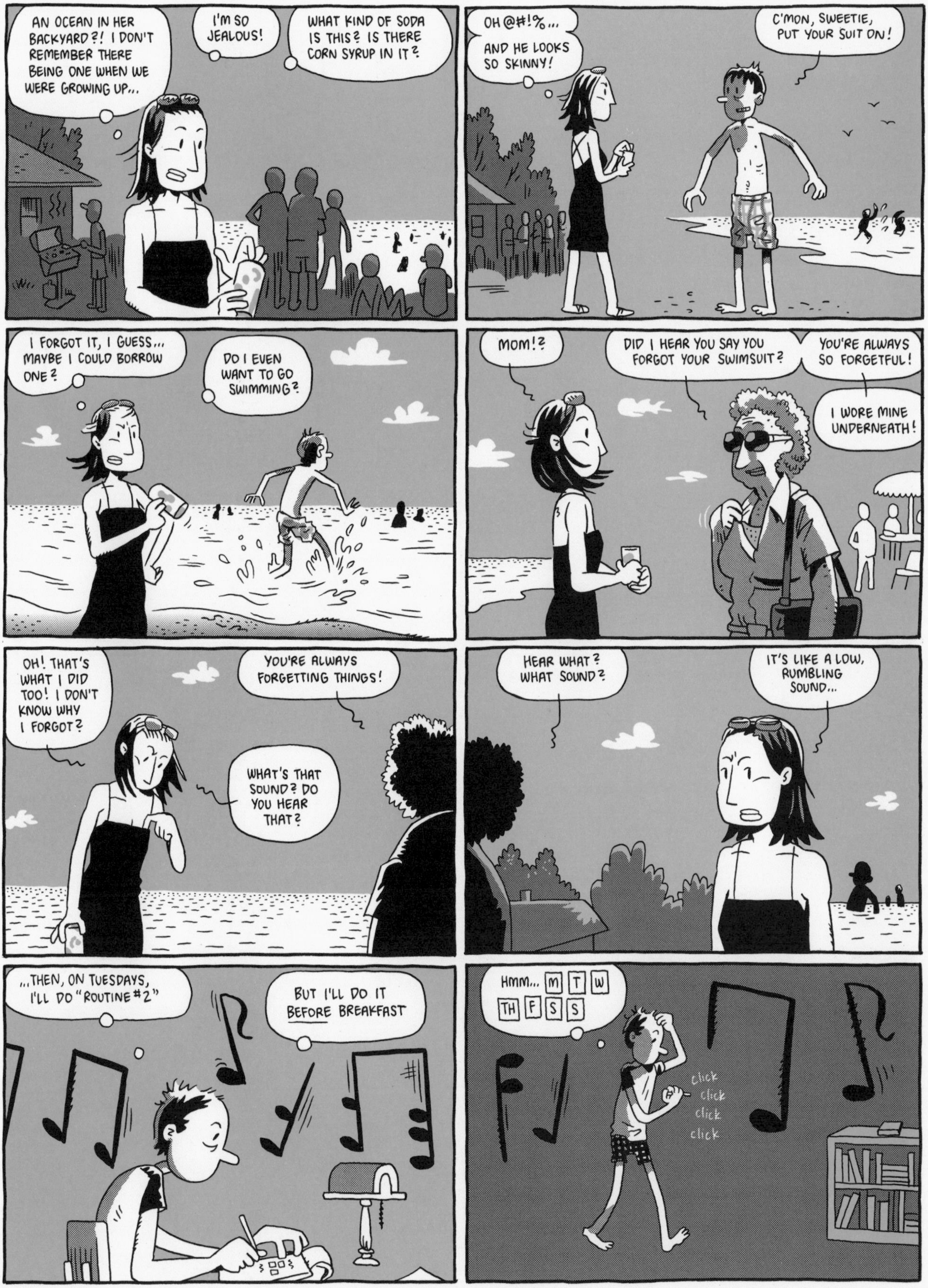
AN OCEAN IN HER BACKYARD?! I DON'T REMEMBER THERE BEING ONE WHEN WE WERE GROWING UP...
I'M SO JEALOUS!
WHAT KIND OF SODA IS THIS? IS THERE CORN SYRUP IN IT?
OH @#!%...
AND HE LOOKS SO SKINNY!
C'MON, SWEETIE, PUT YOUR SUIT ON!
I FORGOT IT, I GUESS... MAYBE I COULD BORROW ONE?
DO I EVEN WANT TO GO SWIMMING?
MOM!?
DID I HEAR YOU SAY YOU FORGOT YOUR SWIMSUIT?
YOU'RE ALWAYS SO FORGETFUL!
I WORE MINE UNDERNEATH!
OH! THAT'S WHAT I DID TOO! I DON'T KNOW WHY I FORGOT?
YOU'RE ALWAYS FORGETTING THINGS!
WHAT'S THAT SOUND? DO YOU HEAR THAT?
HEAR WHAT? WHAT SOUND?
IT'S LIKE A LOW, RUMBLING SOUND...
...THEN, ON TUESDAYS, I'LL DO "ROUTINE #2"
BUT I'LL DO IT BEFORE BREAKFAST
HMM... M T W TH F S S
click click click click

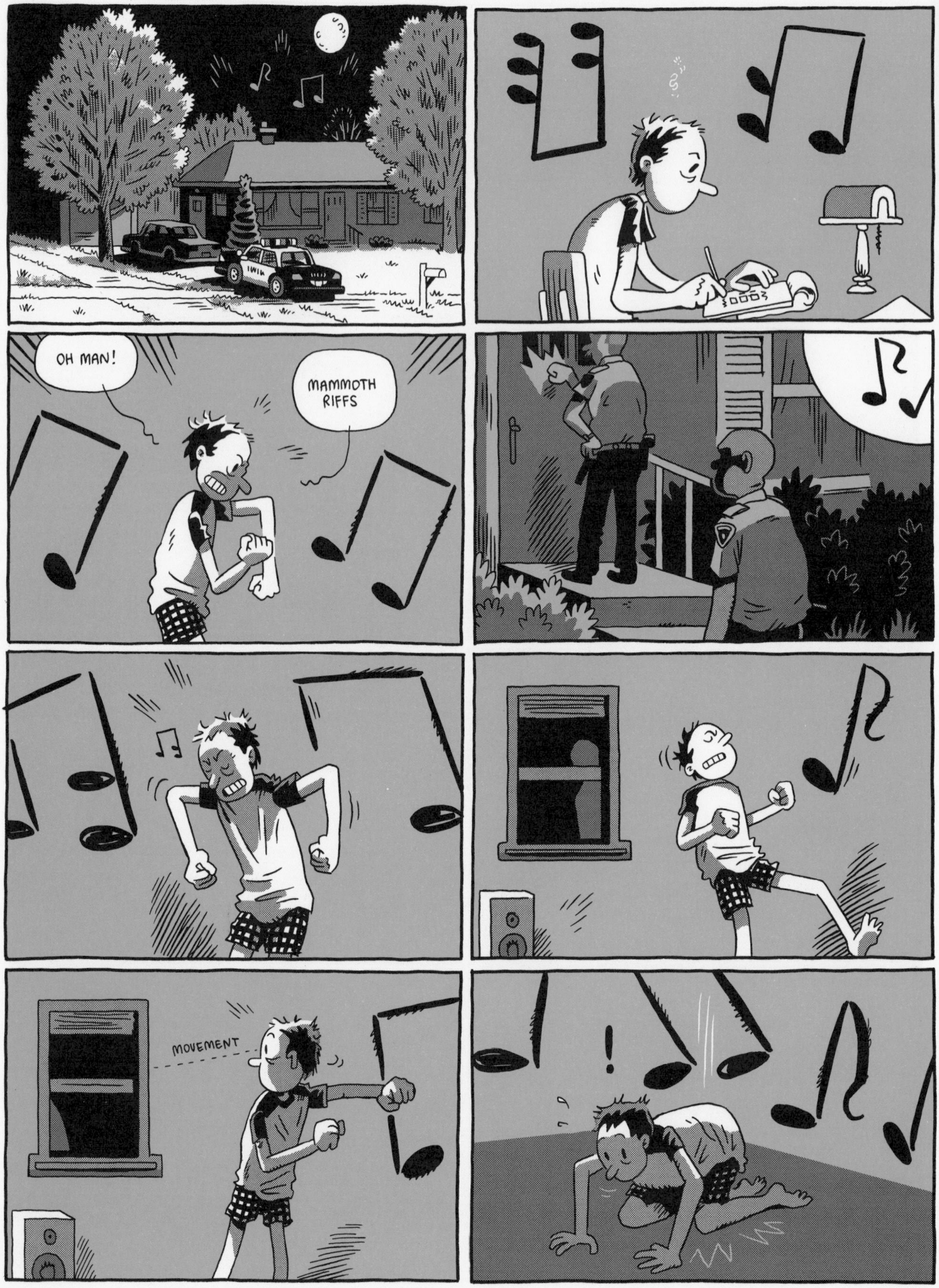
OH MAN!
MAMMOTH RIFFS
MOVEMENT
!

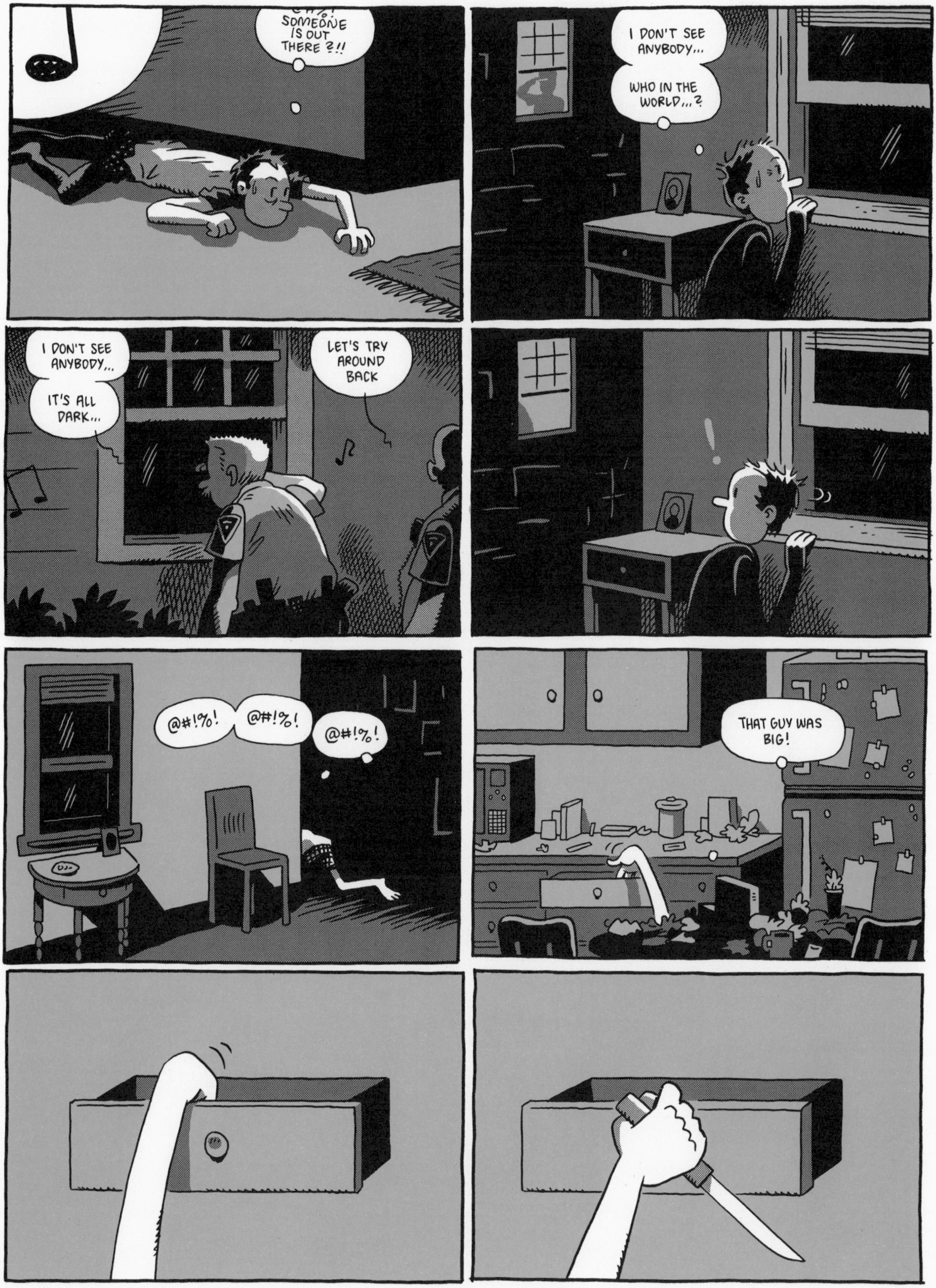
SOMEONE IS OUT THERE ?!!
I DON'T SEE ANYBODY...
WHO IN THE WORLD...?
I DON'T SEE ANYBODY...
IT'S ALL DARK...
LET'S TRY AROUND BACK
!
@#!%!
@#!%!
@#!%!
THAT GUY WAS BIG!

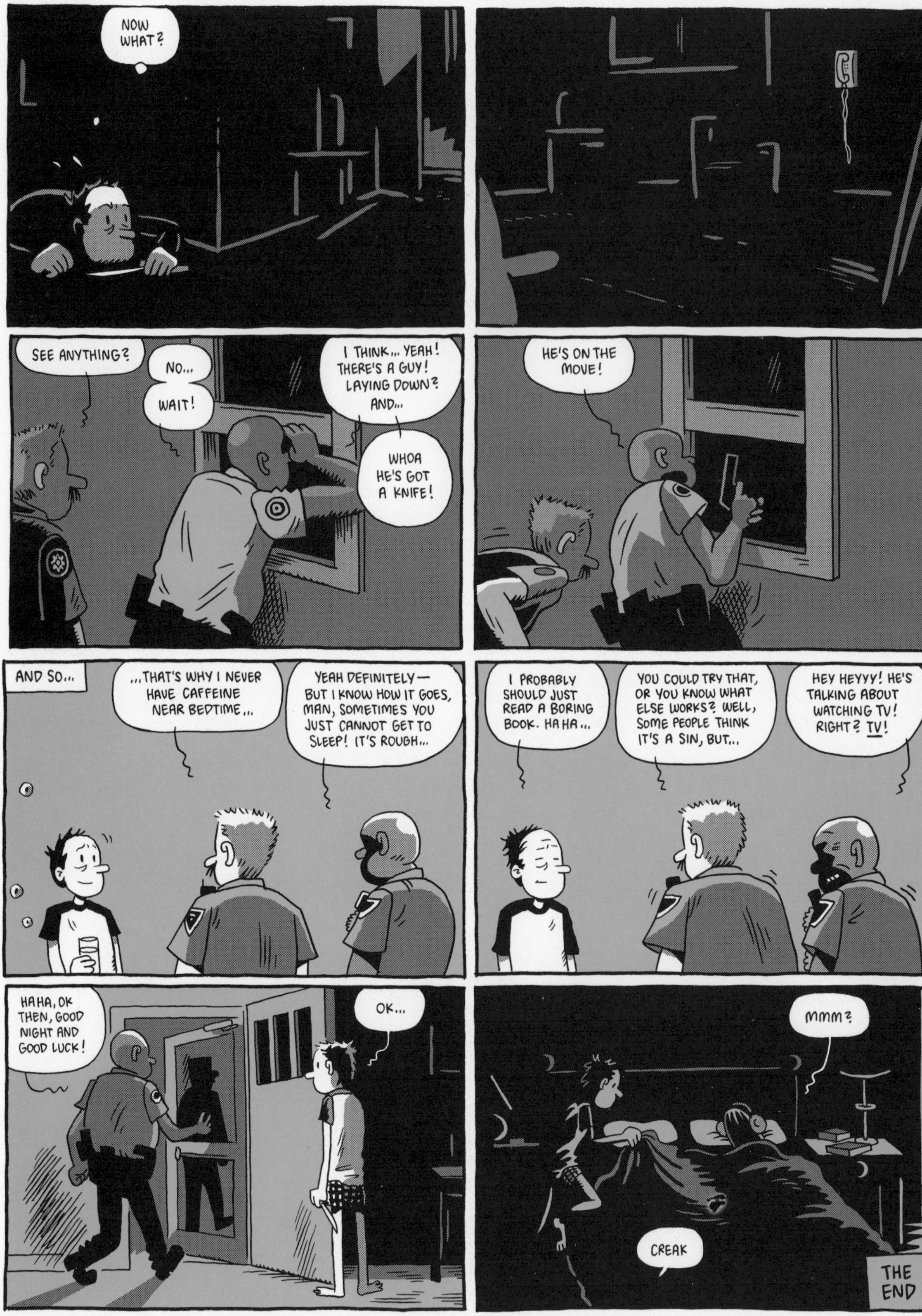
NOW WHAT?
SEE ANYTHING?
NO...
WAIT!
I THINK... YEAH! THERE'S A GUY! LAYING DOWN? AND...
WHOA HE'S GOT A KNIFE!
HE'S ON THE MOVE!
AND SO...
...THAT'S WHY I NEVER HAVE CAFFEINE NEAR BEDTIME...
YEAH DEFINITELY— BUT I KNOW HOW IT GOES, MAN, SOMETIMES YOU JUST CANNOT GET TO SLEEP! IT'S ROUGH...
I PROBABLY SHOULD JUST READ A BORING BOOK. HA HA...
YOU COULD TRY THAT, OR YOU KNOW WHAT ELSE WORKS? WELL, SOME PEOPLE THINK IT'S A SIN, BUT...
HEY HEYYY! HE'S TALKING ABOUT WATCHING TV! RIGHT? TV!
HA HA, OK THEN, GOOD NIGHT AND GOOD LUCK!
OK...
MMM?
CREAK
THE END

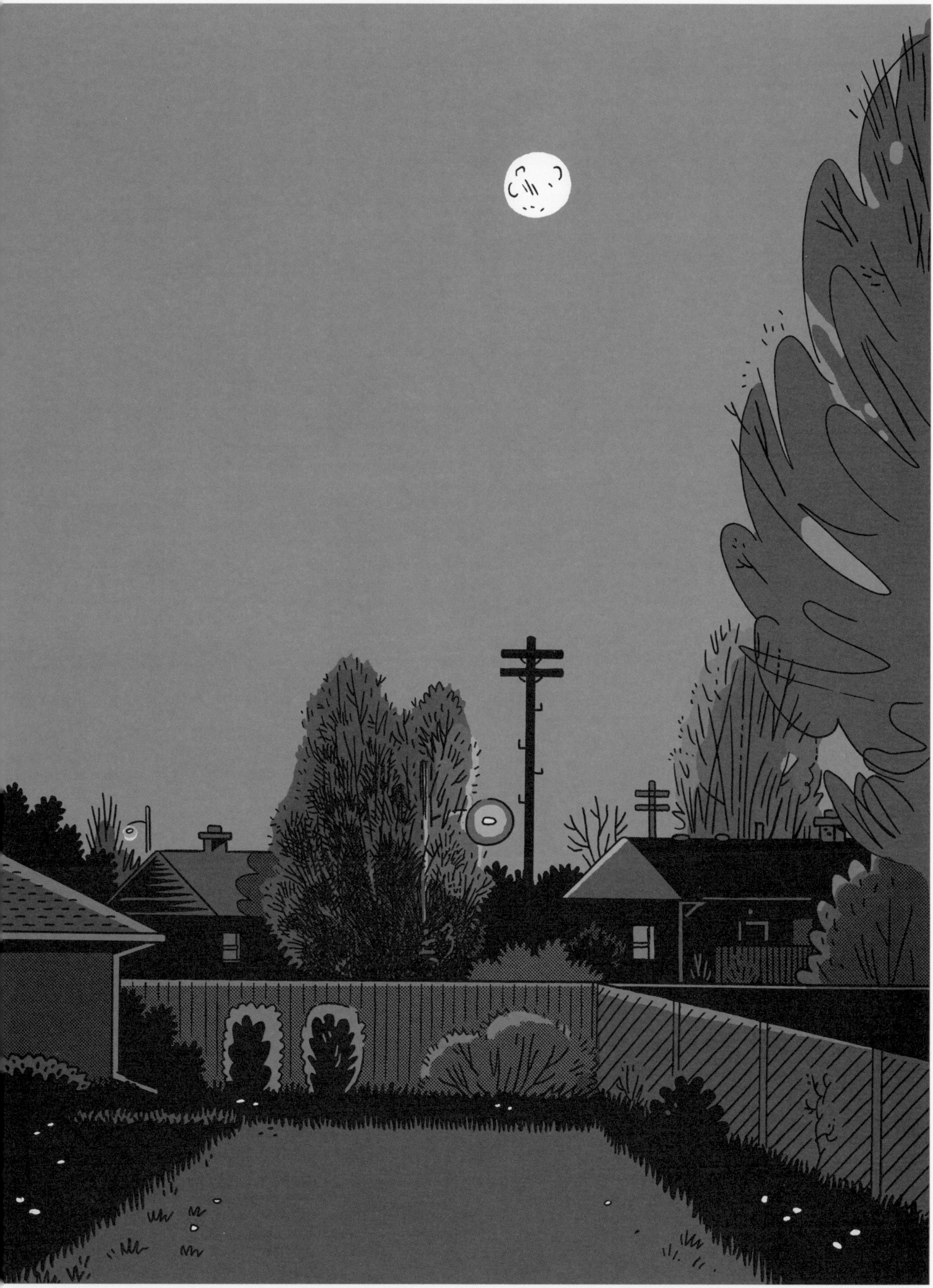

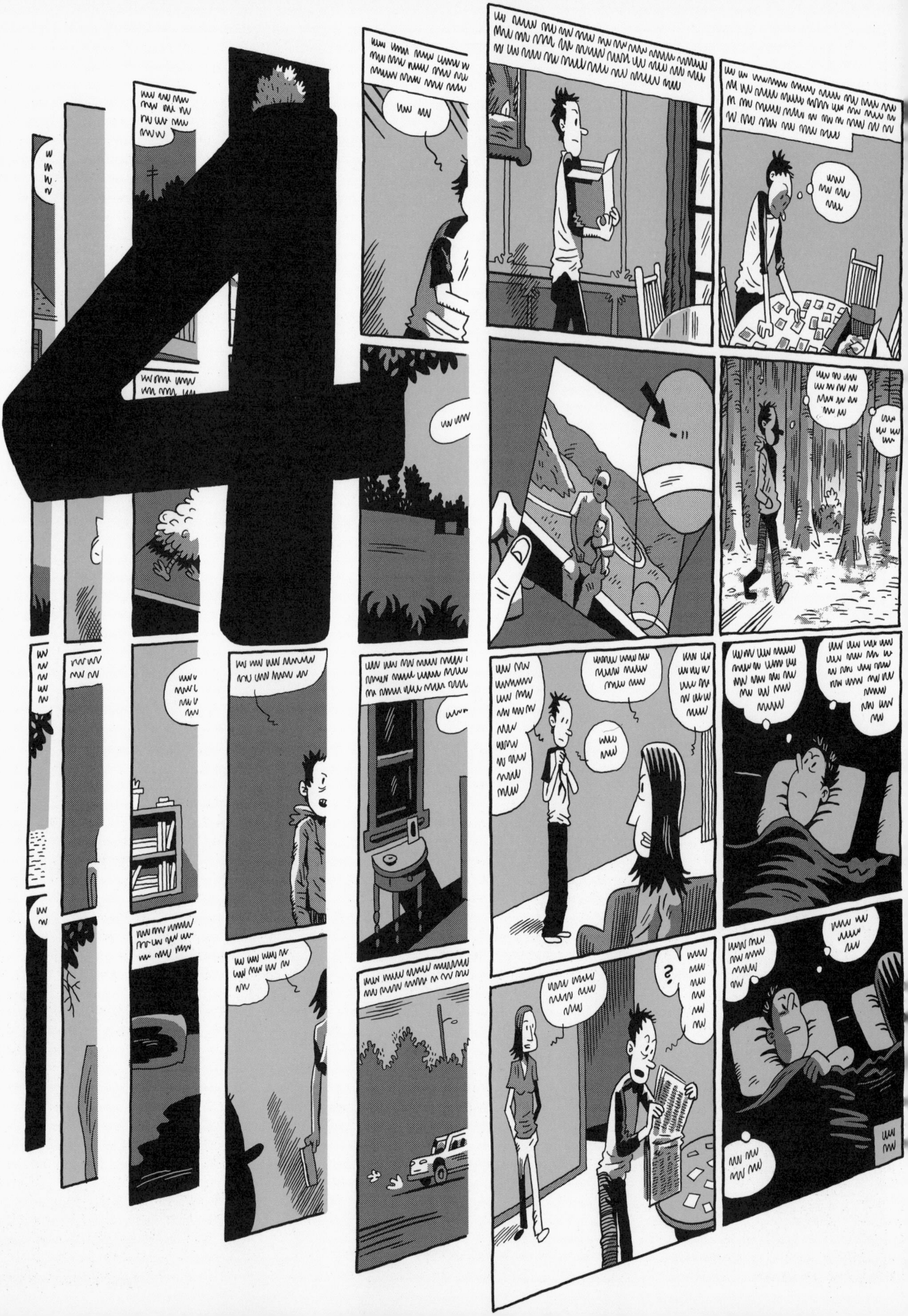
4
?

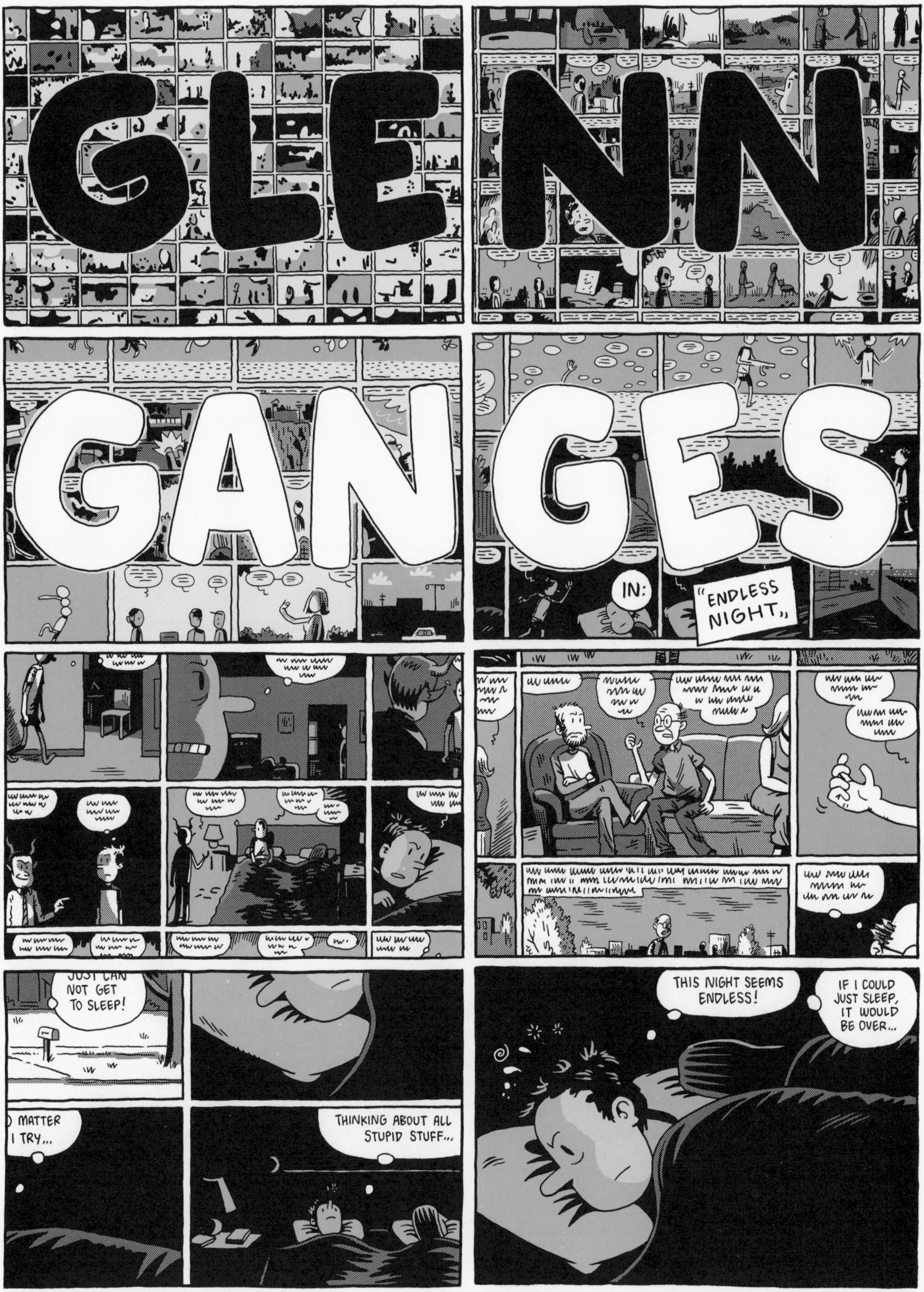
GLENN GANGES
IN:
"ENDLESS NIGHT"
JUST CAN NOT GET TO SLEEP!
MATTER I TRY...
THINKING ABOUT ALL STUPID STUFF...
THIS NIGHT SEEMS ENDLESS!
IF I COULD JUST SLEEP, IT WOULD BE OVER...

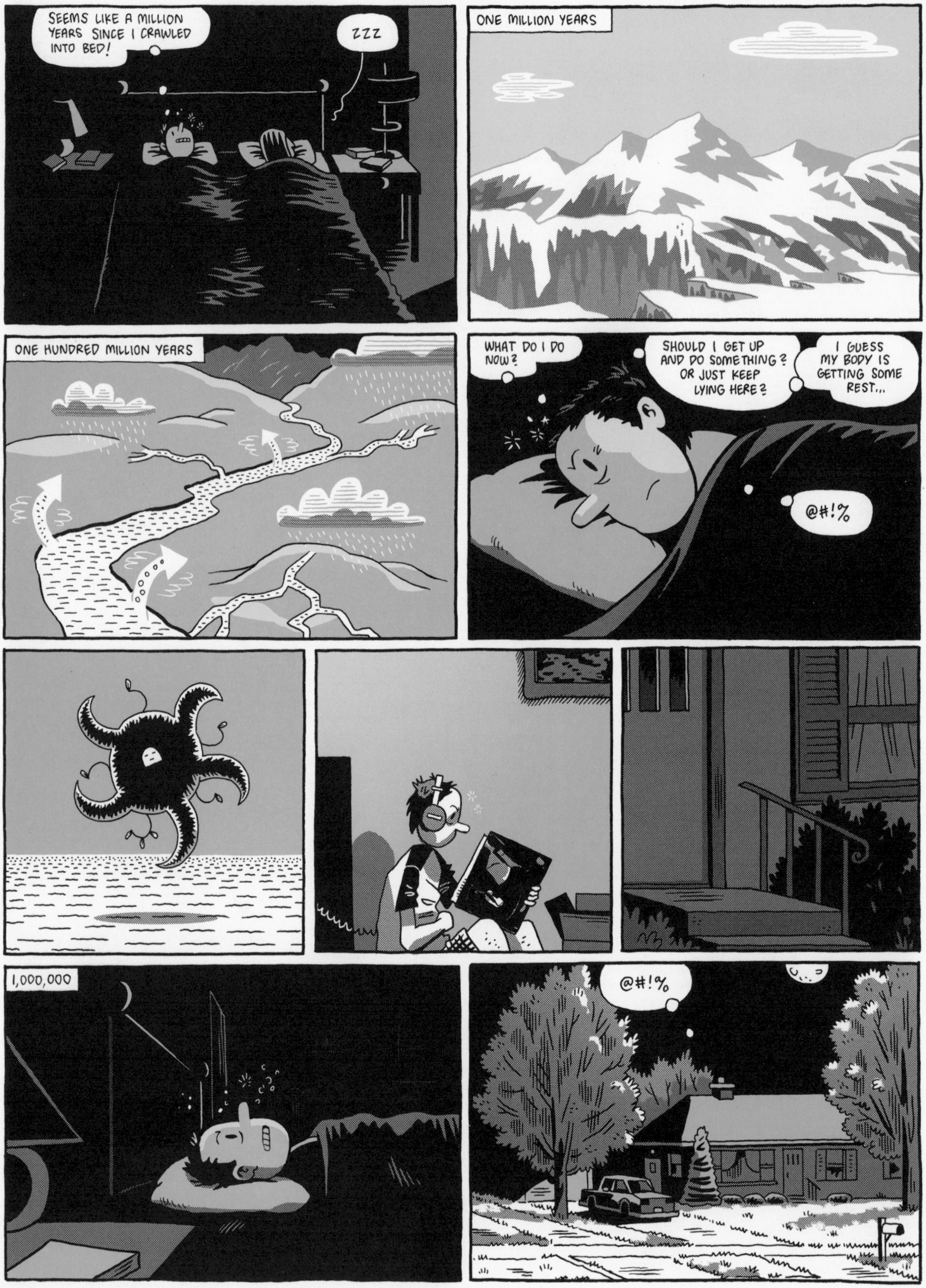
SEEMS LIKE A MILLION YEARS SINCE I CRAWLED INTO BED!
ZZZ
ONE MILLION YEARS
ONE HUNDRED MILLION YEARS
WHAT DO I DO NOW?
SHOULD I GET UP AND DO SOMETHING? OR JUST KEEP LYING HERE?
I GUESS MY BODY IS GETTING SOME REST...
@#!%
1,000,000
@#!%

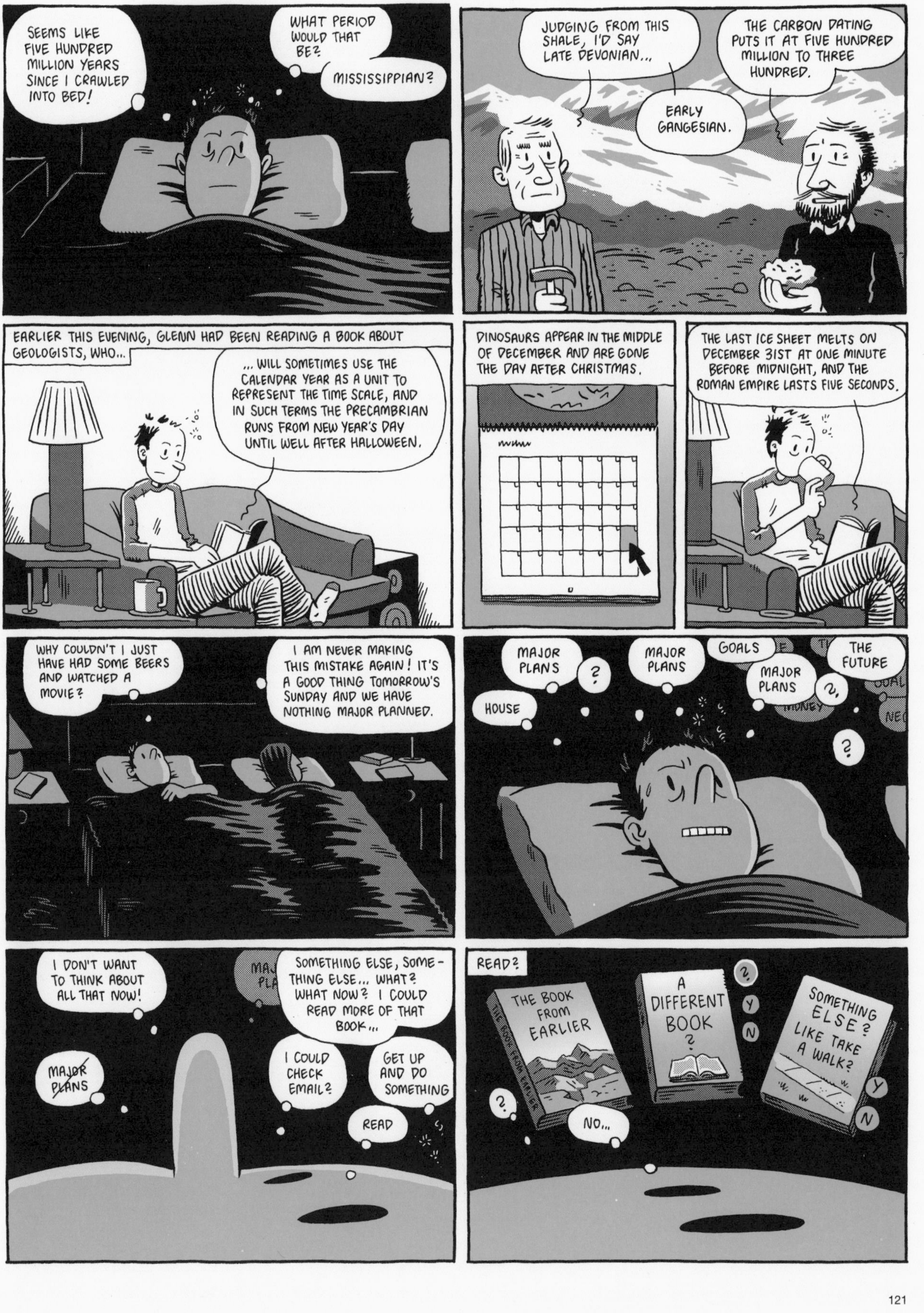
SEEMS LIKE FIVE HUNDRED MILLION YEARS SINCE I CRAWLED INTO BED!
WHAT PERIOD WOULD THAT BE?
MISSISSIPPIAN?
JUDGING FROM THIS SHALE, I'D SAY LATE DEVONIAN...
EARLY GANGESIAN.
THE CARBON DATING PUTS IT AT FIVE HUNDRED MILLION TO THREE HUNDRED.
EARLIER THIS EVENING, GLENN HAD BEEN READING A BOOK ABOUT GEOLOGISTS, WHO...
... WILL SOMETIMES USE THE CALENDAR YEAR AS A UNIT TO REPRESENT THE TIME SCALE, AND IN SUCH TERMS THE PRECAMBRIAN RUNS FROM NEW YEAR'S DAY UNTIL WELL AFTER HALLOWEEN.
DINOSAURS APPEAR IN THE MIDDLE OF DECEMBER AND ARE GONE THE DAY AFTER CHRISTMAS.
THE LAST ICE SHEET MELTS ON DECEMBER 31ST AT ONE MINUTE BEFORE MIDNIGHT, AND THE ROMAN EMPIRE LASTS FIVE SECONDS.
WHY COULDN'T I JUST HAVE HAD SOME BEERS AND WATCHED A MOVIE?
I AM NEVER MAKING THIS MISTAKE AGAIN! IT'S A GOOD THING TOMORROW'S SUNDAY AND WE HAVE NOTHING MAJOR PLANNED.
MAJOR PLANS
?
MAJOR PLANS
GOALS
MAJOR PLANS
THE FUTURE
HOUSE
?
?
I DON'T WANT TO THINK ABOUT ALL THAT NOW!
SOMETHING ELSE, SOMETHING ELSE... WHAT? WHAT NOW? I COULD READ MORE OF THAT BOOK...
MAJOR PLANS
I COULD CHECK EMAIL?
GET UP AND DO SOMETHING
READ
READ?
THE BOOK FROM EARLIER
A DIFFERENT BOOK ?
SOMETHING ELSE? LIKE TAKE A WALK?
?
Y
N
?
NO...
Y
N

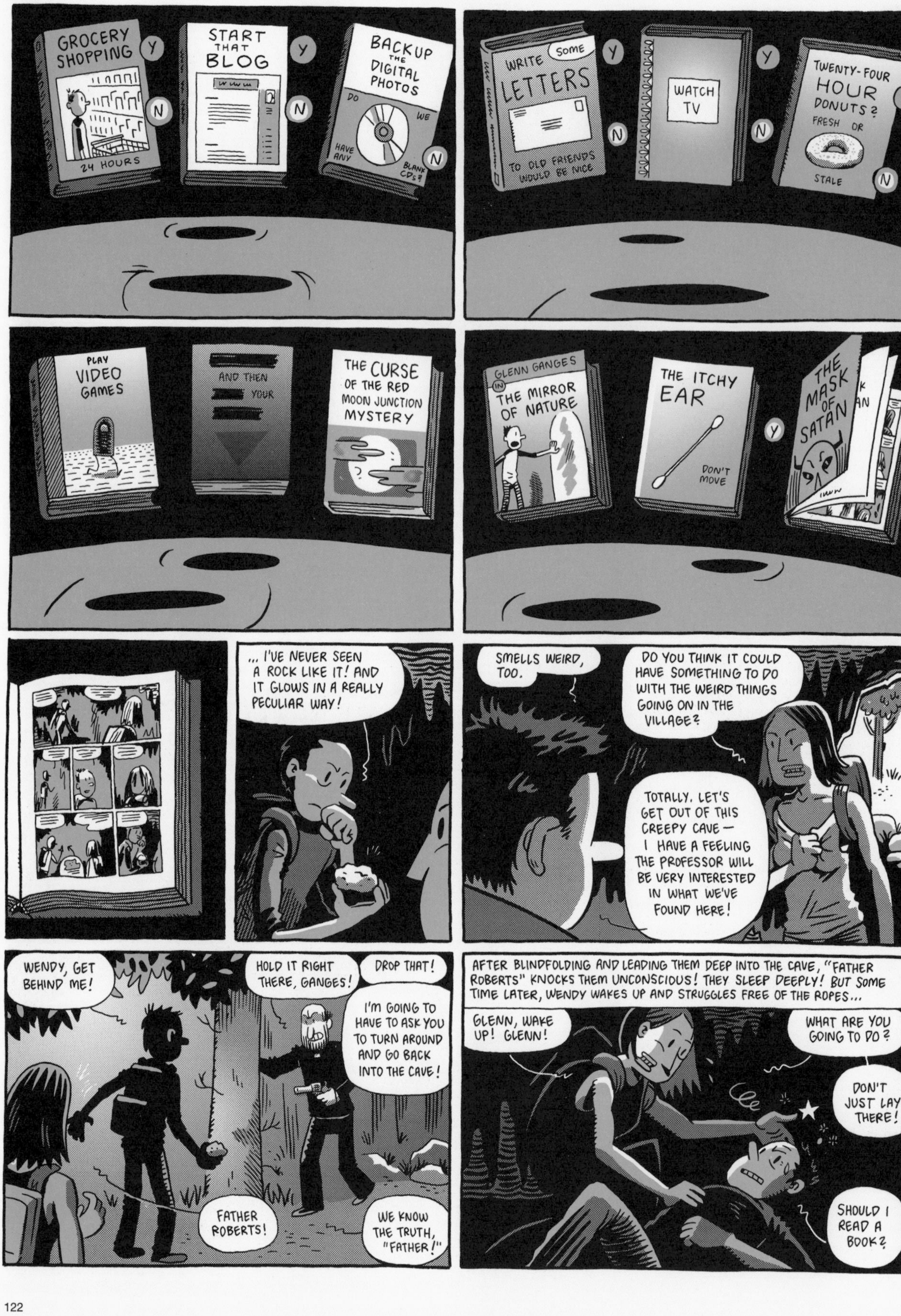
GROCERY SHOPPING
Y
N
24 HOURS
START THAT BLOG
Y
N
BACKUP THE DIGITAL PHOTOS
DO WE HAVE ANY BLANK CDs?
N
WRITE SOME LETTERS
TO OLD FRIENDS WOULD BE NICE
Y
N
WATCH TV
Y
N
TWENTY-FOUR HOUR DONUTS?
FRESH OR STALE
Y
N
PLAY VIDEO GAMES
[redacted] AND THEN [redacted] YOUR [redacted]
THE CURSE OF THE RED MOON JUNCTION MYSTERY
GLENN GANGES IN THE MIRROR OF NATURE
THE ITCHY EAR
DON'T MOVE
Y
THE MASK OF SATAN
... I'VE NEVER SEEN A ROCK LIKE IT! AND IT GLOWS IN A REALLY PECULIAR WAY!
SMELLS WEIRD, TOO.
DO YOU THINK IT COULD HAVE SOMETHING TO DO WITH THE WEIRD THINGS GOING ON IN THE VILLAGE?
TOTALLY. LET'S GET OUT OF THIS CREEPY CAVE — I HAVE A FEELING THE PROFESSOR WILL BE VERY INTERESTED IN WHAT WE'VE FOUND HERE!
WENDY, GET BEHIND ME!
HOLD IT RIGHT THERE, GANGES!
DROP THAT!
I'M GOING TO HAVE TO ASK YOU TO TURN AROUND AND GO BACK INTO THE CAVE!
FATHER ROBERTS!
WE KNOW THE TRUTH, "FATHER!"
AFTER BLINDFOLDING AND LEADING THEM DEEP INTO THE CAVE, "FATHER ROBERTS" KNOCKS THEM UNCONSCIOUS! THEY SLEEP DEEPLY! BUT SOME TIME LATER, WENDY WAKES UP AND STRUGGLES FREE OF THE ROPES...
GLENN, WAKE UP! GLENN!
WHAT ARE YOU GOING TO DO?
DON'T JUST LAY THERE!
SHOULD I READ A BOOK?

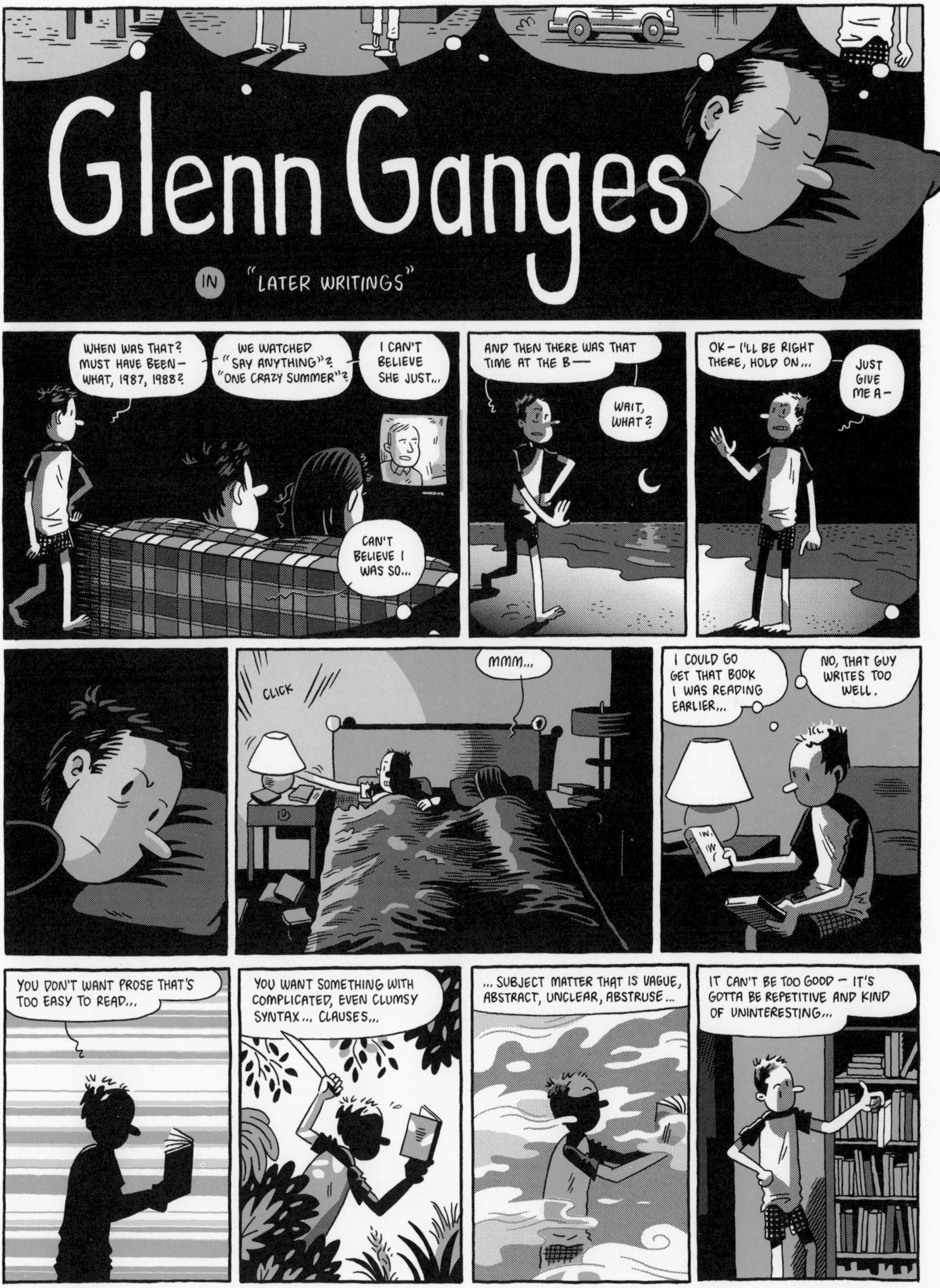

Glenn Ganges
IN "LATER WRITINGS"
WHEN WAS THAT? MUST HAVE BEEN— WHAT, 1987, 1988?
WE WATCHED "SAY ANYTHING"? "ONE CRAZY SUMMER"?
I CAN'T BELIEVE SHE JUST...
CAN'T BELIEVE I WAS SO...
AND THEN THERE WAS THAT TIME AT THE B—
WAIT, WHAT?
OK — I'LL BE RIGHT THERE, HOLD ON...
JUST GIVE ME A—
CLICK
MMM...
I COULD GO GET THAT BOOK I WAS READING EARLIER...
NO, THAT GUY WRITES TOO WELL.
YOU DON'T WANT PROSE THAT'S TOO EASY TO READ...
YOU WANT SOMETHING WITH COMPLICATED, EVEN CLUMSY SYNTAX... CLAUSES...
... SUBJECT MATTER THAT IS VAGUE, ABSTRACT, UNCLEAR, ABSTRUSE...
IT CAN'T BE TOO GOOD — IT'S GOTTA BE REPETITIVE AND KIND OF UNINTERESTING...

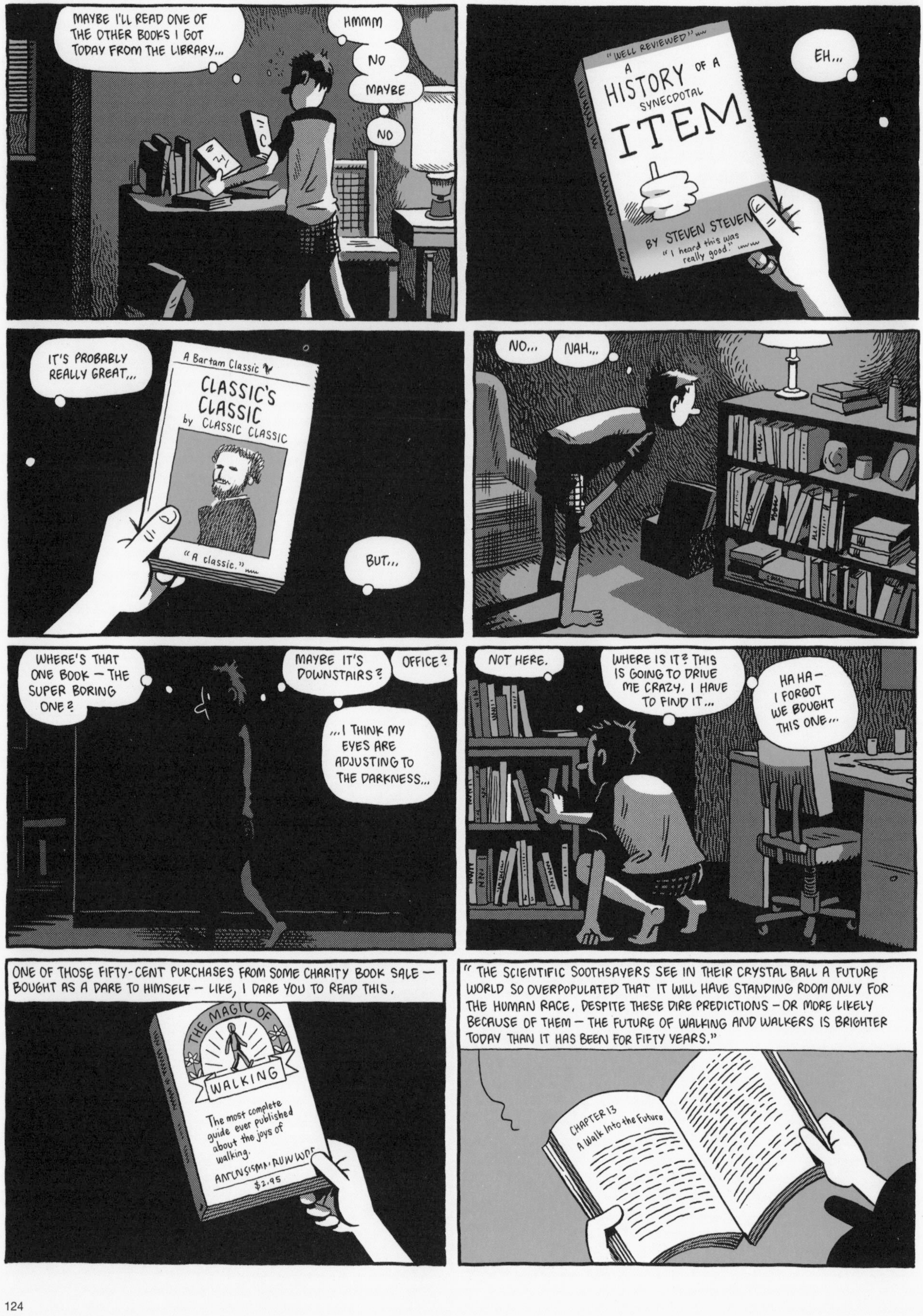

MAYBE I'LL READ ONE OF THE OTHER BOOKS I GOT TODAY FROM THE LIBRARY...
HMMM
NO
MAYBE
NO
"WELL REVIEWED"
A HISTORY OF A SYNECDOTAL ITEM
BY STEVEN STEVEN
"I heard this was really good."
EH...
IT'S PROBABLY REALLY GREAT...
A Bartam Classic
CLASSIC'S CLASSIC
by CLASSIC CLASSIC
"A classic."
BUT...
NO...
NAH...
WHERE'S THAT ONE BOOK — THE SUPER BORING ONE?
MAYBE IT'S DOWNSTAIRS?
OFFICE?
...I THINK MY EYES ARE ADJUSTING TO THE DARKNESS...
NOT HERE.
WHERE IS IT? THIS IS GOING TO DRIVE ME CRAZY. I HAVE TO FIND IT...
HA HA — I FORGOT WE BOUGHT THIS ONE...
ONE OF THOSE FIFTY-CENT PURCHASES FROM SOME CHARITY BOOK SALE — BOUGHT AS A DARE TO HIMSELF — LIKE, I DARE YOU TO READ THIS.
THE MAGIC OF WALKING
The most complete guide ever published about the joys of walking.
$2.95
" THE SCIENTIFIC SOOTHSAYERS SEE IN THEIR CRYSTAL BALL A FUTURE WORLD SO OVERPOPULATED THAT IT WILL HAVE STANDING ROOM ONLY FOR THE HUMAN RACE. DESPITE THESE DIRE PREDICTIONS — OR MORE LIKELY BECAUSE OF THEM — THE FUTURE OF WALKING AND WALKERS IS BRIGHTER TODAY THAN IT HAS BEEN FOR FIFTY YEARS."
CHAPTER 13
A Walk Into the Future

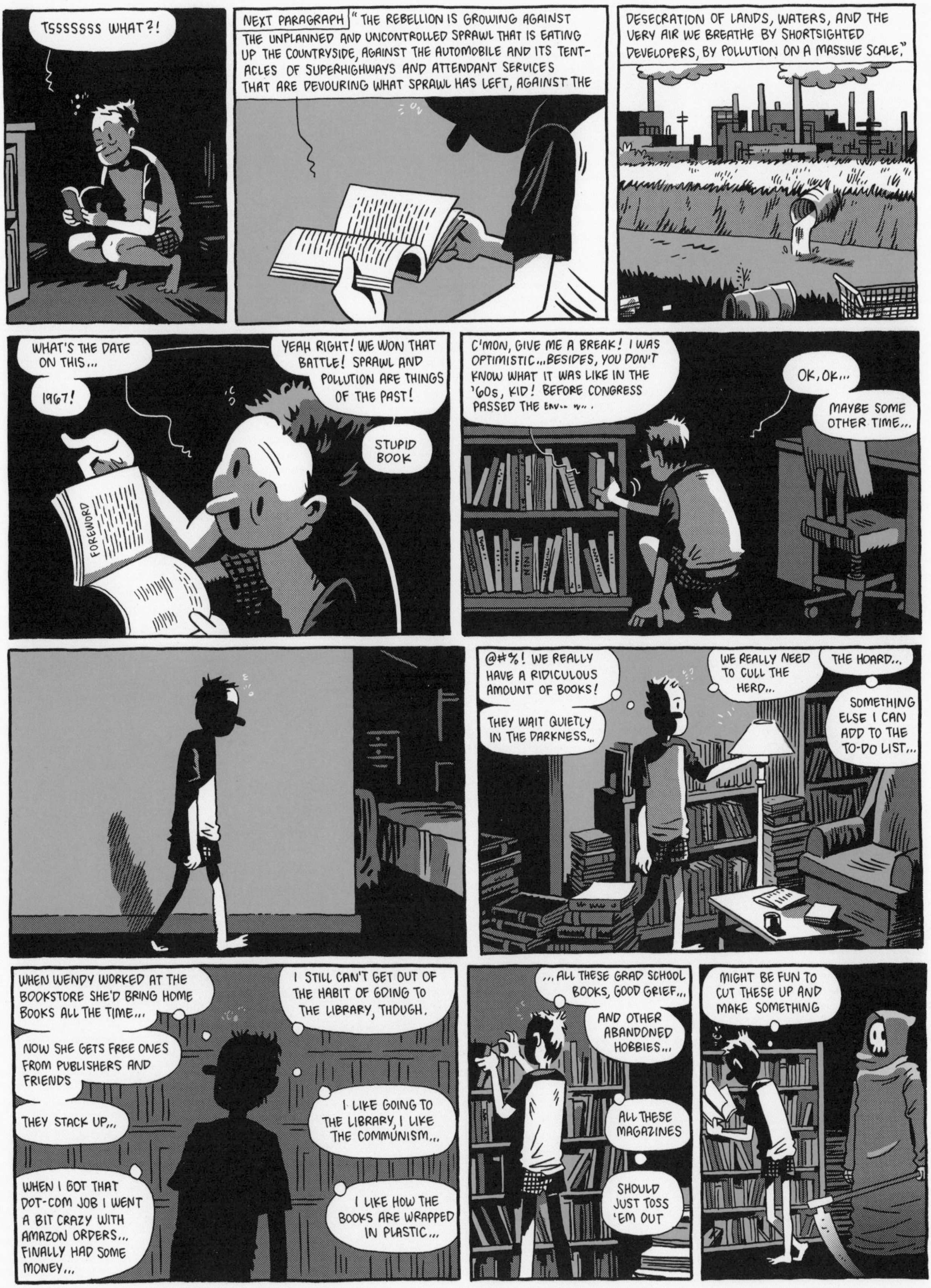
TSSSSSSS WHAT?!
NEXT PARAGRAPH
"THE REBELLION IS GROWING AGAINST THE UNPLANNED AND UNCONTROLLED SPRAWL THAT IS EATING UP THE COUNTRYSIDE, AGAINST THE AUTOMOBILE AND ITS TENTACLES OF SUPERHIGHWAYS AND ATTENDANT SERVICES THAT ARE DEVOURING WHAT SPRAWL HAS LEFT, AGAINST THE
DESECRATION OF LANDS, WATERS, AND THE VERY AIR WE BREATHE BY SHORTSIGHTED DEVELOPERS, BY POLLUTION ON A MASSIVE SCALE."
WHAT'S THE DATE ON THIS...
1967!
FOREWORD
YEAH RIGHT! WE WON THAT BATTLE! SPRAWL AND POLLUTION ARE THINGS OF THE PAST!
STUPID BOOK
C'MON, GIVE ME A BREAK! I WAS OPTIMISTIC... BESIDES, YOU DON'T KNOW WHAT IT WAS LIKE IN THE '60s, KID! BEFORE CONGRESS PASSED THE
OK, OK...
MAYBE SOME OTHER TIME...
@#%! WE REALLY HAVE A RIDICULOUS AMOUNT OF BOOKS!
THEY WAIT QUIETLY IN THE DARKNESS...
WE REALLY NEED TO CULL THE HERD...
THE HOARD...
SOMETHING ELSE I CAN ADD TO THE TO-DO LIST...
WHEN WENDY WORKED AT THE BOOKSTORE SHE'D BRING HOME BOOKS ALL THE TIME...
NOW SHE GETS FREE ONES FROM PUBLISHERS AND FRIENDS
THEY STACK UP...
WHEN I GOT THAT DOT-COM JOB I WENT A BIT CRAZY WITH AMAZON ORDERS... FINALLY HAD SOME MONEY...
I STILL CAN'T GET OUT OF THE HABIT OF GOING TO THE LIBRARY, THOUGH.
I LIKE GOING TO THE LIBRARY, I LIKE THE COMMUNISM...
I LIKE HOW THE BOOKS ARE WRAPPED IN PLASTIC...
...ALL THESE GRAD SCHOOL BOOKS, GOOD GRIEF...
AND OTHER ABANDONED HOBBIES...
ALL THESE MAGAZINES
SHOULD JUST TOSS 'EM OUT
MIGHT BE FUN TO CUT THESE UP AND MAKE SOMETHING

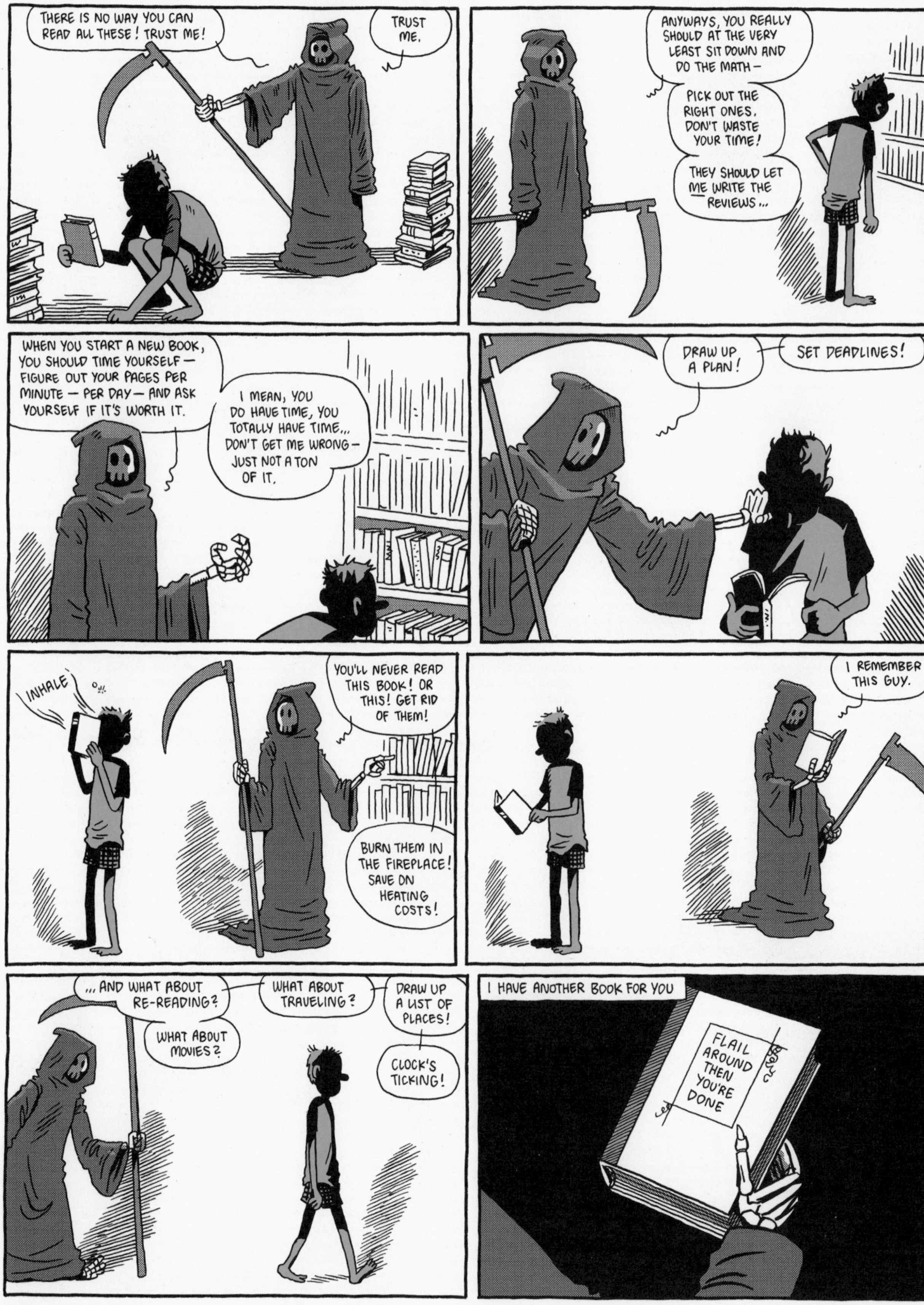
THERE IS NO WAY YOU CAN READ ALL THESE! TRUST ME!
TRUST ME.
ANYWAYS, YOU REALLY SHOULD AT THE VERY LEAST SIT DOWN AND DO THE MATH—
PICK OUT THE RIGHT ONES. DON'T WASTE YOUR TIME!
THEY SHOULD LET ME WRITE THE REVIEWS...
WHEN YOU START A NEW BOOK, YOU SHOULD TIME YOURSELF— FIGURE OUT YOUR PAGES PER MINUTE — PER DAY— AND ASK YOURSELF IF IT'S WORTH IT.
I MEAN, YOU DO HAVE TIME, YOU TOTALLY HAVE TIME... DON'T GET ME WRONG— JUST NOT A TON OF IT.
DRAW UP A PLAN!
SET DEADLINES!
INHALE
YOU'LL NEVER READ THIS BOOK! OR THIS! GET RID OF THEM!
BURN THEM IN THE FIREPLACE! SAVE ON HEATING COSTS!
I REMEMBER THIS GUY.
...AND WHAT ABOUT RE-READING?
WHAT ABOUT MOVIES?
WHAT ABOUT TRAVELING?
DRAW UP A LIST OF PLACES!
CLOCK'S TICKING!
I HAVE ANOTHER BOOK FOR YOU
FLAIL AROUND THEN YOU'RE DONE

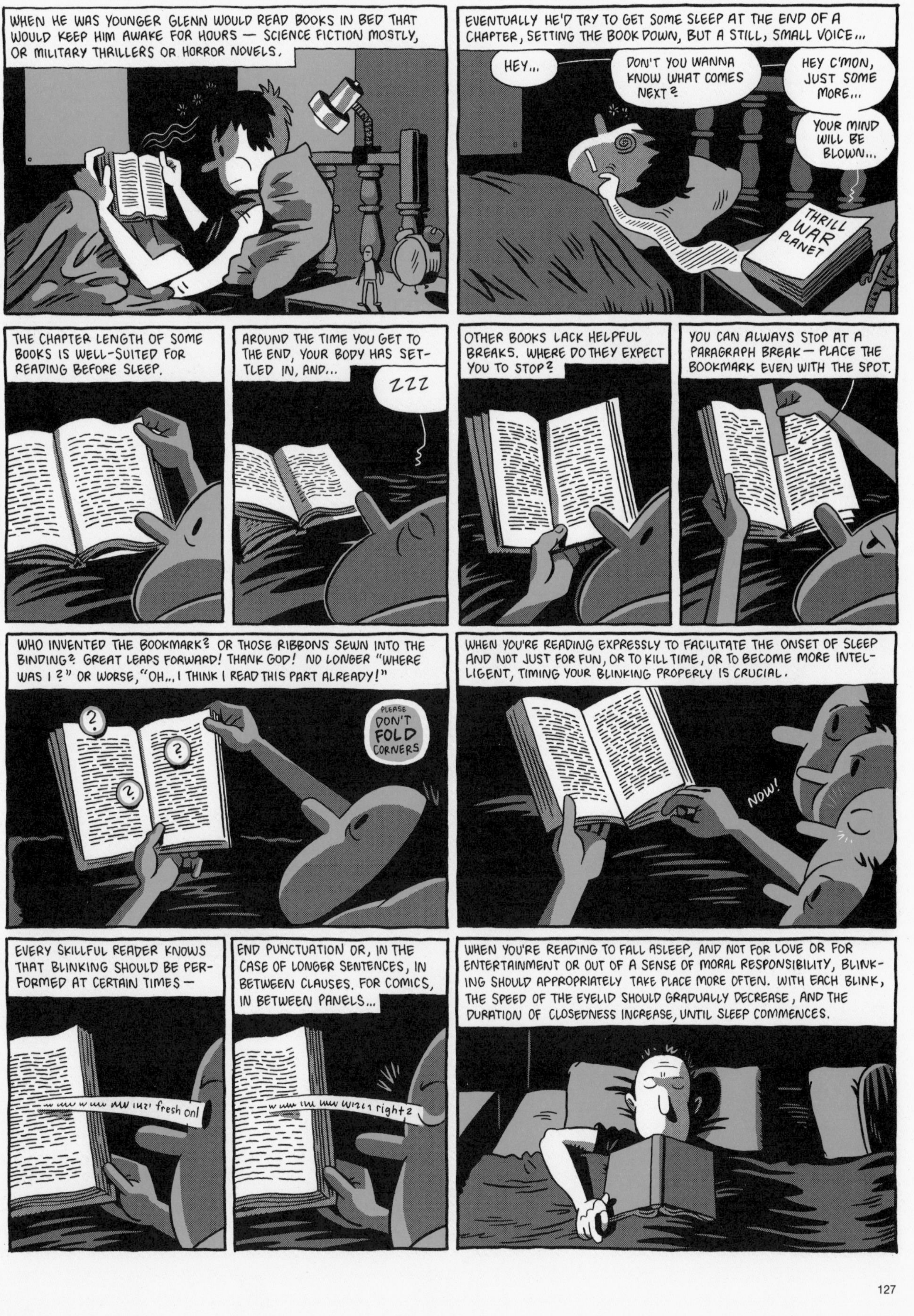
WHEN HE WAS YOUNGER GLENN WOULD READ BOOKS IN BED THAT WOULD KEEP HIM AWAKE FOR HOURS — SCIENCE FICTION MOSTLY, OR MILITARY THRILLERS OR HORROR NOVELS.
EVENTUALLY HE'D TRY TO GET SOME SLEEP AT THE END OF A CHAPTER, SETTING THE BOOK DOWN, BUT A STILL, SMALL VOICE...
HEY...
DON'T YOU WANNA KNOW WHAT COMES NEXT?
HEY C'MON, JUST SOME MORE...
YOUR MIND WILL BE BLOWN...
THRILL WAR PLANET
THE CHAPTER LENGTH OF SOME BOOKS IS WELL-SUITED FOR READING BEFORE SLEEP.
AROUND THE TIME YOU GET TO THE END, YOUR BODY HAS SETTLED IN, AND...
ZZZ
OTHER BOOKS LACK HELPFUL BREAKS. WHERE DO THEY EXPECT YOU TO STOP?
YOU CAN ALWAYS STOP AT A PARAGRAPH BREAK — PLACE THE BOOKMARK EVEN WITH THE SPOT.
WHO INVENTED THE BOOKMARK? OR THOSE RIBBONS SEWN INTO THE BINDING? GREAT LEAPS FORWARD! THANK GOD! NO LONGER "WHERE WAS I?" OR WORSE, "OH... I THINK I READ THIS PART ALREADY!"
PLEASE DON'T FOLD CORNERS
WHEN YOU'RE READING EXPRESSLY TO FACILITATE THE ONSET OF SLEEP AND NOT JUST FOR FUN, OR TO KILL TIME, OR TO BECOME MORE INTELLIGENT, TIMING YOUR BLINKING PROPERLY IS CRUCIAL.
NOW!
EVERY SKILLFUL READER KNOWS THAT BLINKING SHOULD BE PERFORMED AT CERTAIN TIMES —
END PUNCTUATION OR, IN THE CASE OF LONGER SENTENCES, IN BETWEEN CLAUSES. FOR COMICS, IN BETWEEN PANELS...
WHEN YOU'RE READING TO FALL ASLEEP, AND NOT FOR LOVE OR FOR ENTERTAINMENT OR OUT OF A SENSE OF MORAL RESPONSIBILITY, BLINKING SHOULD APPROPRIATELY TAKE PLACE MORE OFTEN. WITH EACH BLINK, THE SPEED OF THE EYELID SHOULD GRADUALLY DECREASE, AND THE DURATION OF CLOSEDNESS INCREASE, UNTIL SLEEP COMMENCES.

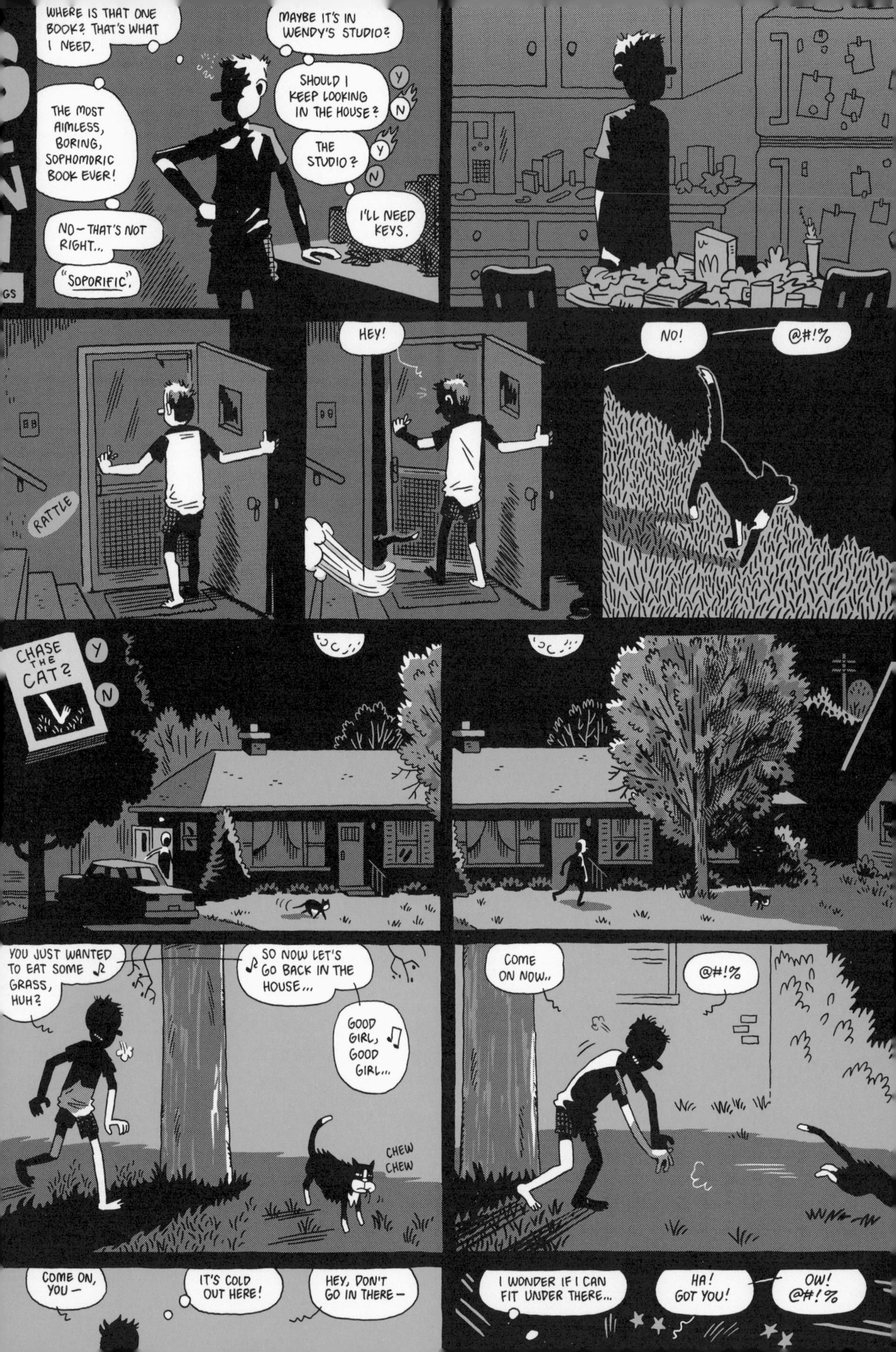
WHERE IS THAT ONE BOOK? THAT'S WHAT I NEED.
THE MOST AIMLESS, BORING, SOPHOMORIC BOOK EVER!
NO— THAT'S NOT RIGHT...
"SOPORIFIC".
MAYBE IT'S IN WENDY'S STUDIO?
SHOULD I KEEP LOOKING IN THE HOUSE?
Y
N
THE STUDIO?
Y
N
I'LL NEED KEYS.
RATTLE
HEY!
NO!
@#!%
CHASE THE CAT?
Y
N
YOU JUST WANTED TO EAT SOME GRASS, HUH?
SO NOW LET'S GO BACK IN THE HOUSE...
GOOD GIRL, GOOD GIRL...
CHEW CHEW
COME ON NOW..
@#!%
COME ON, YOU—
IT'S COLD OUT HERE!
HEY, DON'T GO IN THERE—
I WONDER IF I CAN FIT UNDER THERE...
HA! GOT YOU!
OW! @#!%

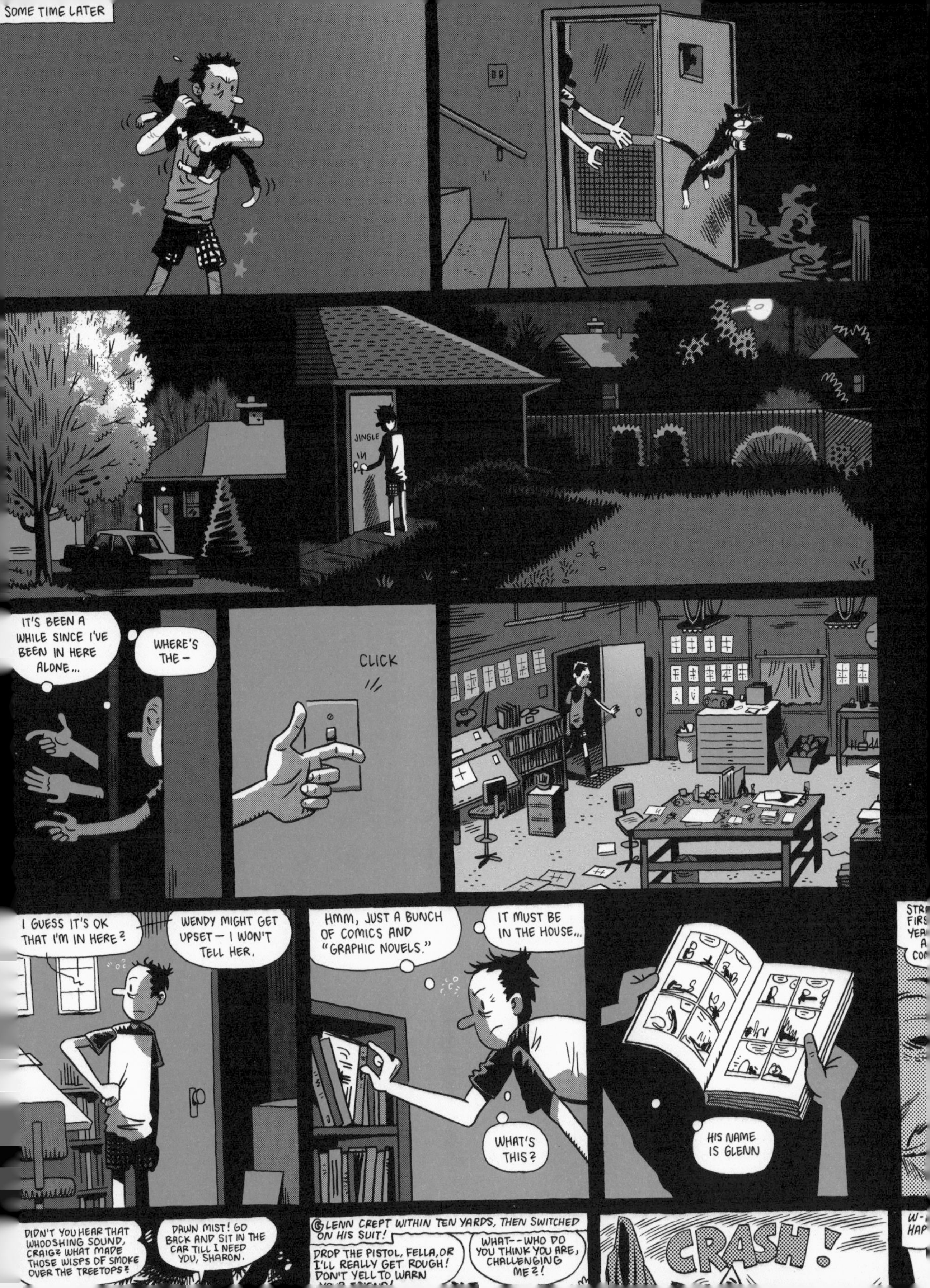
SOME TIME LATER
JINGLE
IT'S BEEN A WHILE SINCE I'VE BEEN IN HERE ALONE...
WHERE'S THE—
CLICK
I GUESS IT'S OK THAT I'M IN HERE?
WENDY MIGHT GET UPSET — I WON'T TELL HER.
HMM, JUST A BUNCH OF COMICS AND "GRAPHIC NOVELS."
IT MUST BE IN THE HOUSE...
WHAT'S THIS?
HIS NAME IS GLENN
DIDN'T YOU HEAR THAT WHOOSHING SOUND, CRAIG? WHAT MADE THOSE WISPS OF SMOKE OVER THE TREETOPS?
DAWN MIST! GO BACK AND SIT IN THE CAR TILL I NEED YOU, SHARON.
GLENN CREPT WITHIN TEN YARDS, THEN SWITCHED ON HIS SUIT!
DROP THE PISTOL, FELLA, OR I'LL REALLY GET ROUGH! DON'T YELL TO WARN
WHAT--WHO DO YOU THINK YOU ARE, CHALLENGING ME?!
CRASH!

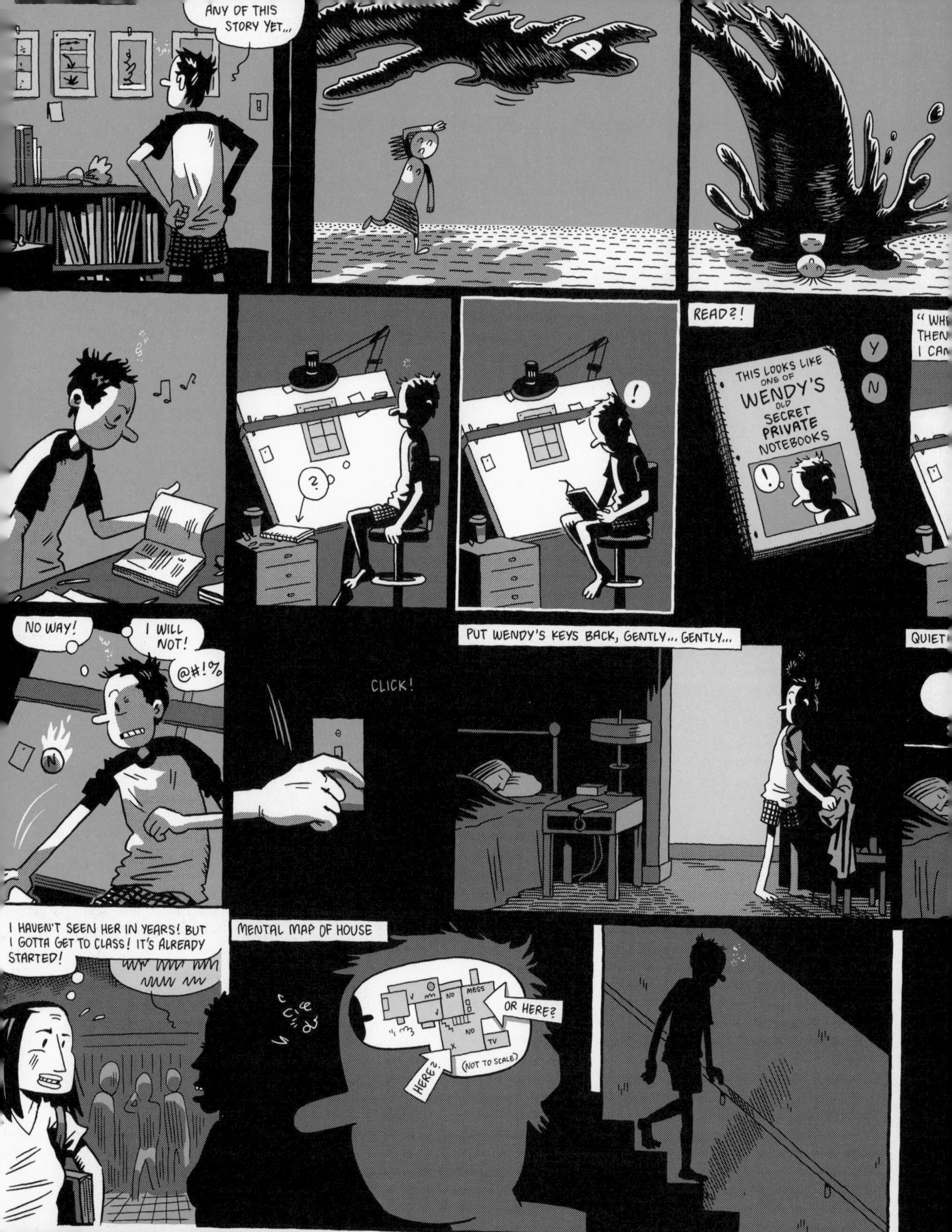

ANY OF THIS STORY YET...
READ?!
THIS LOOKS LIKE ONE OF WENDY'S OLD SECRET PRIVATE NOTEBOOKS
Y
N
NO WAY!
I WILL NOT!
@#!%
CLICK!
PUT WENDY'S KEYS BACK, GENTLY... GENTLY...
I HAVEN'T SEEN HER IN YEARS! BUT I GOTTA GET TO CLASS! IT'S ALREADY STARTED!
MENTAL MAP OF HOUSE
MESS
ND
ND
TV
OR HERE?
HERE?
(NOT TO SCALE)

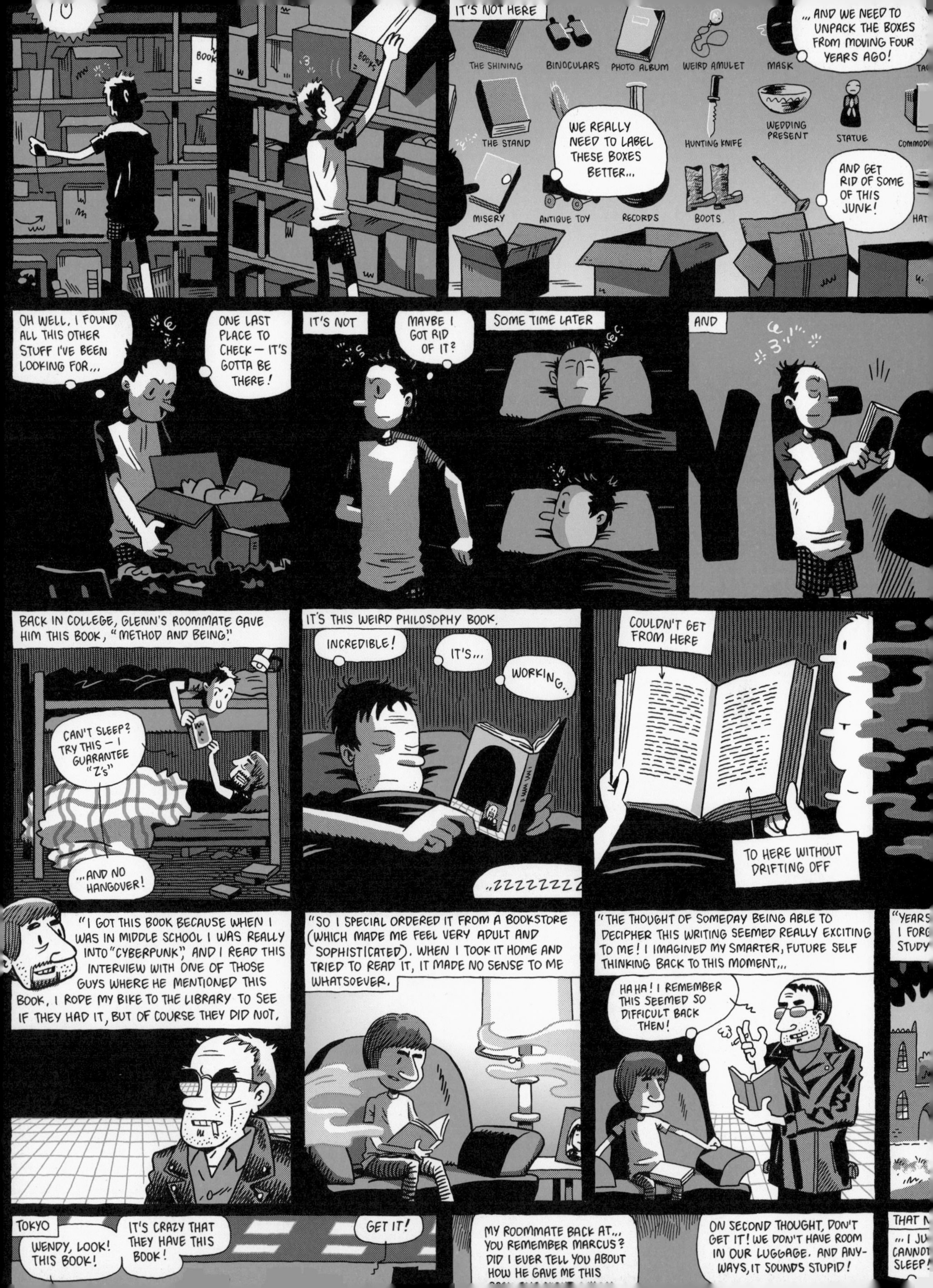

10
BOOKS
IT'S NOT HERE
THE SHINING
BINOCULARS
PHOTO ALBUM
WEIRD AMULET
MASK
...AND WE NEED TO UNPACK THE BOXES FROM MOVING FOUR YEARS AGO!
THE STAND
WE REALLY NEED TO LABEL THESE BOXES BETTER...
HUNTING KNIFE
WEDDING PRESENT
STATUE
AND GET RID OF SOME OF THIS JUNK!
MISERY
ANTIQUE TOY
RECORDS
BOOTS
HAT
OH WELL, I FOUND ALL THIS OTHER STUFF I'VE BEEN LOOKING FOR...
ONE LAST PLACE TO CHECK — IT'S GOTTA BE THERE!
IT'S NOT
MAYBE I GOT RID OF IT?
SOME TIME LATER
AND
BACK IN COLLEGE, GLENN'S ROOMMATE GAVE HIM THIS BOOK, "METHOD AND BEING."
CAN'T SLEEP? TRY THIS — I GUARANTEE "Z's"
...AND NO HANGOVER!
IT'S THIS WEIRD PHILOSOPHY BOOK.
INCREDIBLE!
IT'S...
WORKING...
..ZZZZZZZ
COULDN'T GET FROM HERE
TO HERE WITHOUT DRIFTING OFF
"I GOT THIS BOOK BECAUSE WHEN I WAS IN MIDDLE SCHOOL I WAS REALLY INTO "CYBERPUNK", AND I READ THIS INTERVIEW WITH ONE OF THOSE GUYS WHERE HE MENTIONED THIS BOOK. I RODE MY BIKE TO THE LIBRARY TO SEE IF THEY HAD IT, BUT OF COURSE THEY DID NOT.
"SO I SPECIAL ORDERED IT FROM A BOOKSTORE (WHICH MADE ME FEEL VERY ADULT AND SOPHISTICATED). WHEN I TOOK IT HOME AND TRIED TO READ IT, IT MADE NO SENSE TO ME WHATSOEVER.
"THE THOUGHT OF SOMEDAY BEING ABLE TO DECIPHER THIS WRITING SEEMED REALLY EXCITING TO ME! I IMAGINED MY SMARTER, FUTURE SELF THINKING BACK TO THIS MOMENT...
HA HA! I REMEMBER THIS SEEMED SO DIFFICULT BACK THEN!
TOKYO
WENDY, LOOK! THIS BOOK!
IT'S CRAZY THAT THEY HAVE THIS BOOK!
GET IT!
MY ROOMMATE BACK AT... YOU REMEMBER MARCUS? DID I EVER TELL YOU ABOUT HOW HE GAVE ME THIS
ON SECOND THOUGHT, DON'T GET IT! WE DON'T HAVE ROOM IN OUR LUGGAGE. AND ANYWAYS, IT SOUNDS STUPID!

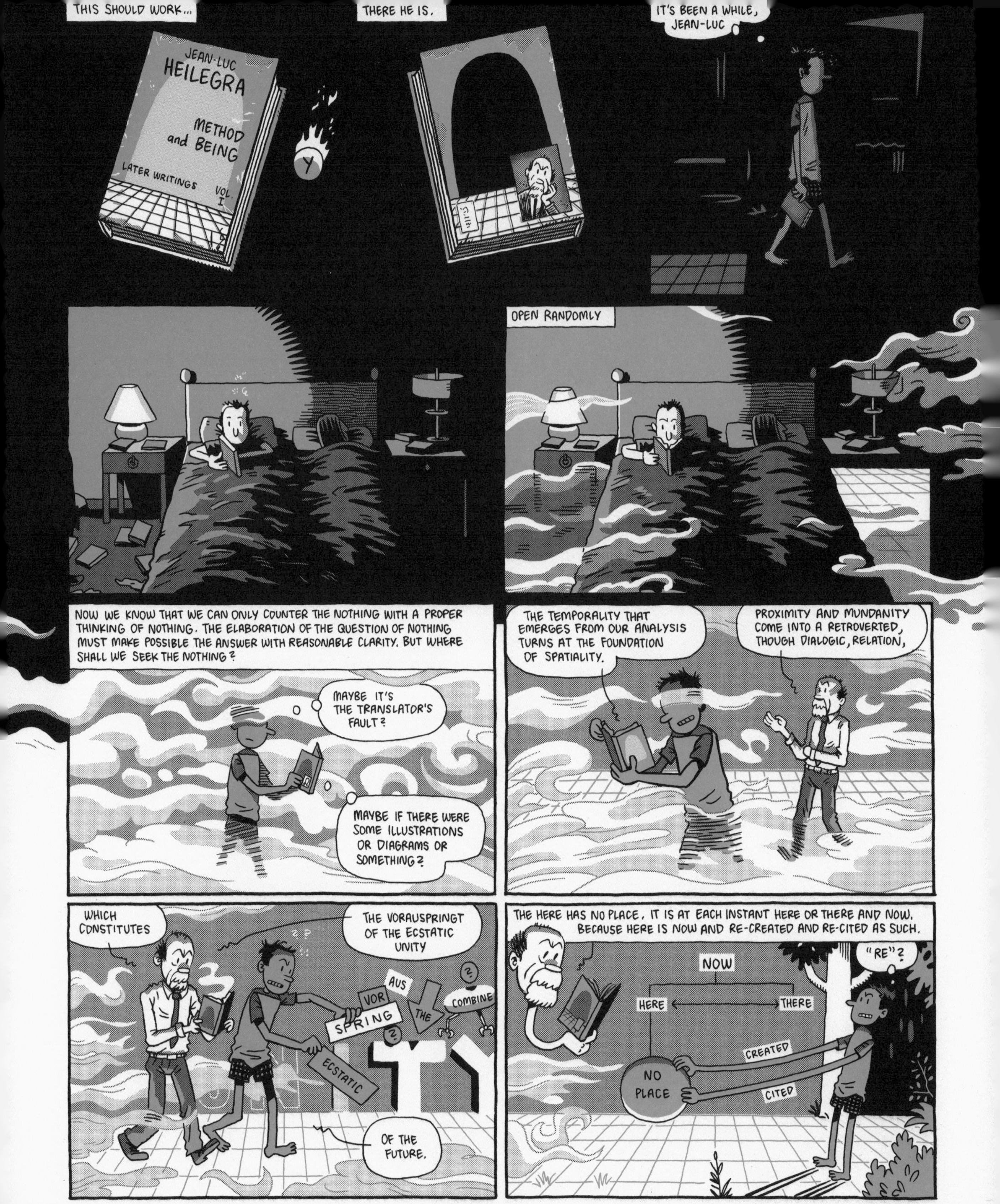
THIS SHOULD WORK...
JEAN-LUC HEILEGRA
METHOD and BEING
LATER WRITINGS
VOL. I
THERE HE IS.
IT'S BEEN A WHILE, JEAN-LUC
OPEN RANDOMLY
NOW WE KNOW THAT WE CAN ONLY COUNTER THE NOTHING WITH A PROPER THINKING OF NOTHING. THE ELABORATION OF THE QUESTION OF NOTHING MUST MAKE POSSIBLE THE ANSWER WITH REASONABLE CLARITY. BUT WHERE SHALL WE SEEK THE NOTHING?
MAYBE IT'S THE TRANSLATOR'S FAULT?
MAYBE IF THERE WERE SOME ILLUSTRATIONS OR DIAGRAMS OR SOMETHING?
THE TEMPORALITY THAT EMERGES FROM OUR ANALYSIS TURNS AT THE FOUNDATION OF SPATIALITY.
PROXIMITY AND MUNDANITY COME INTO A RETROVERTED, THOUGH DIALOGIC, RELATION,
WHICH CONSTITUTES
THE VORAUSPRINGT OF THE ECSTATIC UNITY
AUS
VOR
SPRING
THE
COMBINE
ECSTATIC
OF THE FUTURE.
THE HERE HAS NO PLACE. IT IS AT EACH INSTANT HERE OR THERE AND NOW. BECAUSE HERE IS NOW AND RE-CREATED AND RE-CITED AS SUCH.
NOW
HERE
THERE
"RE"?
CREATED
NO PLACE
CITED

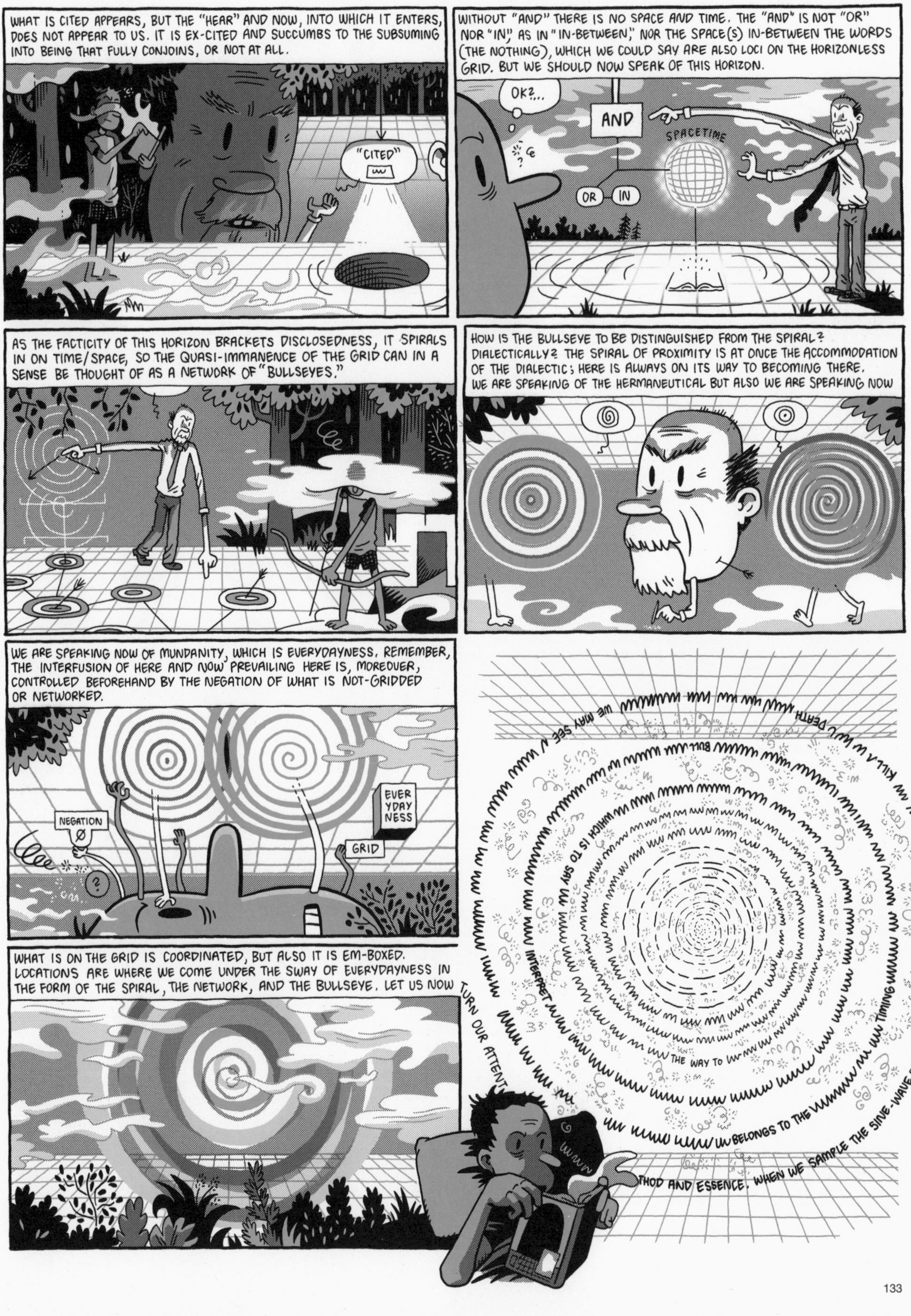

WHAT IS CITED APPEARS, BUT THE "HEAR" AND NOW, INTO WHICH IT ENTERS, DOES NOT APPEAR TO US. IT IS EX-CITED AND SUCCUMBS TO THE SUBSUMING INTO BEING THAT FULLY CONJOINS, OR NOT AT ALL.
"CITED"
WITHOUT "AND" THERE IS NO SPACE AND TIME. THE "AND" IS NOT "OR" NOR "IN", AS IN "IN-BETWEEN," NOR THE SPACE(S) IN-BETWEEN THE WORDS (THE NOTHING), WHICH WE COULD SAY ARE ALSO LOCI ON THE HORIZONLESS GRID. BUT WE SHOULD NOW SPEAK OF THIS HORIZON.
OK?...
AND
SPACETIME
OR
IN
AS THE FACTICITY OF THIS HORIZON BRACKETS DISCLOSEDNESS, IT SPIRALS IN ON TIME/SPACE, SO THE QUASI-IMMANENCE OF THE GRID CAN IN A SENSE BE THOUGHT OF AS A NETWORK OF "BULLSEYES."
HOW IS THE BULLSEYE TO BE DISTINGUISHED FROM THE SPIRAL? DIALECTICALLY? THE SPIRAL OF PROXIMITY IS AT ONCE THE ACCOMMODATION OF THE DIALECTIC; HERE IS ALWAYS ON ITS WAY TO BECOMING THERE. WE ARE SPEAKING OF THE HERMANEUTICAL BUT ALSO WE ARE SPEAKING NOW
WE ARE SPEAKING NOW OF MUNDANITY, WHICH IS EVERYDAYNESS. REMEMBER, THE INTERFUSION OF HERE AND NOW PREVAILING HERE IS, MOREOVER, CONTROLLED BEFOREHAND BY THE NEGATION OF WHAT IS NOT-GRIDDED OR NETWORKED.
NEGATION
Ø
EVERYDAYNESS
GRID
WHAT IS ON THE GRID IS COORDINATED, BUT ALSO IT IS EM-BOXED. LOCATIONS ARE WHERE WE COME UNDER THE SWAY OF EVERYDAYNESS IN THE FORM OF THE SPIRAL, THE NETWORK, AND THE BULLSEYE. LET US NOW TURN OUR ATTENT
WE MAY SEE
DEATH
KILL
BULLSEYE
WHICH IS TO SAY
INTERPRET
THE WAY TO
TIMING
BELONGS TO THE
WHEN WE SAMPLE THE SINE-WAVE SPIRAL
OF THE
THOD AND ESSENCE.

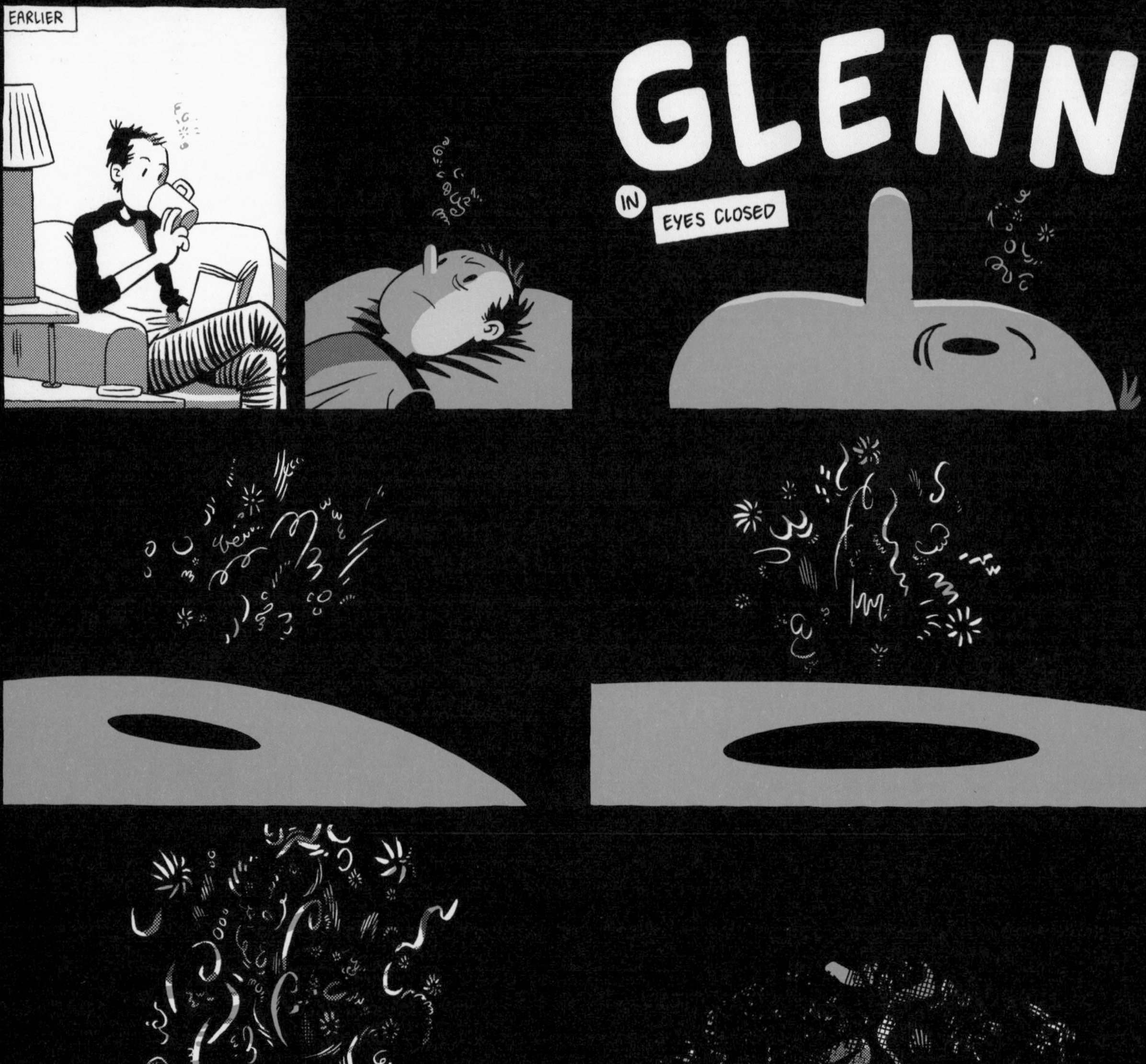
EARLIER
GLENN
IN
EYES CLOSED

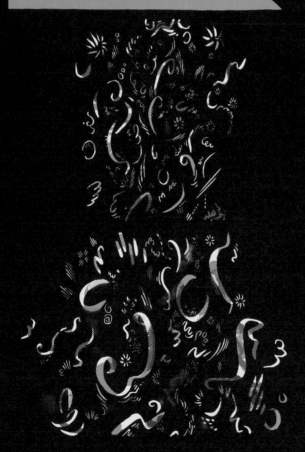

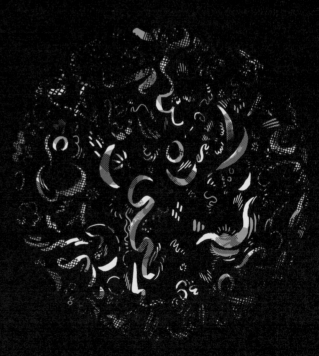

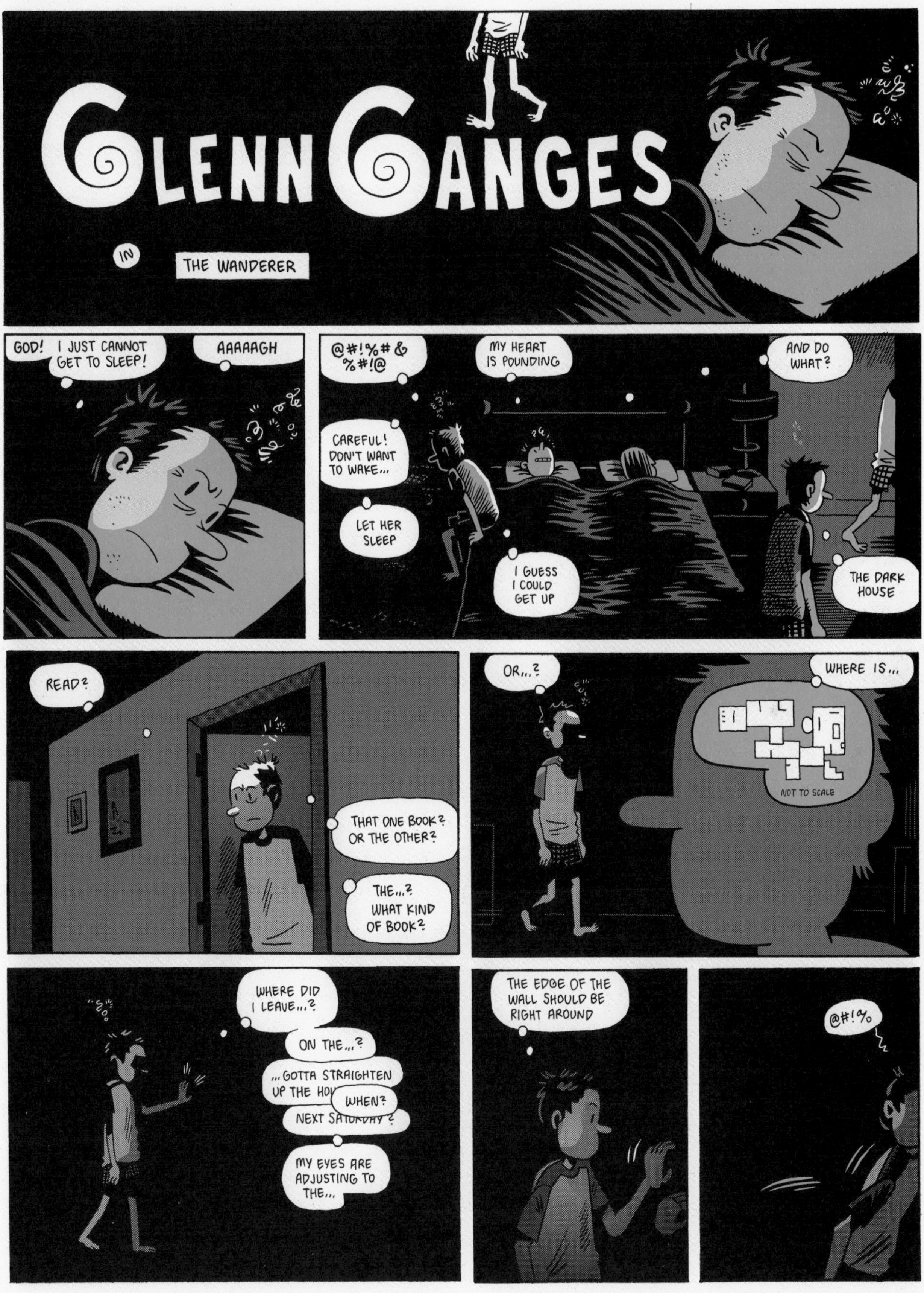
GLENN GANGES
IN
THE WANDERER
GOD! I JUST CANNOT GET TO SLEEP!
AAAAAGH
@#!%#& %#!@
MY HEART IS POUNDING
CAREFUL! DON'T WANT TO WAKE...
LET HER SLEEP
I GUESS I COULD GET UP
AND DO WHAT?
THE DARK HOUSE
READ?
THAT ONE BOOK? OR THE OTHER?
THE...? WHAT KIND OF BOOK?
OR...?
WHERE IS...
NOT TO SCALE
WHERE DID I LEAVE...?
ON THE...?
...GOTTA STRAIGHTEN UP THE HO
WHEN?
NEXT SATURDAY?
MY EYES ARE ADJUSTING TO THE...
THE EDGE OF THE WALL SHOULD BE RIGHT AROUND
@#!%

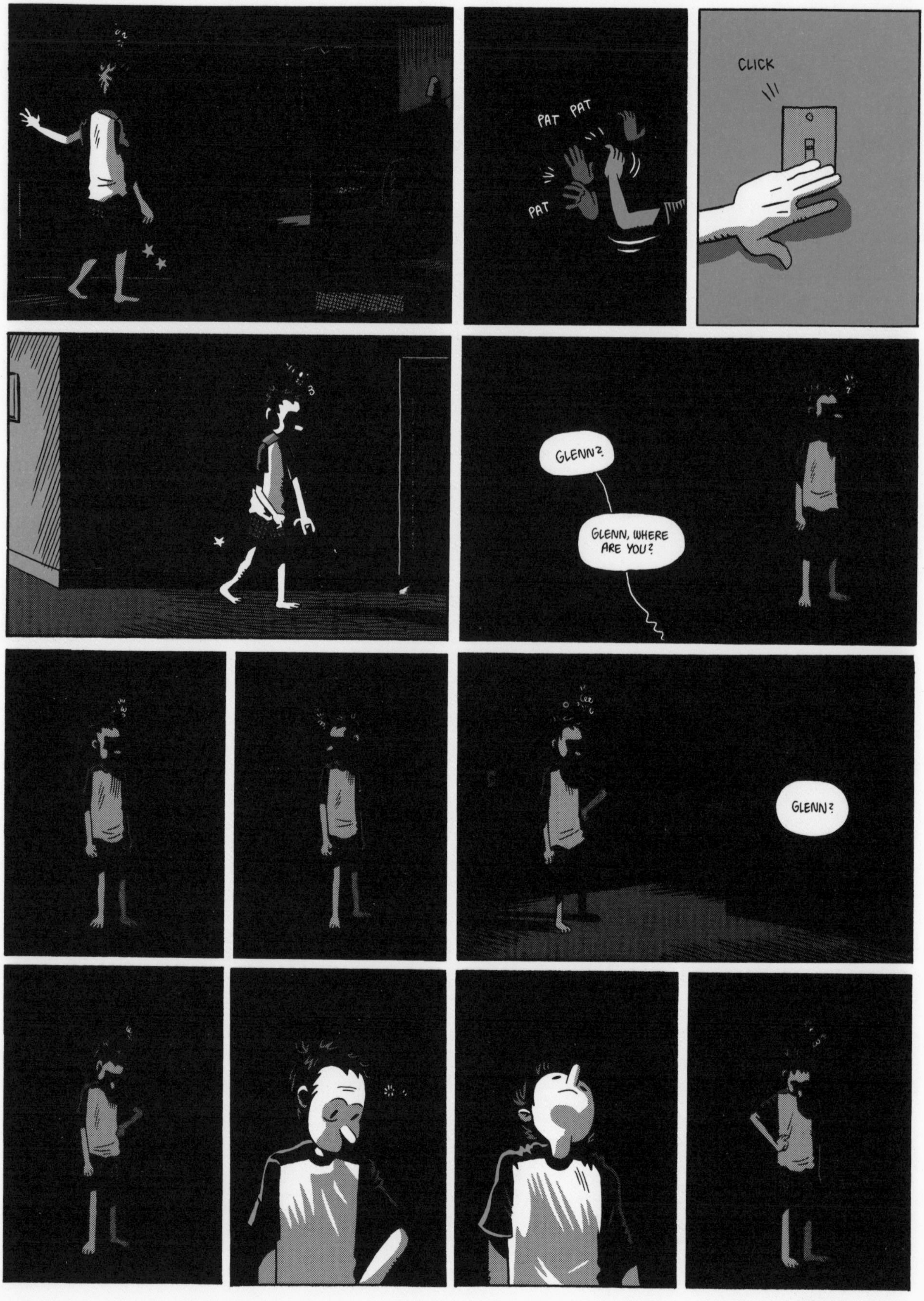
PAT PAT
PAT
CLICK
GLENN?
GLENN, WHERE ARE YOU?
GLENN?

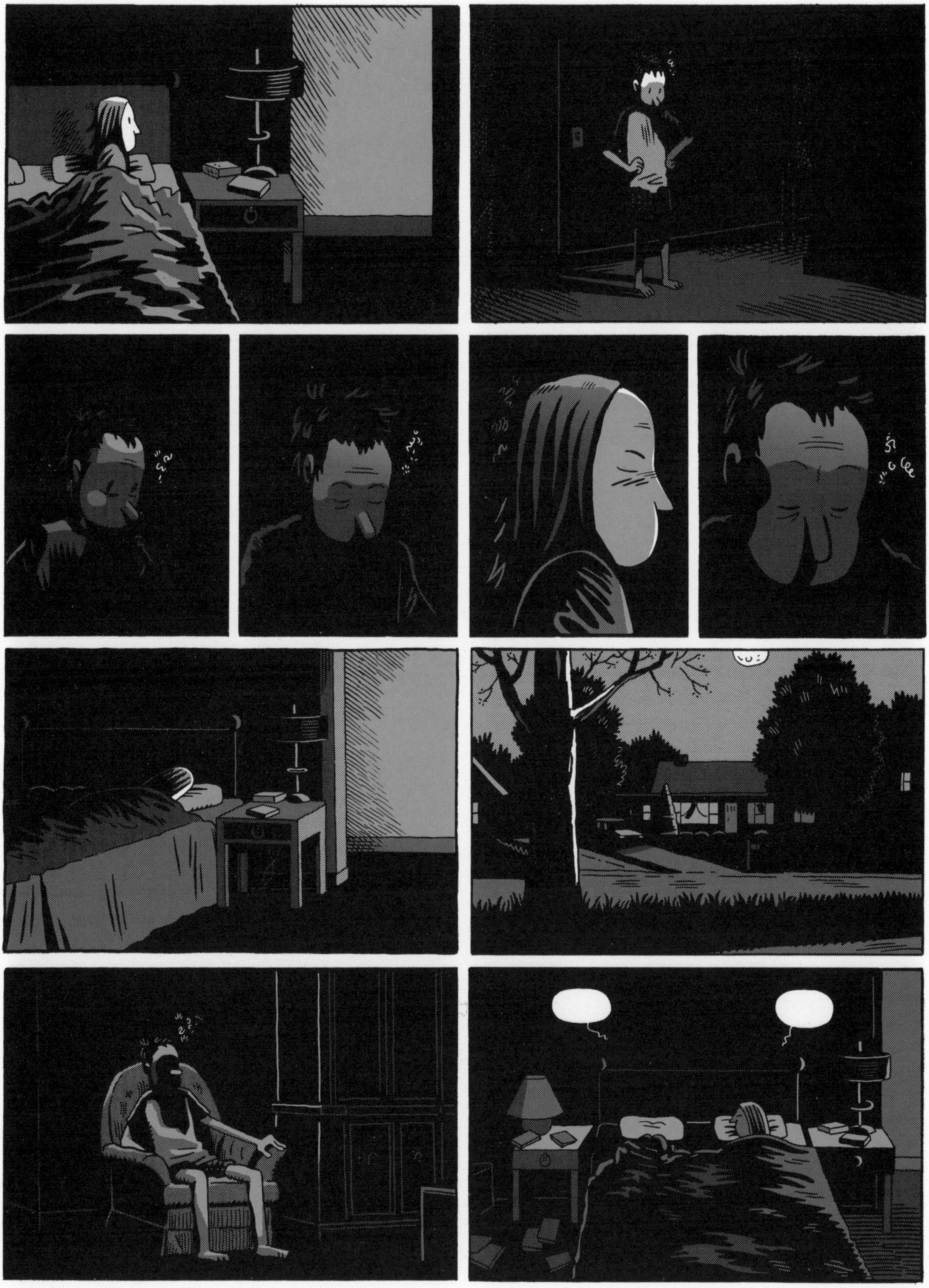

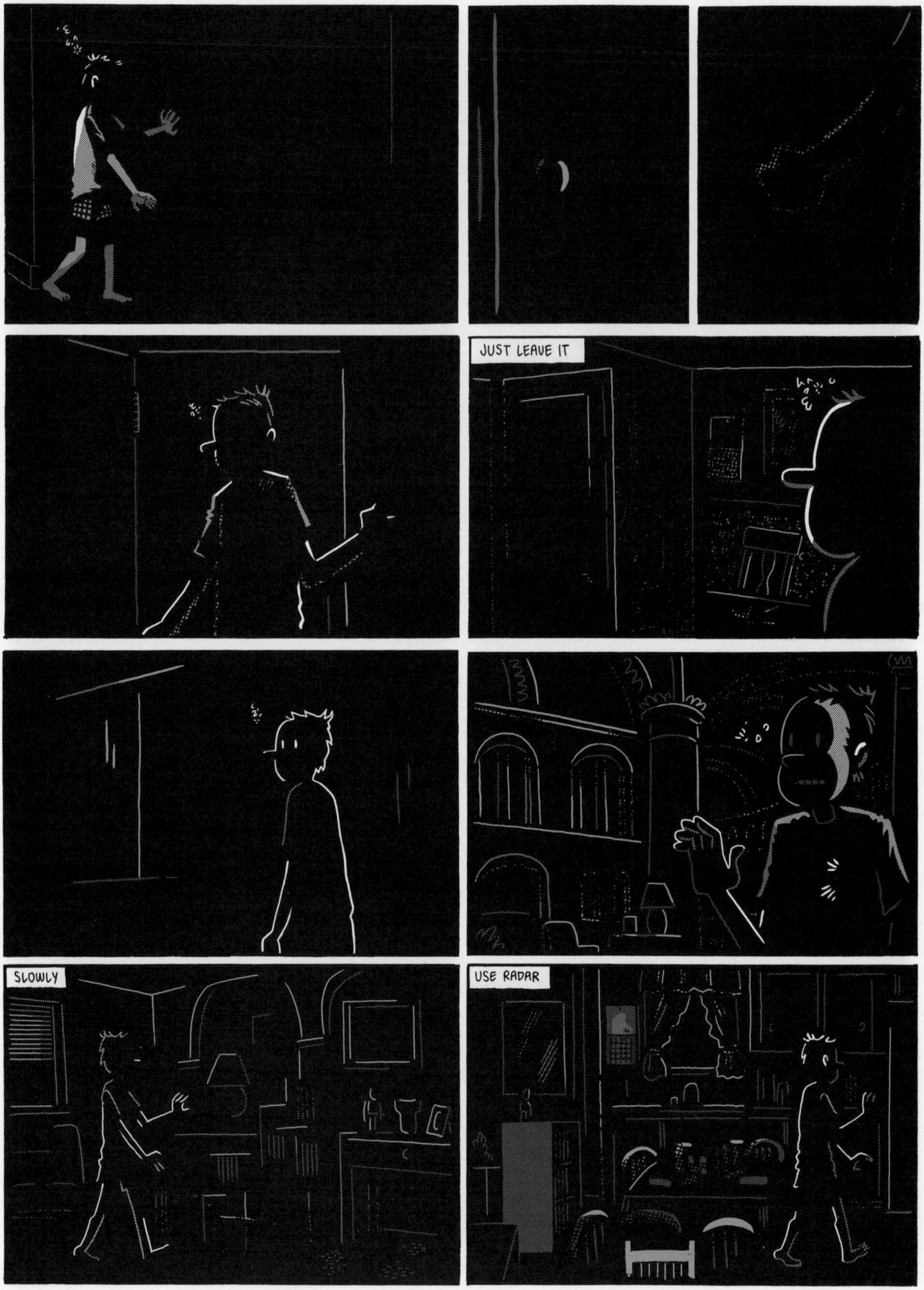
JUST LEAVE IT
SLOWLY
USE RADAR

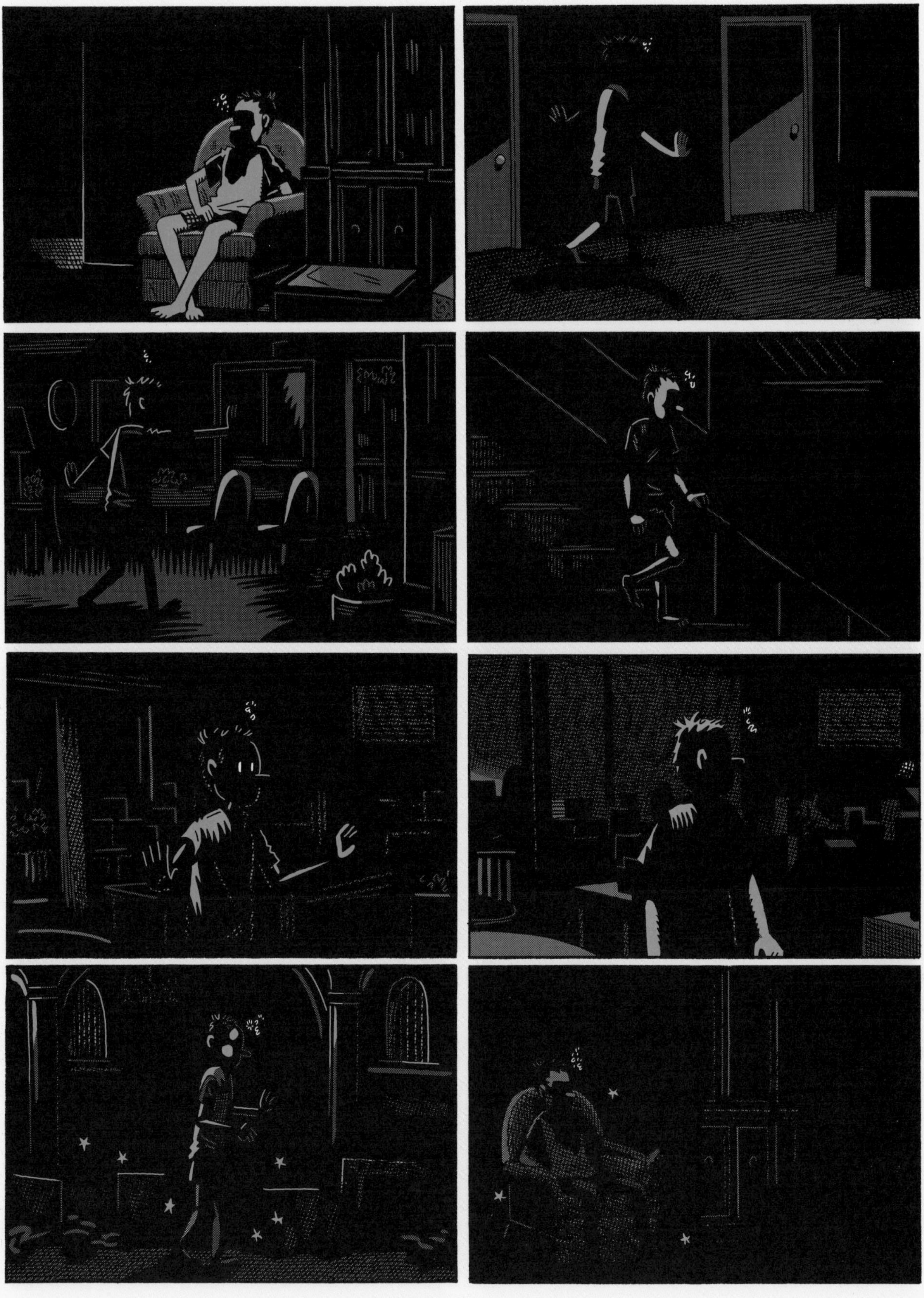

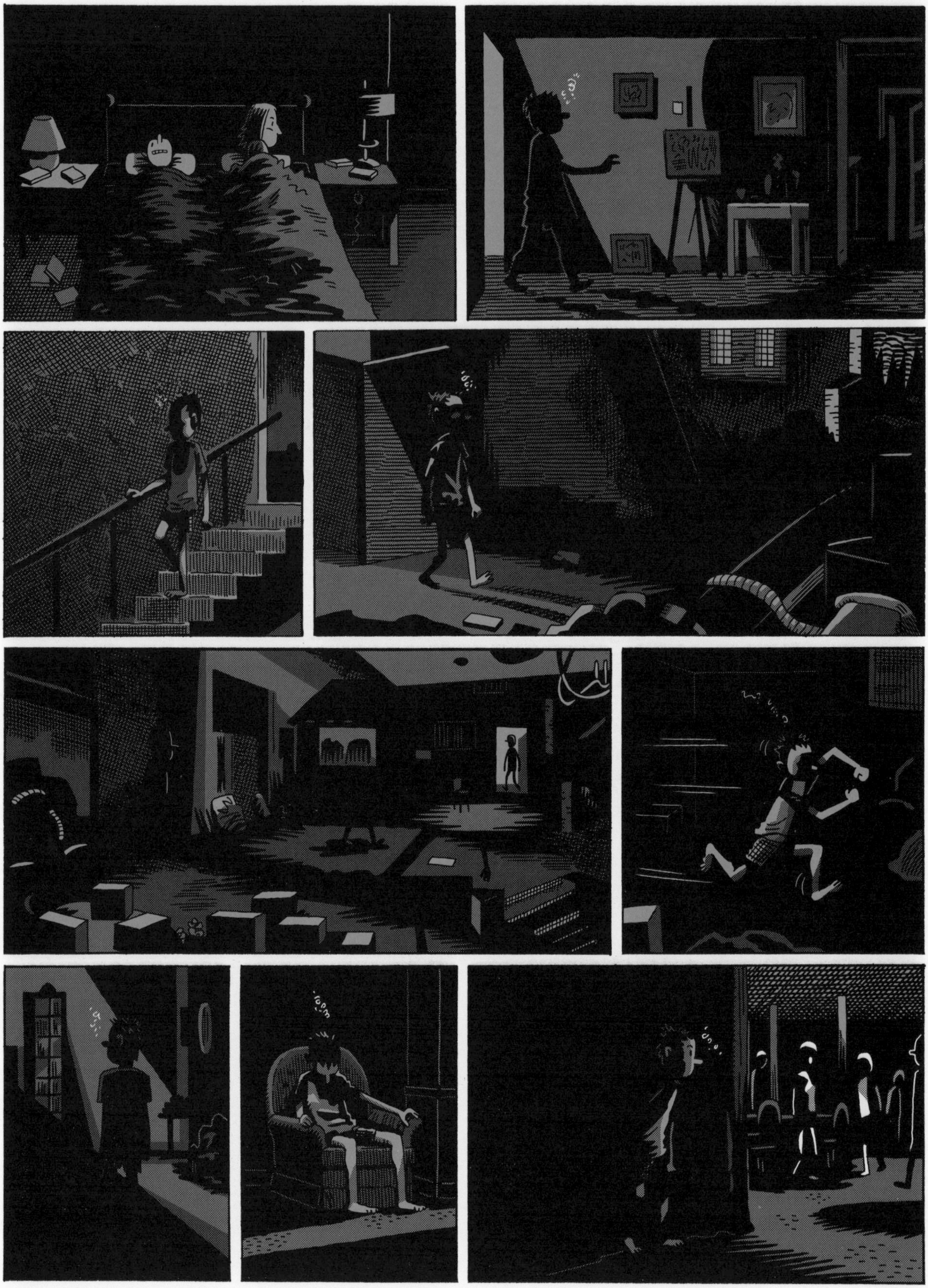

SIGH

ALL THE

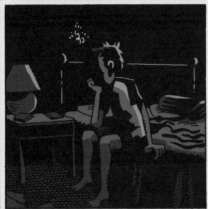

WHY DID I

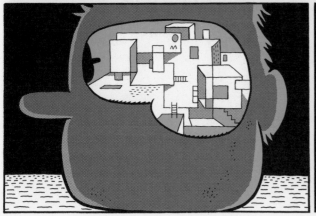

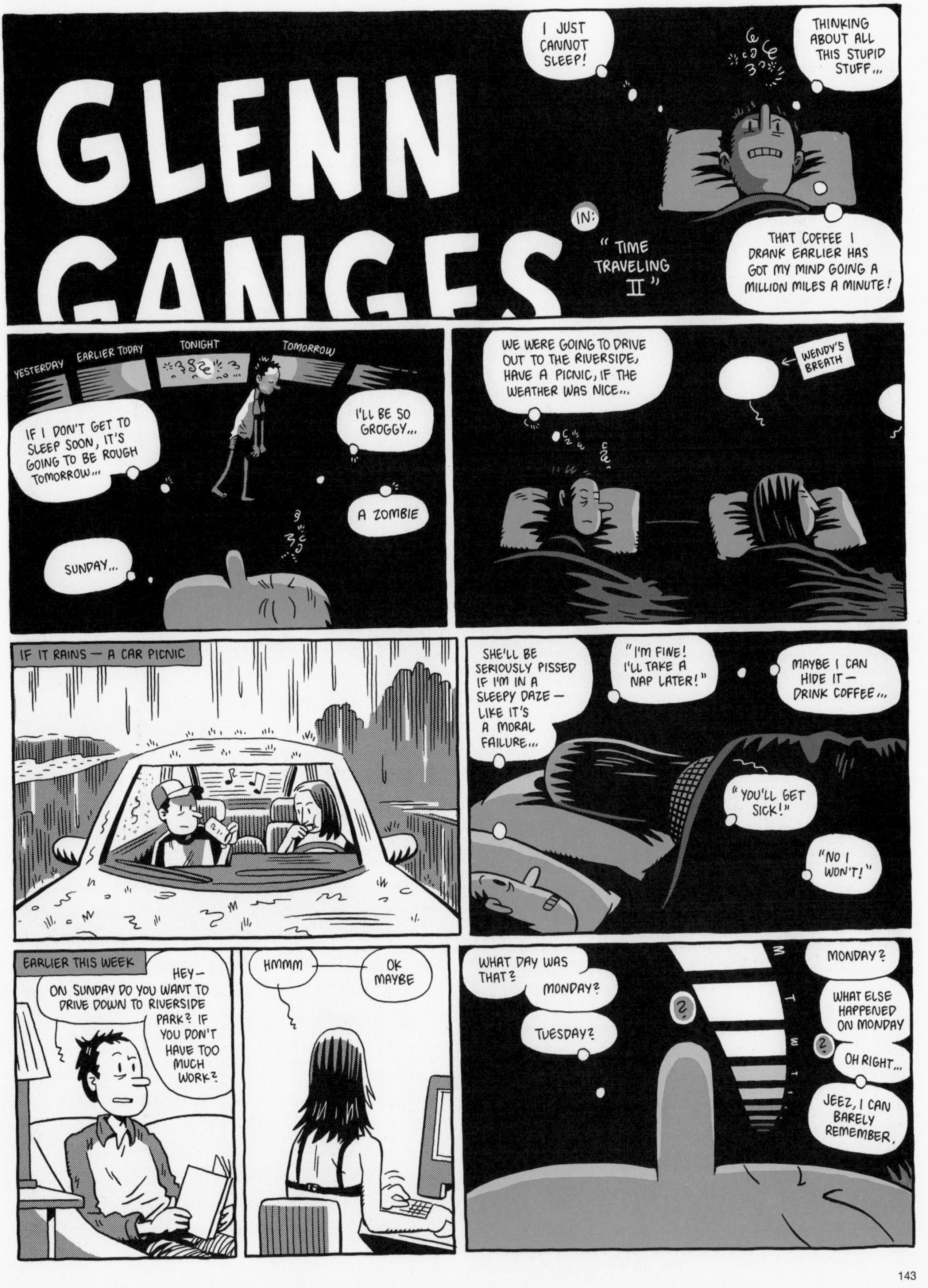
GLENN GANGES
IN:
"TIME TRAVELING II"
I JUST CANNOT SLEEP!
THINKING ABOUT ALL THIS STUPID STUFF...
THAT COFFEE I DRANK EARLIER HAS GOT MY MIND GOING A MILLION MILES A MINUTE!
YESTERDAY
EARLIER TODAY
TONIGHT
TOMORROW
IF I DON'T GET TO SLEEP SOON, IT'S GOING TO BE ROUGH TOMORROW...
I'LL BE SO GROGGY...
A ZOMBIE
SUNDAY...
WE WERE GOING TO DRIVE OUT TO THE RIVERSIDE, HAVE A PICNIC, IF THE WEATHER WAS NICE...
WENDY'S BREATH
IF IT RAINS — A CAR PICNIC
SHE'LL BE SERIOUSLY PISSED IF I'M IN A SLEEPY DAZE — LIKE IT'S A MORAL FAILURE...
"I'M FINE! I'LL TAKE A NAP LATER!"
MAYBE I CAN HIDE IT — DRINK COFFEE...
"YOU'LL GET SICK!"
"NO I WON'T!"
EARLIER THIS WEEK
HEY— ON SUNDAY DO YOU WANT TO DRIVE DOWN TO RIVERSIDE PARK? IF YOU DON'T HAVE TOO MUCH WORK?
HMMM
OK MAYBE
WHAT DAY WAS THAT?
MONDAY?
TUESDAY?
MONDAY?
WHAT ELSE HAPPENED ON MONDAY
OH RIGHT...
JEEZ, I CAN BARELY REMEMBER.

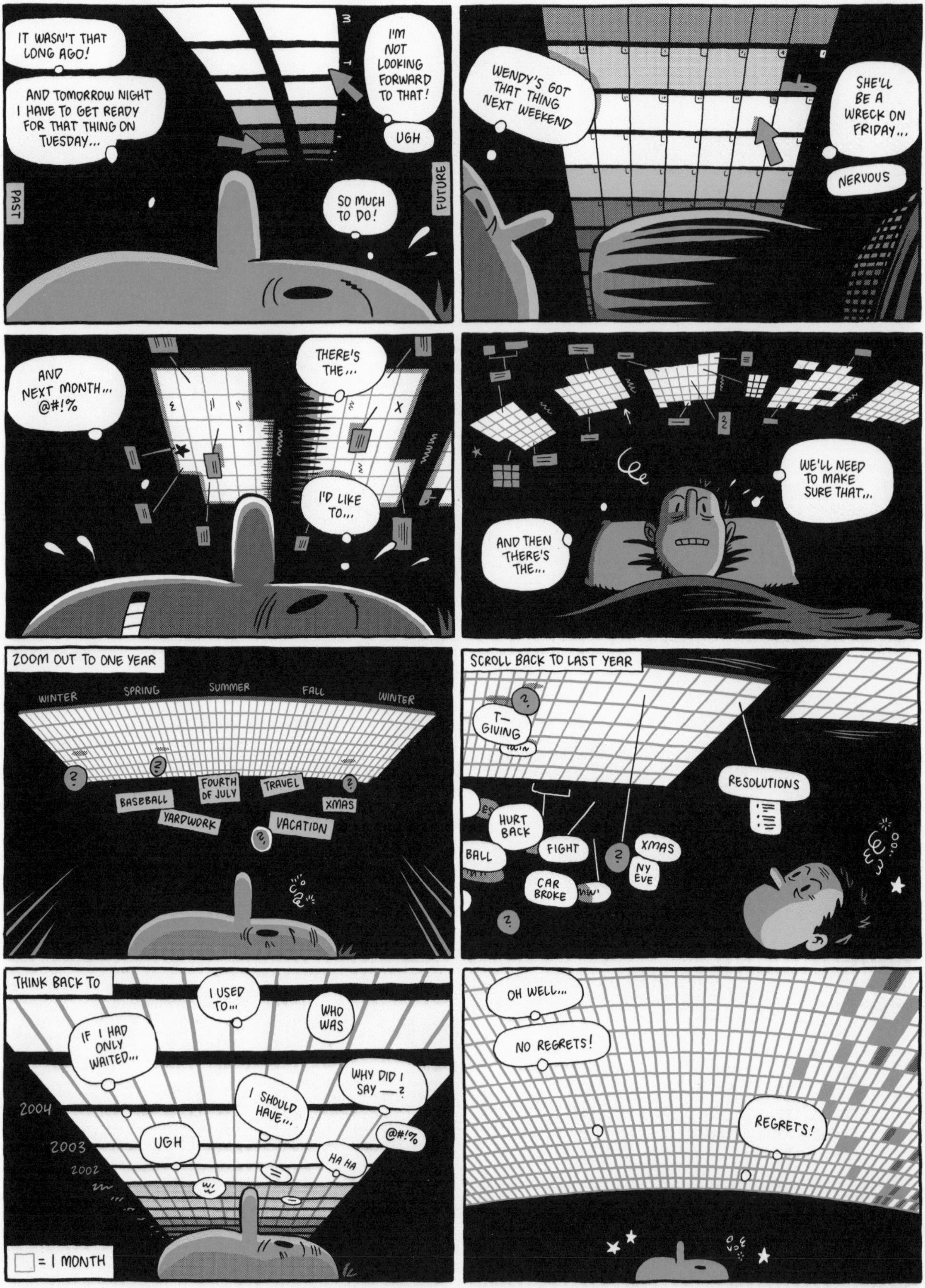

IT WASN'T THAT LONG AGO!
AND TOMORROW NIGHT I HAVE TO GET READY FOR THAT THING ON TUESDAY...
I'M NOT LOOKING FORWARD TO THAT!
UGH
PAST
FUTURE
SO MUCH TO DO!
WENDY'S GOT THAT THING NEXT WEEKEND
SHE'LL BE A WRECK ON FRIDAY...
NERVOUS
AND NEXT MONTH... @#!%
THERE'S THE...
I'D LIKE TO...
WE'LL NEED TO MAKE SURE THAT...
AND THEN THERE'S THE...
ZOOM OUT TO ONE YEAR
WINTER
SPRING
SUMMER
FALL
WINTER
FOURTH OF JULY
TRAVEL
BASEBALL
XMAS
YARDWORK
VACATION
SCROLL BACK TO LAST YEAR
T-GIVING
RESOLUTIONS
HURT BACK
FIGHT
XMAS
BALL
NY EVE
CAR BROKE
THINK BACK TO
I USED TO...
WHO WAS
IF I HAD ONLY WAITED...
WHY DID I SAY __?
I SHOULD HAVE...
2004
UGH
@#!%
2003
HA HA
2002
= 1 MONTH
OH WELL...
NO REGRETS!
REGRETS!

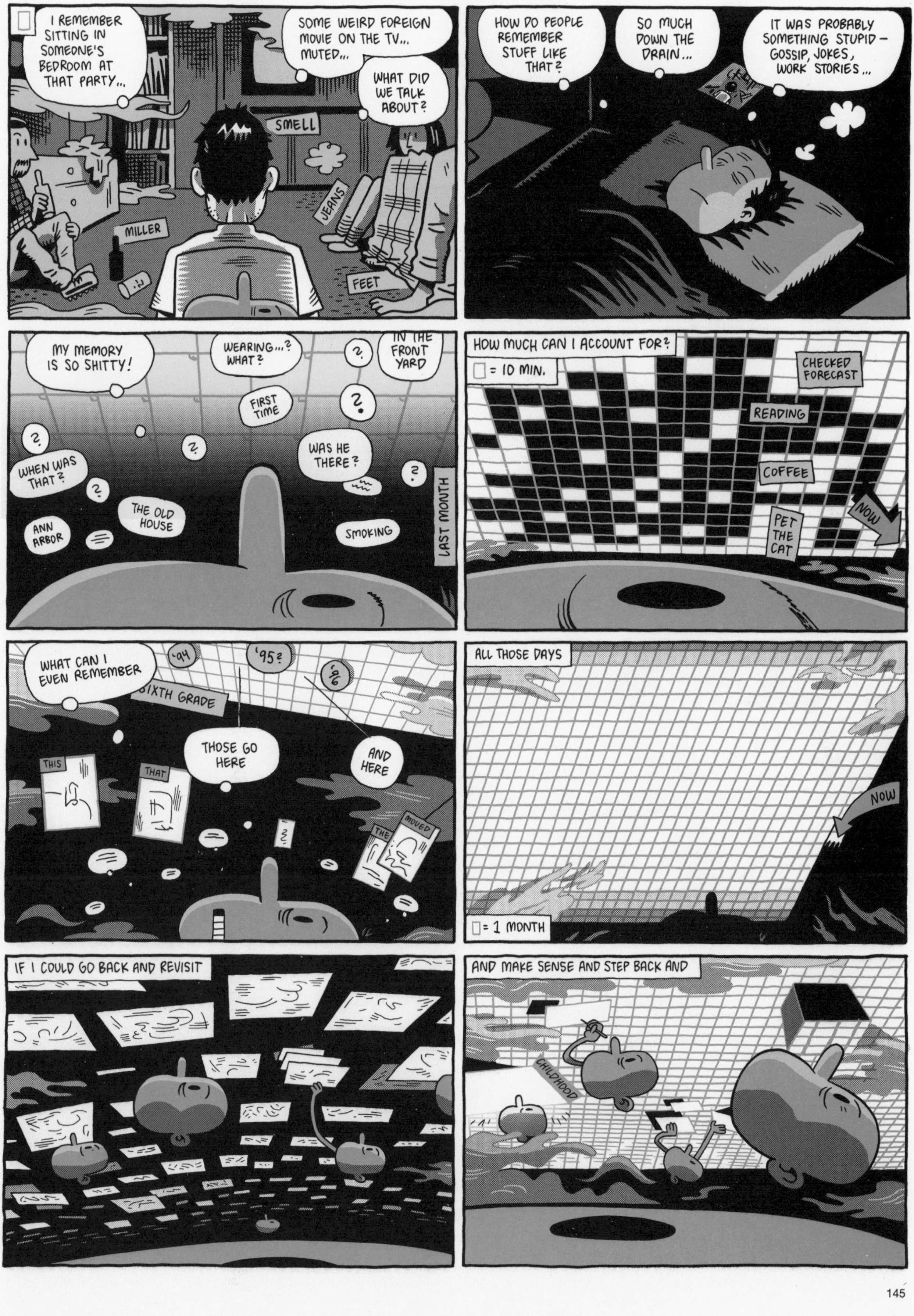

I REMEMBER SITTING IN SOMEONE'S BEDROOM AT THAT PARTY...
SOME WEIRD FOREIGN MOVIE ON THE TV... MUTED...
WHAT DID WE TALK ABOUT?
SMELL
JEANS
MILLER
FEET
HOW DO PEOPLE REMEMBER STUFF LIKE THAT?
SO MUCH DOWN THE DRAIN...
IT WAS PROBABLY SOMETHING STUPID - GOSSIP, JOKES, WORK STORIES...
MY MEMORY IS SO SHITTY!
WEARING...? WHAT?
IN THE FRONT YARD
FIRST TIME
WAS HE THERE?
WHEN WAS THAT?
THE OLD HOUSE
ANN ARBOR
SMOKING
LAST MONTH
HOW MUCH CAN I ACCOUNT FOR?
= 10 MIN.
CHECKED FORECAST
READING
COFFEE
PET THE CAT
NOW
WHAT CAN I EVEN REMEMBER
'94
'95?
'96
SIXTH GRADE
THOSE GO HERE
AND HERE
THIS
THAT
THE
MOVED
ALL THOSE DAYS
NOW
= 1 MONTH
IF I COULD GO BACK AND REVISIT
AND MAKE SENSE AND STEP BACK AND
CHILDHOOD

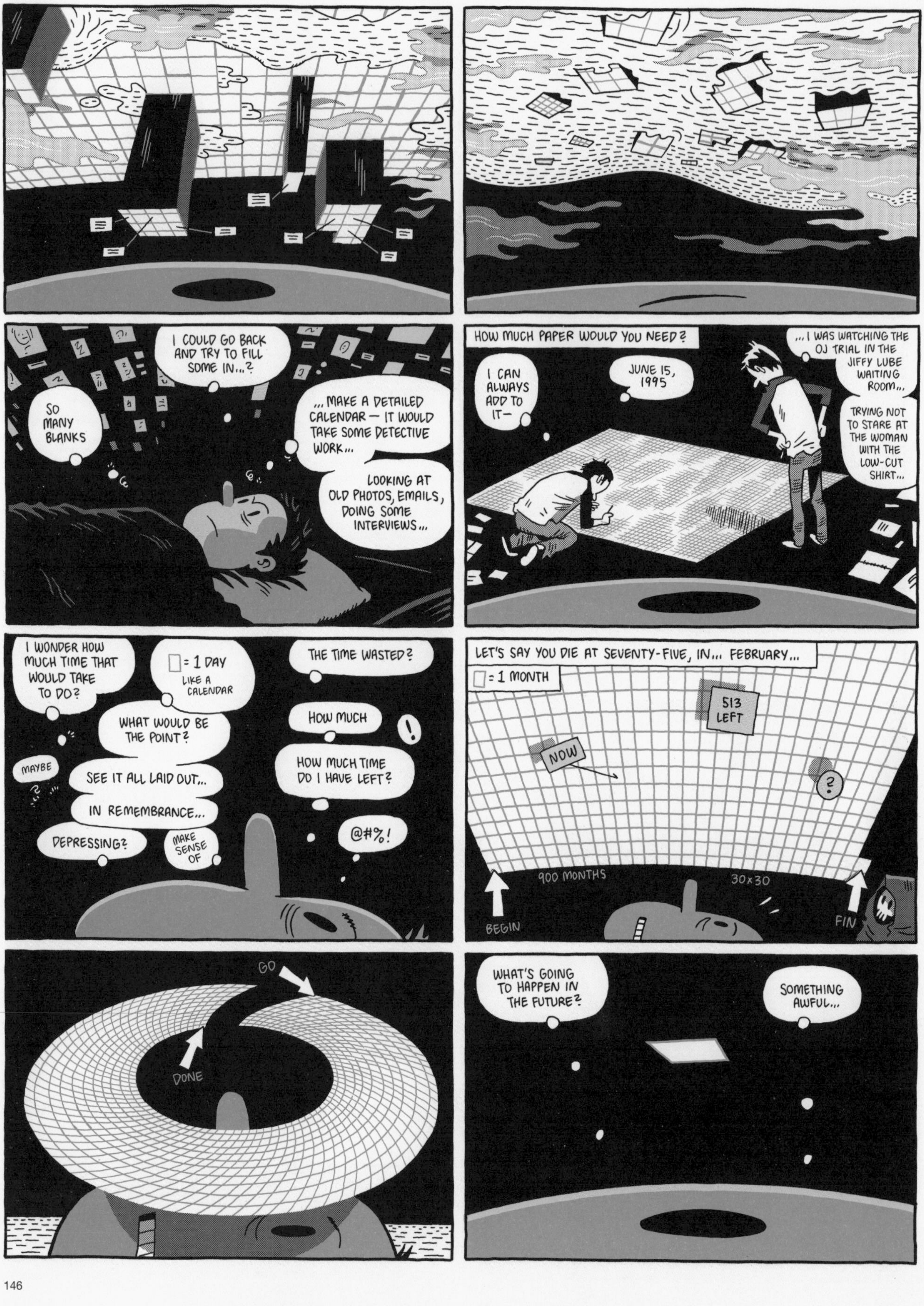
I COULD GO BACK AND TRY TO FILL SOME IN...?
SO MANY BLANKS
...MAKE A DETAILED CALENDAR — IT WOULD TAKE SOME DETECTIVE WORK...
LOOKING AT OLD PHOTOS, EMAILS, DOING SOME INTERVIEWS...
HOW MUCH PAPER WOULD YOU NEED?
I CAN ALWAYS ADD TO IT—
JUNE 15, 1995
...I WAS WATCHING THE OJ TRIAL IN THE JIFFY LUBE WAITING ROOM...
TRYING NOT TO STARE AT THE WOMAN WITH THE LOW-CUT SHIRT...
I WONDER HOW MUCH TIME THAT WOULD TAKE TO DO?
= 1 DAY LIKE A CALENDAR
WHAT WOULD BE THE POINT?
MAYBE
SEE IT ALL LAID OUT...
IN REMEMBRANCE...
DEPRESSING?
MAKE SENSE OF
THE TIME WASTED?
HOW MUCH
!
HOW MUCH TIME DO I HAVE LEFT?
@#%!
LET'S SAY YOU DIE AT SEVENTY-FIVE, IN... FEBRUARY...
= 1 MONTH
513 LEFT
NOW
?
900 MONTHS
30x30
BEGIN
FIN
GO
DONE
WHAT'S GOING TO HAPPEN IN THE FUTURE?
SOMETHING AWFUL...

□ = 1 YEAR   (32 YEARS)

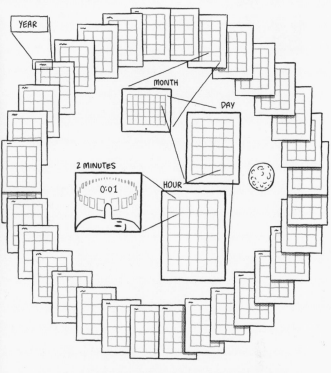

YEAR

MONTH

DAY

HOUR

2 MINUTES

0:01

PICK A BOX AND ZOOM IN AND ENTER IT LIKE A GHOST...

APRIL 17, 199—

I WAS A DIFFERENT PERSON BACK THEN

...REPLAY IT FROM DIFFERENT ANGLES...

ADD TAG   LIKE

I WISH I COULD HAVE A 3D REPLICA OF EVERYTHING SO FAR

COULD YOU DO THAT? WITH COMPUTERS?

PROBABLY SOMEDAY...

LASERS TO MEASURE THE...

YOU COULDN'T RECORD DREAMING, THOUGH

DREAM JOURNAL

OR THOUGHTS

AND THEN THE INEVITABLE DOUBLING AS THE SYSTEM HAS TO ACCOUNT FOR TIME SPENT INSIDE ITSELF...

HAUNTING THE PAST

HAUNTING WENDY'S

TERRIFYING

THERE'S A LOT OF OVERLAP, RIGHT?

BUT RIGHT NOW SHE'S OFF THE GRID

ZZZZ

WAKE HER UP?

AND THEN THERE'S ALL THE INTERSECTIONS WITH...

ALL THE OTHER PEOPLE IN YOUR...

IN THE...

...

I'M NOT GOING TO TRY TO PICTURE THAT...

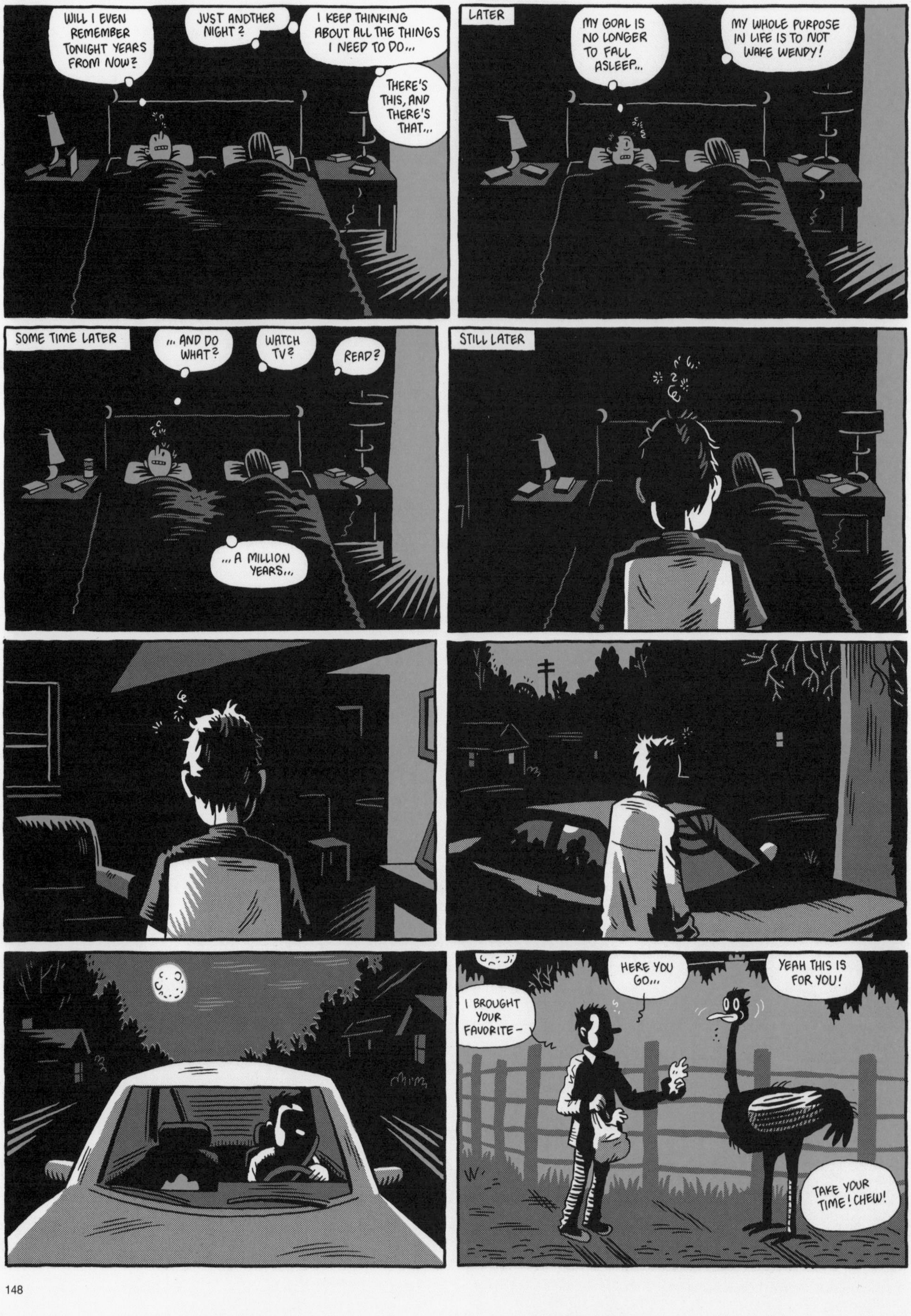
WILL I EVEN REMEMBER TONIGHT YEARS FROM NOW?
JUST ANOTHER NIGHT?
I KEEP THINKING ABOUT ALL THE THINGS I NEED TO DO...
THERE'S THIS, AND THERE'S THAT...
LATER
MY GOAL IS NO LONGER TO FALL ASLEEP...
MY WHOLE PURPOSE IN LIFE IS TO NOT WAKE WENDY!
SOME TIME LATER
... AND DO WHAT?
WATCH TV?
READ?
... A MILLION YEARS...
STILL LATER
I BROUGHT YOUR FAVORITE-
HERE YOU GO...
YEAH THIS IS FOR YOU!
TAKE YOUR TIME! CHEW!

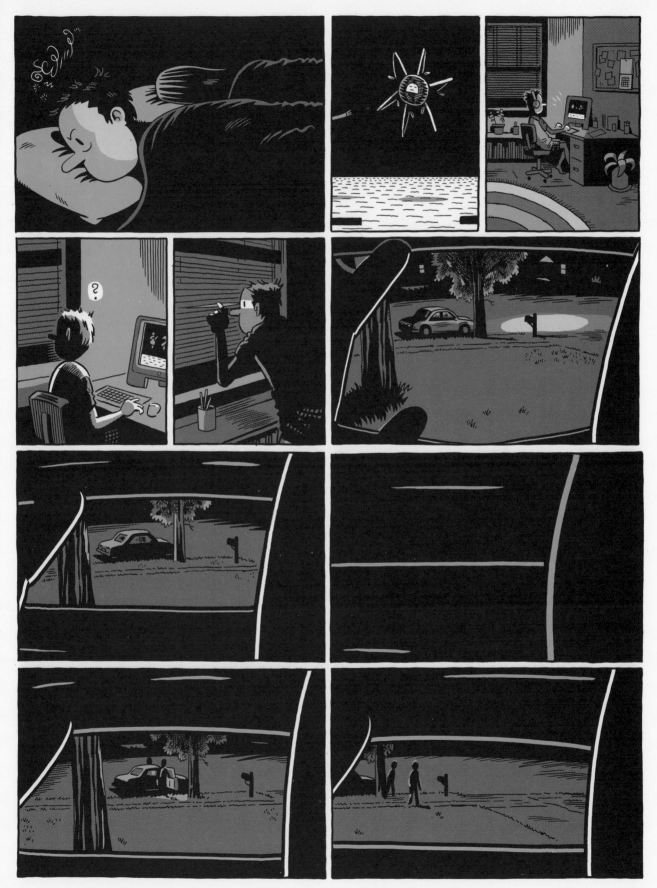

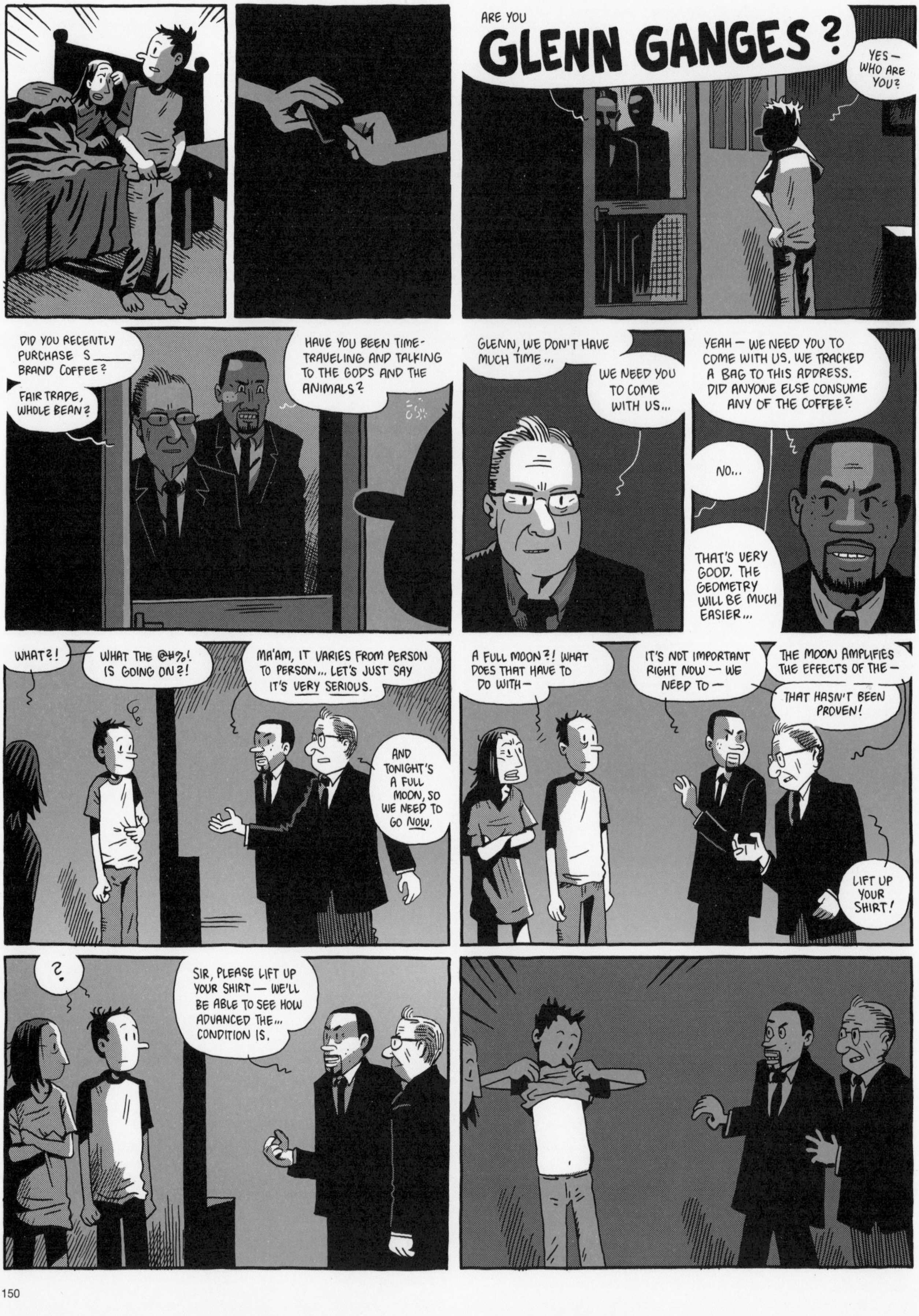
ARE YOU GLENN GANGES?
YES— WHO ARE YOU?
DID YOU RECENTLY PURCHASE S_____ BRAND COFFEE?
FAIR TRADE, WHOLE BEAN?
HAVE YOU BEEN TIME-TRAVELING AND TALKING TO THE GODS AND THE ANIMALS?
GLENN, WE DON'T HAVE MUCH TIME...
WE NEED YOU TO COME WITH US...
YEAH — WE NEED YOU TO COME WITH US. WE TRACKED A BAG TO THIS ADDRESS. DID ANYONE ELSE CONSUME ANY OF THE COFFEE?
NO...
THAT'S VERY GOOD. THE GEOMETRY WILL BE MUCH EASIER...
WHAT?!
WHAT THE @#%! IS GOING ON?!
MA'AM, IT VARIES FROM PERSON TO PERSON... LET'S JUST SAY IT'S VERY SERIOUS.
AND TONIGHT'S A FULL MOON, SO WE NEED TO GO NOW.
A FULL MOON?! WHAT DOES THAT HAVE TO DO WITH—
IT'S NOT IMPORTANT RIGHT NOW — WE NEED TO—
THE MOON AMPLIFIES THE EFFECTS OF THE—
THAT HASN'T BEEN PROVEN!
LIFT UP YOUR SHIRT!
?
SIR, PLEASE LIFT UP YOUR SHIRT — WE'LL BE ABLE TO SEE HOW ADVANCED THE... CONDITION IS.

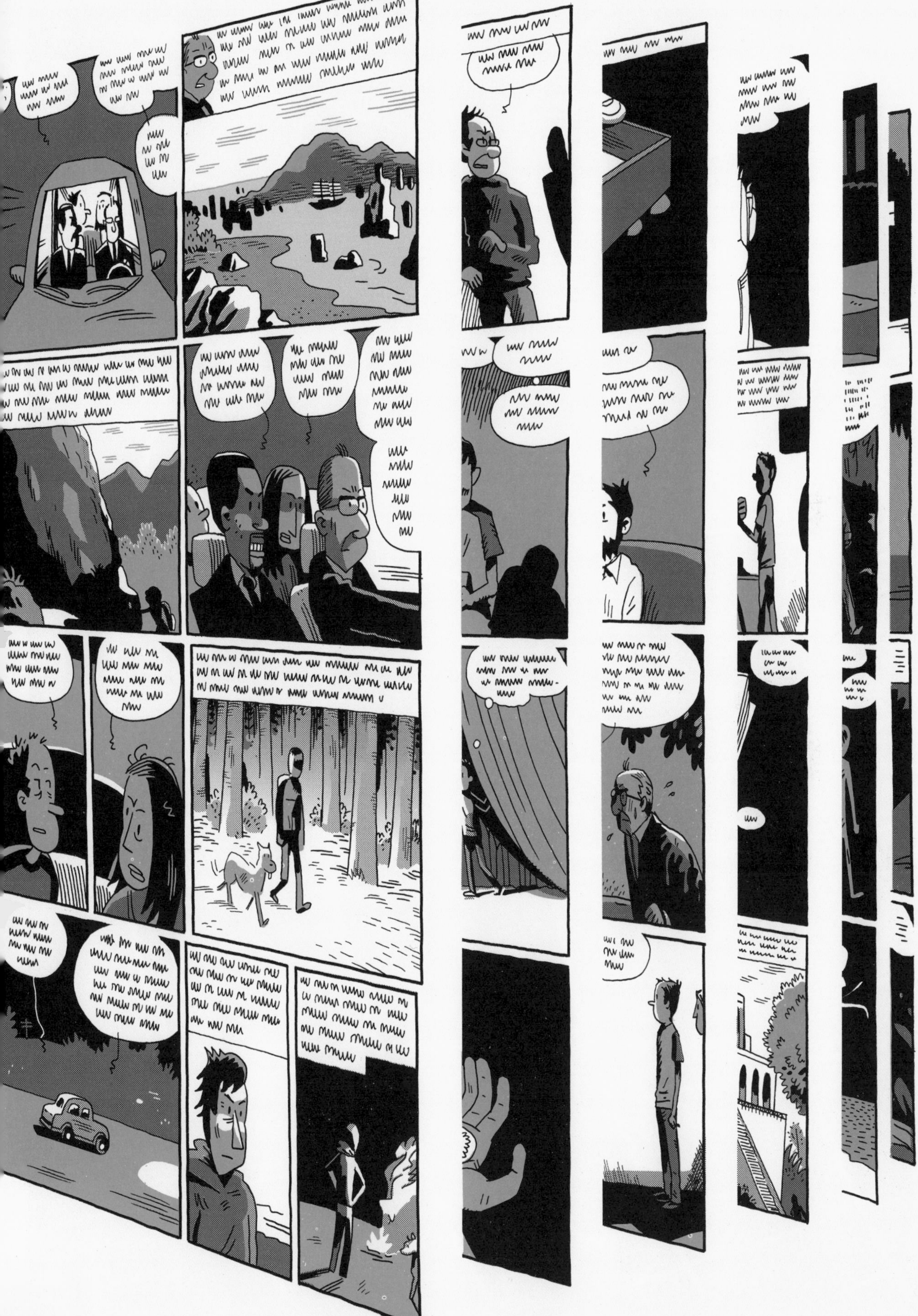

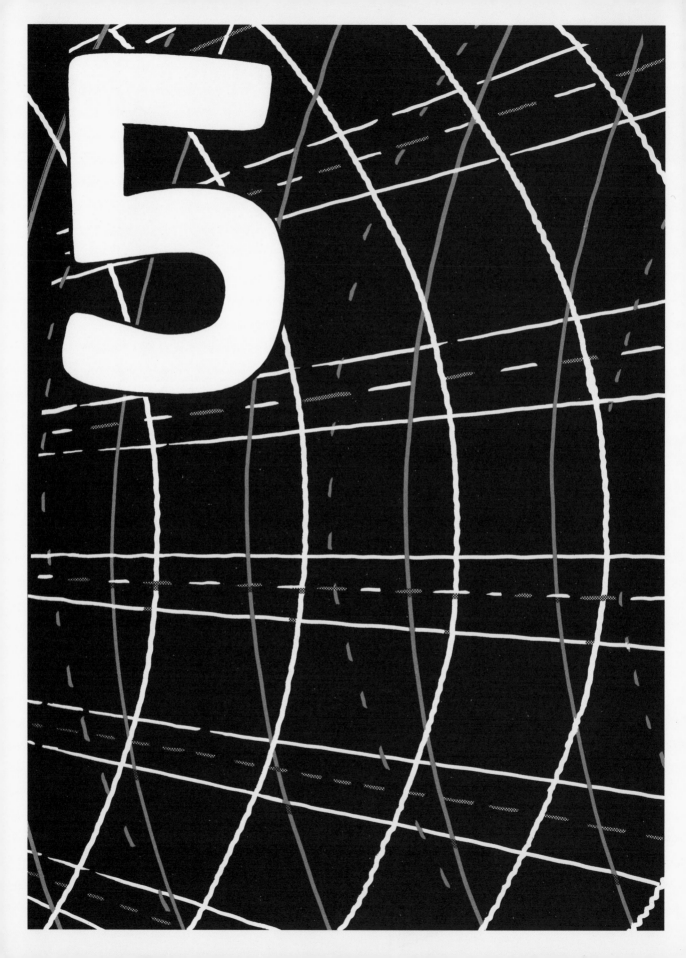

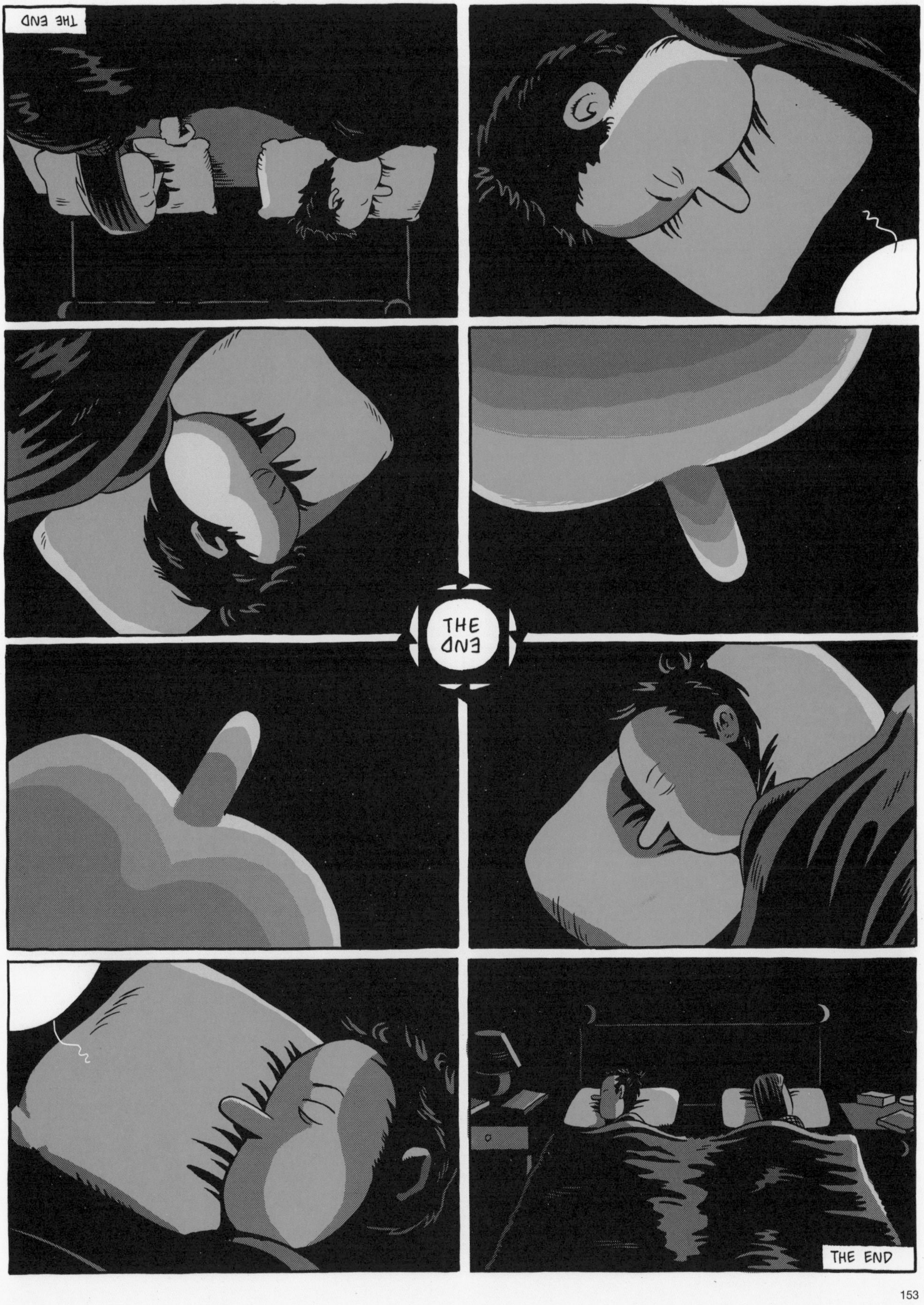
THE END
THE END
THE END

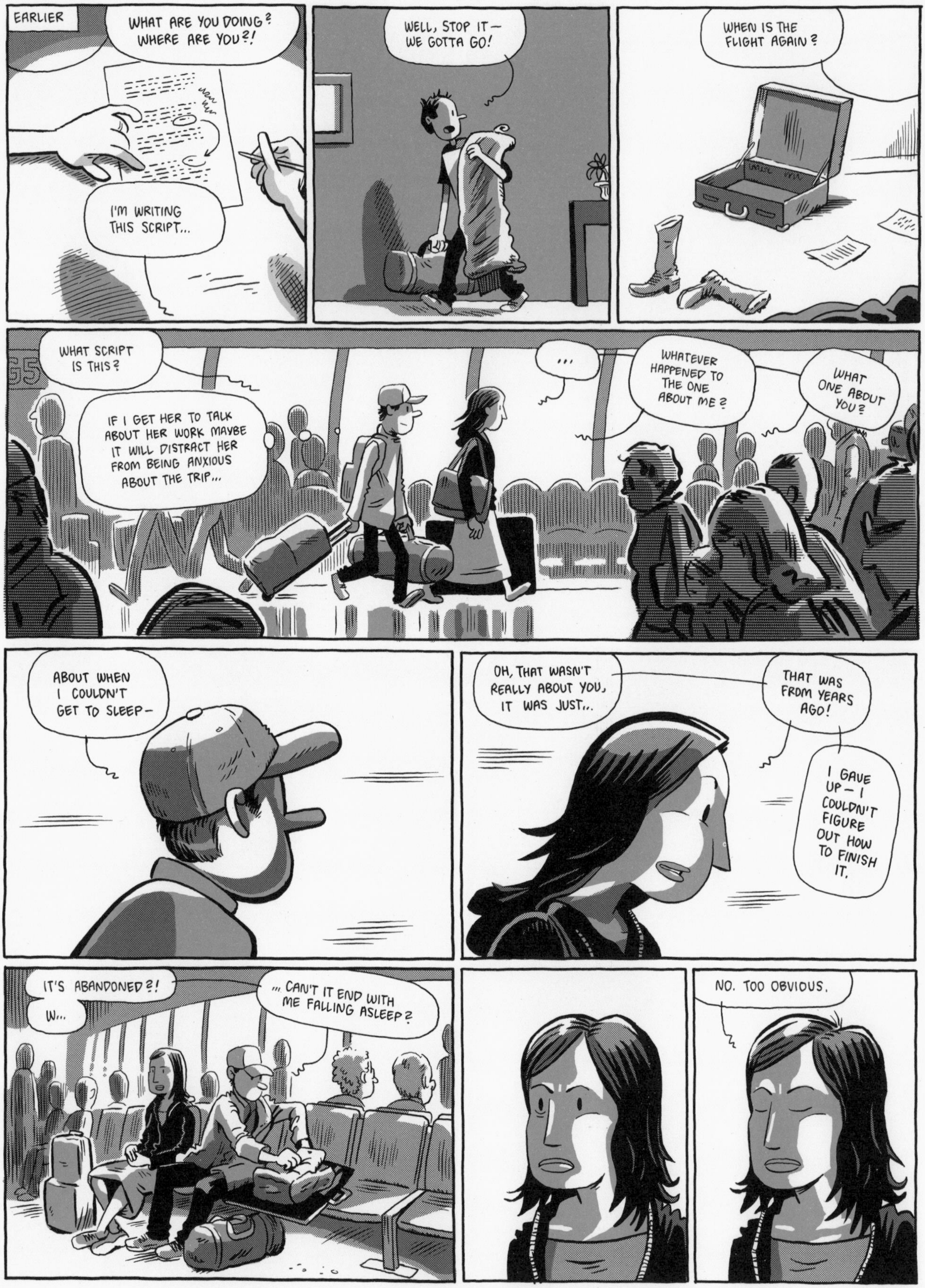
EARLIER
WHAT ARE YOU DOING? WHERE ARE YOU?!
I'M WRITING THIS SCRIPT...
WELL, STOP IT— WE GOTTA GO!
WHEN IS THE FLIGHT AGAIN?
WHAT SCRIPT IS THIS?
IF I GET HER TO TALK ABOUT HER WORK MAYBE IT WILL DISTRACT HER FROM BEING ANXIOUS ABOUT THE TRIP...
...
WHATEVER HAPPENED TO THE ONE ABOUT ME?
WHAT ONE ABOUT YOU?
ABOUT WHEN I COULDN'T GET TO SLEEP—
OH, THAT WASN'T REALLY ABOUT YOU, IT WAS JUST...
THAT WAS FROM YEARS AGO!
I GAVE UP— I COULDN'T FIGURE OUT HOW TO FINISH IT.
IT'S ABANDONED?!
W...
... CAN'T IT END WITH ME FALLING ASLEEP?
NO. TOO OBVIOUS.

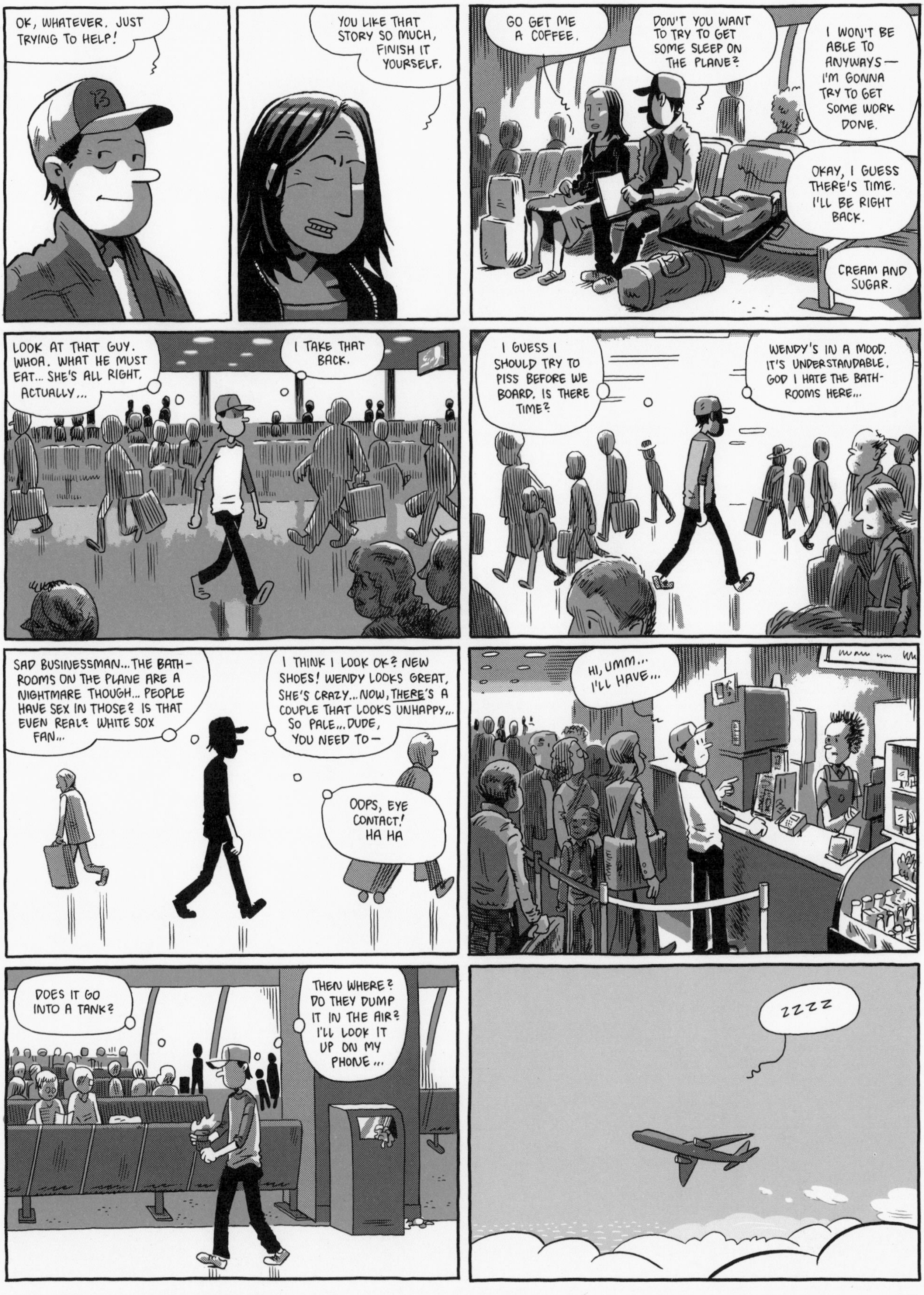

OK, WHATEVER. JUST TRYING TO HELP!
YOU LIKE THAT STORY SO MUCH, FINISH IT YOURSELF.
GO GET ME A COFFEE.
DON'T YOU WANT TO TRY TO GET SOME SLEEP ON THE PLANE?
I WON'T BE ABLE TO ANYWAYS— I'M GONNA TRY TO GET SOME WORK DONE.
OKAY, I GUESS THERE'S TIME. I'LL BE RIGHT BACK.
CREAM AND SUGAR.
LOOK AT THAT GUY. WHOA. WHAT HE MUST EAT... SHE'S ALL RIGHT, ACTUALLY...
I TAKE THAT BACK.
I GUESS I SHOULD TRY TO PISS BEFORE WE BOARD. IS THERE TIME?
WENDY'S IN A MOOD. IT'S UNDERSTANDABLE. GOD I HATE THE BATHROOMS HERE...
SAD BUSINESSMAN... THE BATHROOMS ON THE PLANE ARE A NIGHTMARE THOUGH... PEOPLE HAVE SEX IN THOSE? IS THAT EVEN REAL? WHITE SOX FAN...
I THINK I LOOK OK? NEW SHOES! WENDY LOOKS GREAT, SHE'S CRAZY... NOW, THERE'S A COUPLE THAT LOOKS UNHAPPY... SO PALE... DUDE, YOU NEED TO—
OOPS, EYE CONTACT! HA HA
HI, UMM... I'LL HAVE...
DOES IT GO INTO A TANK?
THEN WHERE? DO THEY DUMP IT IN THE AIR? I'LL LOOK IT UP ON MY PHONE...
ZZZZ

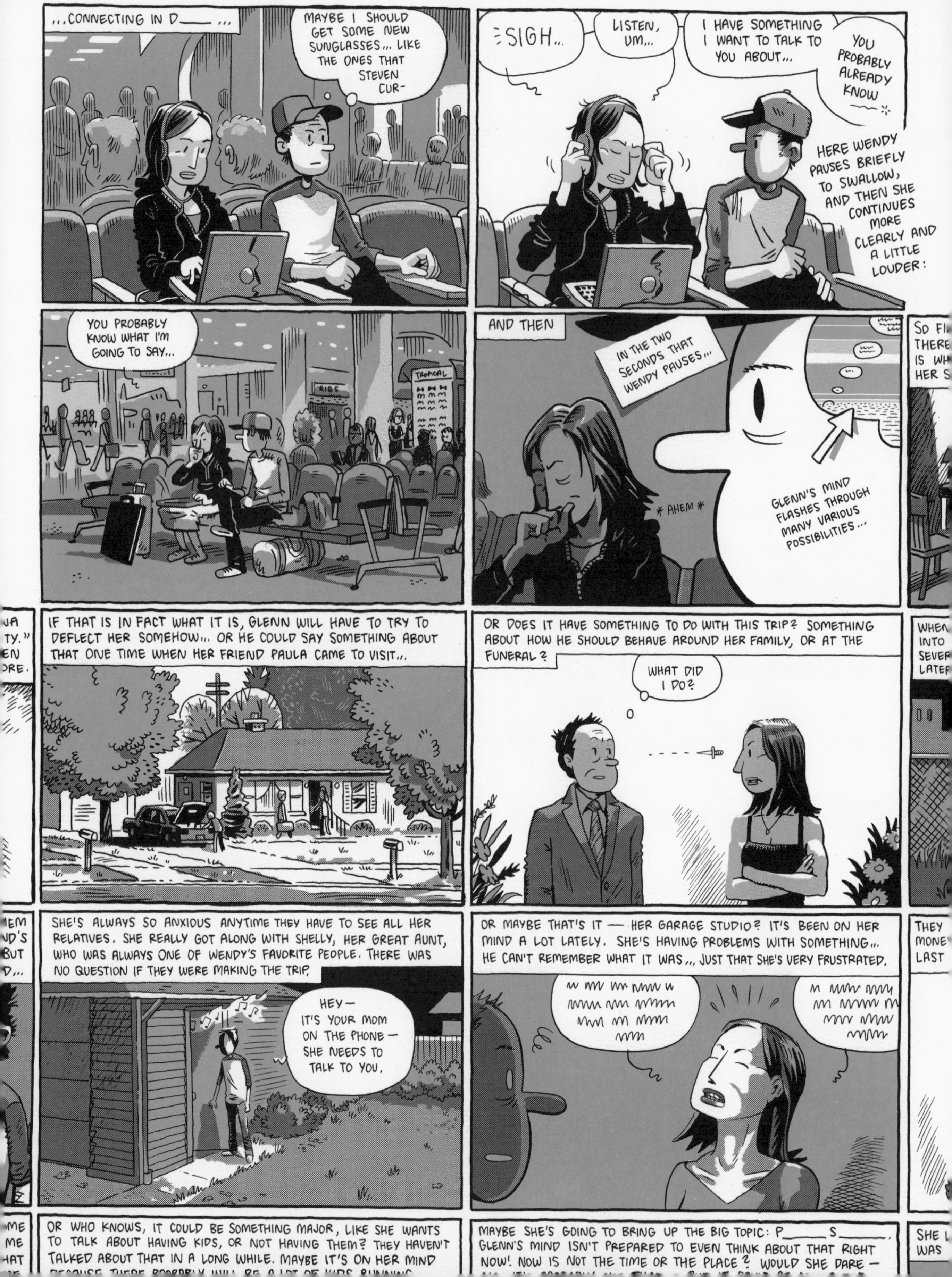
...CONNECTING IN D____ ...
MAYBE I SHOULD GET SOME NEW SUNGLASSES... LIKE THE ONES THAT STEVEN CUR-
SIGH..
LISTEN, UM...
I HAVE SOMETHING I WANT TO TALK TO YOU ABOUT...
YOU PROBABLY ALREADY KNOW
HERE WENDY PAUSES BRIEFLY TO SWALLOW, AND THEN SHE CONTINUES MORE CLEARLY AND A LITTLE LOUDER:
YOU PROBABLY KNOW WHAT I'M GOING TO SAY...
RIBS
TROPICAL
AND THEN
IN THE TWO SECONDS THAT WENDY PAUSES...
* AHEM *
GLENN'S MIND FLASHES THROUGH MANY VARIOUS POSSIBILITIES...
IF THAT IS IN FACT WHAT IT IS, GLENN WILL HAVE TO TRY TO DEFLECT HER SOMEHOW... OR HE COULD SAY SOMETHING ABOUT THAT ONE TIME WHEN HER FRIEND PAULA CAME TO VISIT...
OR DOES IT HAVE SOMETHING TO DO WITH THIS TRIP? SOMETHING ABOUT HOW HE SHOULD BEHAVE AROUND HER FAMILY, OR AT THE FUNERAL?
WHAT DID I DO?
SHE'S ALWAYS SO ANXIOUS ANYTIME THEY HAVE TO SEE ALL HER RELATIVES. SHE REALLY GOT ALONG WITH SHELLY, HER GREAT AUNT, WHO WAS ALWAYS ONE OF WENDY'S FAVORITE PEOPLE. THERE WAS NO QUESTION IF THEY WERE MAKING THE TRIP.
HEY— IT'S YOUR MOM ON THE PHONE— SHE NEEDS TO TALK TO YOU.
OR MAYBE THAT'S IT — HER GARAGE STUDIO? IT'S BEEN ON HER MIND A LOT LATELY. SHE'S HAVING PROBLEMS WITH SOMETHING... HE CAN'T REMEMBER WHAT IT WAS... JUST THAT SHE'S VERY FRUSTRATED.
OR WHO KNOWS, IT COULD BE SOMETHING MAJOR, LIKE SHE WANTS TO TALK ABOUT HAVING KIDS, OR NOT HAVING THEM? THEY HAVEN'T TALKED ABOUT THAT IN A LONG WHILE. MAYBE IT'S ON HER MIND
MAYBE SHE'S GOING TO BRING UP THE BIG TOPIC: P____ S____. GLENN'S MIND ISN'T PREPARED TO EVEN THINK ABOUT THAT RIGHT NOW! NOW IS NOT THE TIME OR THE PLACE? WOULD SHE DARE—

OK, CALM DOWN, IT'S PROBABLY NOT THAT... IT'S PROBABLY, UH...

WHAT DOES THAT TONE OF VOICE *USUALLY* MEAN?

GLENN, YOU *SAID* YOU WERE GOING TO DO X, BUT NOW IT'S ___ DAYS/WEEKS/MONTHS LATER AND...

YEAH... @#!%! REMEMBER WHEN I SAID I'D HELP HER WITH THOSE COMICS PAGES? THAT DIDN'T GO VERY WELL...

 VS.

GLENN   WENDY

F

SUMMER, 200_ :

WHAT ARE YOU DOING ?!

I NEED YOU TO WORK ON THESE PAGES!

I PROMISE I'LL GET TO THEM TOMORROW AT WORK. IT SHOULD BE A QUIET DAY...

SUMMER, 199 _

[FIGHTING ABOUT SOMETHING STUPID]

WHAT IS YOUR DEAL ?!! I'M BARELY IN THE DOOR AND YOU'RE ON MY CASE!

YOU WERE UP HALF THE NIGHT LAST NIGHT — YOU'RE JUST TIRED!

OH SURE, ACT LIKE I'M CRAZY! YOU KNOW I'M RIGHT!

OH, AND! THE LIFE INSURANCE THING CAME IN THE MAIL!

YOU KNOW YOU SAID YOU WOULD TAKE CARE OF IT LIKE TWO MONTHS AGO!

I'LL CALL PAUL TOMORROW!

LATER

@#!%!!

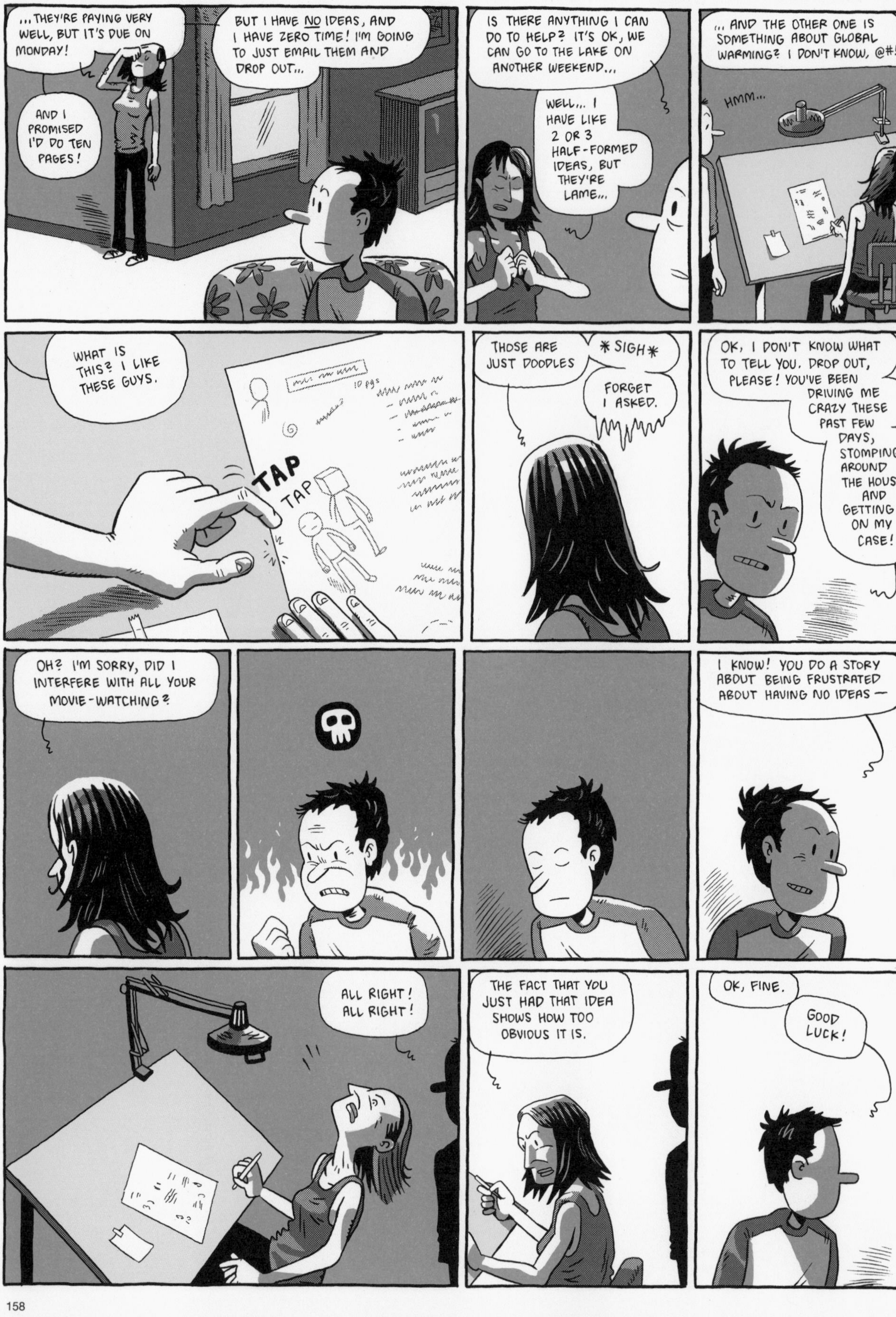

...THEY'RE PAYING VERY WELL, BUT IT'S DUE ON MONDAY!
AND I PROMISED I'D DO TEN PAGES!
BUT I HAVE NO IDEAS, AND I HAVE ZERO TIME! I'M GOING TO JUST EMAIL THEM AND DROP OUT...
IS THERE ANYTHING I CAN DO TO HELP? IT'S OK, WE CAN GO TO THE LAKE ON ANOTHER WEEKEND...
WELL... I HAVE LIKE 2 OR 3 HALF-FORMED IDEAS, BUT THEY'RE LAME...
HMM...
...AND THE OTHER ONE IS SOMETHING ABOUT GLOBAL WARMING? I DON'T KNOW, @#!%!
WHAT IS THIS? I LIKE THESE GUYS.
10 pgs
TAP
TAP
THOSE ARE JUST DOODLES
SIGH
FORGET I ASKED.
OK, I DON'T KNOW WHAT TO TELL YOU. DROP OUT, PLEASE! YOU'VE BEEN DRIVING ME CRAZY THESE PAST FEW DAYS, STOMPING AROUND THE HOUSE AND GETTING ON MY CASE!
OH? I'M SORRY, DID I INTERFERE WITH ALL YOUR MOVIE-WATCHING?
I KNOW! YOU DO A STORY ABOUT BEING FRUSTRATED ABOUT HAVING NO IDEAS —
ALL RIGHT! ALL RIGHT!
THE FACT THAT YOU JUST HAD THAT IDEA SHOWS HOW TOO OBVIOUS IT IS.
OK, FINE.
GOOD LUCK!

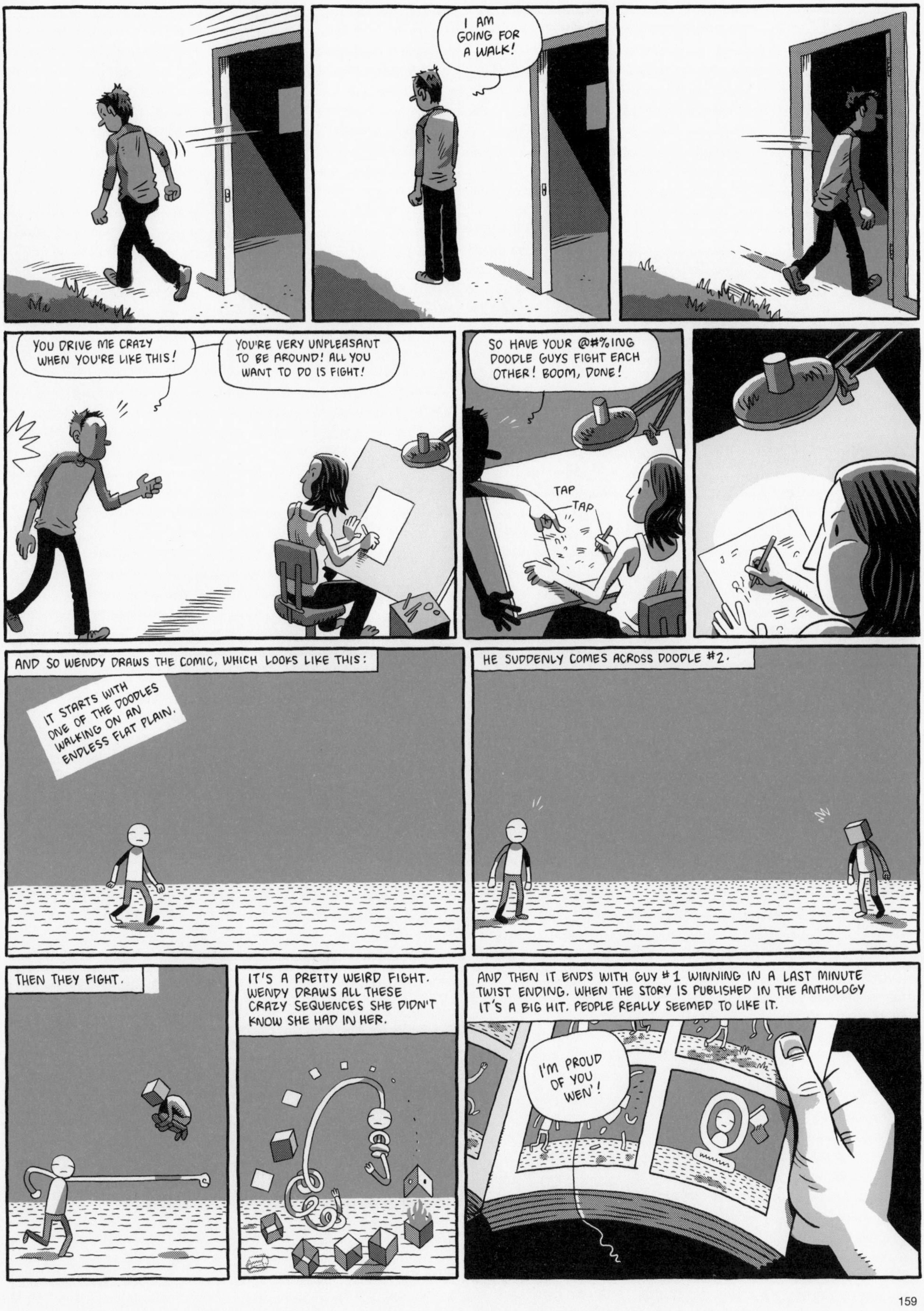
I AM GOING FOR A WALK!
YOU DRIVE ME CRAZY WHEN YOU'RE LIKE THIS!
YOU'RE VERY UNPLEASANT TO BE AROUND! ALL YOU WANT TO DO IS FIGHT!
SO HAVE YOUR @#%ING DOODLE GUYS FIGHT EACH OTHER! BOOM, DONE!
TAP
TAP
AND SO WENDY DRAWS THE COMIC, WHICH LOOKS LIKE THIS:
IT STARTS WITH ONE OF THE DOODLES WALKING ON AN ENDLESS FLAT PLAIN.
HE SUDDENLY COMES ACROSS DOODLE #2.
THEN THEY FIGHT.
IT'S A PRETTY WEIRD FIGHT. WENDY DRAWS ALL THESE CRAZY SEQUENCES SHE DIDN'T KNOW SHE HAD IN HER.
AND THEN IT ENDS WITH GUY #1 WINNING IN A LAST MINUTE TWIST ENDING. WHEN THE STORY IS PUBLISHED IN THE ANTHOLOGY IT'S A BIG HIT. PEOPLE REALLY SEEMED TO LIKE IT.
I'M PROUD OF YOU WEN'!

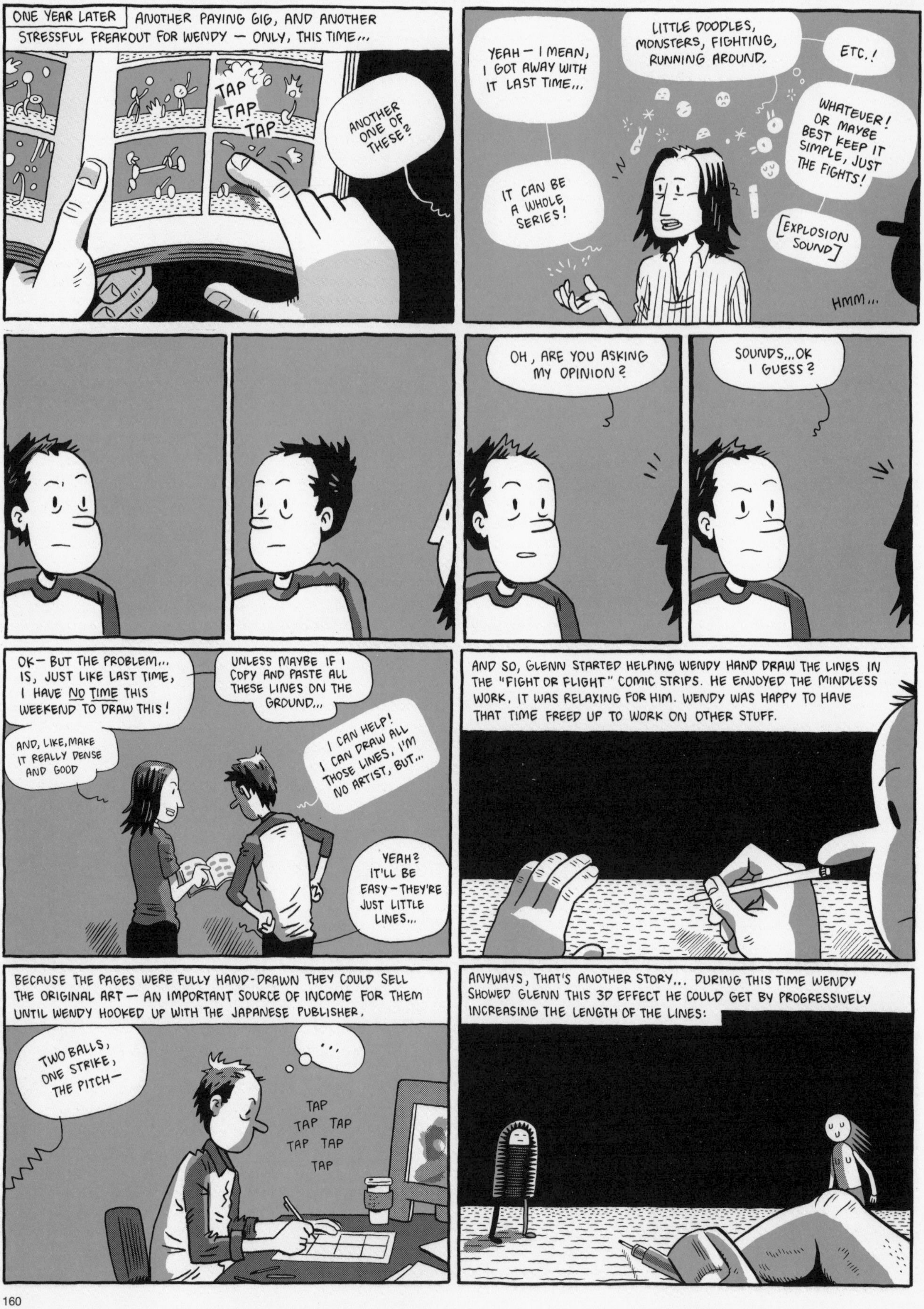
ONE YEAR LATER
ANOTHER PAYING GIG, AND ANOTHER STRESSFUL FREAKOUT FOR WENDY — ONLY, THIS TIME...
TAP TAP TAP
ANOTHER ONE OF THESE?
YEAH — I MEAN, I GOT AWAY WITH IT LAST TIME...
IT CAN BE A WHOLE SERIES!
LITTLE DOODLES, MONSTERS, FIGHTING, RUNNING AROUND,
ETC.!
WHATEVER! OR MAYBE BEST KEEP IT SIMPLE, JUST THE FIGHTS!
[EXPLOSION SOUND]
HMM...
OH, ARE YOU ASKING MY OPINION?
SOUNDS... OK I GUESS?
OK— BUT THE PROBLEM... IS, JUST LIKE LAST TIME, I HAVE NO TIME THIS WEEKEND TO DRAW THIS!
UNLESS MAYBE IF I COPY AND PASTE ALL THESE LINES ON THE GROUND...
AND, LIKE, MAKE IT REALLY DENSE AND GOOD
I CAN HELP! I CAN DRAW ALL THOSE LINES. I'M NO ARTIST, BUT...
YEAH? IT'LL BE EASY — THEY'RE JUST LITTLE LINES...
AND SO, GLENN STARTED HELPING WENDY HAND DRAW THE LINES IN THE "FIGHT OR FLIGHT" COMIC STRIPS. HE ENJOYED THE MINDLESS WORK, IT WAS RELAXING FOR HIM. WENDY WAS HAPPY TO HAVE THAT TIME FREED UP TO WORK ON OTHER STUFF.
BECAUSE THE PAGES WERE FULLY HAND-DRAWN THEY COULD SELL THE ORIGINAL ART — AN IMPORTANT SOURCE OF INCOME FOR THEM UNTIL WENDY HOOKED UP WITH THE JAPANESE PUBLISHER.
TWO BALLS, ONE STRIKE, THE PITCH—
...
TAP TAP TAP TAP TAP TAP
ANYWAYS, THAT'S ANOTHER STORY... DURING THIS TIME WENDY SHOWED GLENN THIS 3D EFFECT HE COULD GET BY PROGRESSIVELY INCREASING THE LENGTH OF THE LINES:

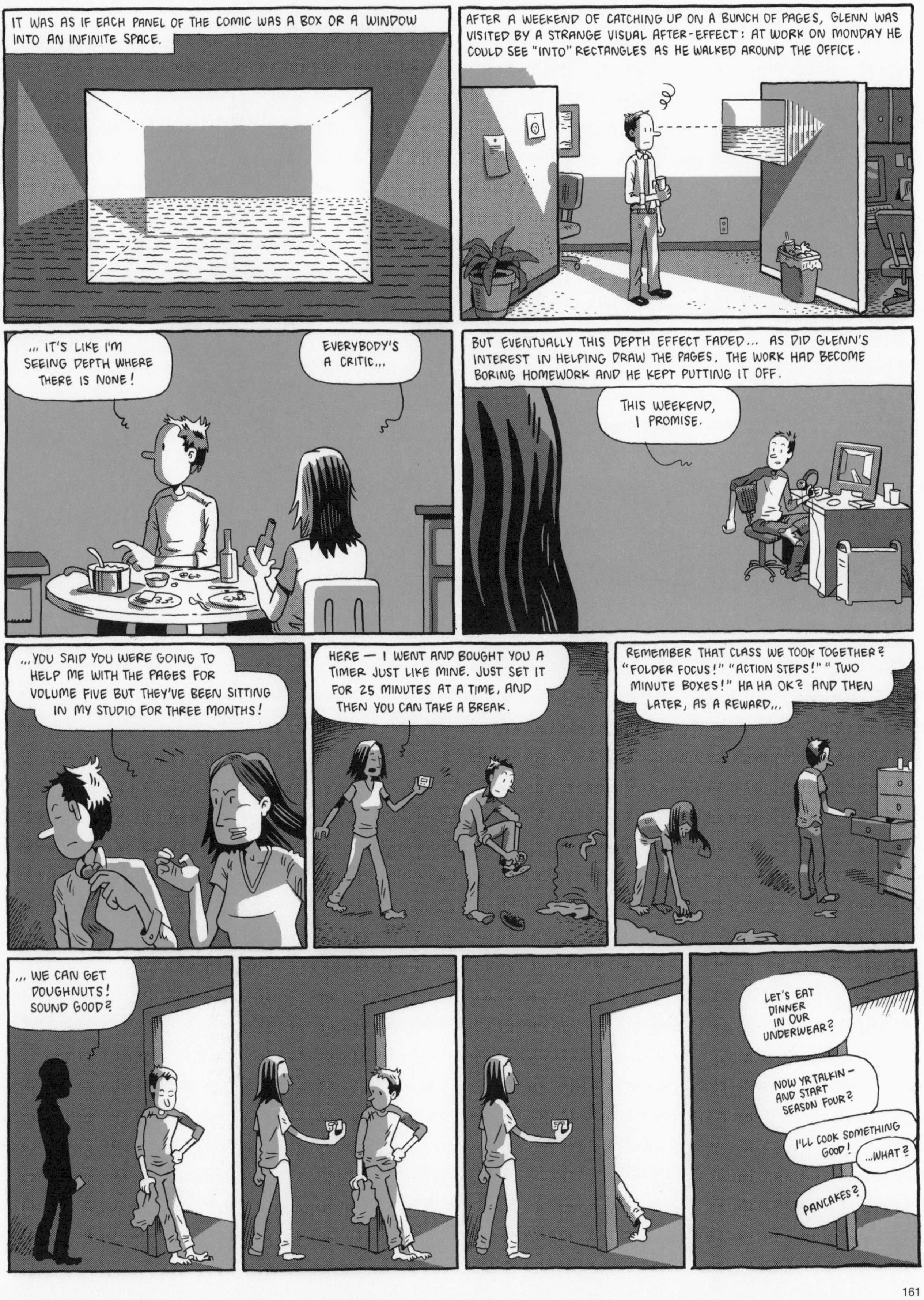
IT WAS AS IF EACH PANEL OF THE COMIC WAS A BOX OR A WINDOW INTO AN INFINITE SPACE.
AFTER A WEEKEND OF CATCHING UP ON A BUNCH OF PAGES, GLENN WAS VISITED BY A STRANGE VISUAL AFTER-EFFECT: AT WORK ON MONDAY HE COULD SEE "INTO" RECTANGLES AS HE WALKED AROUND THE OFFICE.
... IT'S LIKE I'M SEEING DEPTH WHERE THERE IS NONE!
EVERYBODY'S A CRITIC...
BUT EVENTUALLY THIS DEPTH EFFECT FADED... AS DID GLENN'S INTEREST IN HELPING DRAW THE PAGES. THE WORK HAD BECOME BORING HOMEWORK AND HE KEPT PUTTING IT OFF.
THIS WEEKEND, I PROMISE.
...YOU SAID YOU WERE GOING TO HELP ME WITH THE PAGES FOR VOLUME FIVE BUT THEY'VE BEEN SITTING IN MY STUDIO FOR THREE MONTHS!
HERE — I WENT AND BOUGHT YOU A TIMER JUST LIKE MINE. JUST SET IT FOR 25 MINUTES AT A TIME, AND THEN YOU CAN TAKE A BREAK.
REMEMBER THAT CLASS WE TOOK TOGETHER? "FOLDER FOCUS!" "ACTION STEPS!" "TWO MINUTE BOXES!" HA HA OK? AND THEN LATER, AS A REWARD...
... WE CAN GET DOUGHNUTS! SOUND GOOD?
LET'S EAT DINNER IN OUR UNDERWEAR?
NOW YR TALKIN — AND START SEASON FOUR?
I'LL COOK SOMETHING GOOD!
...WHAT?
PANCAKES?

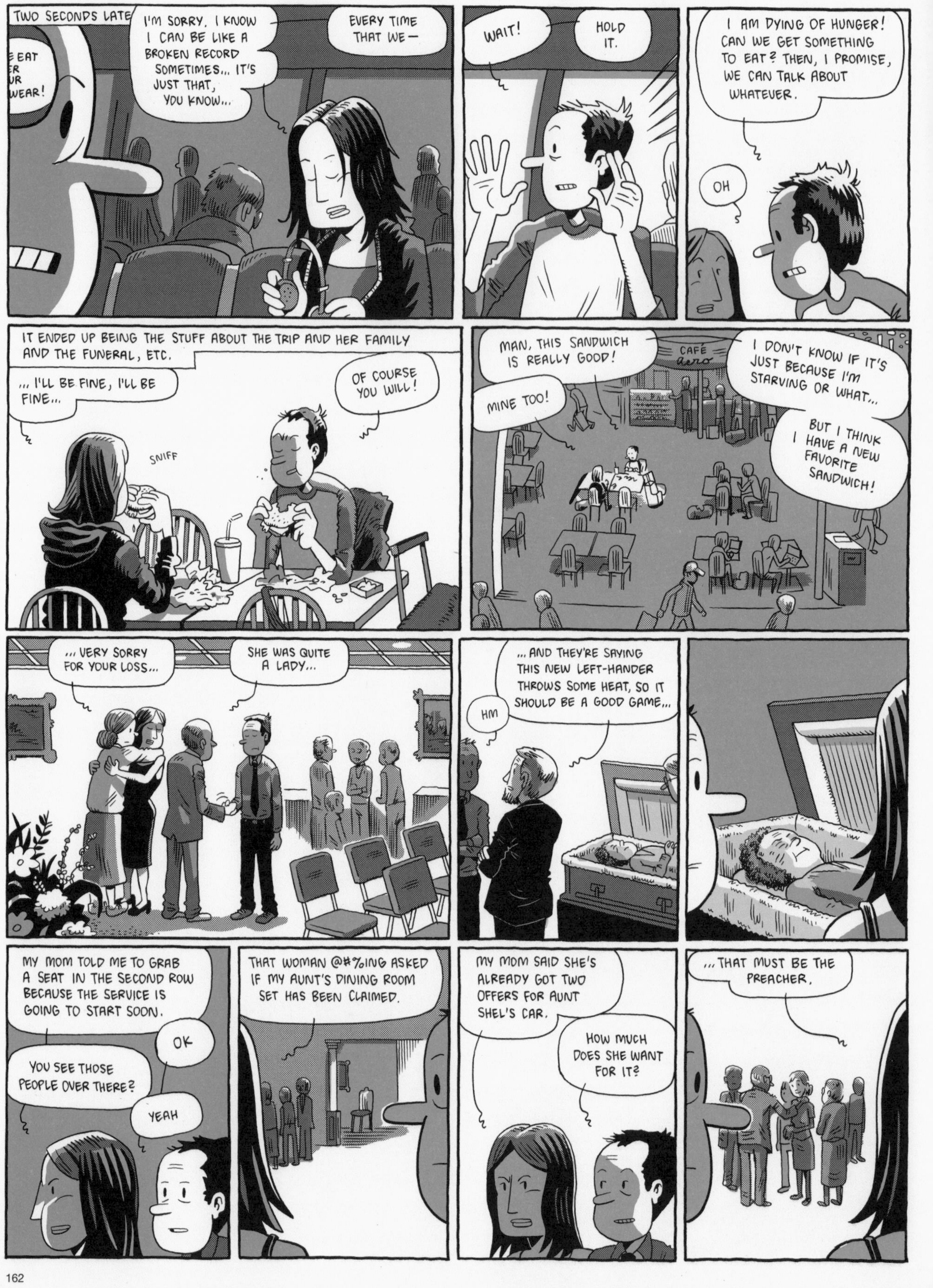
TWO SECONDS LATER
I'M SORRY. I KNOW I CAN BE LIKE A BROKEN RECORD SOMETIMES... IT'S JUST THAT, YOU KNOW...
EVERY TIME THAT WE—
WAIT!
HOLD IT.
I AM DYING OF HUNGER! CAN WE GET SOMETHING TO EAT? THEN, I PROMISE, WE CAN TALK ABOUT WHATEVER.
OH
IT ENDED UP BEING THE STUFF ABOUT THE TRIP AND HER FAMILY AND THE FUNERAL, ETC.
...I'LL BE FINE, I'LL BE FINE...
OF COURSE YOU WILL!
SNIFF
MAN, THIS SANDWICH IS REALLY GOOD!
MINE TOO!
CAFÉ aero
I DON'T KNOW IF IT'S JUST BECAUSE I'M STARVING OR WHAT...
BUT I THINK I HAVE A NEW FAVORITE SANDWICH!
...VERY SORRY FOR YOUR LOSS...
SHE WAS QUITE A LADY...
...AND THEY'RE SAYING THIS NEW LEFT-HANDER THROWS SOME HEAT, SO IT SHOULD BE A GOOD GAME...
HM
MY MOM TOLD ME TO GRAB A SEAT IN THE SECOND ROW BECAUSE THE SERVICE IS GOING TO START SOON.
OK
YOU SEE THOSE PEOPLE OVER THERE?
YEAH
THAT WOMAN @#%ING ASKED IF MY AUNT'S DINING ROOM SET HAS BEEN CLAIMED.
MY MOM SAID SHE'S ALREADY GOT TWO OFFERS FOR AUNT SHEL'S CAR.
HOW MUCH DOES SHE WANT FOR IT?
...THAT MUST BE THE PREACHER.

THE GUY THAT AUNT SHELLY WANTED COULDN'T MAKE IT... IT'S A SHAME BECAUSE SHE REALLY LIKED HIM... HE WAS HER PASTOR FOR MANY YEARS... BAPTIST... BUT HE'S IN FLORIDA OR SOMETHING... SO THEY SENT THIS GUY...

(MY MOM SAID HE SEEMED NICE ON THE PHONE...)

... TO REMEMBER AND TO CELEBRATE THE LIFE OF A BELOVED SISTER, AUNT, AND FRIEND...

SHALL WE BOW OUR HEADS AND PRAY TOGETHER TO PREPARE OUR HEARTS TO HEAR THE WORD OF THE LORD.

OUR GRACIOUS GOD WE ⌇⌇ ⌇⌇⌇⌇ ⌇⌇⌇ ⌇ ⌇⌇⌇ ⌇⌇⌇ ⌇⌇⌇ OH LORD WE ⌇ ⌇⌇⌇ ⌇⌇⌇ ⌇⌇ IN YOUR BOSOM ⌇⌇ ⌇⌇⌇ ⌇⌇⌇ WE KNOW THAT ⌇⌇⌇ ⌇⌇⌇ ⌇⌇⌇ ⌇⌇⌇ ⌇⌇ ⌇⌇⌇ ⌇⌇⌇ ⌇⌇⌇ ⌇⌇ ⌇⌇ ⌇⌇⌇ ⌇⌇⌇ ⌇⌇ ⌇⌇ ⌇⌇⌇

... AMEN.

!

OH MAN, I TOTALLY ZONED OUT...

... I'D LIKE TO READ SOME PASSAGES I KNOW WERE DEAR TO ⌇⌇ ⌇⌇⌇ WERE ⌇⌇ ⌇⌇⌇ CORINTHIANS.

" NOW, THEN, ⌇⌇ ⌇⌇ ⌇⌇⌇⌇ ⌇⌇ ⌇⌇⌇ ⌇⌇⌇⌇ ⌇⌇ ⌇⌇⌇ ⌇⌇⌇ ⌇⌇ ⌇⌇⌇

⌇⌇⌇ ⌇⌇ ⌇⌇⌇ ⌇⌇⌇ ⌇⌇⌇ ⌇⌇⌇ ⌇⌇ ⌇⌇⌇ ⌇⌇⌇ ⌇⌇ ⌇ ⌇⌇⌇ ⌇⌇⌇

I WONDER WHAT WE'RE HAVING FOR LUNCH

NEXT WEEK I'M GONNA BUY THAT GAME

⌇⌇⌇ ⌇ ⌇⌇⌇ ⌇ AND THEN ⌇⌇ ⌇⌇⌇ ⌇ ⌇⌇⌇

⌇⌇⌇ ⌇⌇⌇ ⌇⌇⌇⌇ ⌇⌇⌇ ⌇⌇ ⌇⌇⌇

WHY DID ⌇⌇⌇ ⌇⌇⌇ ⌇ ⌇⌇⌇ ⌇⌇ ⌇⌇⌇⌇

⌇⌇ ⌇⌇⌇

WORLD?

4.5 B

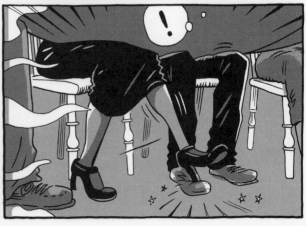

!

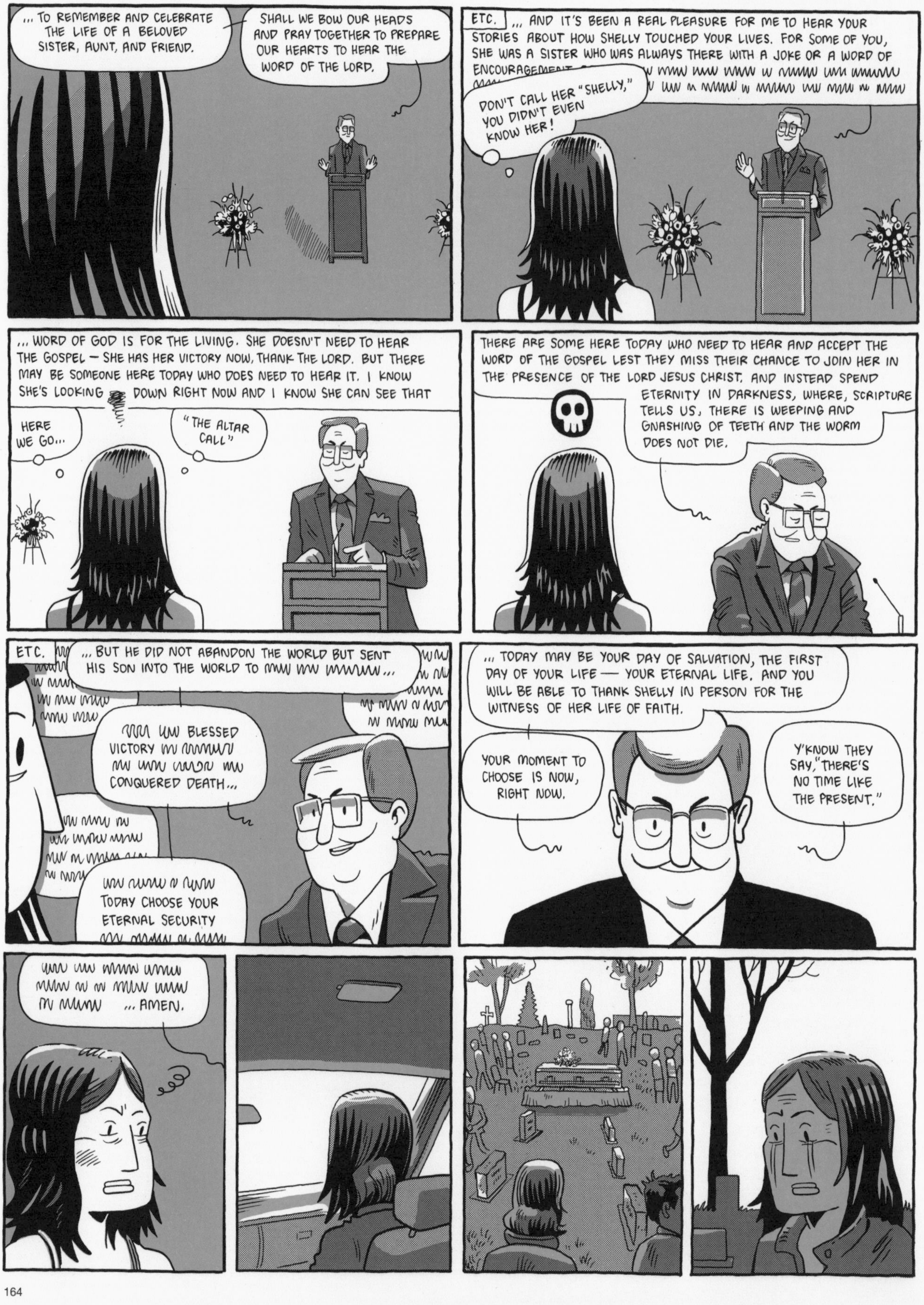
... TO REMEMBER AND CELEBRATE THE LIFE OF A BELOVED SISTER, AUNT, AND FRIEND.
SHALL WE BOW OUR HEADS AND PRAY TOGETHER TO PREPARE OUR HEARTS TO HEAR THE WORD OF THE LORD.
ETC.
... AND IT'S BEEN A REAL PLEASURE FOR ME TO HEAR YOUR STORIES ABOUT HOW SHELLY TOUCHED YOUR LIVES. FOR SOME OF YOU, SHE WAS A SISTER WHO WAS ALWAYS THERE WITH A JOKE OR A WORD OF ENCOURAGEMENT
DON'T CALL HER "SHELLY," YOU DIDN'T EVEN KNOW HER!
... WORD OF GOD IS FOR THE LIVING. SHE DOESN'T NEED TO HEAR THE GOSPEL — SHE HAS HER VICTORY NOW, THANK THE LORD. BUT THERE MAY BE SOMEONE HERE TODAY WHO DOES NEED TO HEAR IT. I KNOW SHE'S LOOKING DOWN RIGHT NOW AND I KNOW SHE CAN SEE THAT
HERE WE GO...
"THE ALTAR CALL"
THERE ARE SOME HERE TODAY WHO NEED TO HEAR AND ACCEPT THE WORD OF THE GOSPEL LEST THEY MISS THEIR CHANCE TO JOIN HER IN THE PRESENCE OF THE LORD JESUS CHRIST, AND INSTEAD SPEND
ETERNITY IN DARKNESS, WHERE, SCRIPTURE TELLS US, THERE IS WEEPING AND GNASHING OF TEETH AND THE WORM DOES NOT DIE.
ETC.
... BUT HE DID NOT ABANDON THE WORLD BUT SENT HIS SON INTO THE WORLD TO ...
BLESSED VICTORY CONQUERED DEATH...
TODAY CHOOSE YOUR ETERNAL SECURITY
... TODAY MAY BE YOUR DAY OF SALVATION, THE FIRST DAY OF YOUR LIFE — YOUR ETERNAL LIFE. AND YOU WILL BE ABLE TO THANK SHELLY IN PERSON FOR THE WITNESS OF HER LIFE OF FAITH.
YOUR MOMENT TO CHOOSE IS NOW, RIGHT NOW.
Y'KNOW THEY SAY, "THERE'S NO TIME LIKE THE PRESENT."
... AMEN.

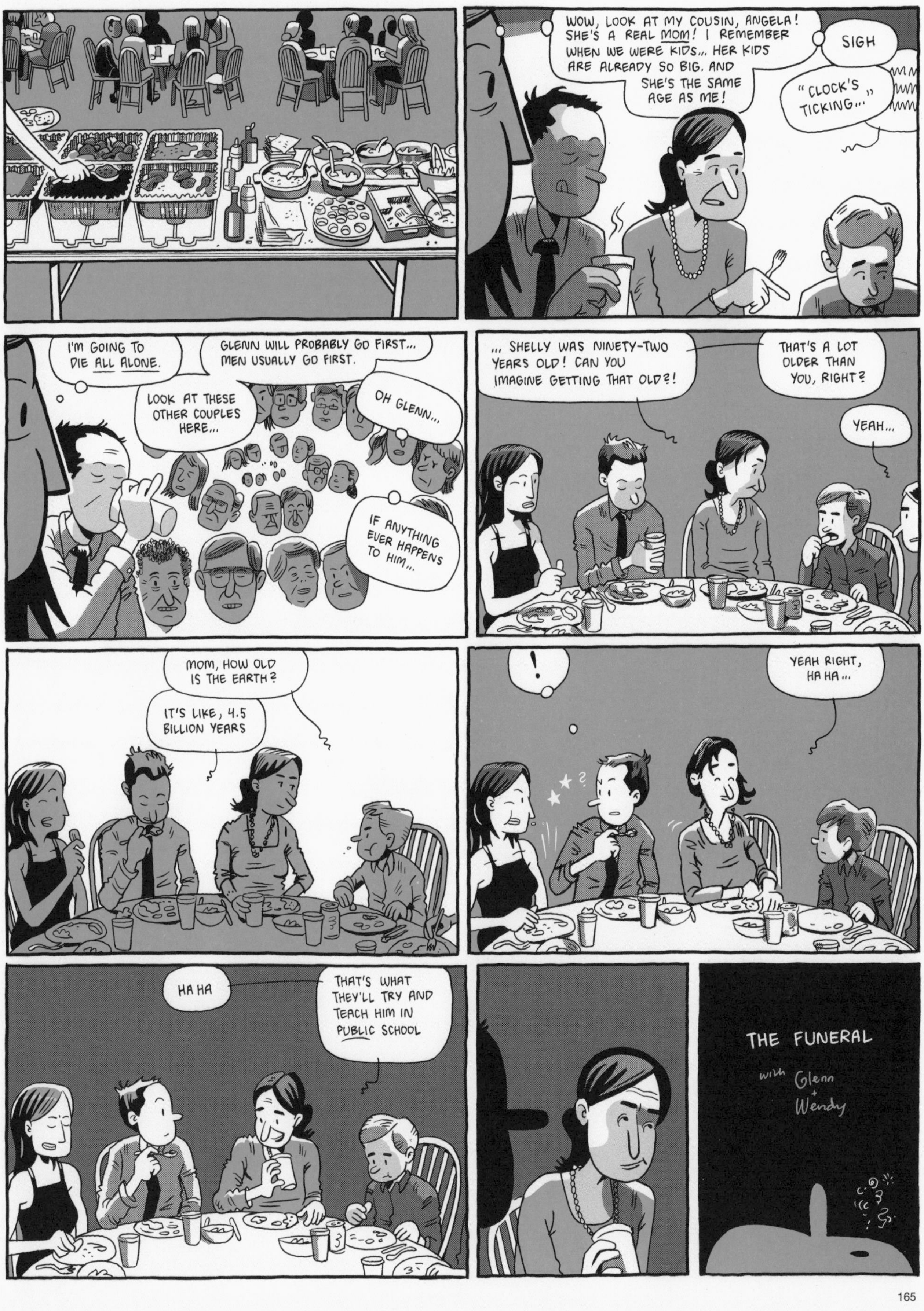
WOW, LOOK AT MY COUSIN, ANGELA! SHE'S A REAL MOM! I REMEMBER WHEN WE WERE KIDS... HER KIDS ARE ALREADY SO BIG. AND SHE'S THE SAME AGE AS ME!
SIGH
"CLOCK'S TICKING..."
I'M GOING TO DIE ALL ALONE.
GLENN WILL PROBABLY GO FIRST... MEN USUALLY GO FIRST.
LOOK AT THESE OTHER COUPLES HERE...
OH GLENN...
IF ANYTHING EVER HAPPENS TO HIM...
... SHELLY WAS NINETY-TWO YEARS OLD! CAN YOU IMAGINE GETTING THAT OLD?!
THAT'S A LOT OLDER THAN YOU, RIGHT?
YEAH...
MOM, HOW OLD IS THE EARTH?
IT'S LIKE, 4.5 BILLION YEARS
!
YEAH RIGHT, HA HA...
HA HA
THAT'S WHAT THEY'LL TRY AND TEACH HIM IN PUBLIC SCHOOL
THE FUNERAL
with Glenn + Wendy

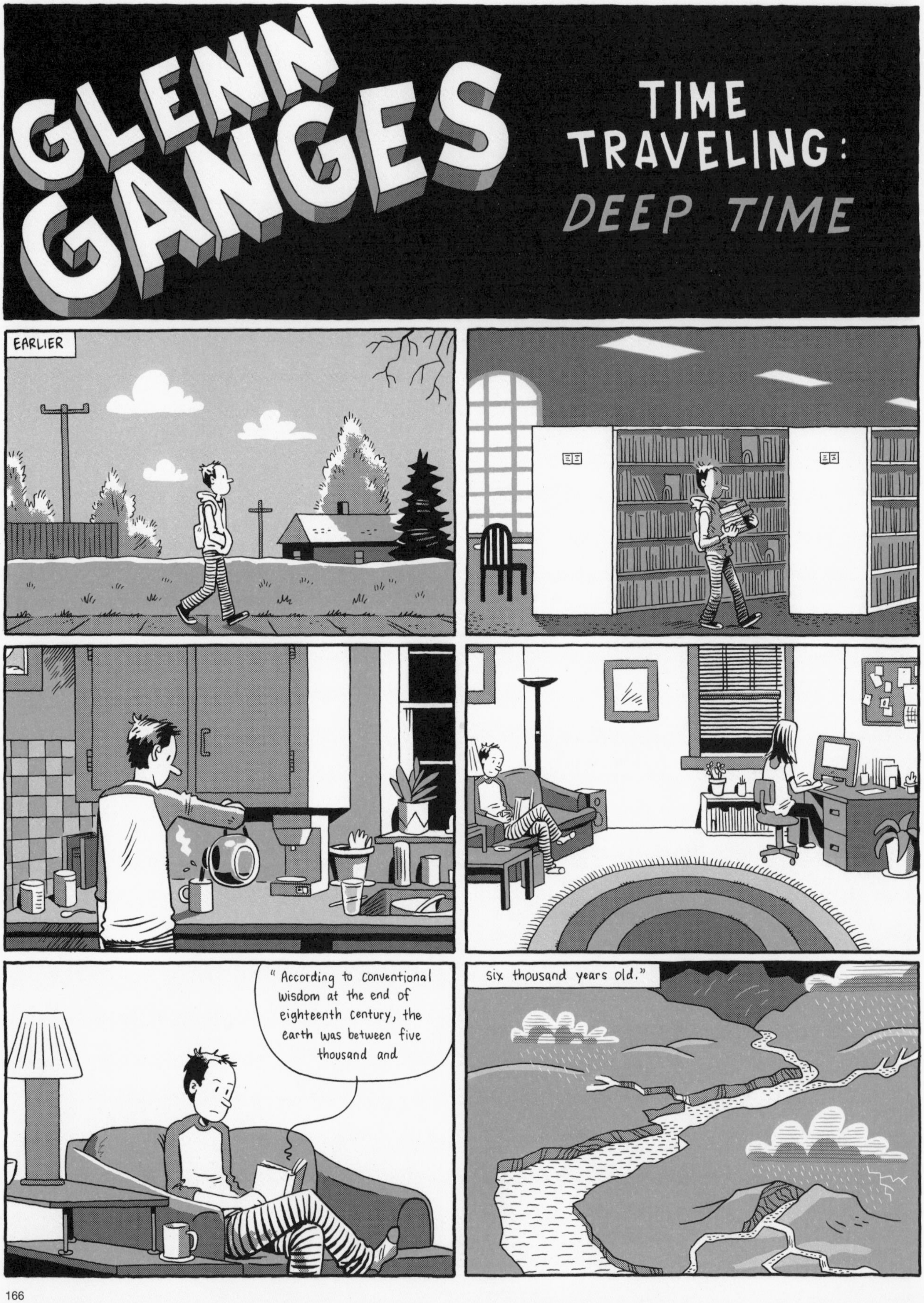
GLENN GANGES
TIME TRAVELING:
DEEP TIME
EARLIER
" According to conventional wisdom at the end of eighteenth century, the earth was between five thousand and
six thousand years old."

"...to make the rock of that lower formation and then tilt it up and wear it down and deposit sediment on it to form the rock above would require an immense quantity of time. You could place your finger on that line and touch forty million years."

THIS BOOK IS GOOD. IT'S MESSING WITH MY HEAD!

...

HISTORICAL STUFF.

SCIENCE STUFF...

MOUNTAINS AND STUFF. BUT THIS PART I'M READING RIGHT NOW IS ABOUT ONE OF THE FIRST GUYS WHO FIGURED OUT THAT THE EARTH IS BILLIONS OF YEARS OLD.

HIS NAME WAS JAMES HUTTON.

ARE YOU LISTENING TO ME?

YES.

HE WAS A SCOTTISH "GENTLEMAN SCIENTIST" WHO'S, LIKE, THE "DARWIN" OF DISCOVERING "DEEP TIME."— (BUT THIS IS ACTUALLY BEFORE DARWIN, IN THE 1700s.)

IT'S PRETTY HARD TO IMAGINE A MILLION YEARS, MUCH LESS A HUNDRED MILLION YEARS...

IT WASN'T UNTIL THE 1950s THAT RADIOACTIVE * DATING SHOWED THAT THE EARTH WAS ACTUALLY 4.5 BILLION YEARS OLD!

OR, LIKE, EIGHT HUNDRED MILLION

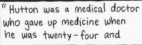
RADIOMETRIC — ed.

HMM.

"Hutton was a medical doctor who gave up medicine when he was twenty-four and

"became a farmer who, at the age of forty-two, retired from the farm... Wherever he went, he found himself drawn to ditches and pits, riverbanks and cutbanks..."

"He was drawn to high cliffs, to look out over the land and wonder. If he saw black shining rocks in the white chalks of Norfolk, or fossil clams in the Cheviot Hills, he wondered why they were there."

"He had become preoccupied with the operations of the earth and he was beginning to discern a gradual and repetitive process measured out in dynamic cycles."

EDINBURGH

WHEN ARE YOU GOING TO COME SEE THESE NEW FOSSILS I'VE ACQUIRED?

EHRM...

FRIEND JOSEPH BLACK, DISCOVERER OF CARBON DIOXIDE, etc.

WHEN ARE YOU GOING TO SPEAK AT THE ROYAL SOCIETY ABOUT YOUR GEOLOGICAL THEORY?

ALL RIGHT... I'LL DO IT...

FOR TOO LONG I'VE BEEN PUTTING OFF THE WRITING DOWN OF IT.

AND SO

... THE PURPOSE OF THIS DISSERTATION IS TO FORM SOME ESTIMATE WITH REGARD TO THE TIME THE GLOBE OF THIS EARTH HAS EXISTED...

MARCH 7, 1785

"As things appear from the perspective of today, Hutton in that lecture became the founder of modern geology. As things appeared to Hutton at the time, he had constructed a theory that to him made eminent sense ..."

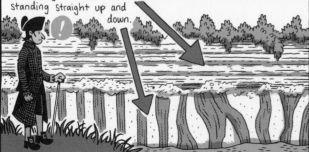

"... but he had better do some more observing and traveling to see if he was right. One day while roaming around near Jedburgh, he found a stream cutbank where water laid bare the flat-lying sandstone, and below it, beds of schistus that were standing straight up and down.

"Alive in a world that thought of itself as six thousand years old, Hutton had no way of knowing that there were seventy million years just in the line that separated them, and many millions in each formation, but he sensed something like it, and as he stood there on the riverbank he was seeing it for all humanity."

SO... THESE ROCK FORMATIONS HE SAW — HOW DID THEY FORM? WHAT FORCES WERE AT WORK? GODS? GIANTS? HOW MUCH TIME DID IT TAKE?

BY THE LATE 1700s, IT WAS GENERALLY UNDERSTOOD BY THE "MAN ON THE STREET" THAT LANDFORMS AND FOSSILS GOT TO BE WHERE THEY WERE DUE TO NOAH'S FLOOD, ETC.

HOWEVER, MANY EDUCATED NATURALISTS AT THE TIME BELIEVED THE EARTH TO BE FAR OLDER THAN THE 20TH CENTURY LITERALIST, "YOUNG EARTH" CREATIONIST TIMESCALE — BUT ONLY BY A FEW HUNDREDS OF THOUSANDS OF YEARS, MAYBE EVEN A FEW MILLION.

MAN ON THE STREET

"SAVANT" IN FRANCE

SEVERAL THOUSAND YEARS

MORE LIKE FIVE MILLION YEARS

BOTH A BIT OFF

THE IDEA THAT TIME WAS ETERNAL AND CYCLICAL WAS AN ANCIENT BUT PAGAN VIEW, OUT OF BOUNDS.

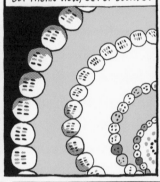

TIME WAS LINEAR AND HISTORICAL FOR BIBLE READERS, WHETHER THEY WERE SOPHISTICATED READERS OR WERE RESISTANT TO SOPHISTICATION.

PAST

FUTURE

THE END

YOU ARE HERE

THE THINKING WAS THAT THE EARTH FORMED THIS WAY: LAND HAD FORMED AS HEAVY ELEMENTS SETTLED AND COMBINED UNDER THE PRESSURE OF AN ANCIENT, PLANET-WIDE SUPER-OCEAN. THESE WERE THE DAYS OF "THE SPIRIT OF GOD MOVING ON THE FACE OF THE WATERS."

GRAVITY

IMMENSE PRESSURE

ALL FUTURE LAND

GIANTS AND EPIC FLOODS, NO — BUT YES, A TIME OF MASSIVE EARTHQUAKES AND CATASTROPHES WHICH CARVED AND FOLDED AND PILED UP MOUNTAINS. BUT OUR PRESENT WORLD HAD CALMED.

THE THINKING WAS THAT OUR PRESENT WORLD WAS THE RUINS (OR THE ROTTING) BROUGHT ABOUT BY THE CATASTROPHIC EVENTS AND THE EROSION OF THE ORIGINAL LANDFORMS. NOW THE EARTH IS IN A TIME OF DECAY, MOVING TOWARD A WARM, SMOOTH, SWAMPY DESTINY... HUTTON HAD DIFFERENT IDEAS —

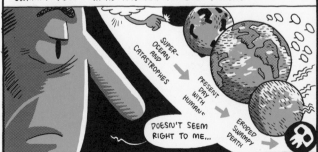

SUPER-OCEAN AND CATASTROPHES

PRESENT DAY WITH HUMANS

ERODED SWAMPY DEATH

DOESN'T SEEM RIGHT TO ME...

SO... HUTTON'S IDEAS — HOW DID THEY FORM? WHAT FORCES WERE AT WORK?

IT WASN'T JUST "COMMON SENSE" OR "PURE SCIENCE." HUTTON THOUGHT DIFFERENTLY THAN SCIENTISTS TODAY. HE WAS LOOKING AT THOSE LAYERS OF ROCK THROUGH LAYERS OF LENSES (OR FILTERS) OF HIS OWN PRECONCEPTIONS. OF COURSE, EVERYONE DOES THIS.
1
SHARP FOCUS
BLURRY
1
PASSES THROUGH
LENS METAPHOR
FILTER METAPHOR
YOU HAVE TO USE SOMETHING TO FILTER AND FOCUS THE BLURRY, BUZZING CONFUSION.
?
WE STEER BY THESE COORDINATES AND THE CYCLE CONTINUES. GROOVES ARE WORN INTO OUR BRAINS, AND LAYERS OF LENSES AND FILTERS FUSE AND CRYSTALLIZE. FILTERS GET FILTERED.
WHAT WERE HIS PRECONCEPTIONS? HUTTON WAS A DEIST — A PRETTY COMMON SETUP IN HIS TIME — HE BELIEVED THAT
God created the world for the purpose of supporting life, and especially Mankind; Science shows us his Wisdom in the makeup of Nature:
a Balanced, Providential System.
ALSO KEEP IN MIND THAT ONE HUNDRED YEARS BEFORE, NEWTON HAD PUBLISHED HIS LAWS OF MOTION AND UNIVERSAL GRAVITATION AND OPENED UP DEEP SPACE.
... THIS FORM? WHAT FORCES...?
NOT TO SCALE
INERTIA AND GRAVITY BALANCE EACH OTHER
AND THE SPHERES TURN IN THEIR CYCLES
LIKE A GIANT MACHINE
THIS HAPPENS EVERYWHERE IN SPACE
IT'S ALL THE SAME
FOR GUYS LIKE HUTTON, IT WAS AS IF NEWTON HAD SEEN THE UNIVERSE FROM OUTSIDE, AS IF HIS MIND, IN PERFECT STILLNESS, HAD SEEN EVERYTHING ELSE STILL IN MOTION. IT WAS AS IF HE STEPPED OUTSIDE THE STORY AND SAW ITS ETERNAL, UNCHANGING FORM.
SO AT THE TIME IT WAS PRETTY COMMON TO WANT TO FOLLOW NEWTON'S LEAD. HUTTON USED NEWTON'S WAY OF THINKING AS A MODEL FOR HIS THEORY OF THE EARTH AS A SLOW AND STEADY CYCLICAL "MACHINE."
N
N

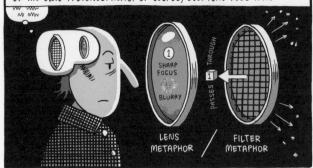

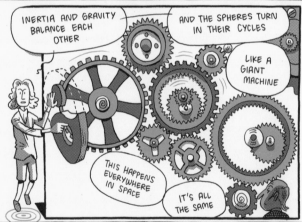

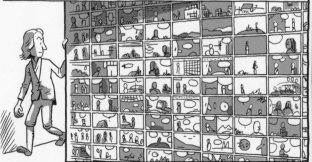

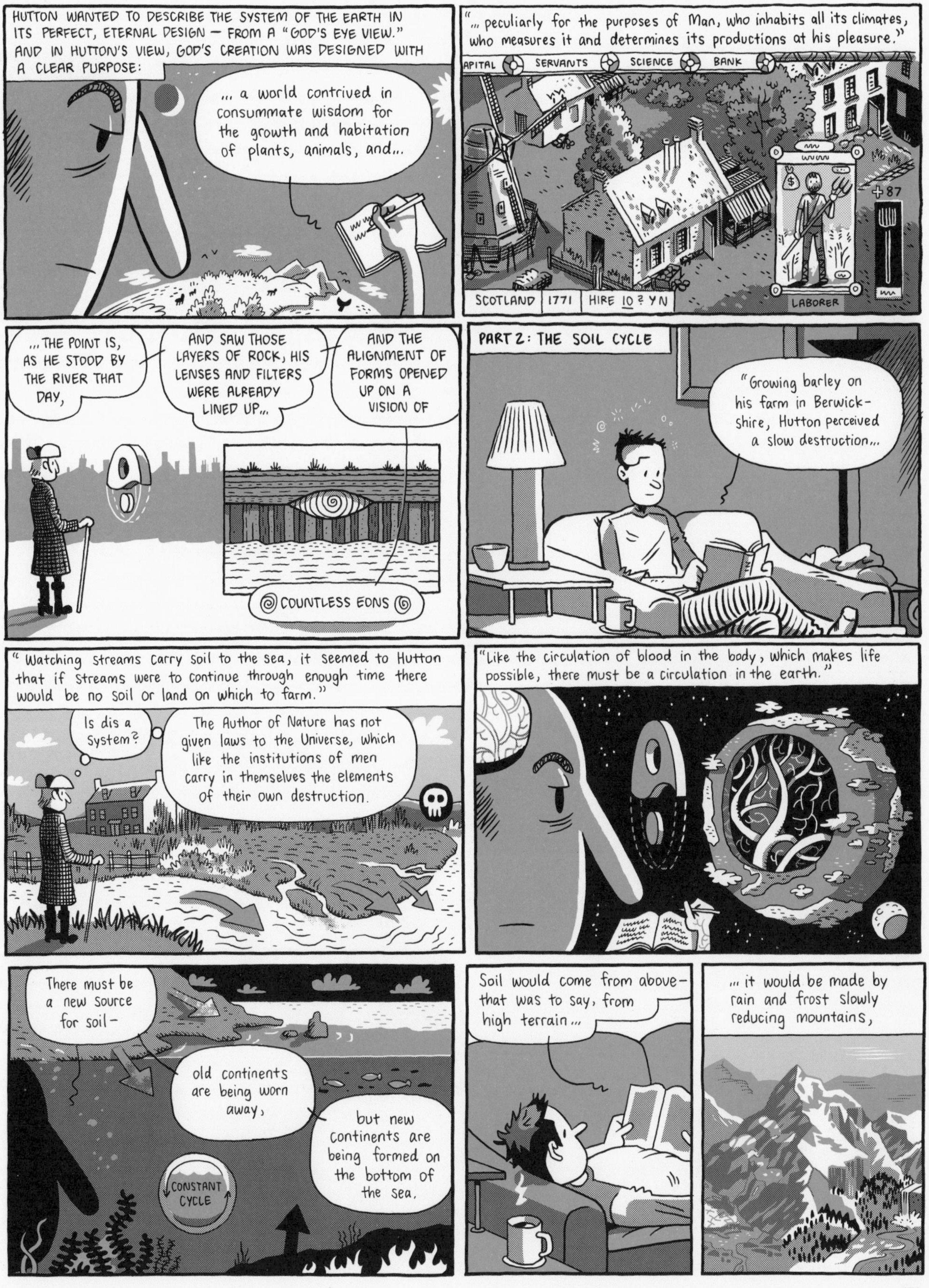
HUTTON WANTED TO DESCRIBE THE SYSTEM OF THE EARTH IN ITS PERFECT, ETERNAL DESIGN — FROM A "GOD'S EYE VIEW." AND IN HUTTON'S VIEW, GOD'S CREATION WAS DESIGNED WITH A CLEAR PURPOSE:
... a world contrived in consummate wisdom for the growth and habitation of plants, animals, and...
"... peculiarly for the purposes of Man, who inhabits all its climates, who measures it and determines its productions at his pleasure."
APITAL
SERVANTS
SCIENCE
BANK
+87
SCOTLAND
1771
HIRE 10 ? YN
LABORER
... THE POINT IS, AS HE STOOD BY THE RIVER THAT DAY,
AND SAW THOSE LAYERS OF ROCK, HIS LENSES AND FILTERS WERE ALREADY LINED UP...
AND THE ALIGNMENT OF FORMS OPENED UP ON A VISION OF
COUNTLESS EONS
PART 2: THE SOIL CYCLE
"Growing barley on his farm in Berwick-shire, Hutton perceived a slow destruction...
"Watching streams carry soil to the sea, it seemed to Hutton that if streams were to continue through enough time there would be no soil or land on which to farm."
Is dis a System?
The Author of Nature has not given laws to the Universe, which like the institutions of men carry in themselves the elements of their own destruction.
"Like the circulation of blood in the body, which makes life possible, there must be a circulation in the earth."
There must be a new source for soil-
old continents are being worn away,
but new continents are being formed on the bottom of the sea.
CONSTANT CYCLE
Soil would come from above-that was to say, from high terrain...
... it would be made by rain and frost slowly reducing mountains,

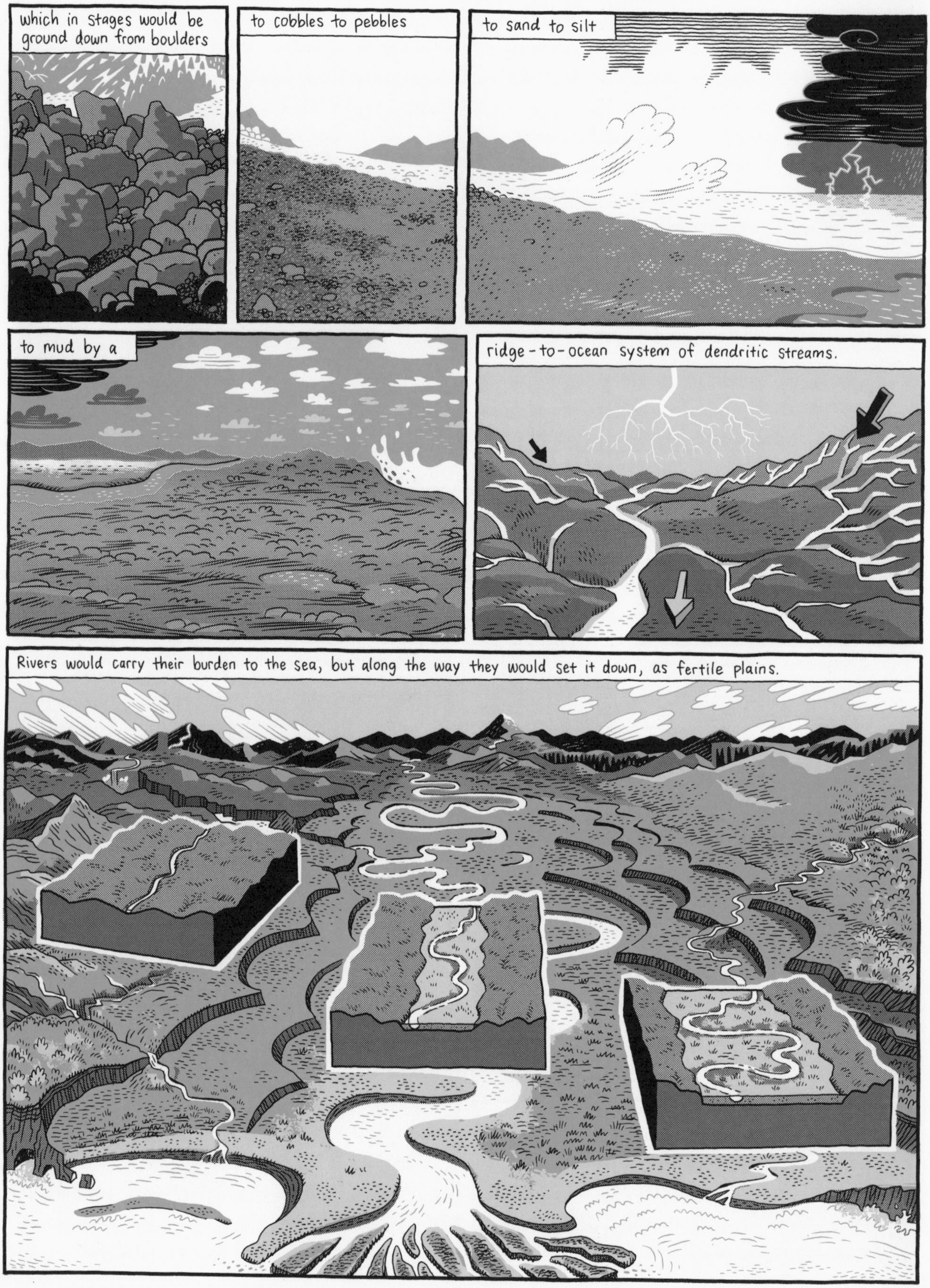
which in stages would be ground down from boulders
to cobbles to pebbles
to sand to silt
to mud by a
ridge-to-ocean system of dendritic streams.
Rivers would carry their burden to the sea, but along the way they would set it down, as fertile plains.

" Rivers come and go. They are far younger than the earth on which they run.

" They reverse themselves and sometimes disappear into holes in the earth,

" or suddenly dry up.

" Their behavior is affected by the shape of the earth below and they in turn change the shape of the earth.

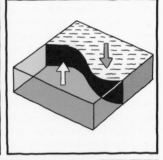

" A river cuts on one side while it fills in on the other, etching out the country, filling in formations, and leaving fertile soil.

FILL

CUT

" And below, the land tilts and bobs on the molten mantle, which flows like slow weather around the Earth's core.

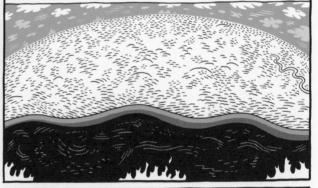

" Seen from high above, with thousands of years speeding by in seconds, a river slithers and jumps around like a drop on a frying pan or rain on a window.

TAP
TAP

" It wanders all over its own valley seeking the shortest path to the ocean and always finds it.

"In still waters, in layers, the mud, silt, sand, and pebbles would pile up until they reached a depth where heat and pressure could cause them to become consolidated, fused, indurated, lithified — rock."

"But the story could hardly end there.

The earth would have long since been ground smooth and be some sort of global swamp."

"There were fossil marine creatures in high places. They had not got there in a flood."

80 MILLION YEARS AGO

"Something had lifted the rock out of the sea

80-50 M. YRS.

"and folded it up as mountains."

"One had only to ponder volcanoes and hot springs to sense that there was a great deal of heat within the earth — much more than could be produced by...

...A SPONTANEOUSLY BURNING SEAM OF COAL.

(which is what some savants theorized)

"and that not only could high heat soften up rock and change it into other forms of rock...

"it could apparently move whole regions of the crust and bend and break them,

"and elevate them

"far above the sea,"

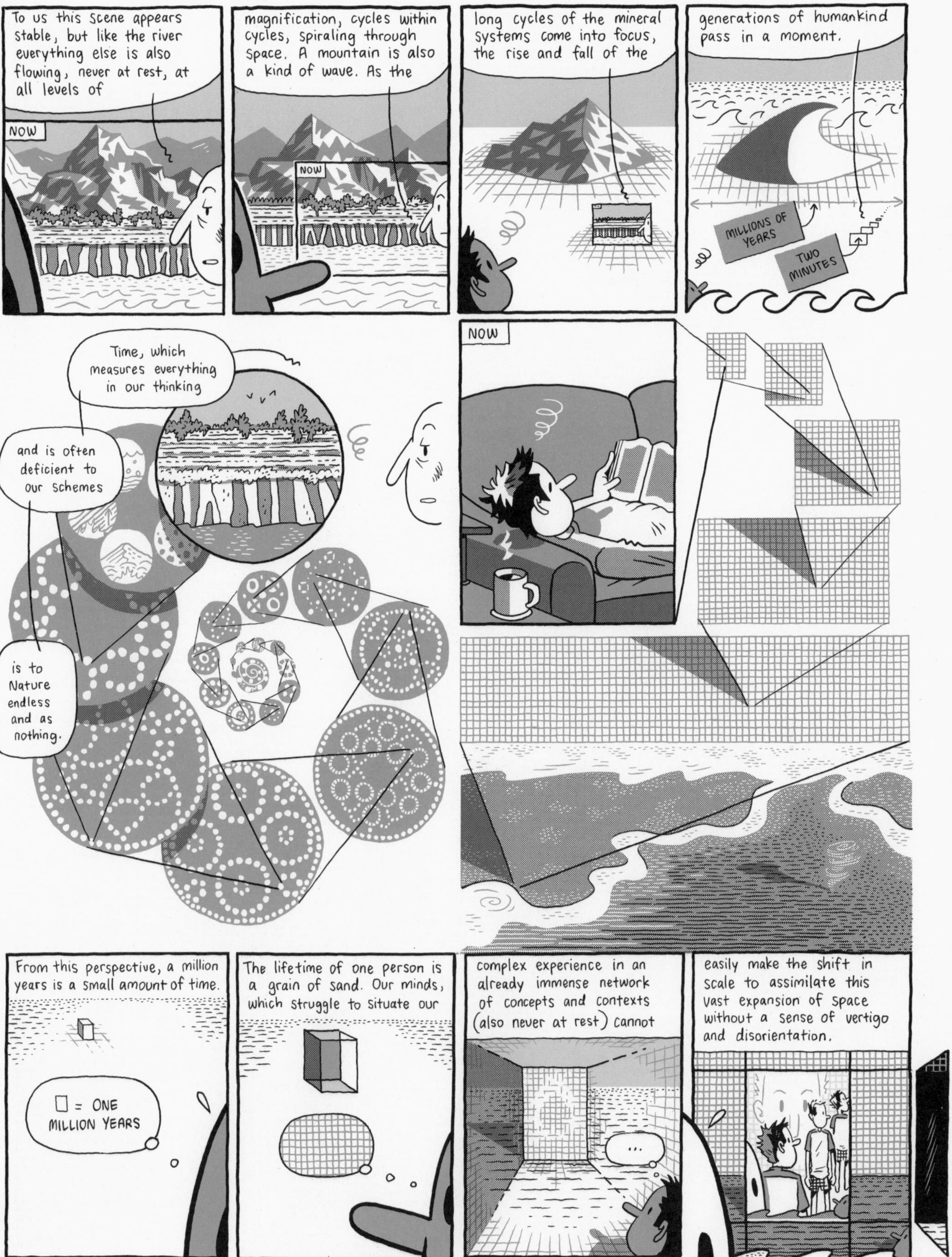

To us this scene appears stable, but like the river everything else is also flowing, never at rest, at all levels of
NOW
magnification, cycles within cycles, spiraling through space. A mountain is also a kind of wave. As the
NOW
long cycles of the mineral systems come into focus, the rise and fall of the
generations of humankind pass in a moment.
MILLIONS OF YEARS
TWO MINUTES
Time, which measures everything in our thinking
and is often deficient to our schemes
is to Nature endless and as nothing.
NOW
From this perspective, a million years is a small amount of time.
☐ = ONE MILLION YEARS
The lifetime of one person is a grain of sand. Our minds, which struggle to situate our
complex experience in an already immense network of concepts and contexts (also never at rest) cannot
...
easily make the shift in scale to assimilate this vast expansion of space without a sense of vertigo and disorientation.

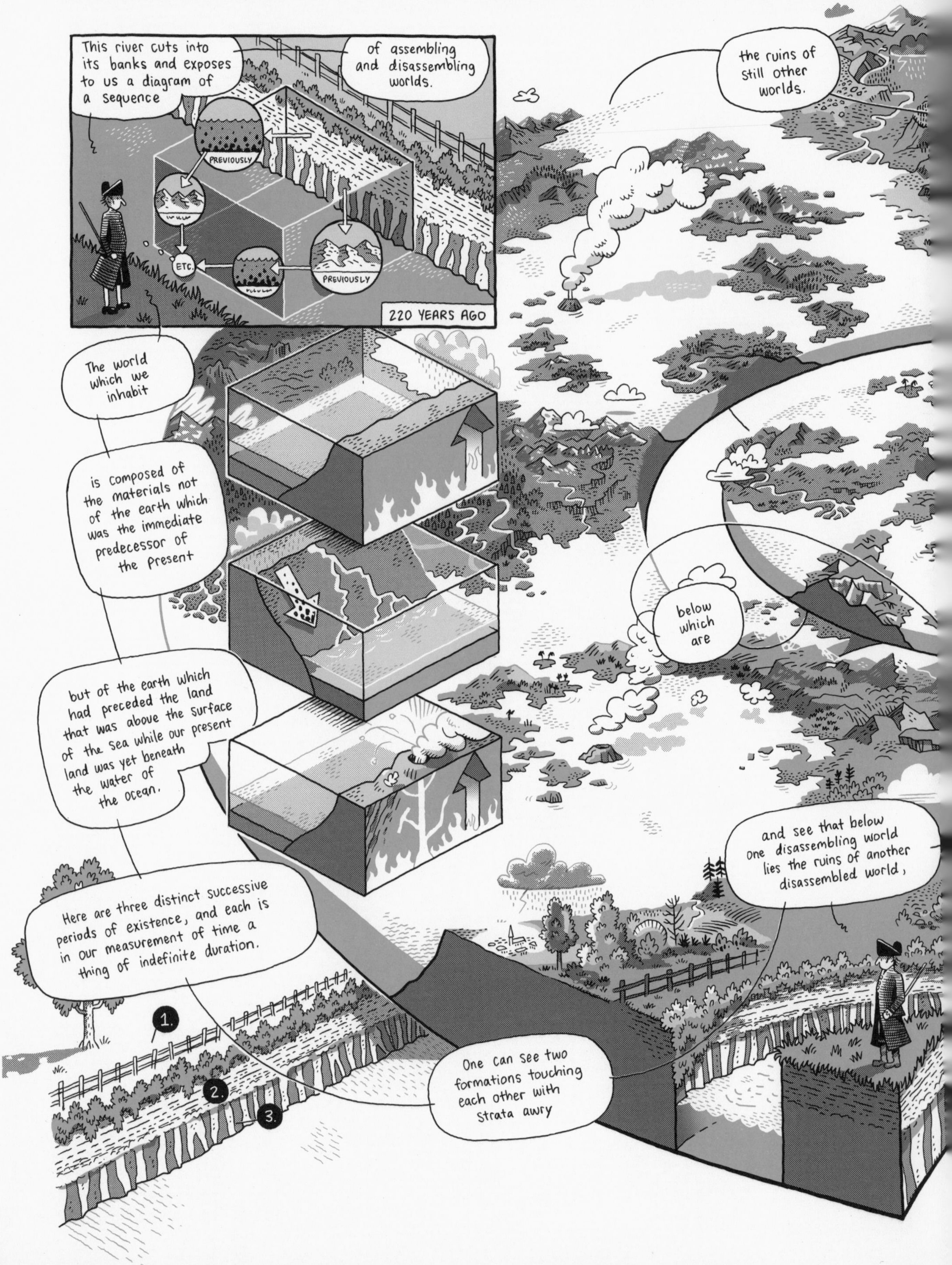
This river cuts into its banks and exposes to us a diagram of a sequence
of assembling and disassembling worlds.
PREVIOUSLY
ETC.
PREVIOUSLY
220 YEARS AGO
the ruins of still other worlds.
The world which we inhabit
is composed of the materials not of the earth which was the immediate predecessor of the present
but of the earth which had preceded the land that was above the surface of the sea while our present land was yet beneath the water of the ocean.
below which are
Here are three distinct successive periods of existence, and each is in our measurement of time a thing of indefinite duration.
and see that below one disassembling world lies the ruins of another disassembled world,
1.
2.
3.
One can see two formations touching each other with strata awry

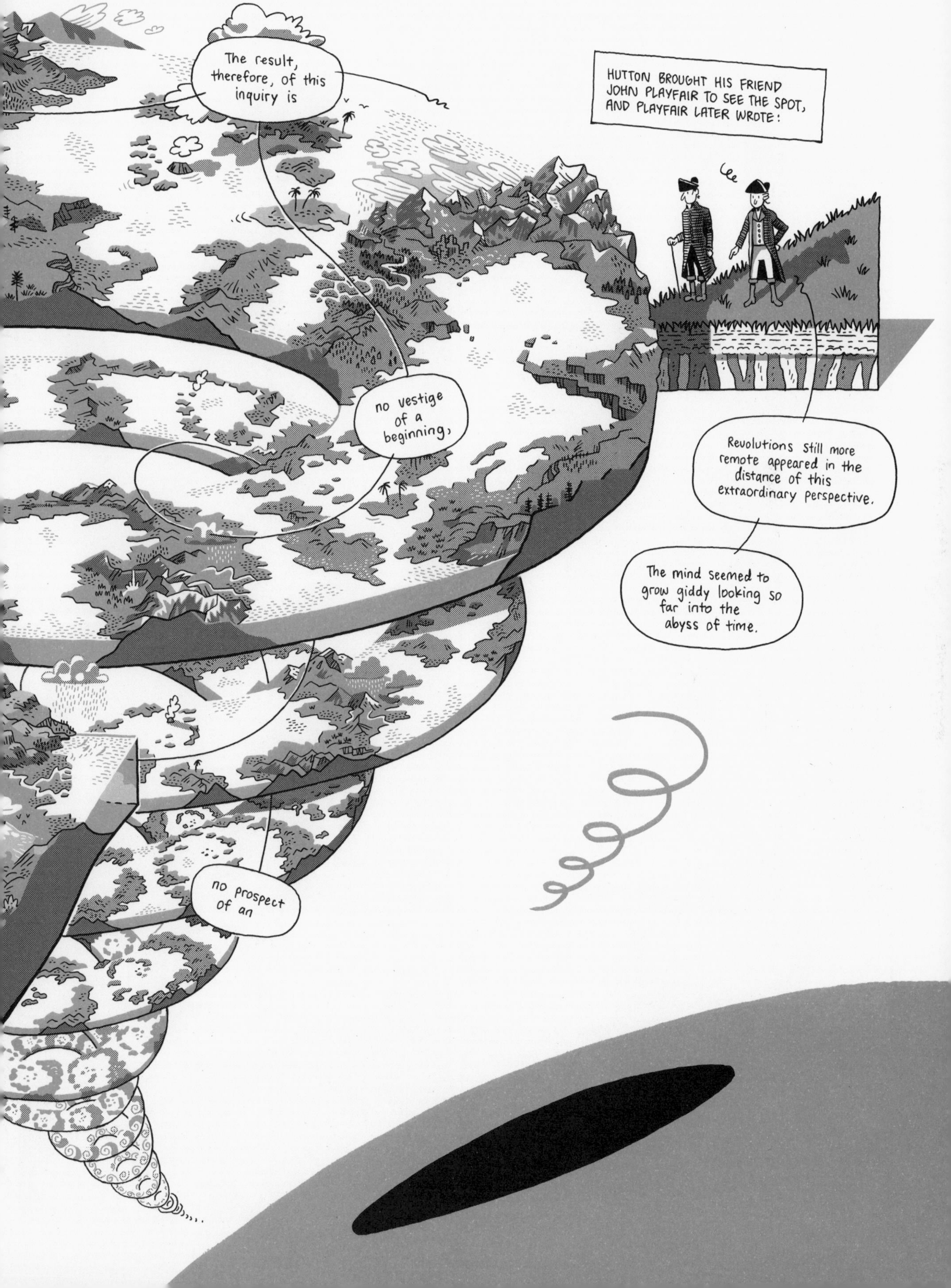
HUTTON BROUGHT HIS FRIEND JOHN PLAYFAIR TO SEE THE SPOT, AND PLAYFAIR LATER WROTE:
Revolutions still more remote appeared in the distance of this extraordinary perspective.
The mind seemed to grow giddy looking so far into the abyss of time.
The result, therefore, of this inquiry is
no vestige of a beginning,
no prospect of an

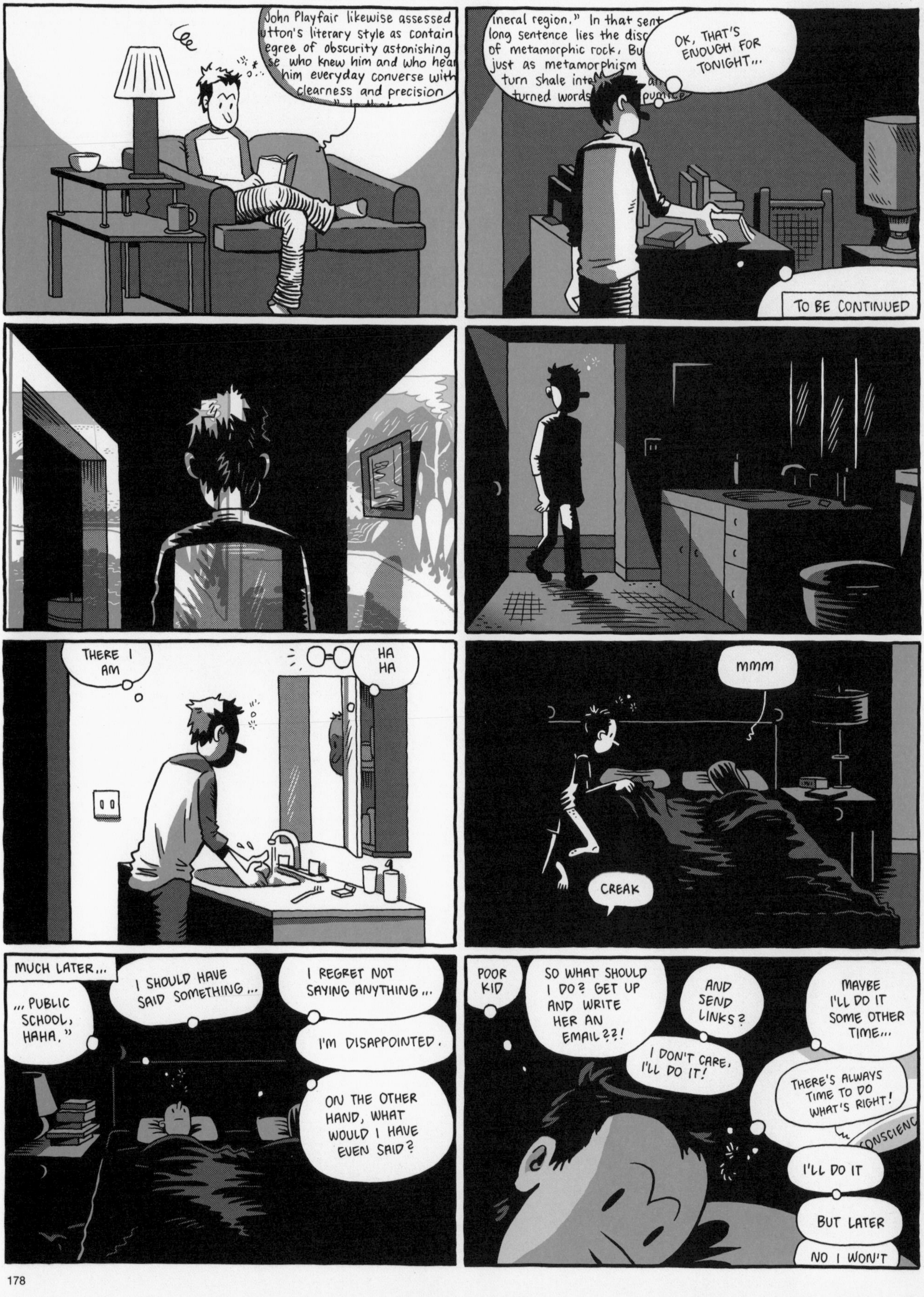
John Playfair likewise assessed
utton's literary style as contain
egree of obscurity astonishing
se who knew him and who hea
him everyday converse with
clearness and precision
ineral region." In that sent
long sentence lies the disc
of metamorphic rock, Bu
just as metamorphism
turn shale int
turned words
OK, THAT'S ENOUGH FOR TONIGHT...
TO BE CONTINUED
THERE I AM
HA HA
mmm
CREAK
MUCH LATER...
... PUBLIC SCHOOL, HAHA."
I SHOULD HAVE SAID SOMETHING...
I REGRET NOT SAYING ANYTHING...
I'M DISAPPOINTED.
ON THE OTHER HAND, WHAT WOULD I HAVE EVEN SAID?
POOR KID
SO WHAT SHOULD I DO? GET UP AND WRITE HER AN EMAIL??!
AND SEND LINKS?
I DON'T CARE, I'LL DO IT!
MAYBE I'LL DO IT SOME OTHER TIME...
THERE'S ALWAYS TIME TO DO WHAT'S RIGHT!
I'LL DO IT
BUT LATER
NO I WON'T

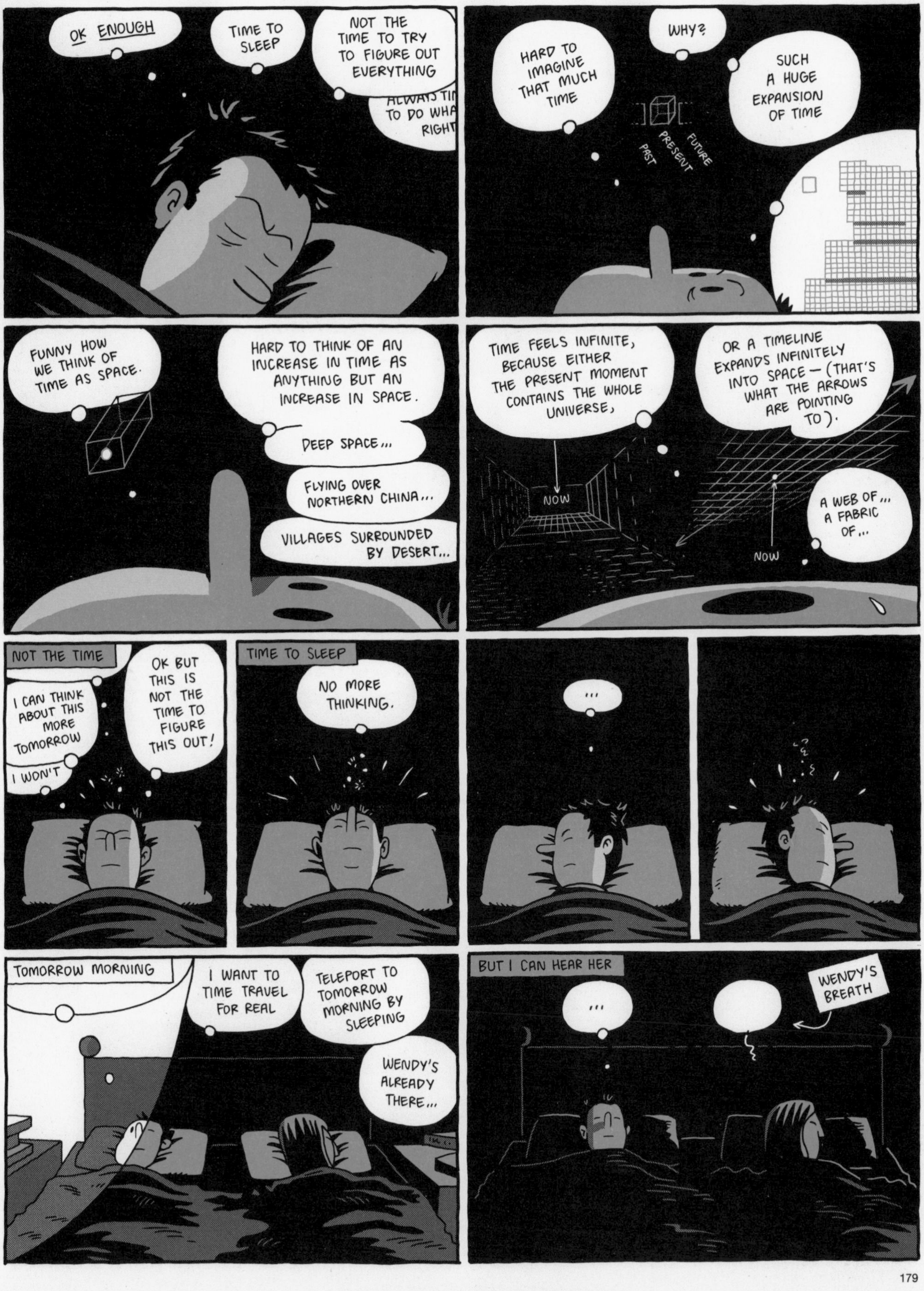
OK ENOUGH
TIME TO SLEEP
NOT THE TIME TO TRY TO FIGURE OUT EVERYTHING
ALWAYS TI[...] TO DO WHA[...] RIGHT
HARD TO IMAGINE THAT MUCH TIME
WHY?
SUCH A HUGE EXPANSION OF TIME
PAST
PRESENT
FUTURE
FUNNY HOW WE THINK OF TIME AS SPACE.
HARD TO THINK OF AN INCREASE IN TIME AS ANYTHING BUT AN INCREASE IN SPACE.
DEEP SPACE...
FLYING OVER NORTHERN CHINA...
VILLAGES SURROUNDED BY DESERT...
TIME FEELS INFINITE, BECAUSE EITHER THE PRESENT MOMENT CONTAINS THE WHOLE UNIVERSE,
OR A TIMELINE EXPANDS INFINITELY INTO SPACE — (THAT'S WHAT THE ARROWS ARE POINTING TO).
NOW
NOW
A WEB OF... A FABRIC OF...
NOT THE TIME
I CAN THINK ABOUT THIS MORE TOMORROW
I WON'T
OK BUT THIS IS NOT THE TIME TO FIGURE THIS OUT!
TIME TO SLEEP
NO MORE THINKING.
...
TOMORROW MORNING
I WANT TO TIME TRAVEL FOR REAL
TELEPORT TO TOMORROW MORNING BY SLEEPING
WENDY'S ALREADY THERE...
BUT I CAN HEAR HER
...
WENDY'S BREATH

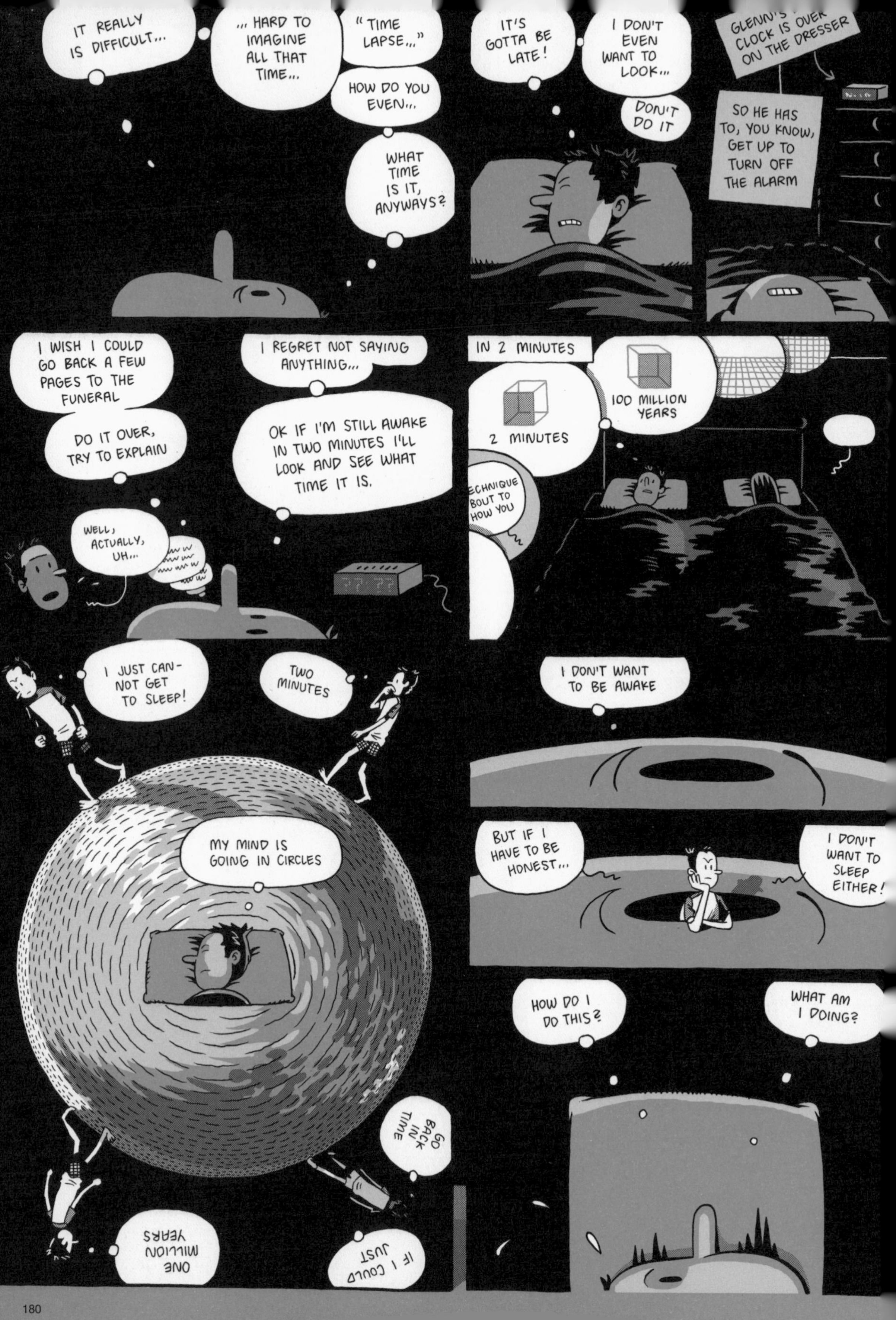

IT REALLY IS DIFFICULT...
... HARD TO IMAGINE ALL THAT TIME...
"TIME LAPSE..."
HOW DO YOU EVEN...
WHAT TIME IS IT, ANYWAYS?
IT'S GOTTA BE LATE!
I DON'T EVEN WANT TO LOOK...
DON'T DO IT
CLOCK IS OVER ON THE DRESSER
SO HE HAS TO, YOU KNOW, GET UP TO TURN OFF THE ALARM
I WISH I COULD GO BACK A FEW PAGES TO THE FUNERAL
DO IT OVER, TRY TO EXPLAIN
WELL, ACTUALLY, UH...
I REGRET NOT SAYING ANYTHING...
OK IF I'M STILL AWAKE IN TWO MINUTES I'LL LOOK AND SEE WHAT TIME IT IS.
IN 2 MINUTES
2 MINUTES
100 MILLION YEARS
I JUST CAN-NOT GET TO SLEEP!
TWO MINUTES
MY MIND IS GOING IN CIRCLES
GO BACK IN TIME
IF I COULD JUST
ONE MILLION YEARS
I DON'T WANT TO BE AWAKE
BUT IF I HAVE TO BE HONEST...
I DON'T WANT TO SLEEP EITHER!
HOW DO I DO THIS?
WHAT AM I DOING?

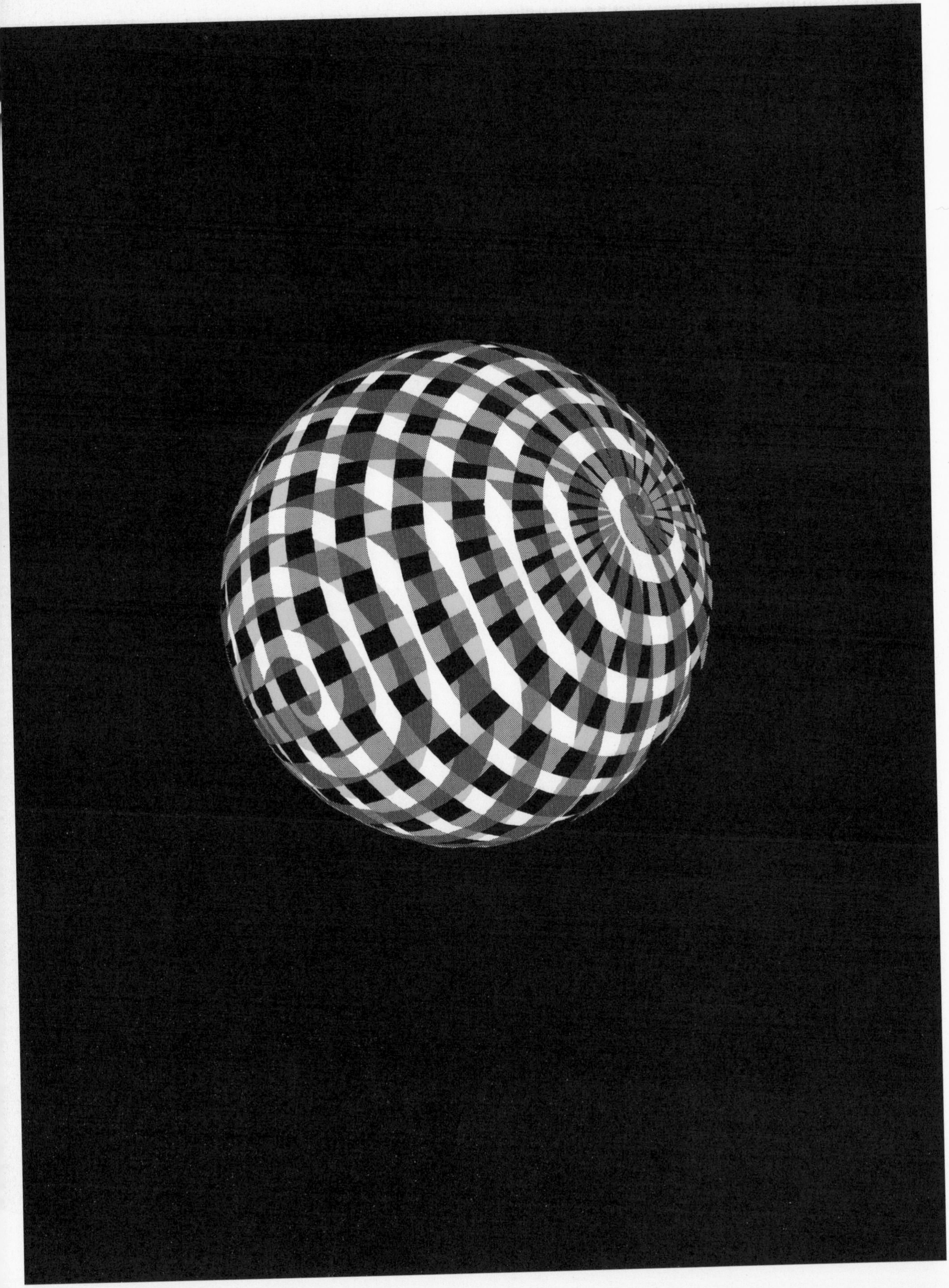

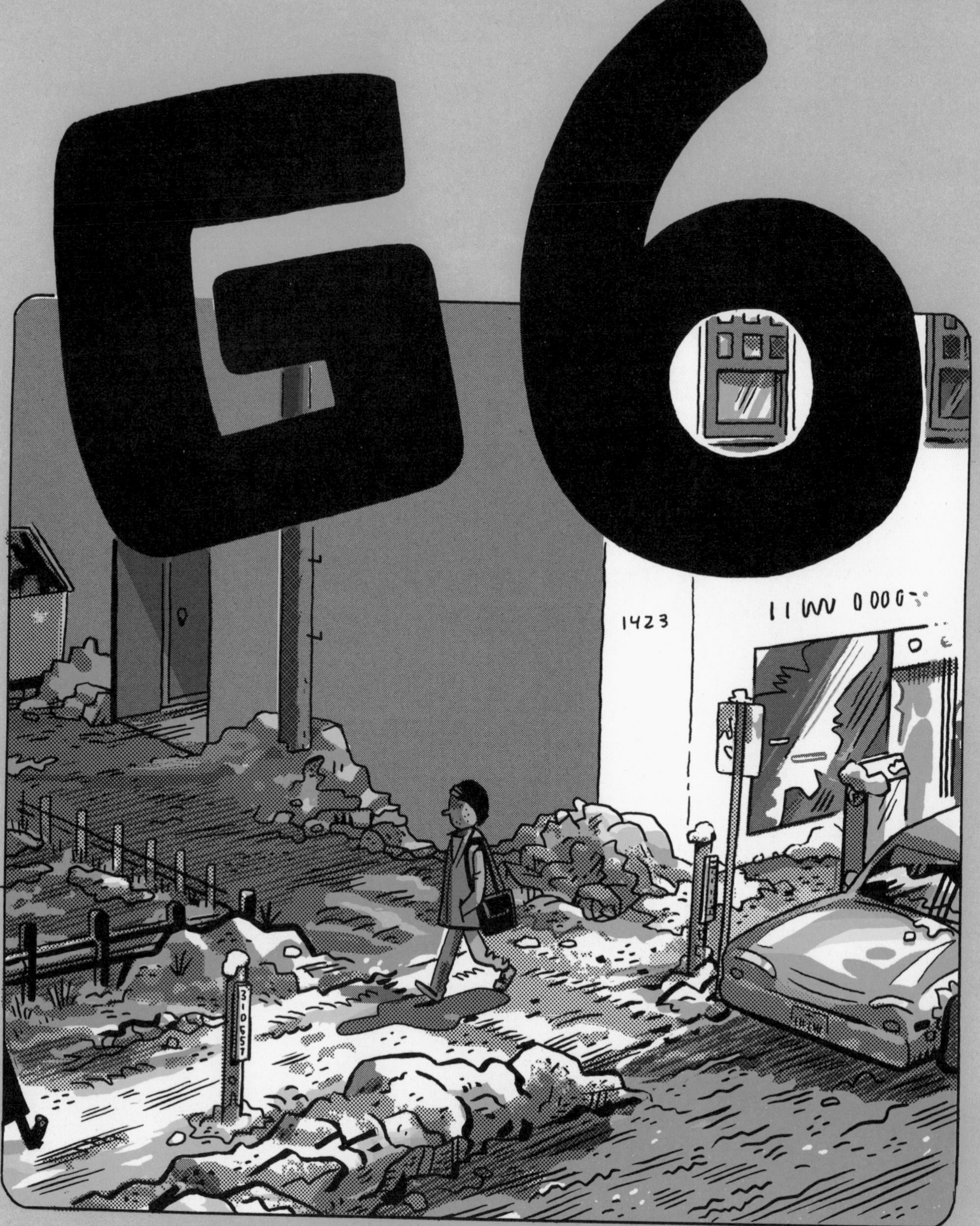
66
1423

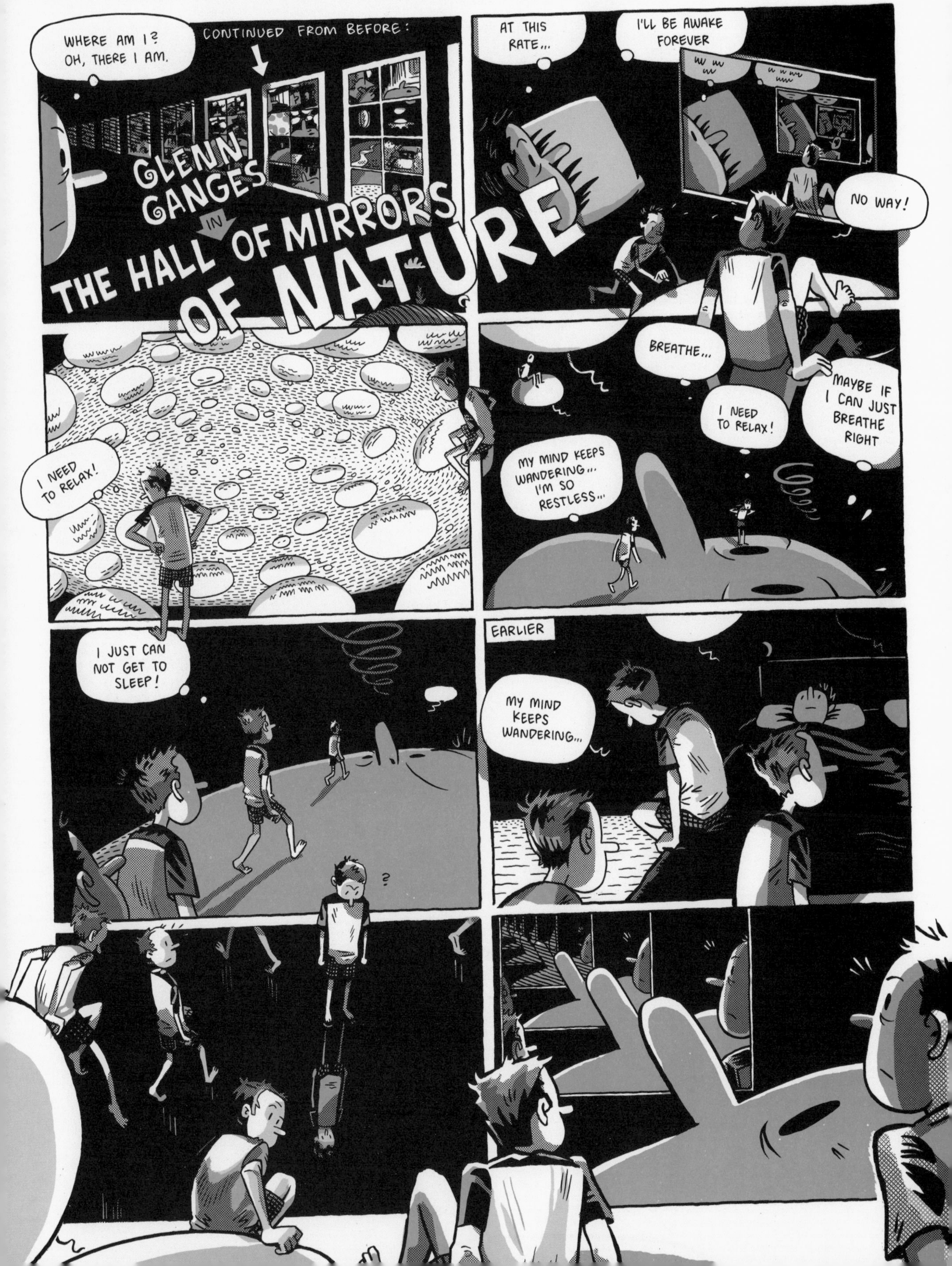
WHERE AM I? OH, THERE I AM.
CONTINUED FROM BEFORE:
GLENN GANGES IN THE HALL OF MIRRORS OF NATURE
AT THIS RATE...
I'LL BE AWAKE FOREVER
NO WAY!
BREATHE...
MAYBE IF I CAN JUST BREATHE RIGHT
I NEED TO RELAX!
I NEED TO RELAX!
MY MIND KEEPS WANDERING... I'M SO RESTLESS...
I JUST CAN NOT GET TO SLEEP!
EARLIER
MY MIND KEEPS WANDERING...

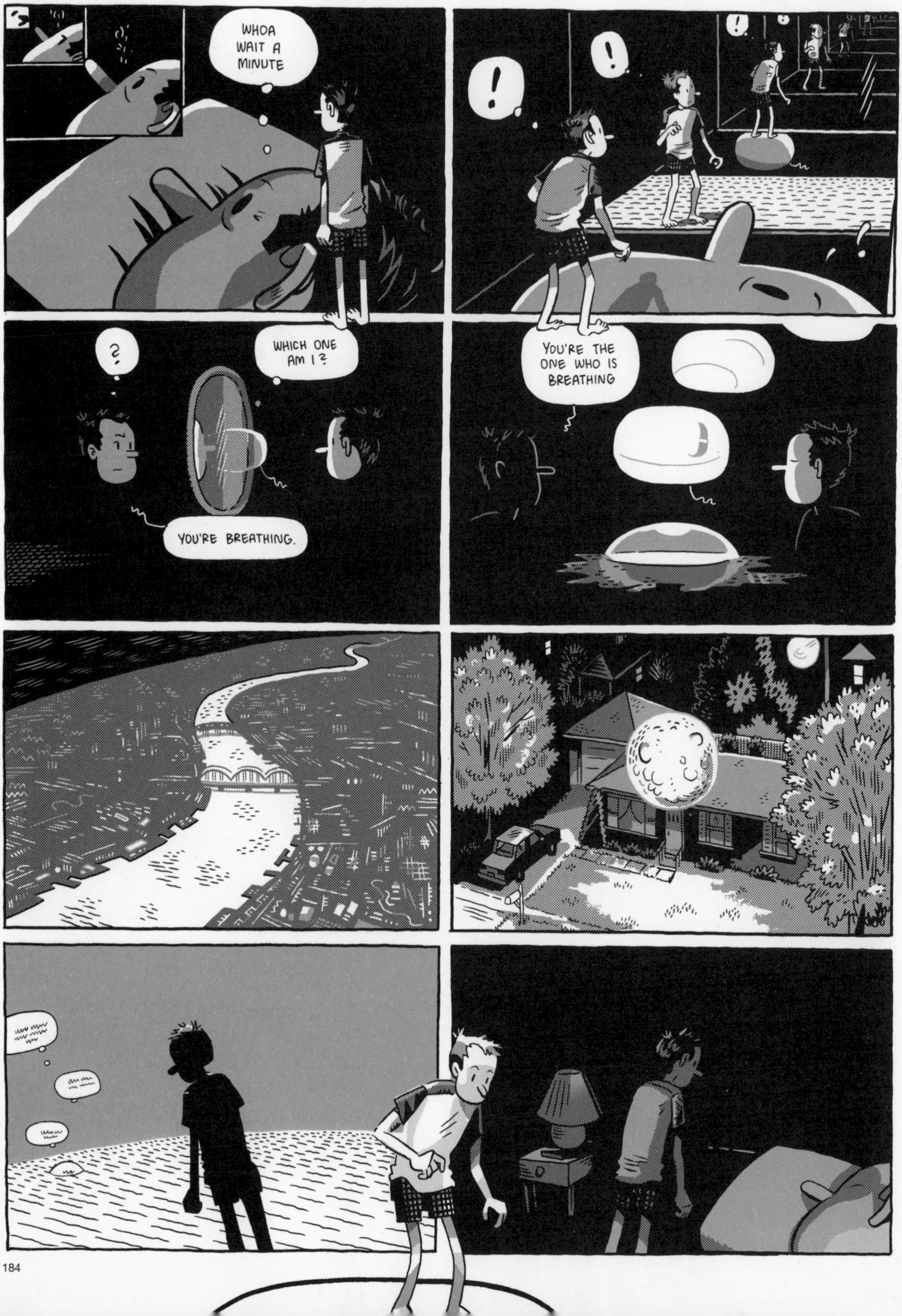
WHOA WAIT A MINUTE
!
!
WHICH ONE AM I?
?
YOU'RE BREATHING.
YOU'RE THE ONE WHO IS BREATHING

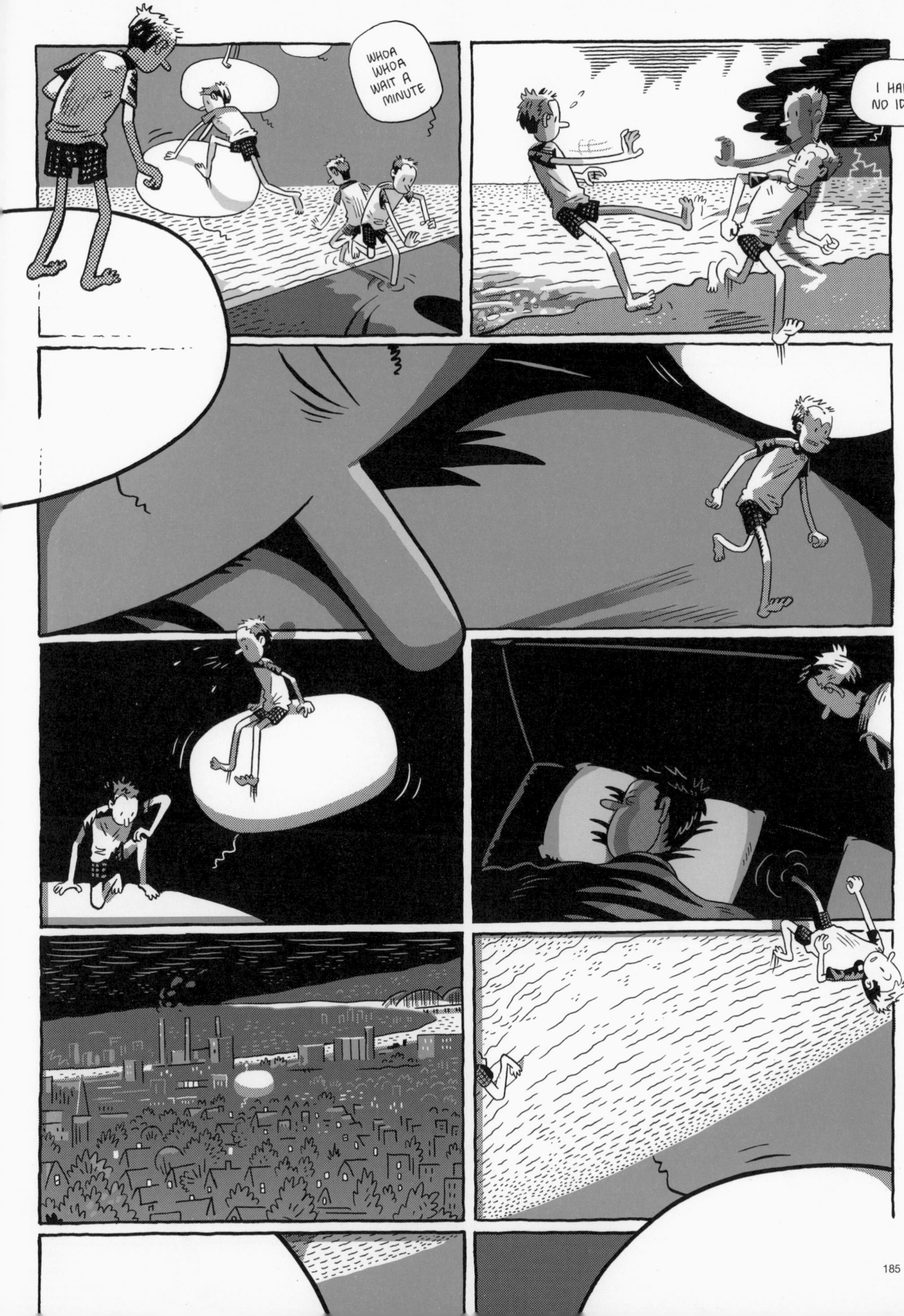
WHOA
WHOA
WAIT A
MINUTE
I HAD
NO IDEA

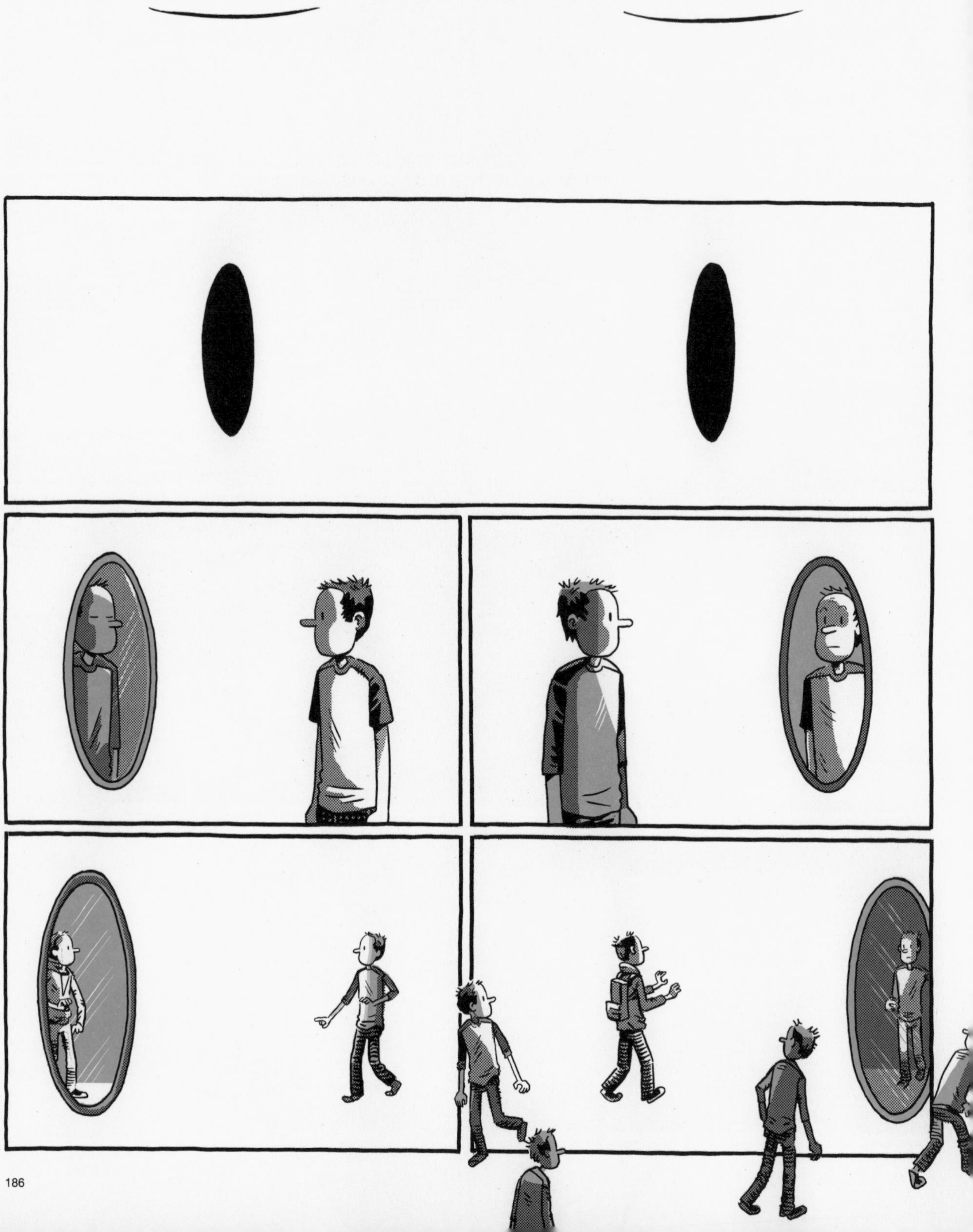

YOU'RE BREATHING

YOU'RE

THINKING

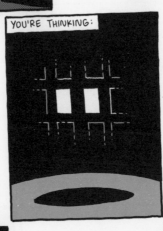

YOU'RE THINKING:

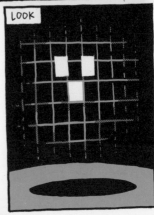

LOOK

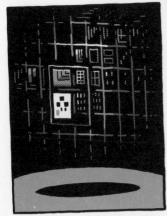

187

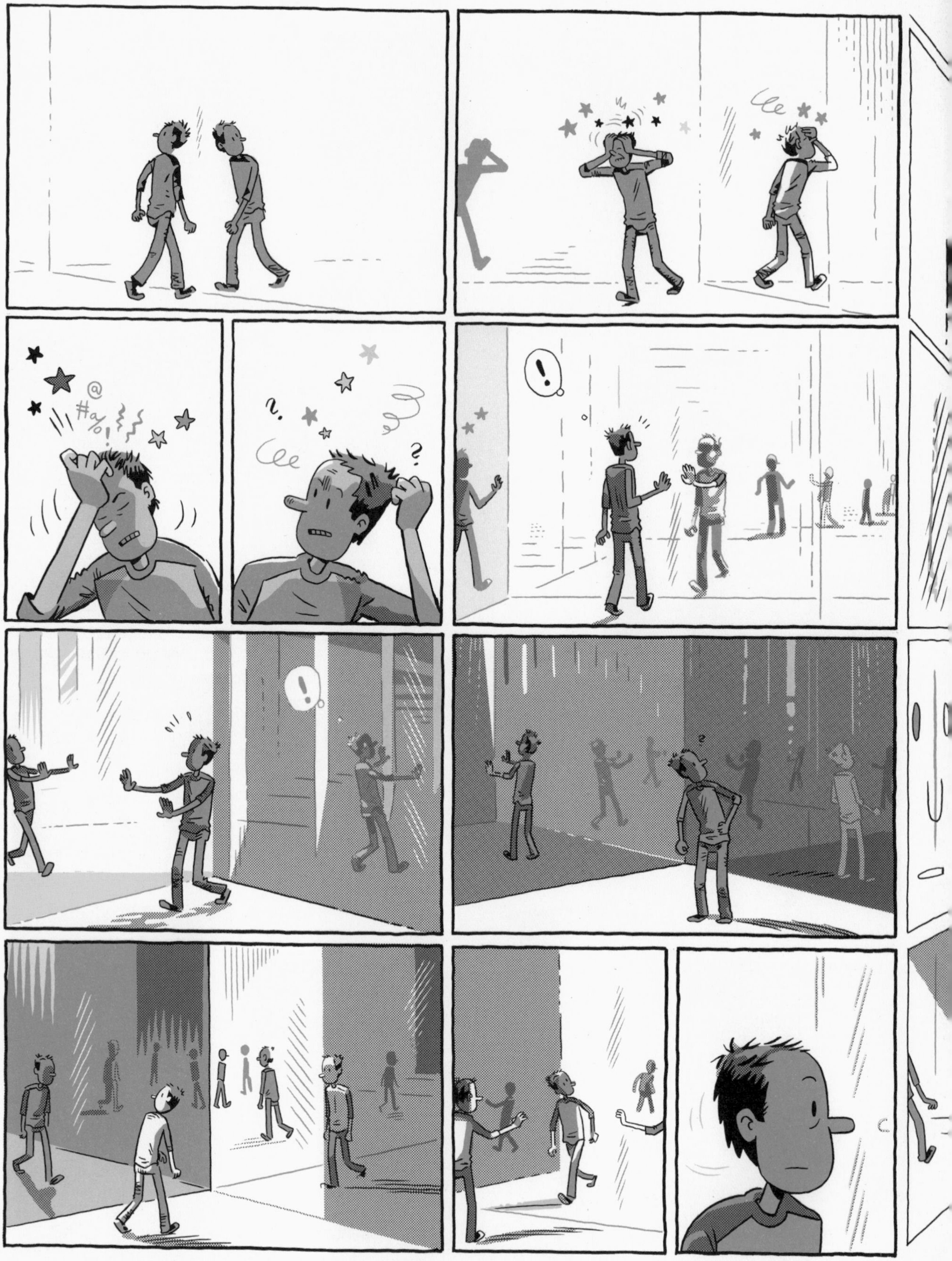

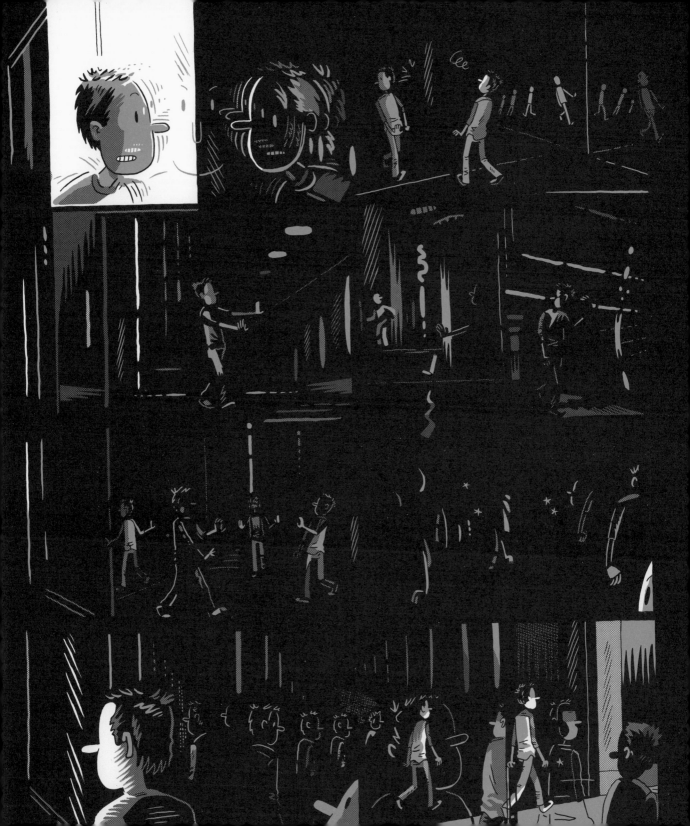

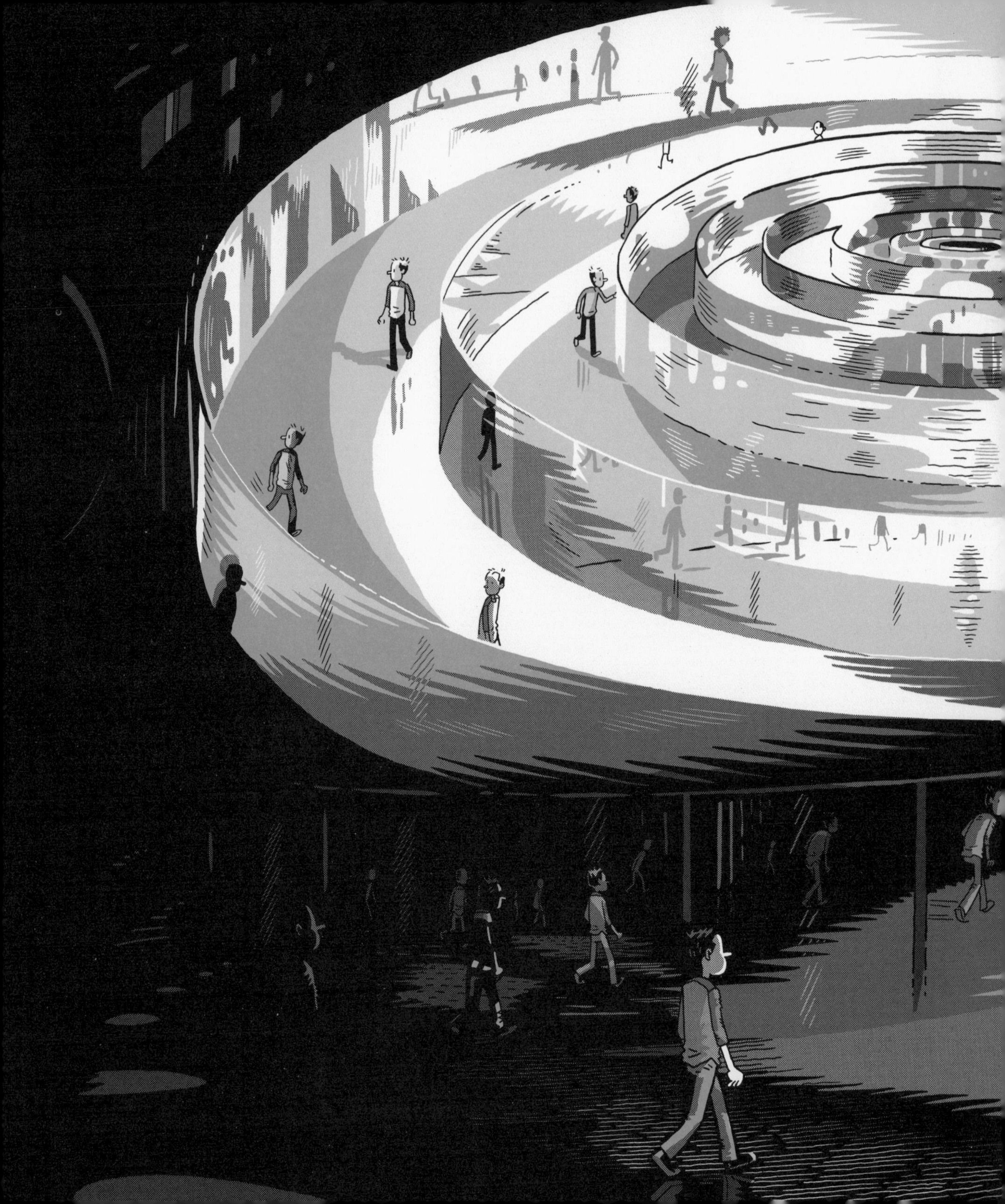

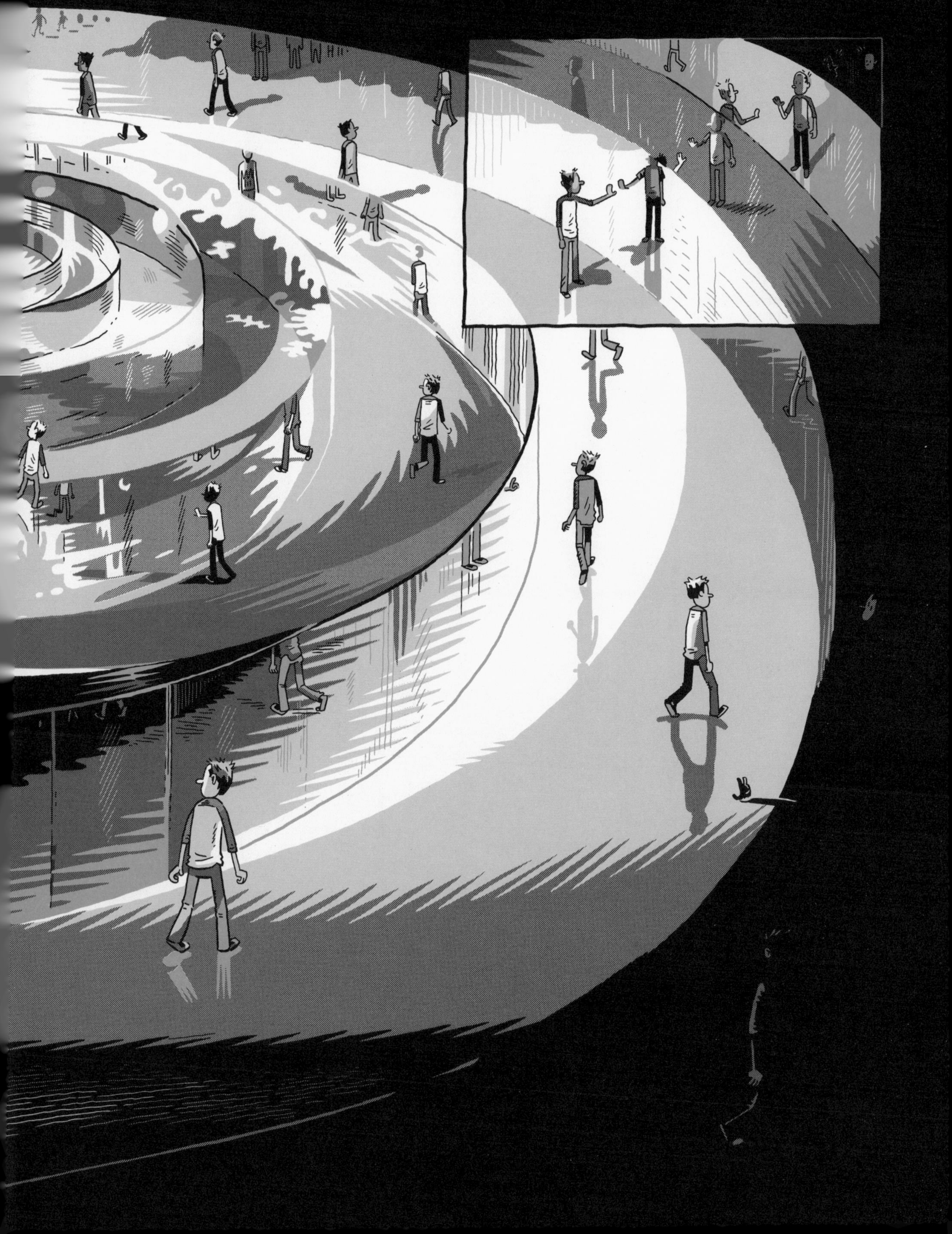

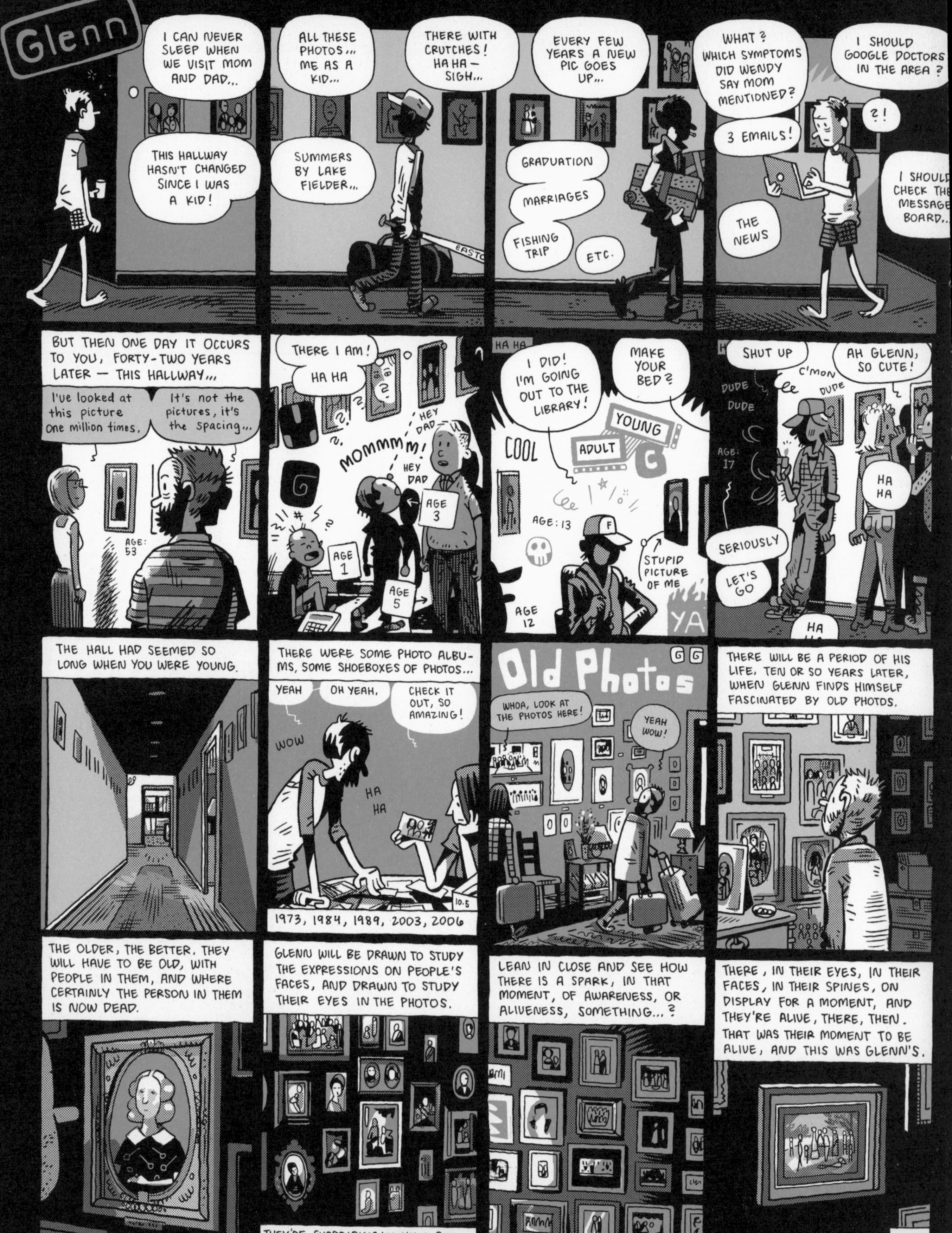
Glenn
I CAN NEVER SLEEP WHEN WE VISIT MOM AND DAD...
THIS HALLWAY HASN'T CHANGED SINCE I WAS A KID!
ALL THESE PHOTOS... ME AS A KID...
THERE WITH CRUTCHES! HA HA — SIGH...
SUMMERS BY LAKE FIELDER...
EVERY FEW YEARS A NEW PIC GOES UP...
GRADUATION
MARRIAGES
FISHING TRIP
ETC.
WHAT? WHICH SYMPTOMS DID WENDY SAY MOM MENTIONED?
3 EMAILS!
THE NEWS
I SHOULD GOOGLE DOCTORS IN THE AREA?
?!
I SHOULD CHECK THE MESSAGE BOARD...
BUT THEN ONE DAY IT OCCURS TO YOU, FORTY-TWO YEARS LATER — THIS HALLWAY...
I've looked at this picture one million times.
It's not the pictures, it's the spacing...
AGE: 53
THERE I AM!
HA HA
MOMMMM!
HEY DAD
HEY DAD
AGE 1
AGE 3
AGE 5
HA HA
I DID! I'M GOING OUT TO THE LIBRARY!
MAKE YOUR BED?
COOL
YOUNG
ADULT
AGE: 13
STUPID PICTURE OF ME
AGE 12
SHUT UP
AH GLENN, SO CUTE!
DUDE
DUDE
C'MON
DUDE
AGE: 17
HA HA
SERIOUSLY
LET'S GO
THE HALL HAD SEEMED SO LONG WHEN YOU WERE YOUNG.
THERE WERE SOME PHOTO ALBUMS, SOME SHOEBOXES OF PHOTOS...
YEAH
OH YEAH.
CHECK IT OUT, SO AMAZING!
WOW
HA HA
1973, 1984, 1989, 2003, 2006
Old Photos
WHOA, LOOK AT THE PHOTOS HERE!
YEAH WOW!
THERE WILL BE A PERIOD OF HIS LIFE, TEN OR SO YEARS LATER, WHEN GLENN FINDS HIMSELF FASCINATED BY OLD PHOTOS.
THE OLDER, THE BETTER. THEY WILL HAVE TO BE OLD, WITH PEOPLE IN THEM, AND WHERE CERTAINLY THE PERSON IN THEM IS NOW DEAD.
GLENN WILL BE DRAWN TO STUDY THE EXPRESSIONS ON PEOPLE'S FACES, AND DRAWN TO STUDY THEIR EYES IN THE PHOTOS.
THEY'RE SURPRISINGLY HIGH-RES...
LEAN IN CLOSE AND SEE HOW THERE IS A SPARK, IN THAT MOMENT, OF AWARENESS, OR ALIVENESS, SOMETHING...?
THERE, IN THEIR EYES, IN THEIR FACES, IN THEIR SPINES, ON DISPLAY FOR A MOMENT, AND THEY'RE ALIVE, THERE, THEN. THAT WAS THEIR MOMENT TO BE ALIVE, AND THIS WAS GLENN'S.
END

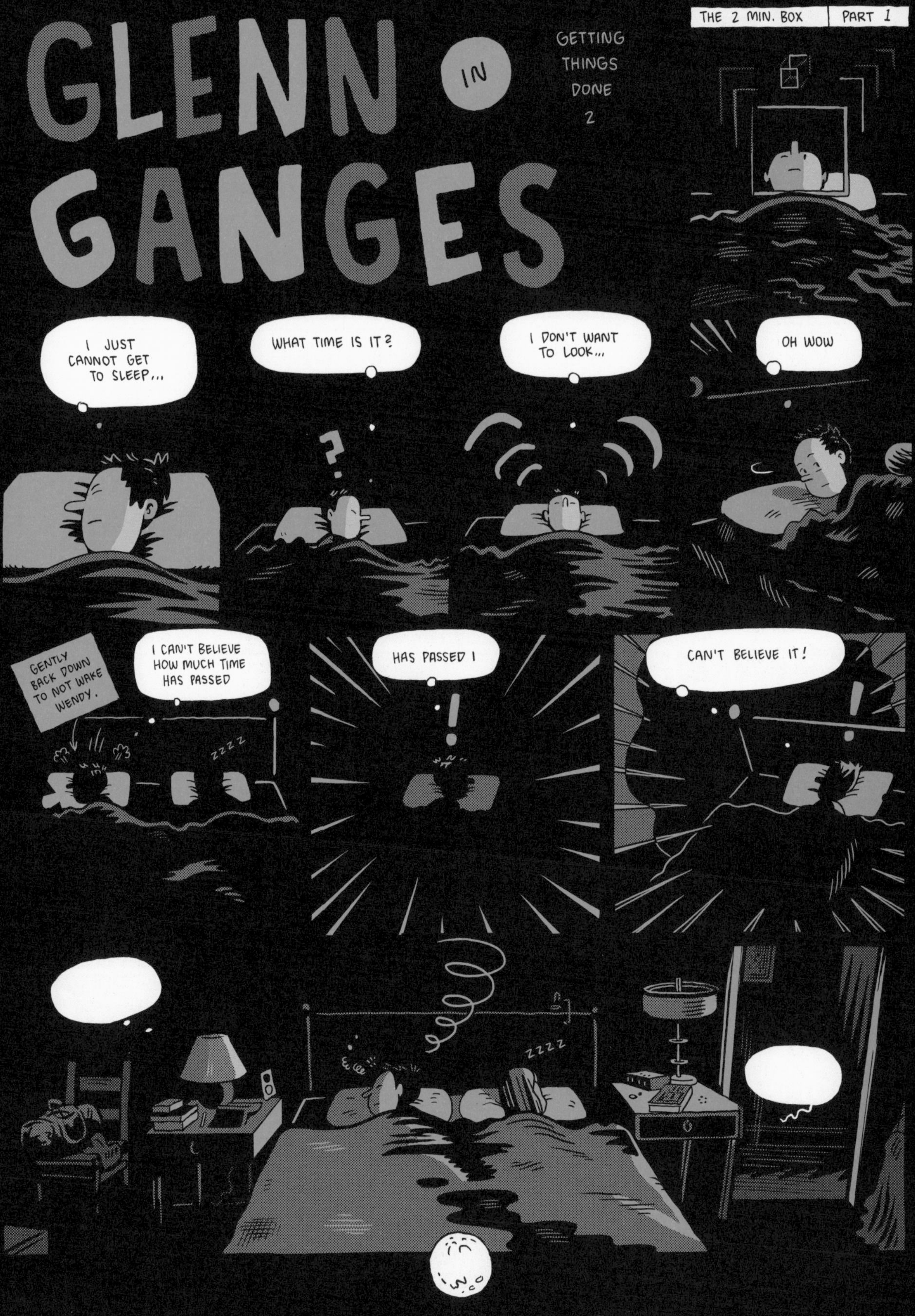
GLENN GANGES IN
GETTING THINGS DONE 2
THE 2 MIN. BOX | PART 1
I JUST CANNOT GET TO SLEEP...
WHAT TIME IS IT?
I DON'T WANT TO LOOK...
OH WOW
GENTLY BACK DOWN TO NOT WAKE WENDY.
I CAN'T BELIEVE HOW MUCH TIME HAS PASSED
ZZZZ
HAS PASSED !
CAN'T BELIEVE IT!
ZZZZ

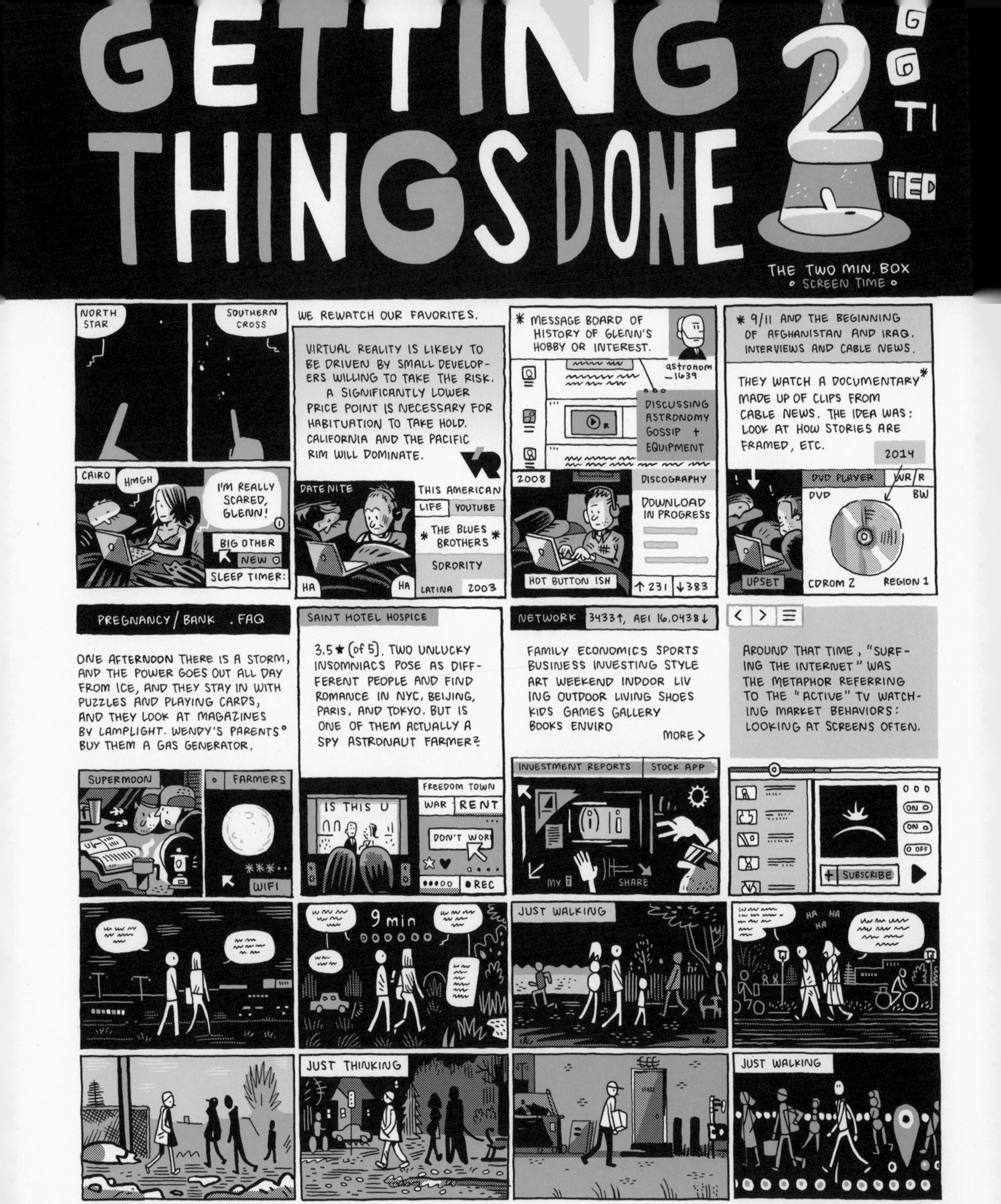
GETTING THINGS DONE 2
G
G
TI
TED
THE TWO MIN. BOX
SCREEN TIME
NORTH STAR
SOUTHERN CROSS
WE REWATCH OUR FAVORITES.
VIRTUAL REALITY IS LIKELY TO BE DRIVEN BY SMALL DEVELOPERS WILLING TO TAKE THE RISK. A SIGNIFICANTLY LOWER PRICE POINT IS NECESSARY FOR HABITUATION TO TAKE HOLD. CALIFORNIA AND THE PACIFIC RIM WILL DOMINATE.
VR
* MESSAGE BOARD OF HISTORY OF GLENN'S HOBBY OR INTEREST.
astronom —1639
DISCUSSING ASTRONOMY GOSSIP + EQUIPMENT
* 9/11 AND THE BEGINNING OF AFGHANISTAN AND IRAQ. INTERVIEWS AND CABLE NEWS.
THEY WATCH A DOCUMENTARY* MADE UP OF CLIPS FROM CABLE NEWS. THE IDEA WAS: LOOK AT HOW STORIES ARE FRAMED, ETC.
2014
CAIRO
HMGH
I'M REALLY SCARED, GLENN!
BIG OTHER
NEW
SLEEP TIMER:
DATE NITE
THIS AMERICAN LIFE
YOUTUBE
* THE BLUES BROTHERS *
SORORITY
LATINA
2003
HA
HA
2008
DISCOGRAPHY
DOWNLOAD IN PROGRESS
HOT BUTTON ISH
↑231 ↓383
DVD PLAYER
WR/R
DVD
BW
UPSET
CDROM Z
REGION 1
PREGNANCY/BANK .FAQ
ONE AFTERNOON THERE IS A STORM, AND THE POWER GOES OUT ALL DAY FROM ICE, AND THEY STAY IN WITH PUZZLES AND PLAYING CARDS, AND THEY LOOK AT MAGAZINES BY LAMPLIGHT. WENDY'S PARENTS° BUY THEM A GAS GENERATOR.
SAINT HOTEL HOSPICE
3.5★ (of 5). TWO UNLUCKY INSOMNIACS POSE AS DIFFERENT PEOPLE AND FIND ROMANCE IN NYC, BEIJING, PARIS, AND TOKYO. BUT IS ONE OF THEM ACTUALLY A SPY ASTRONAUT FARMER?
NETWORK 3433↑, AEI 16.0438↓
FAMILY ECONOMICS SPORTS BUSINESS INVESTING STYLE ART WEEKEND INDOOR LIVING OUTDOOR LIVING SHOES KIDS GAMES GALLERY BOOKS ENVIRO
MORE >
AROUND THAT TIME, "SURFING THE INTERNET" WAS THE METAPHOR REFERRING TO THE "ACTIVE" TV WATCHING MARKET BEHAVIORS: LOOKING AT SCREENS OFTEN.
SUPERMOON
FARMERS
WIFI
FREEDOM TOWN
WAR
RENT
IS THIS U
DON'T WORK
REC
INVESTMENT REPORTS
STOCK APP
MY
SHARE
ON
ON
OFF
SUBSCRIBE
9 min
JUST WALKING
HA HA HA
JUST THINKING
JUST WALKING

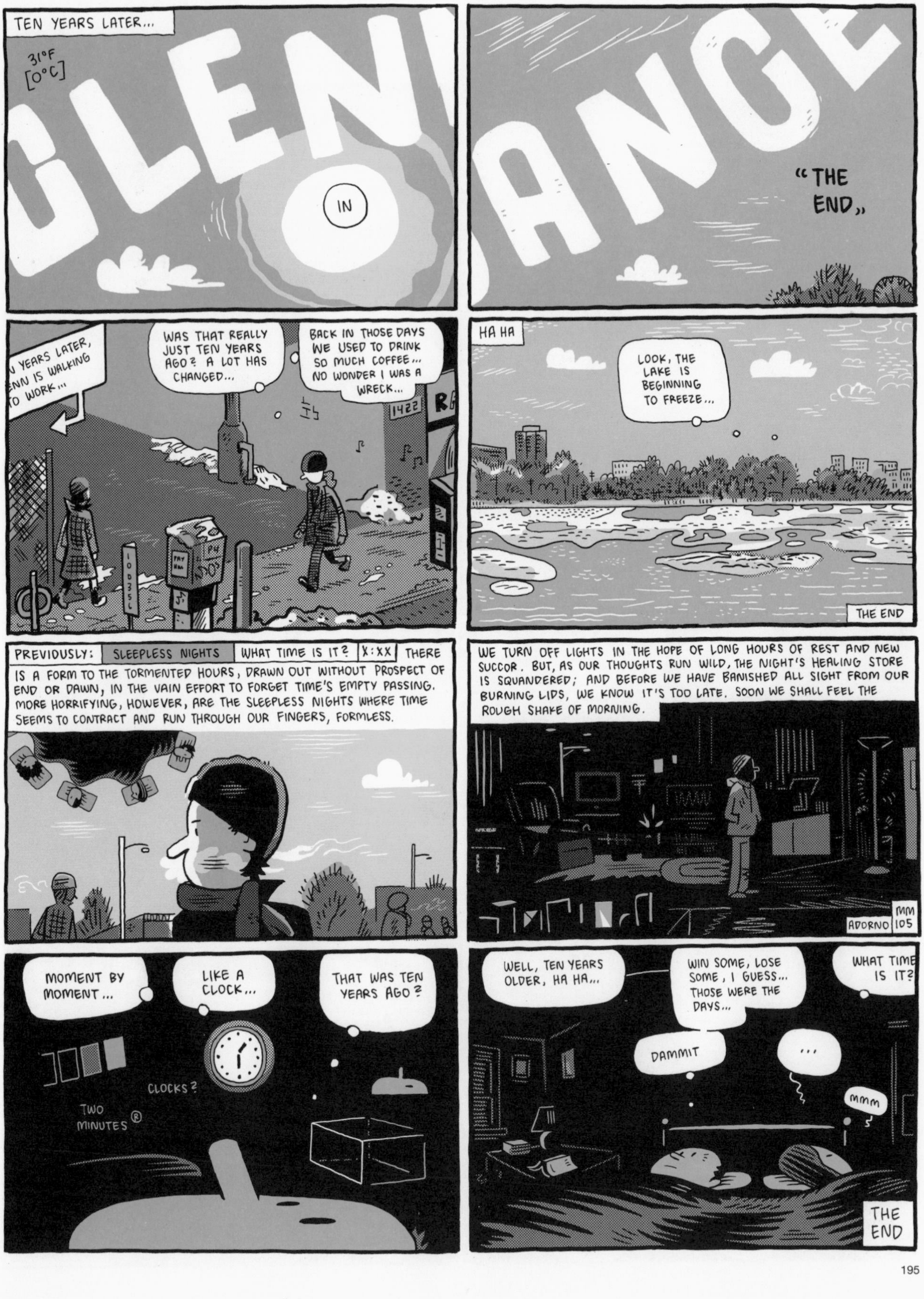

TEN YEARS LATER...
31°F [0°C]
GLEN
IN
ANGE
"THE END,,
N YEARS LATER, ENN IS WALKING TO WORK...
WAS THAT REALLY JUST TEN YEARS AGO? A LOT HAS CHANGED...
BACK IN THOSE DAYS WE USED TO DRINK SO MUCH COFFEE... NO WONDER I WAS A WRECK...
1422
HA HA
LOOK, THE LAKE IS BEGINNING TO FREEZE...
THE END
PREVIOUSLY: SLEEPLESS NIGHTS | WHAT TIME IS IT? | X:XX | THERE IS A FORM TO THE TORMENTED HOURS, DRAWN OUT WITHOUT PROSPECT OF END OR DAWN, IN THE VAIN EFFORT TO FORGET TIME'S EMPTY PASSING. MORE HORRIFYING, HOWEVER, ARE THE SLEEPLESS NIGHTS WHERE TIME SEEMS TO CONTRACT AND RUN THROUGH OUR FINGERS, FORMLESS.
WE TURN OFF LIGHTS IN THE HOPE OF LONG HOURS OF REST AND NEW SUCCOR. BUT, AS OUR THOUGHTS RUN WILD, THE NIGHT'S HEALING STORE IS SQUANDERED; AND BEFORE WE HAVE BANISHED ALL SIGHT FROM OUR BURNING LIDS, WE KNOW IT'S TOO LATE. SOON WE SHALL FEEL THE ROUGH SHAKE OF MORNING.
ADORNO MM 105
MOMENT BY MOMENT...
LIKE A CLOCK...
THAT WAS TEN YEARS AGO?
CLOCKS?
TWO MINUTES®
WELL, TEN YEARS OLDER, HA HA...
WIN SOME, LOSE SOME, I GUESS... THOSE WERE THE DAYS...
WHAT TIME IS IT?
DAMMIT
...
MMM
THE END

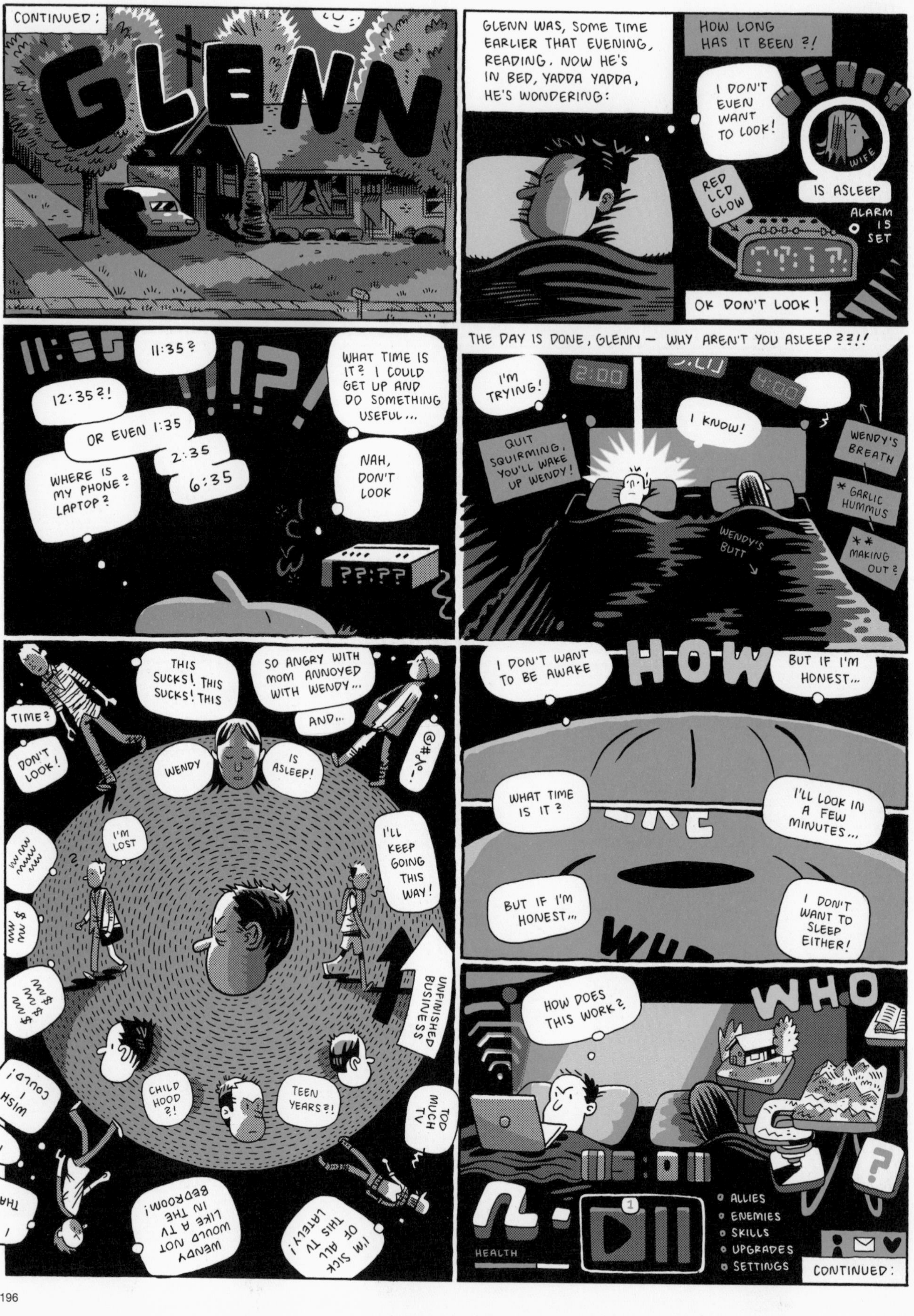
CONTINUED:
GLENN
GLENN WAS, SOME TIME EARLIER THAT EVENING, READING. NOW HE'S IN BED, YADDA YADDA, HE'S WONDERING:
HOW LONG HAS IT BEEN ?!
I DON'T EVEN WANT TO LOOK!
WENDY
WIFE
IS ASLEEP
RED LCD GLOW
ALARM IS SET
OK DON'T LOOK!
11:35
11:35?
!!?!
12:35?!
OR EVEN 1:35
2:35
6:35
WHERE IS MY PHONE? LAPTOP?
WHAT TIME IS IT? I COULD GET UP AND DO SOMETHING USEFUL...
NAH, DON'T LOOK
??:??
THE DAY IS DONE, GLENN — WHY AREN'T YOU ASLEEP ??!!
I'M TRYING!
2:00
4:00
I KNOW!
QUIT SQUIRMING, YOU'LL WAKE UP WENDY!
WENDY'S BREATH
* GARLIC HUMMUS
** MAKING OUT?
WENDY'S BUTT
THIS SUCKS! THIS SUCKS! THIS
SO ANGRY WITH MOM ANNOYED WITH WENDY...
AND...
TIME?
DON'T LOOK!
WENDY
IS ASLEEP!
@#%!
I'M LOST
I'LL KEEP GOING THIS WAY!
UNFINISHED BUSINESS
CHILD HOOD ?!
TEEN YEARS?!
TOO MUCH TV
WISH I COULD!
NAH
I SHOULD WATCH THAT MOVIE
WENDY WOULD NOT LIKE A TV IN THE BEDROOM!
I'M SICK OF ALL THIS TV LATELY!
I DON'T WANT TO BE AWAKE
HOW
BUT IF I'M HONEST...
WHAT TIME IS IT?
I'LL LOOK IN A FEW MINUTES...
BUT IF I'M HONEST...
I DON'T WANT TO SLEEP EITHER!
HOW DOES THIS WORK?
WHO
HEALTH
ALLIES
ENEMIES
SKILLS
UPGRADES
SETTINGS
CONTINUED:

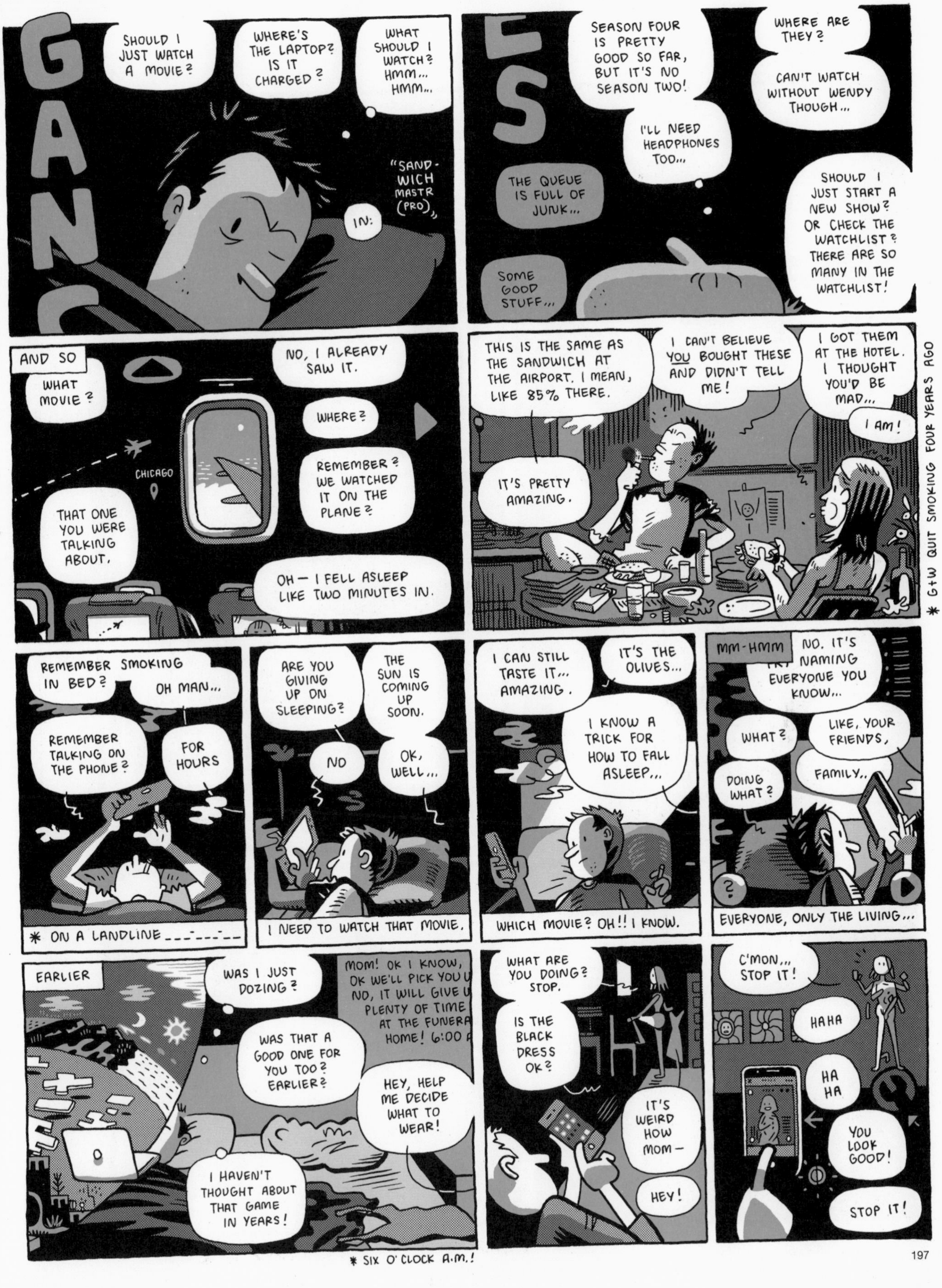
GANG
SHOULD I JUST WATCH A MOVIE?
WHERE'S THE LAPTOP? IS IT CHARGED?
WHAT SHOULD I WATCH? HMM... HMM...
"SAND-WICH MASTR (PRO)"
IN:
ES
SEASON FOUR IS PRETTY GOOD SO FAR, BUT IT'S NO SEASON TWO!
WHERE ARE THEY?
CAN'T WATCH WITHOUT WENDY THOUGH...
I'LL NEED HEADPHONES TOO...
THE QUEUE IS FULL OF JUNK...
SHOULD I JUST START A NEW SHOW? OR CHECK THE WATCHLIST? THERE ARE SO MANY IN THE WATCHLIST!
SOME GOOD STUFF...
AND SO
WHAT MOVIE?
NO, I ALREADY SAW IT.
WHERE?
CHICAGO
REMEMBER? WE WATCHED IT ON THE PLANE?
THAT ONE YOU WERE TALKING ABOUT.
OH — I FELL ASLEEP LIKE TWO MINUTES IN.
THIS IS THE SAME AS THE SANDWICH AT THE AIRPORT. I MEAN, LIKE 85% THERE.
I CAN'T BELIEVE YOU BOUGHT THESE AND DIDN'T TELL ME!
I GOT THEM AT THE HOTEL. I THOUGHT YOU'D BE MAD...
I AM!
IT'S PRETTY AMAZING.
* G+W QUIT SMOKING FOUR YEARS AGO
REMEMBER SMOKING IN BED?
OH MAN...
REMEMBER TALKING ON THE PHONE?
FOR HOURS
* ON A LANDLINE
ARE YOU GIVING UP ON SLEEPING?
THE SUN IS COMING UP SOON.
NO
OK, WELL...
I NEED TO WATCH THAT MOVIE.
I CAN STILL TASTE IT... AMAZING.
IT'S THE OLIVES...
I KNOW A TRICK FOR HOW TO FALL ASLEEP...
WHICH MOVIE? OH!! I KNOW.
MM-HMM
NO. IT'S TRY NAMING EVERYONE YOU KNOW...
WHAT?
LIKE, YOUR FRIENDS,
DOING WHAT?
FAMILY...
EVERYONE, ONLY THE LIVING...
EARLIER
WAS I JUST DOZING?
MOM! OK I KNOW, OK WE'LL PICK YOU U NO, IT WILL GIVE U PLENTY OF TIME AT THE FUNERA HOME! 6:00 A
WAS THAT A GOOD ONE FOR YOU TOO? EARLIER?
HEY, HELP ME DECIDE WHAT TO WEAR!
I HAVEN'T THOUGHT ABOUT THAT GAME IN YEARS!
* SIX O' CLOCK A.M.!
WHAT ARE YOU DOING? STOP.
IS THE BLACK DRESS OK?
IT'S WEIRD HOW MOM—
HEY!
C'MON... STOP IT!
HAHA
HA HA
YOU LOOK GOOD!
STOP IT!

G+W "OUR LOVE" by KnH

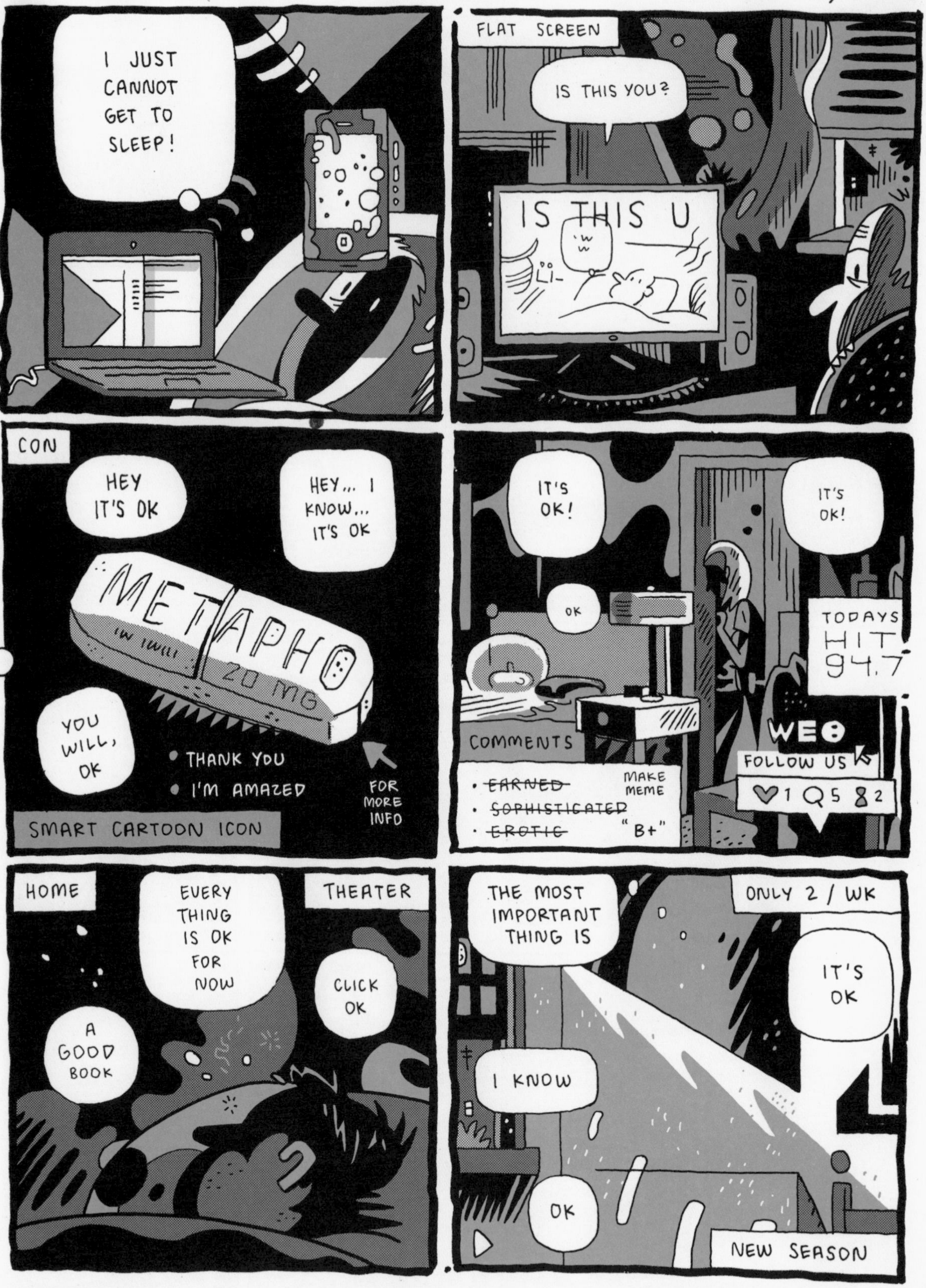
I JUST CANNOT GET TO SLEEP!
FLAT SCREEN
IS THIS YOU?
IS THIS U
CON
HEY IT'S OK
HEY... I KNOW... IT'S OK
METAPHO
20 MG
YOU WILL, OK
• THANK YOU
• I'M AMAZED
FOR MORE INFO
SMART CARTOON ICON
IT'S OK!
IT'S OK!
OK
TODAYS HIT 94.7
COMMENTS
• EARNED
• SOPHISTICATED
• EROTIC
MAKE MEME
"B+"
WEB
FOLLOW US
1 5 2
HOME
EVERY THING IS OK FOR NOW
THEATER
CLICK OK
A GOOD BOOK
THE MOST IMPORTANT THING IS
ONLY 2 / WK
IT'S OK
I KNOW
OK
NEW SEASON

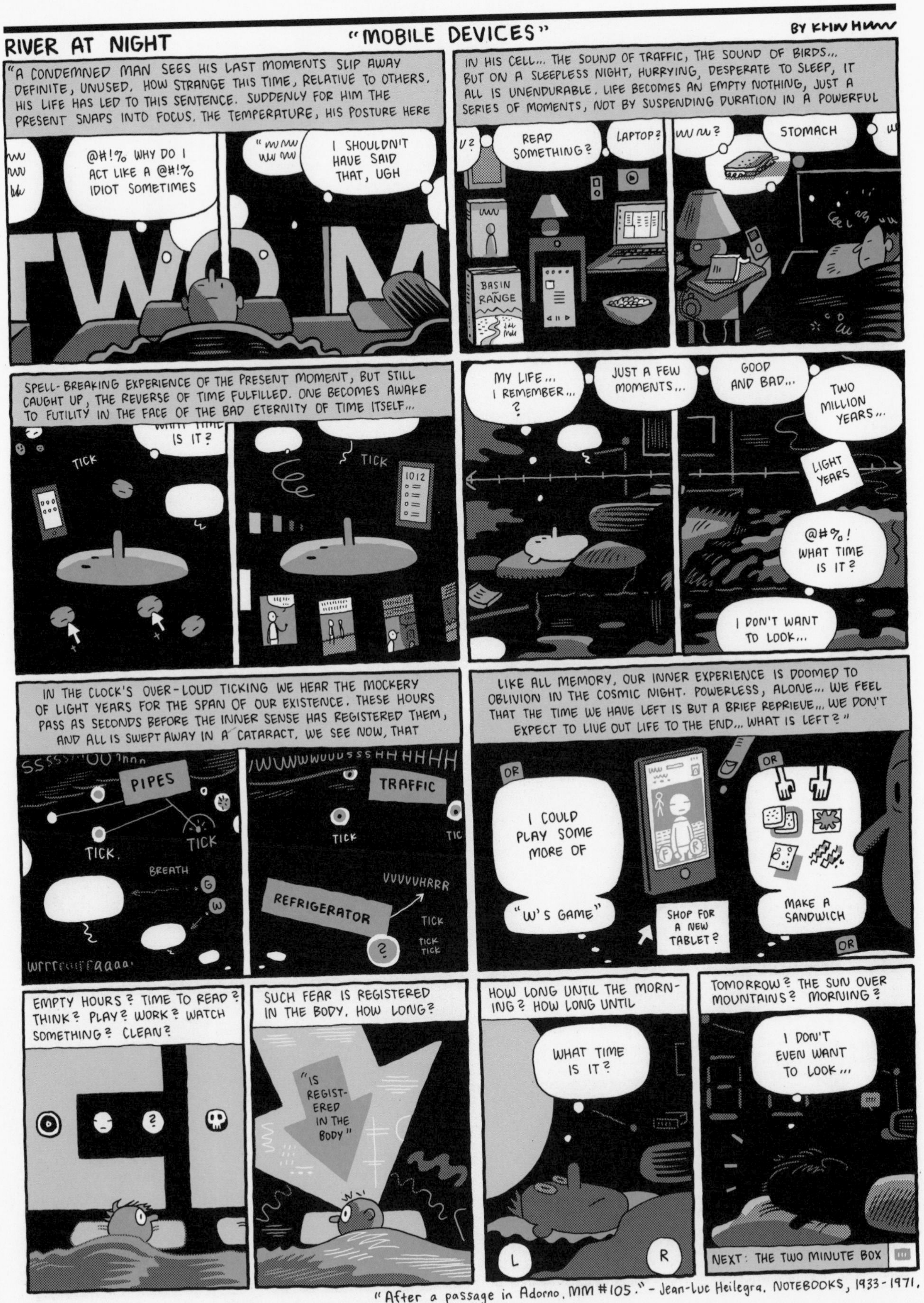
RIVER AT NIGHT
"MOBILE DEVICES"
"A CONDEMNED MAN SEES HIS LAST MOMENTS SLIP AWAY DEFINITE, UNUSED. HOW STRANGE THIS TIME, RELATIVE TO OTHERS. HIS LIFE HAS LED TO THIS SENTENCE. SUDDENLY FOR HIM THE PRESENT SNAPS INTO FOCUS. THE TEMPERATURE, HIS POSTURE HERE
@#!% WHY DO I ACT LIKE A @#!% IDIOT SOMETIMES
I SHOULDN'T HAVE SAID THAT, UGH
TWO M
IN HIS CELL... THE SOUND OF TRAFFIC, THE SOUND OF BIRDS... BUT ON A SLEEPLESS NIGHT, HURRYING, DESPERATE TO SLEEP, IT ALL IS UNENDURABLE. LIFE BECOMES AN EMPTY NOTHING, JUST A SERIES OF MOMENTS, NOT BY SUSPENDING DURATION IN A POWERFUL
READ SOMETHING?
LAPTOP?
STOMACH
BASIN RANGE
SPELL-BREAKING EXPERIENCE OF THE PRESENT MOMENT, BUT STILL CAUGHT UP, THE REVERSE OF TIME FULFILLED. ONE BECOMES AWAKE TO FUTILITY IN THE FACE OF THE BAD ETERNITY OF TIME ITSELF...
IS IT?
TICK
TICK
1012
MY LIFE... I REMEMBER... ?
JUST A FEW MOMENTS...
GOOD AND BAD...
TWO MILLION YEARS...
LIGHT YEARS
@#%! WHAT TIME IS IT?
I DON'T WANT TO LOOK...
IN THE CLOCK'S OVER-LOUD TICKING WE HEAR THE MOCKERY OF LIGHT YEARS FOR THE SPAN OF OUR EXISTENCE. THESE HOURS PASS AS SECONDS BEFORE THE INNER SENSE HAS REGISTERED THEM, AND ALL IS SWEPT AWAY IN A CATARACT. WE SEE NOW, THAT
PIPES
TICK
TICK
BREATH
TRAFFIC
TICK
REFRIGERATOR
VVVVVHRRR
TICK
TICK TICK
LIKE ALL MEMORY, OUR INNER EXPERIENCE IS DOOMED TO OBLIVION IN THE COSMIC NIGHT. POWERLESS, ALONE... WE FEEL THAT THE TIME WE HAVE LEFT IS BUT A BRIEF REPRIEVE... WE DON'T EXPECT TO LIVE OUT LIFE TO THE END... WHAT IS LEFT?"
OR
I COULD PLAY SOME MORE OF
"W'S GAME"
SHOP FOR A NEW TABLET?
OR
MAKE A SANDWICH
OR
EMPTY HOURS? TIME TO READ? THINK? PLAY? WORK? WATCH SOMETHING? CLEAN?
SUCH FEAR IS REGISTERED IN THE BODY. HOW LONG?
"IS REGISTERED IN THE BODY"
HOW LONG UNTIL THE MORNING? HOW LONG UNTIL
WHAT TIME IS IT?
L
R
TOMORROW? THE SUN OVER MOUNTAINS? MORNING?
I DON'T EVEN WANT TO LOOK...
NEXT: THE TWO MINUTE BOX
"After a passage in Adorno, MM #105." - Jean-Luc Heilegra, NOTEBOOKS, 1933-1971.

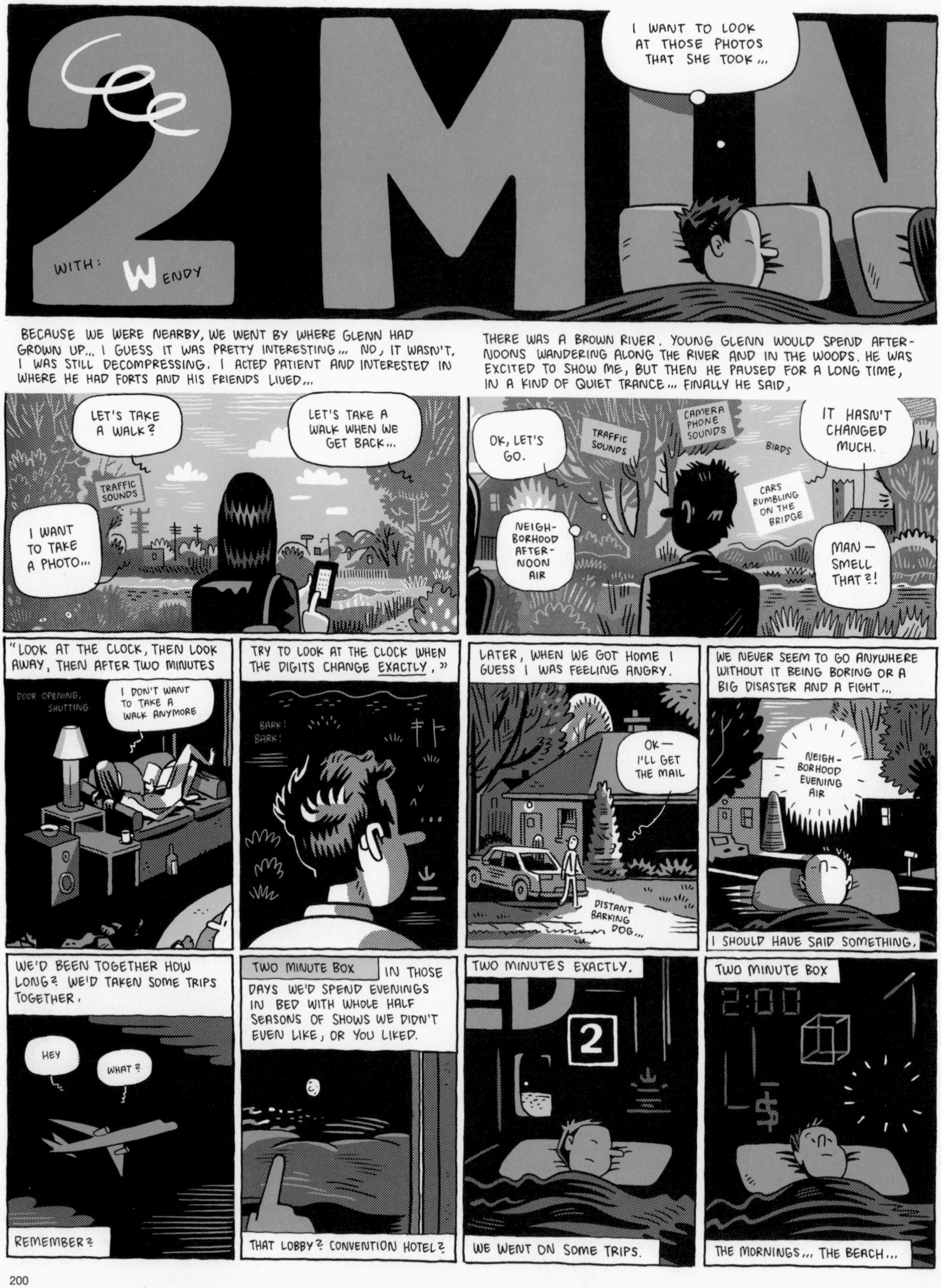
2 MIN
I WANT TO LOOK AT THOSE PHOTOS THAT SHE TOOK...
WITH: WENDY
BECAUSE WE WERE NEARBY, WE WENT BY WHERE GLENN HAD GROWN UP... I GUESS IT WAS PRETTY INTERESTING... NO, IT WASN'T. I WAS STILL DECOMPRESSING. I ACTED PATIENT AND INTERESTED IN WHERE HE HAD FORTS AND HIS FRIENDS LIVED...
THERE WAS A BROWN RIVER. YOUNG GLENN WOULD SPEND AFTERNOONS WANDERING ALONG THE RIVER AND IN THE WOODS. HE WAS EXCITED TO SHOW ME, BUT THEN HE PAUSED FOR A LONG TIME, IN A KIND OF QUIET TRANCE... FINALLY HE SAID,
LET'S TAKE A WALK?
LET'S TAKE A WALK WHEN WE GET BACK...
TRAFFIC SOUNDS
I WANT TO TAKE A PHOTO...
OK, LET'S GO.
TRAFFIC SOUNDS
CAMERA PHONE SOUNDS
BIRDS
IT HASN'T CHANGED MUCH.
CARS RUMBLING ON THE BRIDGE
NEIGH-BORHOOD AFTER-NOON AIR
MAN— SMELL THAT?!
"LOOK AT THE CLOCK, THEN LOOK AWAY, THEN AFTER TWO MINUTES
DOOR OPENING, SHUTTING
I DON'T WANT TO TAKE A WALK ANYMORE
TRY TO LOOK AT THE CLOCK WHEN THE DIGITS CHANGE EXACTLY."
BARK! BARK!
LATER, WHEN WE GOT HOME I GUESS I WAS FEELING ANGRY.
OK— I'LL GET THE MAIL
DISTANT BARKING DOG...
WE NEVER SEEM TO GO ANYWHERE WITHOUT IT BEING BORING OR A BIG DISASTER AND A FIGHT...
NEIGH-BORHOOD EVENING AIR
I SHOULD HAVE SAID SOMETHING.
WE'D BEEN TOGETHER HOW LONG? WE'D TAKEN SOME TRIPS TOGETHER.
HEY
WHAT?
REMEMBER?
TWO MINUTE BOX
IN THOSE DAYS WE'D SPEND EVENINGS IN BED WITH WHOLE HALF SEASONS OF SHOWS WE DIDN'T EVEN LIKE, OR YOU LIKED.
THAT LOBBY? CONVENTION HOTEL?
TWO MINUTES EXACTLY.
2
WE WENT ON SOME TRIPS.
TWO MINUTE BOX
2:00
THE MORNINGS... THE BEACH...

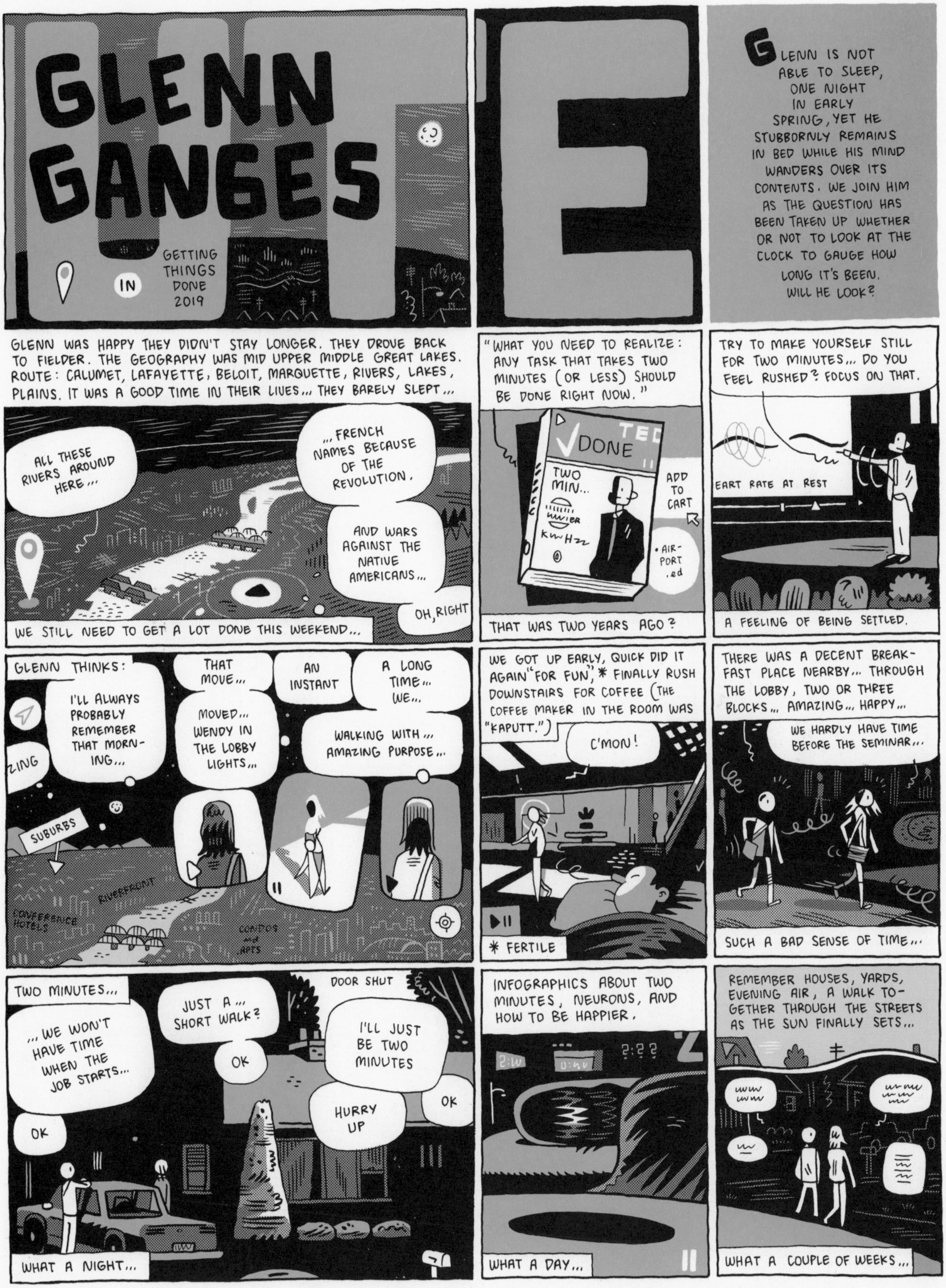
GLENN GANGES
IN
GETTING THINGS DONE 2019
GLENN IS NOT ABLE TO SLEEP, ONE NIGHT IN EARLY SPRING, YET HE STUBBORNLY REMAINS IN BED WHILE HIS MIND WANDERS OVER ITS CONTENTS. WE JOIN HIM AS THE QUESTION HAS BEEN TAKEN UP WHETHER OR NOT TO LOOK AT THE CLOCK TO GAUGE HOW LONG IT'S BEEN. WILL HE LOOK?
GLENN WAS HAPPY THEY DIDN'T STAY LONGER. THEY DROVE BACK TO FIELDER. THE GEOGRAPHY WAS MID UPPER MIDDLE GREAT LAKES. ROUTE: CALUMET, LAFAYETTE, BELOIT, MARQUETTE, RIVERS, LAKES, PLAINS. IT WAS A GOOD TIME IN THEIR LIVES... THEY BARELY SLEPT...
ALL THESE RIVERS AROUND HERE...
...FRENCH NAMES BECAUSE OF THE REVOLUTION.
AND WARS AGAINST THE NATIVE AMERICANS...
OH, RIGHT
WE STILL NEED TO GET A LOT DONE THIS WEEKEND...
"WHAT YOU NEED TO REALIZE: ANY TASK THAT TAKES TWO MINUTES (OR LESS) SHOULD BE DONE RIGHT NOW."
DONE
TWO MIN...
ADD TO CART
THAT WAS TWO YEARS AGO?
TRY TO MAKE YOURSELF STILL FOR TWO MINUTES... DO YOU FEEL RUSHED? FOCUS ON THAT.
EART RATE AT REST
A FEELING OF BEING SETTLED.
GLENN THINKS:
I'LL ALWAYS PROBABLY REMEMBER THAT MORNING...
THAT MOVE...
MOVED... WENDY IN THE LOBBY LIGHTS...
AN INSTANT
A LONG TIME... WE...
WALKING WITH... AMAZING PURPOSE...
SUBURBS
RIVERFRONT
CONFERENCE HOTELS
CONDOS AND APTS
WE GOT UP EARLY, QUICK DID IT AGAIN "FOR FUN",* FINALLY RUSH DOWNSTAIRS FOR COFFEE (THE COFFEE MAKER IN THE ROOM WAS "KAPUTT.")
C'MON!
* FERTILE
THERE WAS A DECENT BREAKFAST PLACE NEARBY... THROUGH THE LOBBY, TWO OR THREE BLOCKS... AMAZING... HAPPY...
WE HARDLY HAVE TIME BEFORE THE SEMINAR...
SUCH A BAD SENSE OF TIME...
TWO MINUTES...
...WE WON'T HAVE TIME WHEN THE JOB STARTS...
JUST A... SHORT WALK?
OK
DOOR SHUT
I'LL JUST BE TWO MINUTES
HURRY UP
OK
OK
WHAT A NIGHT...
INFOGRAPHICS ABOUT TWO MINUTES, NEURONS, AND HOW TO BE HAPPIER.
2:22
WHAT A DAY...
REMEMBER HOUSES, YARDS, EVENING AIR, A WALK TOGETHER THROUGH THE STREETS AS THE SUN FINALLY SETS...
WHAT A COUPLE OF WEEKS...

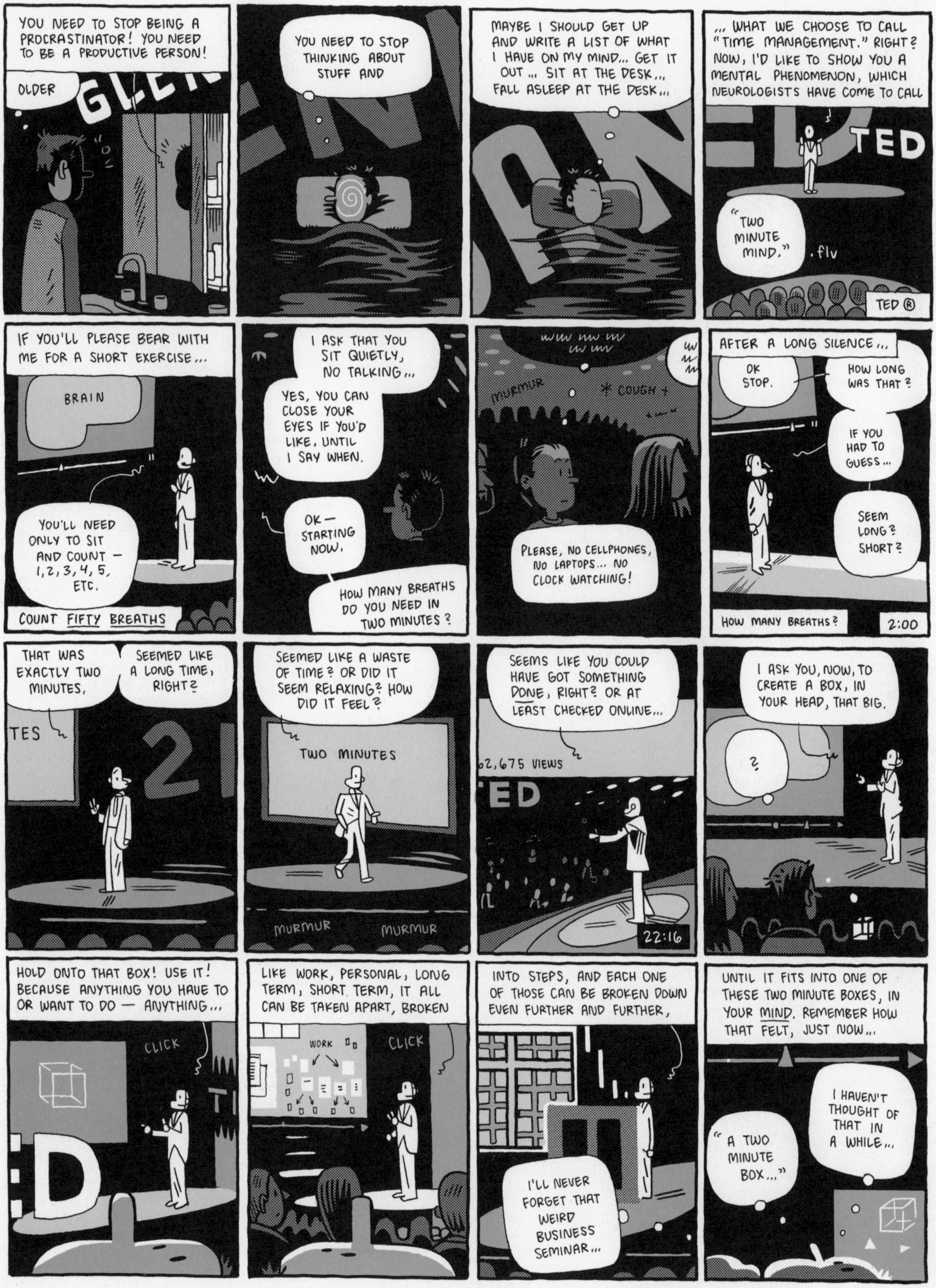
YOU NEED TO STOP BEING A PROCRASTINATOR! YOU NEED TO BE A PRODUCTIVE PERSON!
OLDER
YOU NEED TO STOP THINKING ABOUT STUFF AND
MAYBE I SHOULD GET UP AND WRITE A LIST OF WHAT I HAVE ON MY MIND... GET IT OUT... SIT AT THE DESK... FALL ASLEEP AT THE DESK...
... WHAT WE CHOOSE TO CALL "TIME MANAGEMENT." RIGHT? NOW, I'D LIKE TO SHOW YOU A MENTAL PHENOMENON, WHICH NEUROLOGISTS HAVE COME TO CALL
TED
"TWO MINUTE MIND."
.flv
TED ®
IF YOU'LL PLEASE BEAR WITH ME FOR A SHORT EXERCISE...
BRAIN
YOU'LL NEED ONLY TO SIT AND COUNT — 1, 2, 3, 4, 5, ETC.
COUNT FIFTY BREATHS
I ASK THAT YOU SIT QUIETLY, NO TALKING...
YES, YOU CAN CLOSE YOUR EYES IF YOU'D LIKE, UNTIL I SAY WHEN.
OK — STARTING NOW.
HOW MANY BREATHS DO YOU NEED IN TWO MINUTES?
MURMUR
* COUGH *
PLEASE, NO CELLPHONES, NO LAPTOPS... NO CLOCK WATCHING!
AFTER A LONG SILENCE...
OK STOP.
HOW LONG WAS THAT?
IF YOU HAD TO GUESS...
SEEM LONG? SHORT?
HOW MANY BREATHS?
2:00
THAT WAS EXACTLY TWO MINUTES.
SEEMED LIKE A LONG TIME, RIGHT?
SEEMED LIKE A WASTE OF TIME? OR DID IT SEEM RELAXING? HOW DID IT FEEL?
TWO MINUTES
MURMUR
MURMUR
SEEMS LIKE YOU COULD HAVE GOT SOMETHING DONE, RIGHT? OR AT LEAST CHECKED ONLINE...
VIEWS
TED
22:16
I ASK YOU, NOW, TO CREATE A BOX, IN YOUR HEAD, THAT BIG.
?
HOLD ONTO THAT BOX! USE IT! BECAUSE ANYTHING YOU HAVE TO OR WANT TO DO — ANYTHING...
CLICK
LIKE WORK, PERSONAL, LONG TERM, SHORT TERM, IT ALL CAN BE TAKEN APART, BROKEN
WORK
CLICK
INTO STEPS, AND EACH ONE OF THOSE CAN BE BROKEN DOWN EVEN FURTHER AND FURTHER,
I'LL NEVER FORGET THAT WEIRD BUSINESS SEMINAR...
UNTIL IT FITS INTO ONE OF THESE TWO MINUTE BOXES, IN YOUR MIND. REMEMBER HOW THAT FELT, JUST NOW...
"A TWO MINUTE BOX..."
I HAVEN'T THOUGHT OF THAT IN A WHILE...

THE TWO MINUTE BOX

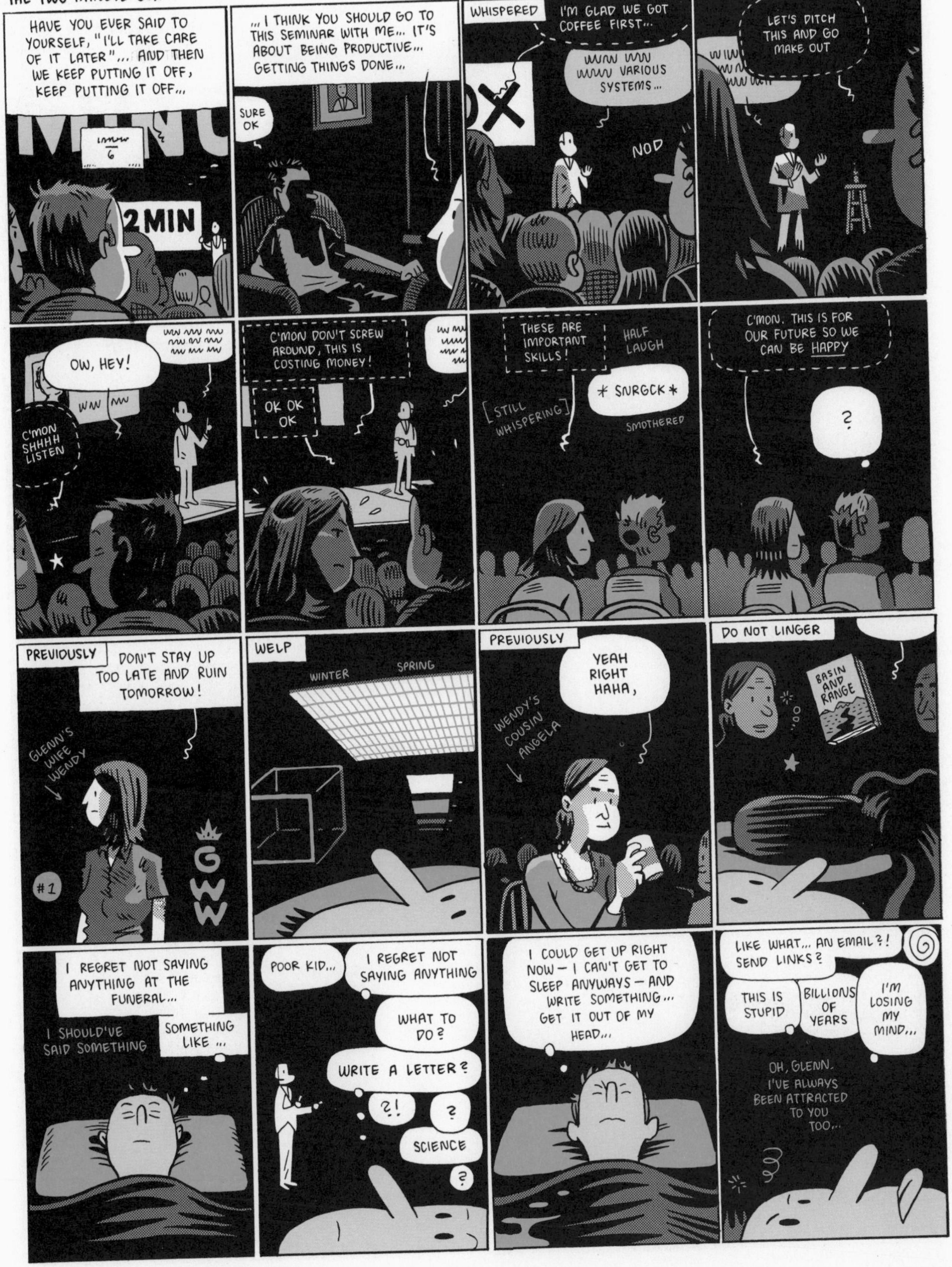
HAVE YOU EVER SAID TO YOURSELF, "I'LL TAKE CARE OF IT LATER"... AND THEN WE KEEP PUTTING IT OFF, KEEP PUTTING IT OFF...
2 MIN
... I THINK YOU SHOULD GO TO THIS SEMINAR WITH ME... IT'S ABOUT BEING PRODUCTIVE... GETTING THINGS DONE...
SURE OK
WHISPERED
I'M GLAD WE GOT COFFEE FIRST...
VARIOUS SYSTEMS...
NOD
LET'S DITCH THIS AND GO MAKE OUT
OW, HEY!
C'MON SHHHH LISTEN
C'MON DON'T SCREW AROUND, THIS IS COSTING MONEY!
OK OK OK
THESE ARE IMPORTANT SKILLS!
HALF LAUGH
[STILL WHISPERING]
* SNRGCK *
SMOTHERED
C'MON. THIS IS FOR OUR FUTURE SO WE CAN BE HAPPY
?
PREVIOUSLY
DON'T STAY UP TOO LATE AND RUIN TOMORROW!
GLENN'S WIFE WENDY
#1
GWW
WELP
WINTER
SPRING
PREVIOUSLY
YEAH RIGHT HAHA,
WENDY'S COUSIN ANGELA
DO NOT LINGER
BASIN AND RANGE
I REGRET NOT SAYING ANYTHING AT THE FUNERAL...
I SHOULD'VE SAID SOMETHING
SOMETHING LIKE ...
POOR KID...
I REGRET NOT SAYING ANYTHING
WHAT TO DO?
WRITE A LETTER?
?!
?
SCIENCE
?
I COULD GET UP RIGHT NOW — I CAN'T GET TO SLEEP ANYWAYS — AND WRITE SOMETHING... GET IT OUT OF MY HEAD...
LIKE WHAT... AN EMAIL?! SEND LINKS?
THIS IS STUPID
BILLIONS OF YEARS
I'M LOSING MY MIND...
OH, GLENN. I'VE ALWAYS BEEN ATTRACTED TO YOU TOO...

"TED TALK"

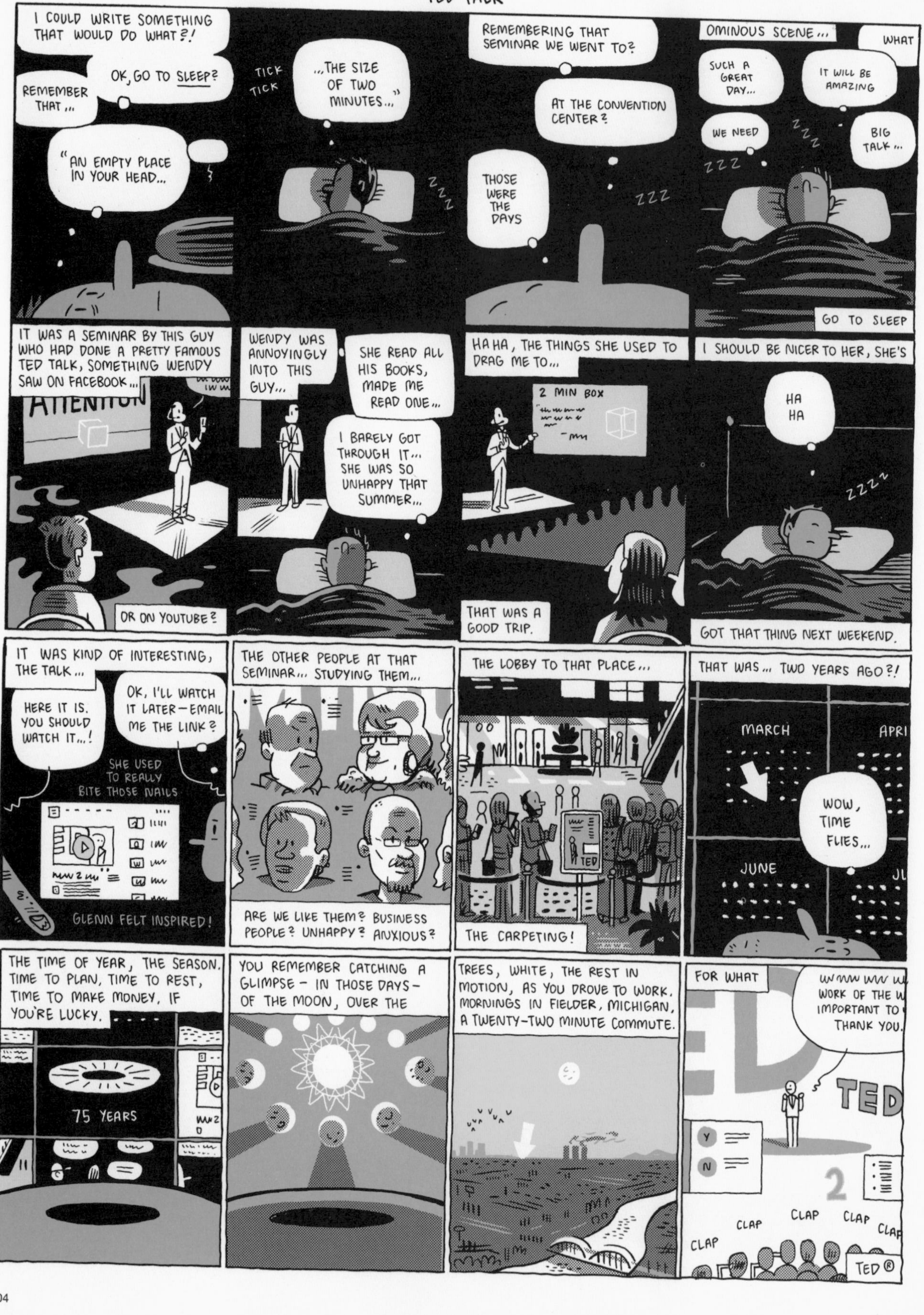
I COULD WRITE SOMETHING THAT WOULD DO WHAT?!
OK, GO TO SLEEP?
REMEMBER THAT...
"AN EMPTY PLACE IN YOUR HEAD...
TICK TICK
..."THE SIZE OF TWO MINUTES..."
REMEMBERING THAT SEMINAR WE WENT TO?
AT THE CONVENTION CENTER?
THOSE WERE THE DAYS
ZZZ
OMINOUS SCENE...
WHAT
SUCH A GREAT DAY...
IT WILL BE AMAZING
WE NEED
BIG TALK...
ZZZ
GO TO SLEEP
IT WAS A SEMINAR BY THIS GUY WHO HAD DONE A PRETTY FAMOUS TED TALK, SOMETHING WENDY SAW ON FACEBOOK...
ATTENTION
OR ON YOUTUBE?
WENDY WAS ANNOYINGLY INTO THIS GUY...
SHE READ ALL HIS BOOKS, MADE ME READ ONE...
I BARELY GOT THROUGH IT... SHE WAS SO UNHAPPY THAT SUMMER...
HA HA, THE THINGS SHE USED TO DRAG ME TO...
2 MIN BOX
THAT WAS A GOOD TRIP.
I SHOULD BE NICER TO HER, SHE'S
HA HA
ZZZZ
GOT THAT THING NEXT WEEKEND.
IT WAS KIND OF INTERESTING, THE TALK...
HERE IT IS. YOU SHOULD WATCH IT...!
OK, I'LL WATCH IT LATER—EMAIL ME THE LINK?
SHE USED TO REALLY BITE THOSE NAILS
GLENN FELT INSPIRED!
THE OTHER PEOPLE AT THAT SEMINAR... STUDYING THEM...
ARE WE LIKE THEM? BUSINESS PEOPLE? UNHAPPY? ANXIOUS?
THE LOBBY TO THAT PLACE...
TED
THE CARPETING!
THAT WAS... TWO YEARS AGO?!
MARCH
APRI
WOW, TIME FLIES...
JUNE
THE TIME OF YEAR, THE SEASON. TIME TO PLAN, TIME TO REST, TIME TO MAKE MONEY, IF YOU'RE LUCKY.
75 YEARS
YOU REMEMBER CATCHING A GLIMPSE – IN THOSE DAYS – OF THE MOON, OVER THE
TREES, WHITE, THE REST IN MOTION, AS YOU DROVE TO WORK. MORNINGS IN FIELDER, MICHIGAN, A TWENTY-TWO MINUTE COMMUTE.
FOR WHAT
WORK OF THE W IMPORTANT TO THANK YOU.
TED
Y
N
2
CLAP CLAP CLAP CLAP CLAP
TED®

"YOUR ATTENTION, PLEASE"

IN THOSE DAYS THERE WERE SOME SLEEPLESS NIGHTS... GOOD ONES, BAD ONES...
AFTER LUNCH WALKS
SOMETIMES TO THE LIBRARY
INTO TOWN
IF YOU COULD ADD THEM ALL UP... HOW MUCH TIME WAS THAT, HOW MANY YEARS?
MORNINGS IN BED...
TOMORROW MORNING...
THIS MORNING
TIME SPENT IN BED... SMELLS, CURVES, SKIN...
WE ALWAYS MADE THE BED IN THAT APARTMENT...
WORRIES, THINGS UNDONE...
TIME SPENT WITH GLOWING SCREENS, STREAMING, TAPPING, SWIPING, READING...
WORK...
WORK
REMEMBER?
SOMETIMES HEADPHONES...
SONGS IN THE DARKNESS, OUT THE WINDOW, INTO THE YARD, DOWN THE STREET,
COOL NIGHT AIR. VALLEY AIR.
YOUR FIRST NEIGHBORHOOD, RAINY SATURDAYS, MUDDY ALLEYWAYS, TREES MEMORIZED, OLD FENCES, WEEDS,
OH GOD THE EMPTY IN-BETWEEN PLACES, THE SUN SHINING, THE COOL SHADOWS, OH GOD!!! WHERE DOES THE TIME GO?
THE 2 MINUTE MIND ®
"THE MIND THAT UNDERSTANDS ITSELF AND ITS WORK IS A MIND THAT KNOWS HOW TO WORK WHEN NECESSARY AND THEN LET GO OF WORK WHEN IT IS NECESSARY; TO PLAY AND LET GO OF PLAY WHEN IT IS NECESSARY..."
9:42P
CHAPTER TWO
"TAKE CHARGE OF YOUR MIND"
TED 2008
SEMINAR EXERCISE
NOW I KNOW IT IS GOING TO SOUND CRAZY BUT
TWO MIN
LET'S DO THAT AGAIN.
AGAIN, PLEASE STAY OFF THE INTERNET DURING THIS, IF YOU WOULD, PLEASE...
TE
I KNOW MANY OF US DEPEND FOR OUR LIVELIHOOD ON THAT RIVER OF CHATTER, HAVE ADAPTED TO ITS SPEED... DON'T WORRY, YOU CAN JUMP BACK IN... "TWO MINUTES."
I'LL PUT A CLOCK UP ON THE SCREEN... TRY TO REMEMBER THE "SIZE" OF TWO MINUTES IN YOUR MENTAL EXPERIENCE...
HERE WE GO... READY?
CLOSE YOUR EYES...
...AND WHEN YOU THINK TWO MINUTES HAS PASSED CHECK THE CLOCK -
0:00
YOU WANT TO BE LOOKING
AT THE MOMENT IT CHANGES.
0:01
THAT WEEKEND TRIP NORTH...
...AND THAT'S HOW YOU GET YOUR
"TWO MINUTE MIND"
SOMETHING SOMETHING SOMETHING...
TED
0:02
REMEMBERING, REPLAYING.
YOU WANT TO SNAP OUT OF IT.
SNAP
2
AT THE MOMENT IT CHANGES
WHEN IT CHANGES
SNAP OUT OF IT.
CRAZY
I'LL TRY THAT NOW
NOTHING FOR TWO MINUTES.
STARTING NOW.

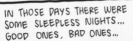

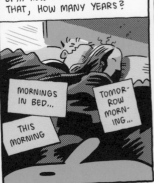

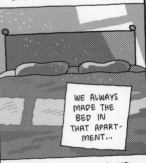

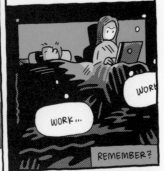

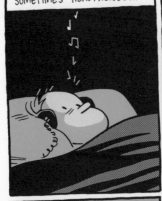

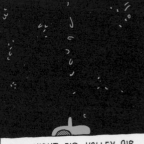

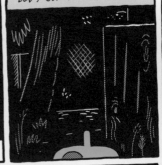

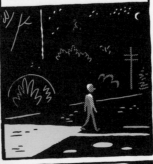

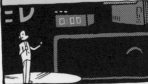

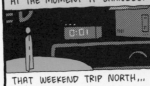

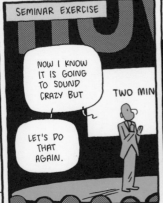

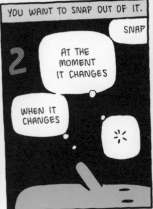

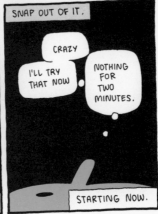

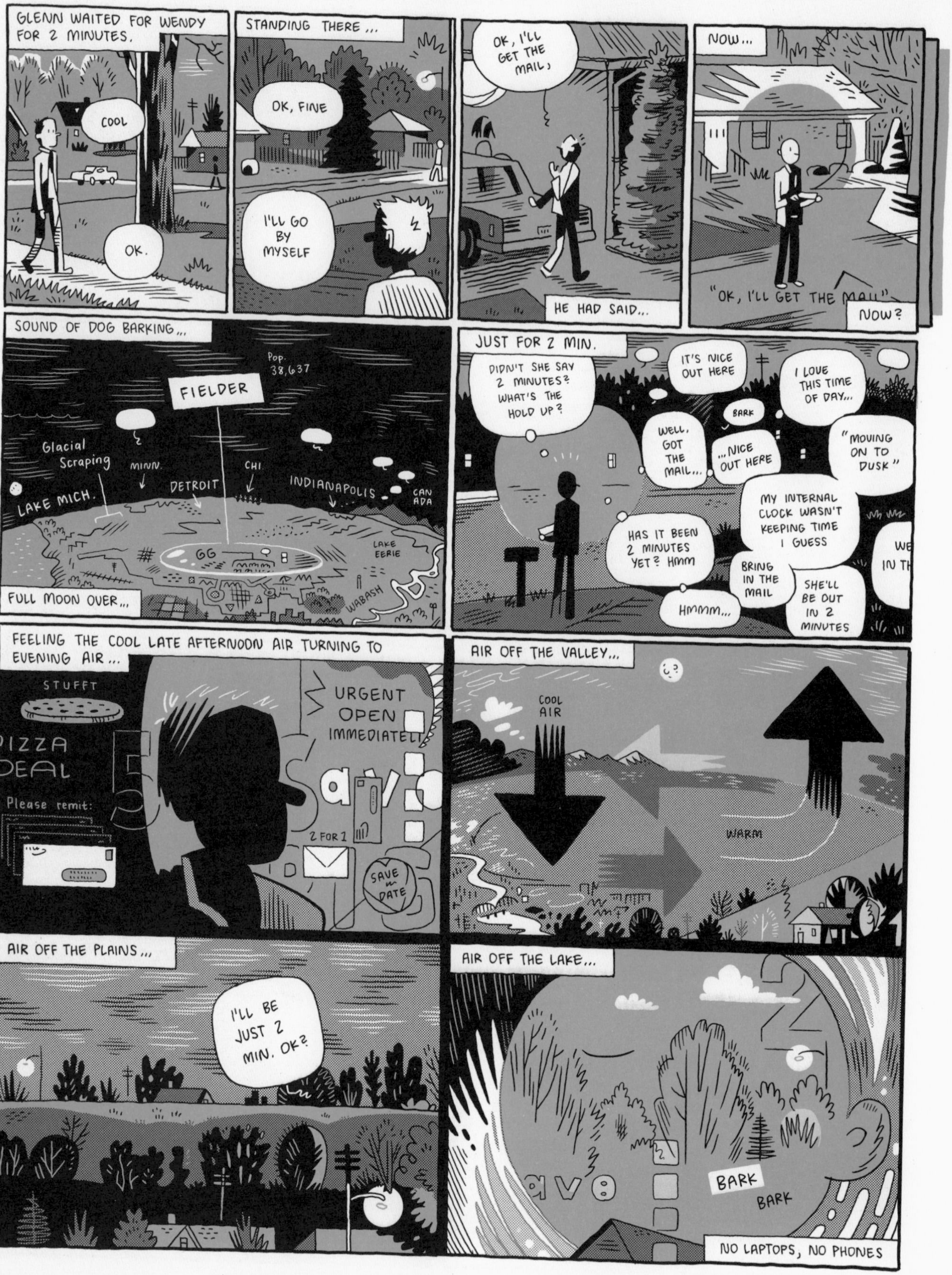
GLENN WAITED FOR WENDY FOR 2 MINUTES.
COOL
OK.
STANDING THERE ...
OK, FINE
I'LL GO BY MYSELF
OK, I'LL GET THE MAIL,
HE HAD SAID...
NOW...
"OK, I'LL GET THE MAIL"
NOW?
SOUND OF DOG BARKING...
Pop. 38,637
FIELDER
Glacial Scraping
MINN.
CHI.
DETROIT
INDIANAPOLIS
CAN ADA
LAKE MICH.
GG
LAKE EERIE
WABASH
FULL MOON OVER...
JUST FOR 2 MIN.
DIDN'T SHE SAY 2 MINUTES? WHAT'S THE HOLD UP?
IT'S NICE OUT HERE
I LOVE THIS TIME OF DAY...
BARK
WELL, GOT THE MAIL...
...NICE OUT HERE
"MOVING ON TO DUSK"
MY INTERNAL CLOCK WASN'T KEEPING TIME I GUESS
HAS IT BEEN 2 MINUTES YET? HMM
BRING IN THE MAIL
SHE'LL BE OUT IN 2 MINUTES
HMMM...
FEELING THE COOL LATE AFTERNOON AIR TURNING TO EVENING AIR ...
STUFFT
PIZZA DEAL
Please remit:
URGENT OPEN IMMEDIATELY
2 FOR 1
SAVE DATE
AIR OFF THE VALLEY...
COOL AIR
WARM
AIR OFF THE PLAINS...
I'LL BE JUST 2 MIN. OK?
AIR OFF THE LAKE...
BARK
BARK
NO LAPTOPS, NO PHONES

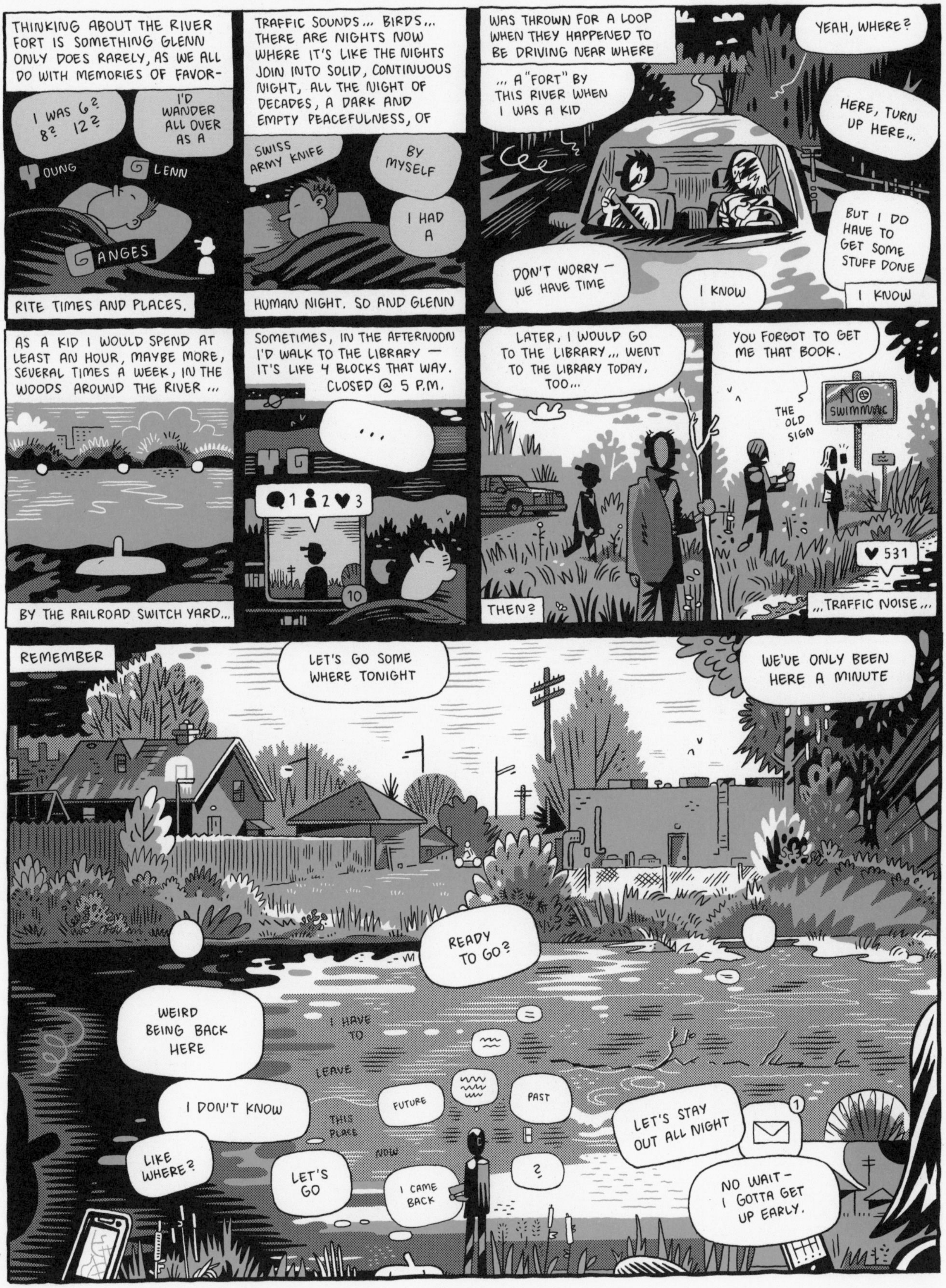
THINKING ABOUT THE RIVER FORT IS SOMETHING GLENN ONLY DOES RARELY, AS WE ALL DO WITH MEMORIES OF FAVOR-
I WAS 6? 8? 12?
I'D WANDER ALL OVER AS A
YOUNG
GLENN
GANGES
RITE TIMES AND PLACES.
TRAFFIC SOUNDS... BIRDS... THERE ARE NIGHTS NOW WHERE IT'S LIKE THE NIGHTS JOIN INTO SOLID, CONTINUOUS NIGHT, ALL THE NIGHT OF DECADES, A DARK AND EMPTY PEACEFULNESS, OF
SWISS ARMY KNIFE
BY MYSELF
I HAD A
HUMAN NIGHT. SO AND GLENN
WAS THROWN FOR A LOOP WHEN THEY HAPPENED TO BE DRIVING NEAR WHERE
... A "FORT" BY THIS RIVER WHEN I WAS A KID
YEAH, WHERE?
HERE, TURN UP HERE...
BUT I DO HAVE TO GET SOME STUFF DONE
DON'T WORRY — WE HAVE TIME
I KNOW
I KNOW
AS A KID I WOULD SPEND AT LEAST AN HOUR, MAYBE MORE, SEVERAL TIMES A WEEK, IN THE WOODS AROUND THE RIVER...
BY THE RAILROAD SWITCH YARD...
SOMETIMES, IN THE AFTERNOON I'D WALK TO THE LIBRARY — IT'S LIKE 4 BLOCKS THAT WAY.
CLOSED @ 5 P.M.
...
YG
1 2 3
10
LATER, I WOULD GO TO THE LIBRARY... WENT TO THE LIBRARY TODAY, TOO...
YOU FORGOT TO GET ME THAT BOOK.
THE OLD SIGN
NO SWIMMING
531
THEN?
...TRAFFIC NOISE...
REMEMBER
LET'S GO SOME WHERE TONIGHT
WE'VE ONLY BEEN HERE A MINUTE
READY TO GO?
WEIRD BEING BACK HERE
I HAVE TO
LEAVE
I DON'T KNOW
FUTURE
PAST
THIS PLACE
NOW
LET'S STAY OUT ALL NIGHT
1
LIKE WHERE?
LET'S GO
I CAME BACK
?
NO WAIT — I GOTTA GET UP EARLY.

12:34

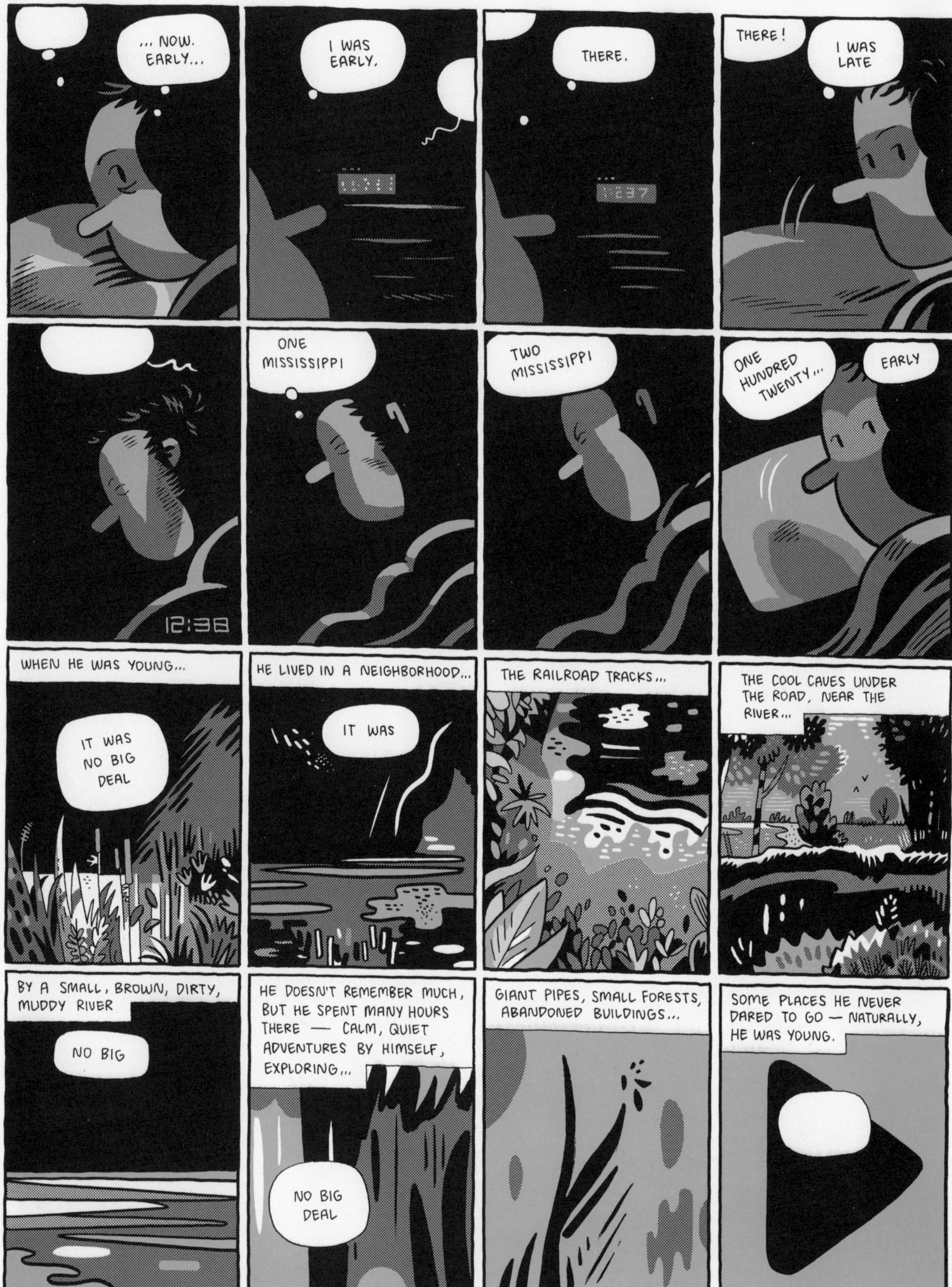
... NOW. EARLY...
I WAS EARLY.
THERE.
THERE!
I WAS LATE
ONE MISSISSIPPI
TWO MISSISSIPPI
ONE HUNDRED TWENTY...
EARLY
12:38
WHEN HE WAS YOUNG...
IT WAS NO BIG DEAL
HE LIVED IN A NEIGHBORHOOD...
IT WAS
THE RAILROAD TRACKS...
THE COOL CAVES UNDER THE ROAD, NEAR THE RIVER...
BY A SMALL, BROWN, DIRTY, MUDDY RIVER
NO BIG
HE DOESN'T REMEMBER MUCH, BUT HE SPENT MANY HOURS THERE — CALM, QUIET ADVENTURES BY HIMSELF, EXPLORING...
NO BIG DEAL
GIANT PIPES, SMALL FORESTS, ABANDONED BUILDINGS...
SOME PLACES HE NEVER DARED TO GO — NATURALLY, HE WAS YOUNG.

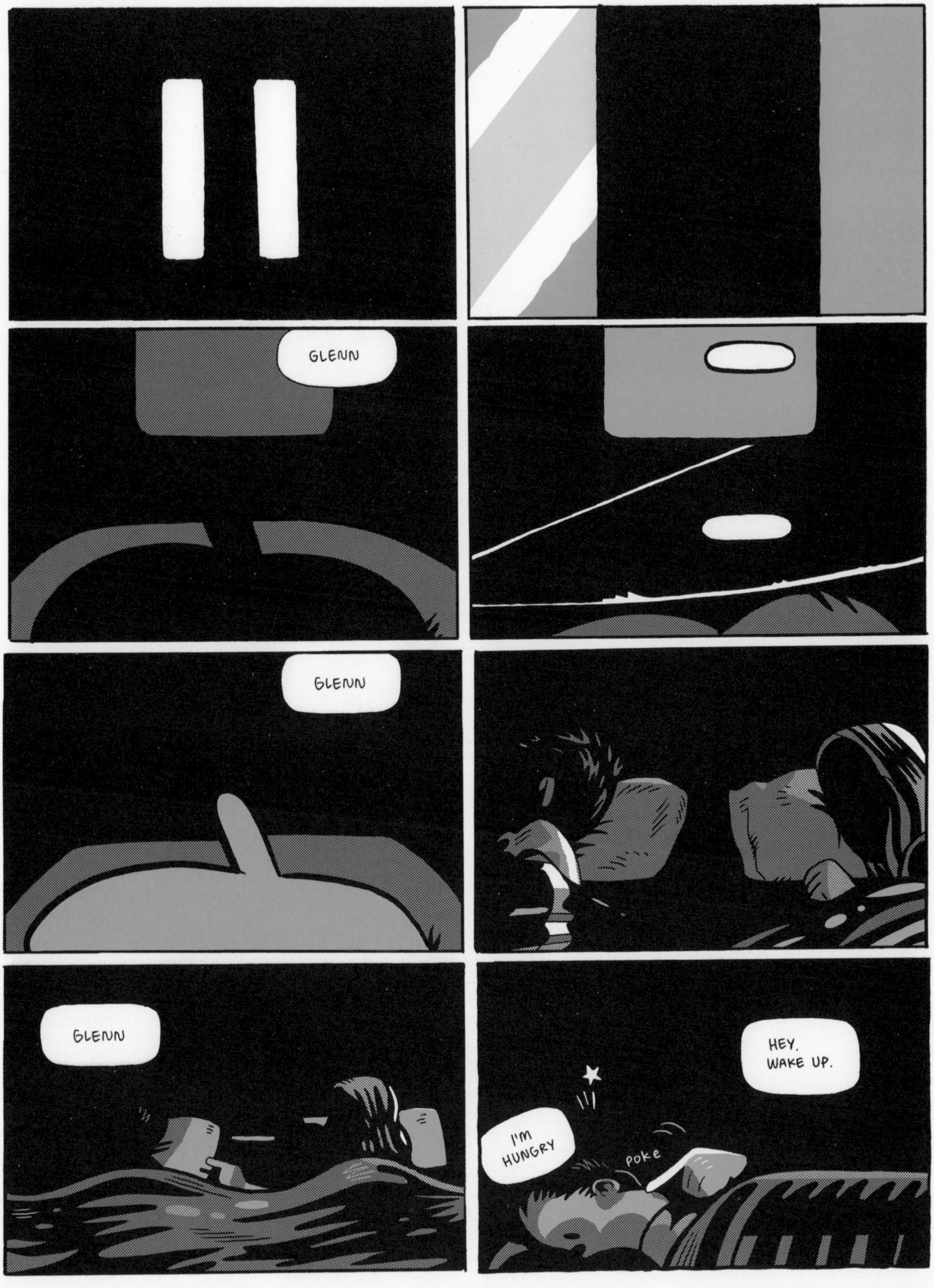
GLENN
GLENN
GLENN
HEY. WAKE UP.
I'M HUNGRY
POKE

G+W

"AIRPORT MEMORIES"

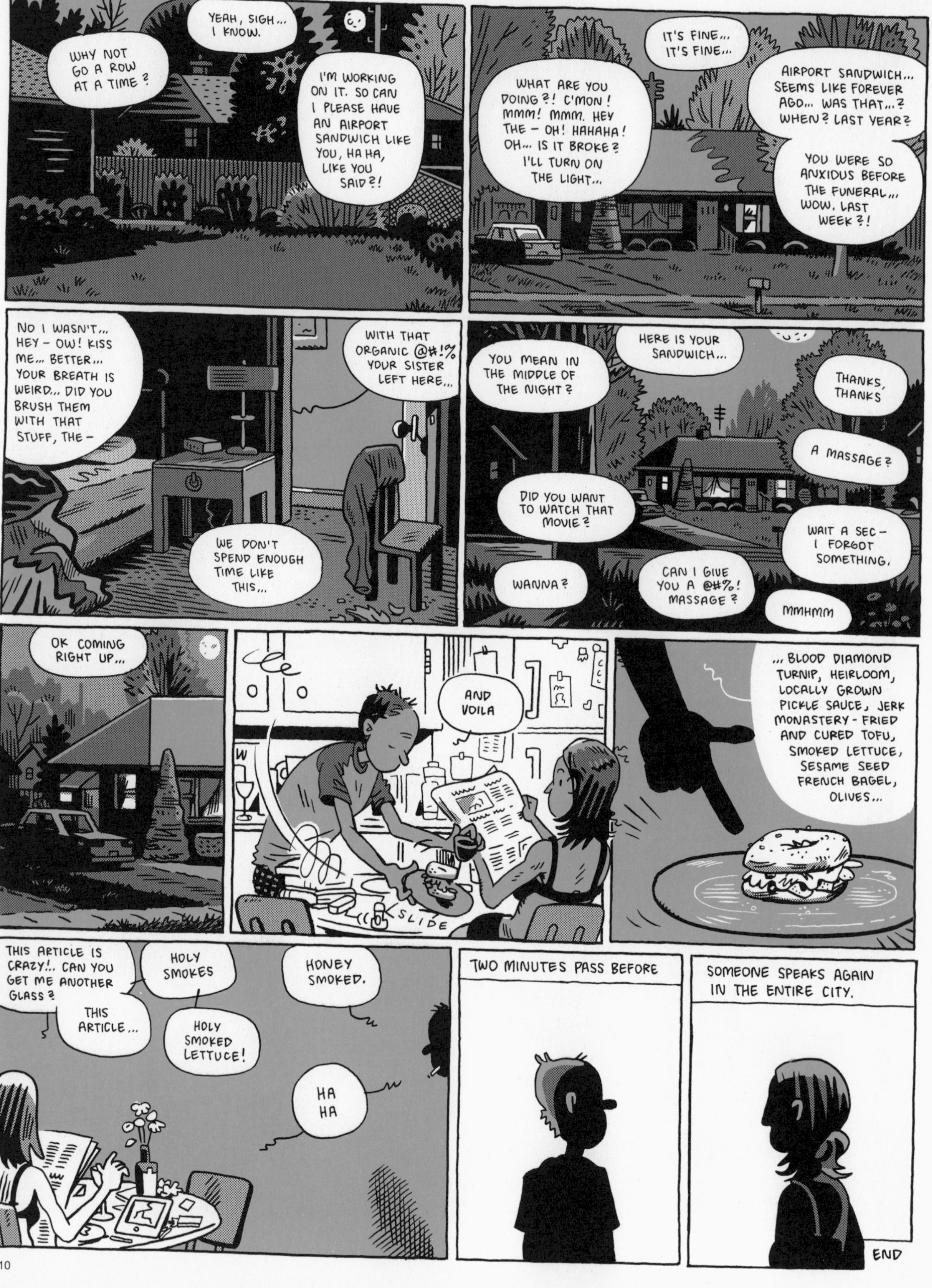
WHY NOT GO A ROW AT A TIME?
YEAH, SIGH... I KNOW.
I'M WORKING ON IT. SO CAN I PLEASE HAVE AN AIRPORT SANDWICH LIKE YOU, HA HA, LIKE YOU SAID?!
WHAT ARE YOU DOING?! C'MON! MMM! MMM. HEY THE - OH! HAHAHA! OH... IS IT BROKE? I'LL TURN ON THE LIGHT...
IT'S FINE... IT'S FINE...
AIRPORT SANDWICH... SEEMS LIKE FOREVER AGO... WAS THAT...? WHEN? LAST YEAR?
YOU WERE SO ANXIOUS BEFORE THE FUNERAL... WOW. LAST WEEK?!
NO I WASN'T... HEY - OW! KISS ME... BETTER... YOUR BREATH IS WEIRD... DID YOU BRUSH THEM WITH THAT STUFF, THE -
WITH THAT ORGANIC @#!% YOUR SISTER LEFT HERE...
WE DON'T SPEND ENOUGH TIME LIKE THIS...
YOU MEAN IN THE MIDDLE OF THE NIGHT?
HERE IS YOUR SANDWICH...
THANKS, THANKS
A MASSAGE?
DID YOU WANT TO WATCH THAT MOVIE?
WAIT A SEC - I FORGOT SOMETHING.
WANNA?
CAN I GIVE YOU A @#%! MASSAGE?
MMHMM
OK COMING RIGHT UP...
AND VOILA
SLIDE
... BLOOD DIAMOND TURNIP, HEIRLOOM, LOCALLY GROWN PICKLE SAUCE, JERK MONASTERY - FRIED AND CURED TOFU, SMOKED LETTUCE, SESAME SEED FRENCH BAGEL, OLIVES...
THIS ARTICLE IS CRAZY!.. CAN YOU GET ME ANOTHER GLASS?
HOLY SMOKES
HONEY SMOKED.
THIS ARTICLE...
HOLY SMOKED LETTUCE!
HA HA
TWO MINUTES PASS BEFORE
SOMEONE SPEAKS AGAIN IN THE ENTIRE CITY.
END

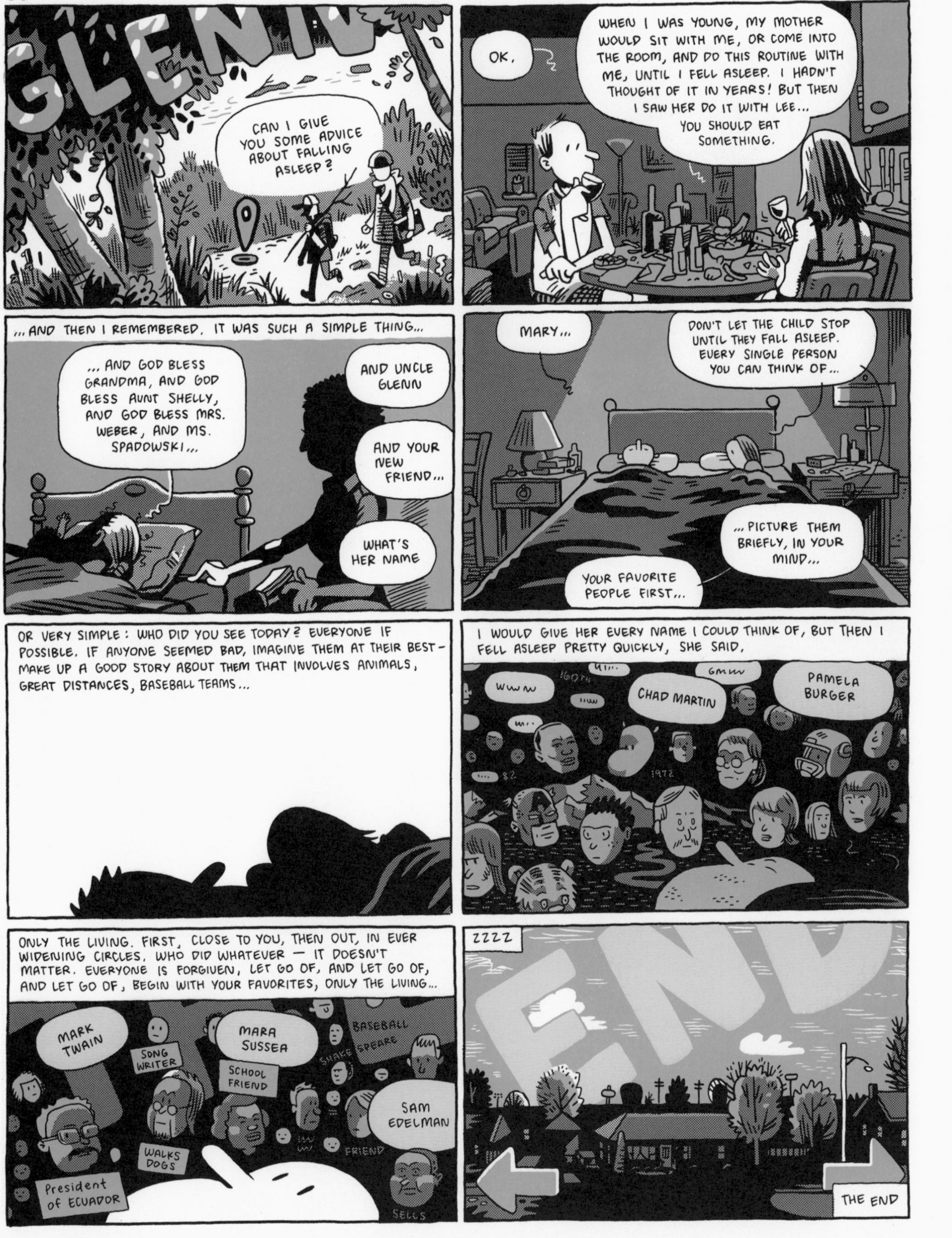
GLENN
CAN I GIVE YOU SOME ADVICE ABOUT FALLING ASLEEP?
OK.
WHEN I WAS YOUNG, MY MOTHER WOULD SIT WITH ME, OR COME INTO THE ROOM, AND DO THIS ROUTINE WITH ME, UNTIL I FELL ASLEEP. I HADN'T THOUGHT OF IT IN YEARS! BUT THEN I SAW HER DO IT WITH LEE...
YOU SHOULD EAT SOMETHING.
...AND THEN I REMEMBERED. IT WAS SUCH A SIMPLE THING...
...AND GOD BLESS GRANDMA, AND GOD BLESS AUNT SHELLY, AND GOD BLESS MRS. WEBER, AND MS. SPADOWSKI...
AND UNCLE GLENN
AND YOUR NEW FRIEND...
WHAT'S HER NAME
MARY...
DON'T LET THE CHILD STOP UNTIL THEY FALL ASLEEP. EVERY SINGLE PERSON YOU CAN THINK OF...
...PICTURE THEM BRIEFLY, IN YOUR MIND...
YOUR FAVORITE PEOPLE FIRST...
OR VERY SIMPLE: WHO DID YOU SEE TODAY? EVERYONE IF POSSIBLE. IF ANYONE SEEMED BAD, IMAGINE THEM AT THEIR BEST - MAKE UP A GOOD STORY ABOUT THEM THAT INVOLVES ANIMALS, GREAT DISTANCES, BASEBALL TEAMS...
I WOULD GIVE HER EVERY NAME I COULD THINK OF, BUT THEN I FELL ASLEEP PRETTY QUICKLY, SHE SAID.
CHAD MARTIN
PAMELA BURGER
ONLY THE LIVING. FIRST, CLOSE TO YOU, THEN OUT, IN EVER WIDENING CIRCLES, WHO DID WHATEVER — IT DOESN'T MATTER. EVERYONE IS FORGIVEN, LET GO OF, AND LET GO OF, AND LET GO OF, BEGIN WITH YOUR FAVORITES, ONLY THE LIVING...
MARK TWAIN
SONG WRITER
MARA SUSSEA
SCHOOL FRIEND
BASEBALL
SHAKESPEARE
SAM EDELMAN
WALKS DOGS
FRIEND
President of ECUADOR
SELLS
ZZZZ
END
THE END

ABOUT THE AUTHOR

KEVIN HUIZENGA grew up near Chicago in the village of South Holland, and has lived in Michigan, Missouri, and Minnesota. In college he started drawing the influential mini-comic *Supermonster*. He has written and drawn several comic book series, including *Or Else* and *Ganges*, as well as numerous mini-comics and zines. His graphic novels include *Curses*, *The Wild Kingdom*, and *Gloriana*. His work has been translated into six languages; won five Ignatz awards and been nominated for Harvey and Eisner awards; and has appeared in *Time*, *The New Yorker*, *Kramers Ergot*, and others. He currently lives and teaches in Minneapolis and sleeps just fine.

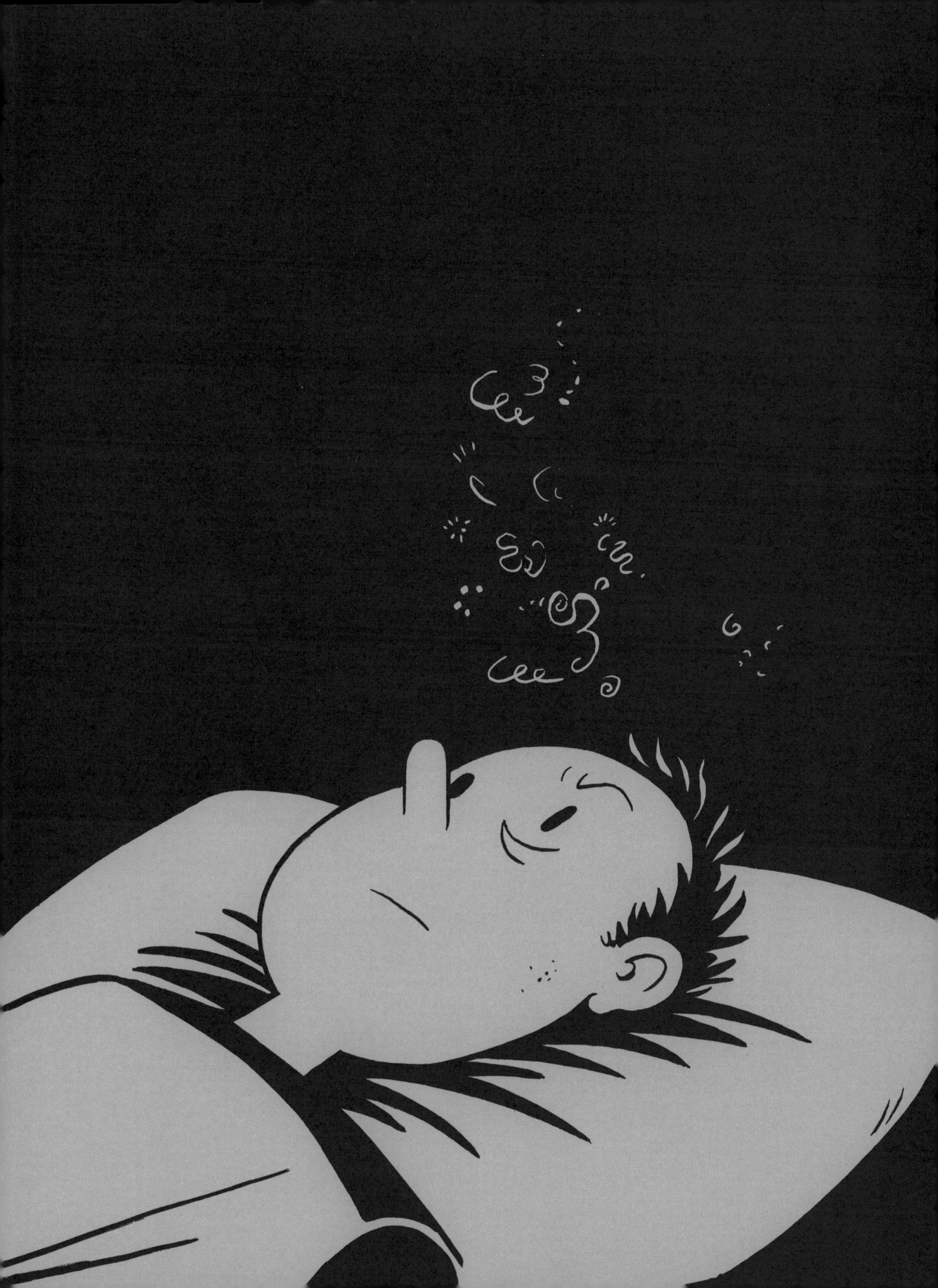

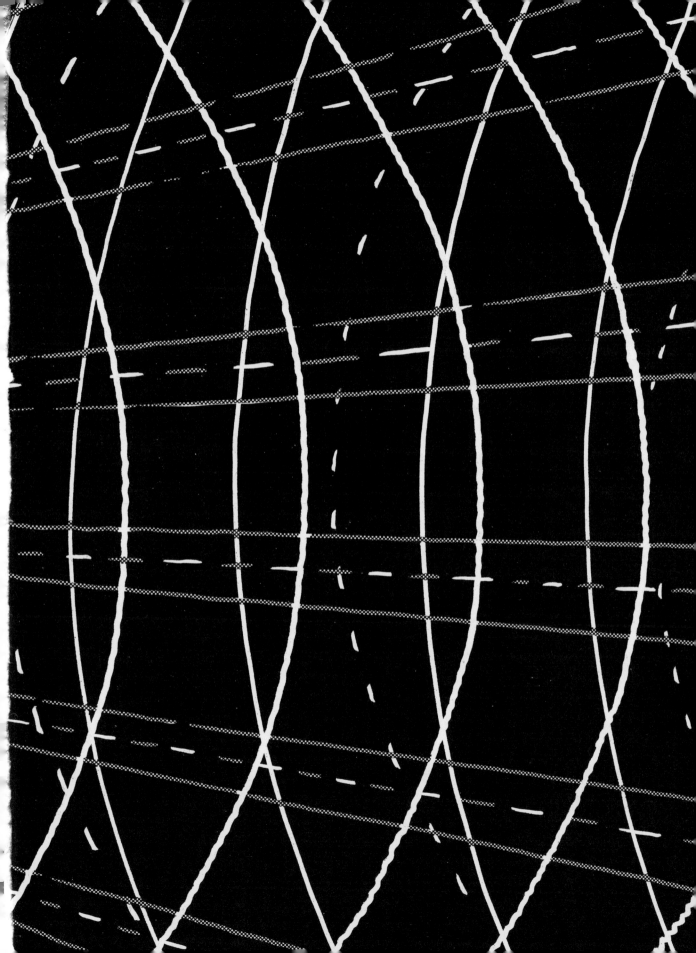

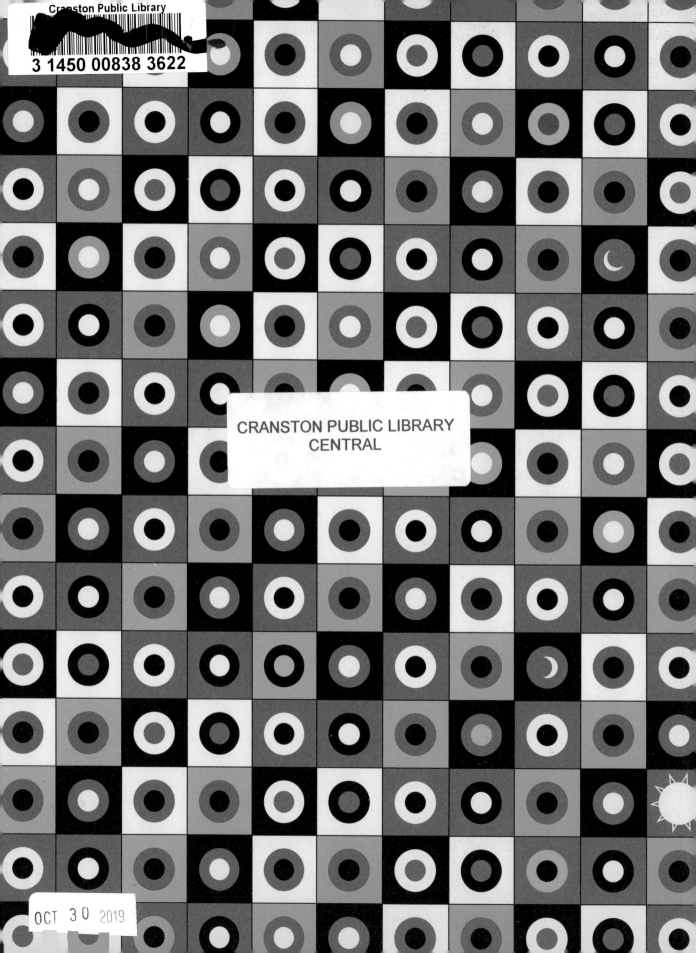